SOLDIERS, CIVILIANS, AND DEMOCRACY

SOLDIERS,

CIVILIANS,

Post-Franco Spain
in Comparative
Perspective

THE JOHNS HOPKINS UNIVERSITY PRESS

AND DEMOCRACY

Felipe Agüero

BALTIMORE AND LONDON

The Johns Hopkins University Press
2715 North Charles Street
Baltimore, Maryland 21218-4319
The Johns Hopkins Press, Ltd., London

Library of Congress Cataloging-in-Publication Data

Agüero, Felipe.
   Soldiers, civilians, and democracy : Post-Franco Spain in
comparative perspective / Felipe Agüero.
      p.   cm.
   Includes bibliographical references and index.
   ISBN 0-8018-5085-1 (alk. paper)
      1. Spain—Politics and government—1975-   2. Civil supremacy
over the military—Spain—History—20th century.   3. Comparative government.   4. Democracy.   I. Title.
DP272.A35   1995
322'.5'094609047—dc20
                                                95-3399
                                                CIP

A catalog record of this book is available from the British Library.

Contents

Figures and Tables

List of Figures and Tables

Preface

This book is about the establishment of civilian supremacy in postauthoritarian democratization. When I first conceived it, democratization advanced only timidly in South American countries that were just moving out of repressive military regimes. Uncertainty consumed victims, hopeful successors, powerful technocrats, and generals alike. Would actual retribution be possible in Uruguay? Would the Brazilian military really retreat? Would Argentine officers cooperate with the new government and the courts? Would Peruvian generals stand idle in the midst of crisis? Would Pinochet stand by the constitutional clause forced upon him which called for a plebiscite?

Spain, at that time, looked, as it later did for East Europeans, as a stalwart bastion of successful regime change. Without really breaking with anybody, Franquist or anti-Franquist, reformers nonetheless cleanly broke with the authoritarian past. The hope that success also crown the efforts of South American democrats facing pervasive military establishments fully justified an all-out immersion into the interstices of the Spanish case, and especially into the always feared and seldom transparent military domains. Two things became clearer as soon as I began surfacing from this immersion: that Spain's democratization was different from most other cases, in many respects unique; and that it shared at least one feature with the other cases—Spaniards had also been, at every turn of the road, consumed by uncertainty.

Since beginning this study, many things have changed about the cases I consider. One has to do with the nature of uncertainties facing the major actors. In the most successful cases these uncertainties now revolve around "normal" issues of well-established European democracies. In Spain, for instance, they concern the benefits of European integration, the future of the arrangement on the *comunidades autónomas,* and the possibility that the Right will get back into government. Uncertainties focused on the military disappeared completely. The military simply ceased to be a source of uncertainty. Even in Portugal, which started the transition so dangerously close to a civil war and in which the military remained so politically prominent until recently, the military was no longer a threat.

Also in South American countries many old problems disappeared, and new ones emerged, such as the challenge of succeeding in regional economic integration, trade liberalization, or state reform. Unfortunately, and despite the differences that sprang up among its members as they moved further away from the authoritarian past, the military remained a source of uncertainty. Even in those countries that made the most progress in reducing military unrest, actors still wondered, if often quietly, whether the militaries were not just dodging an inauspicious period before asserting themselves again. This book deals with the different ability of new democracies in southern Europe and South America to rid themselves of this unhealthy uncertainty. It also contains the hope that further strides will be made toward this goal.

Doing this study was an enjoyable endeavor, and I am grateful to all those who helped me bring it to fruition. Research in Spain was made possible by an International Doctoral Dissertation Fellowship from the Joint Committee on Western Europe of the Social Science Research Council and the American Council of Learned Societies; a grant from the National Science Foundation (SES-8606733); a research fellowship of the Instituto de Cooperación Iberoamericano; and a summer travel grant from the Center for International Studies at Duke University, with funds provided by the Tinker Foundation. Writing was facilitated by the R. Taylor Cole Instructorship in Political Science at Duke University, a Faculty Fellowship at the Helen Kellogg Institute for International Studies at the University of Notre Dame, and support from the Mershon Center of Ohio State University and the Institute for Advanced Study in Princeton.

In Madrid numerous colleagues and "practitioners" collaborated in various ways to help this study. Valentina Fernández Vargas provided a hospitable welcome at the Jaime Balmes Institute of Sociology, which housed the activities and documents of the Comité de Investigaciones Fuerzas Armadas-Sociedad (CIFAS), giving me a first in-depth introduction, in situ, to the subject of my research. CIFAS's president at the time, professor Julio Busquets Bragulat, gave useful suggestions and leads. Charles T. Powell, of the Fundación Ortega y Gasset, kindly made available tapes of the series of interviews he organized in 1985 with lead-

ways. Fernando Reinlein and Carlos Yárnoz provided valuable help in gaining access to materials at *Diario 16* and *El País,* respectively. My thanks to all of them.

I am thankful to those who carefully commented on the manuscript. Arturo Valenzuela, Juan J. Linz, Allan Kornberg, and especially Peter Lange offered helpful suggestions at the early proposal stage. Scott Mainwaring, Guillermo O'Donnell, and David Pion-Berlin made helpful comments on one chapter of an early version. Paulette Higgins, a harsh and implacable critic, generously and decisively helped to improve both form and substance. Peter Lange's careful and critical reading of more than one version of the entire manuscript greatly aided its refinement. Gary Gereffi and Margaret McKean made useful suggestions. J. Samuel Fitch, Richard Gunther, and Arturo Valenzuela were thorough and helpful readers. Pradeep Chhibber and Mariano Torcal painstakingly and dedicatedly read the (next-to) final version and gave timely and consistently good advice. Many thanks to all of them.

There would not even have been a manuscript had it not been for the timely, efficient, and generous support of Duke University president, Keith Brodie, and vice presidents William Griffith and Joel Fleishman at one point, in Madrid, when my health took a precipitous plunge. Peter Lange, with agile initiative and friendly concern, coordinated their efforts to make sure that I got taken care of and could resume my study the following year. I would not have recuperated from this difficult time without Juan Eduardo Costa's and Gisela González's immeasurable amounts of hospitality and generosity, while I was in Madrid, and their consistently high standards in sense of humor. Their efforts helped save a lot more than just this study, and they deserve my gratitude.

My good friend Guillermo Geisse provided warm hospitality in between my two trips to Madrid. Mary Moore was always willing to help with efficient and uplifting support. And, in Princeton, Susan Whitney did her part, brightening the final stretch with charm, wit, and unwavering zest.

The manuscript would have no figures without the skillful help of Rodrigo Garretón and would certainly look a lot less tidy without the kind and efficient support of Ruthe Foster and Lucille Allsen. Manuel Mindreau and Margaret Peirce kindly helped with proofreading and preparation of the index. Many thanks to all of them.

Preface

I   Introduction

Uncertainty, the Military, and Democratization

Retrieving Uncertainty

HOPEFUL REFORMERS within the ailing authoritarian regimes of the late 1980s often turned for inspiration to the earlier success of the Spanish transition to democracy. The ease with which Spanish elites executed a clean break with the Franquist authoritarian regime from within its own institutions was a source of encouragement for those elsewhere who sought to advance change without the peril of violent confrontation. Hastened, however, by the eagerness of late reformers, this turn to the Spanish case inadvertently effected a transmutation in its perceived character. Instead of being the successful outcome of a very complex process, it became an ideal model.[1] In this metamorphosis only those constructive factors behind the outcome, such as the moderation shown by those involved and agreement among political elites, remained.[2] What this ideal model left out, however, were the remaining cleavages, faltering commitments, thinning of popular support, escalating levels of terrorism, and violent military attempts to reverse change, all of which made the outcome very uncertain.[3]

Uncertainty such as in the case of Spanish democratization was partly shared by the transitions in Greece and Portugal and, later, by the movement toward democracy in South America.[4] The transitions that had taken place immediately after World War II in Europe and Japan, in contrast, were far more predictable, given that they followed a script imposed by the military victors. The transitions of the 1970s and 1980s in southern Europe and South America had, instead, simultaneously to produce and act out a script, with no offstage direction. In these cases democratization started out rather tentatively, encountering numerous problems and resistance at every turn.

Democratization in southern Europe and South America was more visibly the result of domestic variables. The transitions took place at a time when the cold war was still on and in countries within the sphere of influence of the United States. In the cold war climate the United States and other Western powers were more concerned with strategic balance than with pulling straggling Western allies to the democratic flock. Earlier, after World War II, Western victors had promoted the democratization of West Germany and Japan to consolidate their side in the emerging bipolar world. Later, when communist rule in Eastern Europe started to crumble, Western powers firmly encouraged democratization because it would also lead to unraveling the military block they formed. The transitions of the 1970s in southern Europe, however, occurred within a well-established Western alliance.[5] Democratization there lacked the sense of international urgency surrounding both the immediate post–World War II transitions and those that transpired in the communist bloc. Left mostly to themselves, and despite the presence of other favorable international factors, the transitions of the 1970s and 1980s highlighted domestic variables, with all the uncertainties associated with them.

In addition, the domestic scenario at the time of the transitions in southern Europe and South America had experienced important changes since the pre-authoritarian period, especially in those cases in which the authoritarian regime lasted longer. Authoritarianism was not a mere interlude, and reformers could not simply resort to a reenactment of whatever political arrangement had existed before. In most countries new constitutions had been set in place, leaving democratic reformers with new institutional realities to confront. The economies had often expanded and diversified, helping create new interests and cleavages that replaced, or expanded on, previously existing ones. New social and political actors emerged, with varying levels of organization, while others became substantially weaker or almost completely disappeared. How old and new political identities and parties would stand in the new scenarios was one of the greatest uncertainties.[6]

Uncertainty and Military Opposition

A weightier uncertainty, however, rested with the military, which continued to be powerful — often the single most powerful institution. With its
monopoly of armed force and political clout, it remained the only organization that could forcefully and drastically reverse political processes
and the transition itself. Obviously, other actors and difficulties also
presented threats to democratization, but none had the power and consequence of threats by the military. In post–World War II Europe defeated armies clearly could not stand in the way of democratization
imposed by the victors; neither could the long-subdued armies in most
of the disappearing communist regimes in the 1990s.[7] In southern Europe and South America, in contrast, the military remained prominent
throughout the transition and well beyond it, enabling it to remain a significant threat to democratization.

Adding to the uncertainty were important changes affecting the military during authoritarianism which were not fully comprehended. Often
the tasks and strains of governance had themselves created new sources
of intramilitary divisions. Also, changing conditions over time infused
generations of officers with different socialization experiences and ideas
about their professional roles.

The exact impact of these changes on the outlook of military officers
in regard to questions of a new regime was totally unknown. Reformist
civilians from within and outside authoritarian regimes speculated,
with little information, on the support, opposition, or neutrality that the
military would show toward regime change. Contradictory and shifting
forecasts inevitably added to a general state of uncertainty. For instance,
in Spain the emergence in 1974 of a group of officers organized clan-
destinely for the purpose of bolstering democratization raised hopes
among the opposition. The subsequent repression of this group, however, coupled with expressions by military leaders of diehard loyalty to
Franquism restored a sense of realism: the bulk of the military were
against changes to the fundamental features of Franquist institutions.
Also, in most other cases the militaries stood, in varying degrees, for the
maintenance of fundamental continuities with the authoritarian regimes they had sustained. Only in Portugal was the military intent on
breaking sharply with the previous regime, although, as the role of the
Armed Forces Movement indicated, this was not tantamount to an
unfettered inauguration of democracy.

Why, then, was it possible for democratic reformers in southern Europe to succeed in the establishment and strengthening of democratic regimes? What factors came to the aid of reformers facing resistance from the military? How did they empower themselves to lead the military to tolerate the establishment of a political regime it initially did not favor? These questions — the central focus of this book — are especially pertinent to the case of Spain. This country had extraordinary success during the 1980s, when military opposition to democracy was finally quieted. Yet, in contrast to Greece, Portugal, and Argentina, democratization in Spain did not start from a collapse of the previous regime. On the contrary, it originated from within Franquist legality and was marked by important continuities. This continuity was most evident in the military, which faced none of the purges experienced by the military in Greece, Portugal, and Argentina.

It must be pointed out that the Spanish generals and admirals who stayed throughout the transition and beyond owed their political outlooks to their formative years during the 1936–39 civil war. They had fought in the victor army, which defeated Republicans and "reds" and which remained sworn to defend Franquist institutions and ideals against the forces of "anti-Spain." As members of "the *Movimiento*," the official Franquist organization, it was the duty of top military officers to preserve the fundamental principles of "the Crusade," which was victorious in 1939.

As most other regime sectors in the mid-1970s, however, the military knew that, after Franco died, some changes would be inevitable. But the changes they had in mind were the same as those entertained by Franquist functionaries seeking to adjust the regime to new conditions without fundamentally altering it. The actual amount and speed of change which followed Franco's death was totally unexpected for the military, especially since it was promoted by former partners in the perishing regime. And yet, the military ended up accepting the transition, albeit grudgingly and with occasional spurts of forceful opposition.

Furthermore, having acknowledged the regime inaugurated by the 1978 constitution, the military was then led to condone the dismantlement of institutions that had previously kept it autonomous and free of direct governmental control. The separate ministries that each of the armed services held in the cabinet were eliminated in 1977 and replaced by a single defense ministry. The subsequent gradual empowerment and civilianization of this ministry, together with the elimination of the Joint Chiefs as the top organ in the military chain of command, unequivocally asserted the supremacy of civilian authorities. And, starting in 1982, a Socialist defense minister persistently pursued and obtained the liquidation of remaining military prerogatives that encumbered full-fledged civilian supremacy.

How was this possible? How did initial uncertainty turn into a well-grounded confidence in the military's respect for the legitimacy of democratically elected officials? What made it possible for these officials gradually to circumscribe the military to nonpolitical roles and to create sound structures for civilian control? Without an answer to these questions, which this book provides, the account of Spain's success in democratization remains incomplete.

Explaining Spain's Success

Spain's startling success in the transition gave rise to a plethora of monographs and scholarly studies.[8] The most theoretical among them generally have agreed on the principal factors standing behind this successful democratization. First, robust economic growth took place in the decades that preceded the transition. Policies initiated in the 1960s gave way to impressive rates of economic development, based mostly on the dynamism of industrial growth, and this in turn reflected in high rates of urbanization. Second, interaction with European economies greatly increased during those decades, via markets, competition, tourism, and seasonal labor migrations. In this context some liberalization of industrial relations took place as well. Third, economic expansion, urbanization, and Europeanization led to improved standards of living and expanded spheres of social pluralism. Also, more tolerant attitudes developed among the population, mollifying some of the historical cleavages. These economic and social changes translated into pressures against the regime's authoritarian mold. Fourth, the consequences of the previous factors coupled with the aging of Franco (*el Caudillo*) and the elimination of his closest collaborator, Admiral Carrero Blanco, precipitated stalemating crises within the regime. This opened up space for reformist, innovative leadership and for King Juan Carlos, himself, to initiate negotiations for change when *el Caudillo* finally passed away.

Fifth, moderation in the opposition and skillful elite leadership facilitated negotiations and compromise, yielding a transition path of accorded reforms that broke with Franquist authoritarian rule.[9]

Individual authors arranged these factors in different ways according to their different approaches. Comprehensive accounts took a sequential view to argue that development, liberalization, and pluralization under Franquism influenced public and elite attitudes and set the stage for the regime's crisis. Franco's death then provided the opportunity for change, which contending elites faced with uncertainty as they mustered strength and delineated competing agendas and strategies. This view (as expounded, for instance, by Juan Linz and Jose María Maravall) emphasized elements of uncertainty and contingency in the way elite choices and mass mobilization unfolded but also made sure to point to preceding structural trends and the institutional opportunities and constraints that bound those choices.[10]

The ostensible role of elite negotiation and compromise led others (such as Richard Gunther and Donald Share) to focus on the conditions and processes of elite transformation. Without such transformation, especially in contrast to the levels of elite polarization which doomed the Second Republic, agreement and unity would not have been possible. Procedural factors as well as values, behavioral styles, and historical memories were invoked to account for what was depicted as elite settlement, a particular mode of elite transformation toward consensual unity.[11] From a different angle Josep Colomer deemed a similar set of social and cultural factors critical in determining which actors, and with what preferences, would emerge as the most relevant during the transition. With these actors and preferences identified, he proceeded to a game-theoretic depiction of the situation to account for what he called a successful transition by agreement. Essential to this success, however, was that maximalist positions be weak or absent and that actors be subjectively predisposed to cooperation or compromise. In the case of Spain this was possible primarily as a result of learning from the experience of civil war.[12]

Another view also considered the weight of preceding social and cultural factors but specifically to downgrade the independent role of elites in fostering coalescent behavior. Victor Pérez-Díaz argued that liberal societal traditions formed during Franquism and the political culture forged during the transition itself rendered the role of elites more like that of rule followers than choice makers. It was "the previous emergence of liberal democratic traditions in society" which shaped elite preferences and choices and which, therefore, explained the success of democratization.[13]

These explanations, with their different approaches, go a long way in helping us understand Spain's extraordinary success. Yet they do not address questions about the role of the military, nor do they shed light on the fact that opposition from within the military to democratization remained active all the way through the 1982 elections. It is indeed instructive that, while these accounts were explaining success, many of their authors, at the same time, were reminding us of the fragility of the new democracy well after the end of the transition.[14] Those accounts, in fact, do not integrate this puzzle within the schemes used to explain success, nor do they explain the changes toward civilian supremacy which started developing in 1982–83.[15]

Pérez-Díaz, however, singled out an important role for the military in his explanatory framework. Political elites, he argued, were successful not because they led the public but, rather, "because they were able to learn from and follow the public mood": "This learning reached the elite mainly from two quarters: from society and from the army. Societal traditions gave support to moderate policies, and the army threatened sanctions on immoderate ones." If politicians' learning from society still remained faulty—that is, if they were unable to absorb society's moderating influence—then the presence of the army served to keep any biases in check.[16]

This view of the military's role is problematic because it reduces it merely to providing constraints. While it is true that fear of the army moderated the stance of some sectors of the elite, especially during the early stages of the transition, it also is true that ridding the political process of these constraints was essential to the success of democratization. Pérez-Díaz's view holds constant the role of the army, a role that, in fact, changed during the process and which, furthermore, *had* to be changed for democratization to succeed. Pérez-Díaz's view of the army's role to threaten sanctions on immoderate policies ignores the fact that the army itself, or at least very significant sectors of it, either promoted immoderate policies (such as coup attempts) or aligned itself with elite sectors favoring those policies. Who, then, was to threaten sanctions on immoderate policies coming from this side? Successful constraints imposed on immoderate stances in the military ended up changing the military's position. And this change came about not as a result of the sheer weight of societal traditions but mostly by the concerted action of elites, with strong public support, and their institutional designs.

The military dimension of Spain's democratic consolidation cannot be subsumed within these general approaches. It is obvious that liberalization, growth, and modernization under Franquism, as well as other factors that facilitated elite unity and compromise, were favorable to democratization. The pressures that these factors exerted for reform were certainly great. But it also is obvious that the military was one of the institutions most resistant to these pressures. While changes in society and among the elites had an impact on the military, this impact was not always positive, often eliciting defensive attitudes and staunch corporate resistance. In addition, the military was perhaps the institution least touched by the wave of modernization which had reached other areas of state and society, and it certainly did not participate in the move toward consensual unity among the elites.

Does this mean that if military contestation had been more successful the military would have been able to reverse the process entirely, overcoming counterpressures and establishing a well-entrenched and firmly repressive post-Franquist military-authoritarian regime? Probably not. But, instead, it could have significantly delayed reform or steered its course in a very different direction, restraining democratization, repressing regional demands for autonomy, altering alignments among civilian elites, and establishing tutelage over the post-Franquist regime. The possibility was there, attempts were made, yet democratization took the successful course we have learned to associate with the Spanish model. Both this possibility and its failure need to be explained in order fully to account for Spain's successful democratic transition and consolidation.

To fulfill this task one must look at the relative empowerment possibilities available to military elites and civilian reformers, first during the transition from authoritarianism and then during the ensuing post-transition process. This requires attention to the initial conditions and institutional setting that provided variable resources, opportunities, and constraints to the strategies and counterstrategies with which the main actors contended as well as to the changes taking place in all these elements as the process unfolded.[17]

The Argument

A study of the assertion of civilian supremacy cannot be approached other than from the angle of changes in the relative empowerment of civilian reformers and the military. If, as I shall elaborate in the following chapter, civilian democratizing elites pursue control over the military and the military resists this pursuit, civilian supremacy will be asserted only as the result of overpowering military resistance.

The basic assumption is that the central issues in civil-military relations in transition periods of the kind studied here are issues of power.[18] This, however, is not the same as saying that civilian supremacy is attained exclusively, or even necessarily, as the result of an imposition. It is often the case that institutional changes lead all actors involved, including the military, to find positive grounds to support democratic civilian control. Still, especially in transition periods, these institutional changes come about as the result of bargaining backed by powerful resources that differentially affect actors' possibilities in the pursuit of, or resistance to, change.

The analysis must, therefore, follow changes in the relative empowerment of civilians and the military and determine which factors influenced these shifts. A study of these changes in cases of transition from authoritarian rule must first establish the relative strengths of the actors at the time of demise of the authoritarian regime. This is the starting point for the process studied here, which also provides the initial conditions that influence the relative position of civilian and military actors at the outset of the transition. These conditions also affect subsequent power relations and influence the chances of completing democratization by advancing civilian supremacy in the post-transition stage.

Relevant initial conditions, I argue, are the position of the military in the outgoing authoritarian regime and the specific nature of the transition path. The relevance of these conditions lies in their impact upon the extent of control that the military exerts over the transition. This can be grasped fully only within a comparative context. Initial conditions in Spain, for instance, contrasted sharply with those found in the rest of southern Europe and South America. The military in Spain, albeit occupying important positions in the Franquist regime, was not situated at the core decision-making sites at the time of the regime's demise and thus had little influence over the transition's agenda. This, in turn, influenced the actual inability of the military to prevent the successful outcome of the transition sealed in the 1978 constitution.

The structuration of democratically consistent patterns of authority over the military extends, however, beyond the end of the transition.[19] Ridding democratization of uncertainty with regard to the loyalty of the military to legitimate civilian authority is a process that takes time. In Spain, for instance, military loyalty could not have been taken for granted right after the establishment of democracy, as the major coup attempt of February 1981, three years after the transition was completed, clearly indicated. And democratization involves not only removing the military from political concerns and eliminating military contestation; it also involves the assertion of prerogatives of civilian officials in military and defense affairs. These tasks, if pursued successfully, are likely to be completed only after the end of the transition, and it is thus necessary to extend the analysis to the distinct *post-transition* process.

The distinctness of this process lies in the new sets of rules it inaugurates, which unevenly distribute the burdens and costs of political action.[20] The costs are higher for those who seek to change already accorded rules in order to better accommodate their interests and demands than for those who are satisfied with the recently established rules. In Spain, for instance, the military felt uneasy in the new democratic situation because it was far more pluralistic than most officers had anticipated and opened the way for the development of the national-regional *autonomías,* which the military overtly disliked. Yet the constitutional and popular legitimacy of the new regime made it very costly for the military to attempt to reverse the changes that had already occurred in order to limit democratization.

The civilians, in turn, had to advance beyond the rules accorded by the transition if they wanted civilian supremacy. The transition had granted procedural democracy but had also allowed much autonomy for the military. Reforms to diminish this autonomy would cause tension in the military, which was costly for civilians, although less costly than risking erosion of popular support or the institutionalized setting of excessive military prerogatives. The end of the transition formalizes a power distribution between the military and civilian authorities which affect their capacity to subsequently redress their new statuses. But, while initial conditions help shape the early outcome of the transition, other factors influence civil-military interaction during the post-transition process in ways not necessarily anticipated at the end of the transition. The new elements brought to bear eventually weaken civilian or military actors or, alternatively, empower them, encouraging the reinforcement or modification of the redistribution of power formalized by the end of the transition. For instance, internal cohesion of the military, or of a ruling civilian coalition, and the extent of public support they can exhibit, are important elements influencing their relative power. A unified civilian coalition with persistent and substantial electoral backing will find it easier to promote reforms that weaken military resistance to civilian control. In turn, a cohesive military facing a divided government lacking strong public support may be better able to deter civilian initiatives or even to strengthen military prerogatives altogether. In Spain, for instance, increasing factionalism in the government party coupled with decreasing public support gave confidence to military hard-liners — who attempted the 1981 coup d'état — to try to redress the disregard for military preferences which democratic inauguration had formalized. The post-transition process is thus critical for the affirmation or reversal of conditions inherited from the transition period and which favor either civilian or military interests. Initial conditions matter, especially in exacting variable levels of effort from actors engaged in redressing their relative status, but, as a comparative exploration will submit, these conditions do not foreclose substantial institutional alterations later in the process.[21]

Organization and Presentation of the Argument

Chapter 2, which closes part 1, presents a discussion of the conceptual and methodological issues involved in the study of the military in the democratization process. It examines the concepts of democracy and civilian supremacy and identifies the principal factors affecting the relative empowerment of military and civilian actors in their bargaining relationship.

Part 2 concentrates on initial conditions and the transition period. Chapter 3 outlines initial conditions in the successful southern European cases, particularly in Spain, and contrasts them with those in the more fragile cases of democratization in South America. The extent of militarization of outgoing authoritarian regimes and the nature of the transition paths are presented in comparative fashion to highlight the way these factors variably influenced the degree of military control of the transition.

Chapter 4 addresses specific ways in which initial conditions are connected with the ensuing processes of civilian and military empowerment and details the way in which these conditions facilitated civilian empowerment in Spain. Here, I will argue, the military was initially positioned in a way that precluded its chances of anticipating changes and thus of effectively opposing them. Civilian reformers presented the military with a sequence of choices which left it with no alternative other than to acquiesce. Also strengthened by their unity and popular support, civilian officials managed to overpower the military and neutralize its resistance. The situation in the South American transitions was radically different; there the military played more prominent roles and could carve out important guarantees for itself.

Chapter 5 addresses the role of internal divisions in the military as a specific source of weakness. The bulk of the military adhered to rigid Franquist tenets and despised reforms, but there had emerged a small number of officers in high grades who thought otherwise. The military was thus not monolithic, and a focus on the interaction of different tendencies in the military with the reformist dynamics unleashed by the government helps to further account for the weakness of initial military opposition. In the South American militaries, multiple sources of division were mitigated by doctrinal developments and the homogeneously defensive posture adopted vis-à-vis civilian charges of human rights' violations.

Part 3 focuses on the changes that take place in the strength of civilians and the military during the post-transition process and, specifically, on the struggle in Spain to overcome hardened military obstacles to the consolidation of the new democratic regime. While initial conditions there helped civilian reformers advance the transition with no military tutelage, military contestation rose dramatically during the inaugural years of the democratic regime.

Chapter 6 addresses the reawakening of the military's contestation capabilities in new democracies, particularly in Spain, and examines its relationship to a number of factors, such as the fragility of government and the ruling party, the spread of civil violence or the formation of violent groups, and the timing of military reform.

Chapter 7 focuses on the culmination of rising military opposition in the attempted coup of February 1981 in Spain. Accumulated military grievances directed against a weakened civilian leadership led to a showdown of enormous consequence. Showdowns usually lead, as happened in this case, to the irretrievable weakening of one of the colliding sides, opening the way for unconstrained reforms (or reaction). The failure of revolt in Argentina, for instance, and other cases, such as the coup attempt of August 1991 in the former Soviet Union, illustrate that possibility.[22] The failure of the February 1981 attempt in Spain may be construed as a turning point that irretrievably weakened the hard-line faction and facilitated the gradual evaporation of all alternatives to democratization.

Chapter 8 turns to the factors that permitted civilian officials to take advantage of this opportunity to assert their supremacy. The overwhelming victory of the Socialist Party in 1982 and the ensuing formation of a stable one-party parliamentary majority and, later, NATO membership strengthened the hand of the civilian leadership. The nature of discontent in the military turned from a previous concern with larger political issues to one now centered exclusively around professional problems related to the strain of modernizing policies.

The final chapter, in part 4, presents the Spanish post-transition process in a comparative context, highlighting the factors that facilitated the attainment of civilian supremacy in Spain in contrast to those that have made this goal harder to attain in other postauthoritarian regimes.

Asserting Civilian Supremacy
in Postauthoritarian Regimes

Democracy and Civilian Supremacy

THE NOTION of democracy used here follows Robert Dahl's emphasis on procedures and institutional guarantees. Democracy consists of the opportunity of citizens to formulate and articulate their preferences and to have these preferences represented in the conduct of government, with corresponding institutional guarantees.[1] Dahl spelled out these guarantees in a set of "procedural minimal" conditions: the right of citizens to run for office and to vote in regular free and fair elections and the right to freedom of expression, to alternative sources of information, and to associational autonomy. It was specified as well that "control over government decisions about policy is constitutionally vested in elected officials."[2] This procedural definition thus implicitly contains the more specific notion of civilian supremacy. According to this notion, elected civilian officials control decisions on all areas of government policy, including the critical areas of security, national defense, and the armed forces.[3]

Civilian supremacy over these areas, however, is much too important to be only implicitly included in definitions of democracy. If democratic procedural conditions apply to any large state bureaucracy, the military is one in which these conditions take on crucial importance because of its monopoly over society's coercive power. Democratic guarantees in this area become even more critical as a result of the military's strong sense of corporate interests combined with a feeling of exclusive technocratic expertise, which often leads it to claim autonomy from external control. It would thus be untenable for a working, procedural definition of democracy not to include explicitly the military as subject to the policies formulated by elected individuals holding the highest state offices.[4]

If civilian rule over the areas of security and national defense is central to any democracy, it is particularly so to new democracies just emerging from situations in which the military occupied prominent positions. In these new democracies the issue of control of institutionalized force is all the more germane because the question of exclusive areas of competence for the military and the government is itself a matter of contestation. The experience of democratization in southern Europe and South America reveals that major obstacles were encountered precisely in these areas. Success in democratization could, in fact, be gauged by the ability of civilian officials to exercise the powers assigned to the offices to which they were elected, including powers over the military. In this light the assertion of civilian control could be seen both as a support mechanism for democratic construction and an indicator of the success and extent of postauthoritarian democratization. The concept of civilian supremacy that I will use here highlights the critical position of the military in facilitating or hindering movement toward a situation in which the standards of procedural democracy are met.

Approaches to Civilian Control

No concept of civilian supremacy may be advanced without reference to Samuel Huntington's influential formulation of models of civilian control. Huntington rightly linked civilian control to the minimization of military power, which would allow civilian authorities effectively to make the military "the tool of the state."[5] Of the various ways of achieving this end, one became paramount with the rise of the military as a profession: objective civilian control. This kind of control is based on the maximization of professionalism, which has the consequence of rendering the armed forces "politically sterile and neutral." This minimization of the military's political power is balanced, however, with "the recognition of autonomous military professionalism . . . of an independent military sphere."[6]

ing figures of Spain's transition to democracy. Fernando Rodrigo, a good friend, offered a generous and wonderful opportunity to share views on a subject of common interest to us and to engage in very productive joint research activities. Interviews organized and held by us at the Fundación with leading military figures gave us a chance to contribute to the already rich documentary wealth on Spain's democratization which the Fundación harbors.

Gathering documentary information on the military is, unfortunately, not always easy. I am thankful to Admiral Angel Liberal Lucini and Lieutenant General José María Sáenz de Tejada for facilitating access to documents in their respective services. General Miguel Alonso Baquer helped me gain access to numerous documents in the Joint Schools and the High Army School at the Centro Superior de Estudios de la Defensa Nacional (CESEDEN). Lieutenant Colonel J. Benítez Sánchez-Malo provided invaluable help in locating old theses and documents, and Navy Captain José Luis Tato at the Revista de Marina was equally helpful. At the Defense Ministry Colonel Carlos Gil Muñoz, Colonel Francisco Laguna Sanguirico, Major Jesús del Olmo, Major Miguel Silva Vidal, and Carlos Bruquetas assisted me with insights, information, connections, and documents. I also wish to thank Debby Jakubs, from Duke University's Perkins Library, for her invaluable assistance in the collection of materials that were indispensable to this study.

Interviews were a critical part of this research, and I would like to thank many more than I can here. Special thanks are due Lieutenant General José María Sáenz de Tejada, Admiral Angel Liberal Lucini, Lieutenant General José Gabeiras, and Admiral Jacinto Garau, who several times spent hours with Fernando Rodrigo and me discussing issues of military reform, modernization, and spending. I am equally thankful to lieutenants general Ricardo Arozarena, Federico Gómez de Salazar, and Emilio García Conde for sharing their experiences on critical episodes as well as on less critical, more habitual aspects of their professional lives. Generals Juan Cano Hevia, Alberto Piris, and Francisco de Galinsoga illuminated my research in many areas. Leopoldo Calvo Sotelo and Alberto Oliart found the time to answer my questions on several occasions. Narcís Serra, Gustavo Suárez Pertierra, Rafael Arias Salgado, and Eduardo Serra set time aside in their busy schedules to answer my questions.

Ana Erice, Enrique Gomáriz, Federico Mañero, Ludolfo Paramio, and Javier Pradera helped advance my research in Madrid in various

In contrast to this kind of control stands subjective control, which pre-supposes some degree of military involvement "in institutional, class, and constitutional politics." Control here is exerted via civilianization of the military, by making it "the mirror of the state" and by denying "an independent military sphere."[7]

These notions of civilian control are helpful in discerning patterns of civil-military relations across countries and historical periods. They are less useful, however, for characterizing civilian supremacy in the context of recent cases of democratization. Subjective control is obviously inappropriate in this context because democratization involves a withdrawal of the military from politics. And the notion of military professionalism involved in objective control has often been associated in these countries with levels of autonomy for the military which are far greater than those tolerable in advanced democracies.[8] In addition, autonomous military professionalism has not always rendered the military "politically sterile and neutral." On the contrary, often it has contributed to, or failed to prevent, the expansion of domestic political roles by the military.[9]

A more useful approach for our purposes is found in a study by Timothy Colton of civil-military relations in the Soviet Union. Colton focused on the notion of military participation and disaggregated it along two distinct and continuous dimensions: the *scope* of issues with which a military is concerned (internal, institutional, intermediate, societal) and the *means* it employs (official prerogative, expert advice, political bargaining, force). Military participation was thus considered a matter of degree.[10]

In a democracy, however, the degree of military participation can vary only within well-defined limits. Military participation and influence in government policy-making cannot trespass beyond certain thresholds that are critical for the maintenance of democratic government. The violation of these limits would make it difficult to characterize a given situation as one of civilian supremacy. No civilian supremacy may be in place if the military forces its participation in decisions over societal issues, as it did, for instance, in Brazil after the transfer of power to a civilian president in 1985.[11]

The process of asserting civilian supremacy after authoritarianism normally starts with the gradual removal of the military from societal concerns to intermediate or institutional concerns.[12] In Spain, for instance, with the liquidation of the old Franquist institutions, military members were deprived of participation in the Cortes, the legislative body. Later the military was denied a say about whether the Communist Party would be allowed to take part in national elections. Military discontent over a number of issues of a societal nature was manifest until the failed coup attempt of February 1981. After this, however, tensions in civil-military relations revolved almost exclusively around institutional matters.

This view helps clarify my own — namely, that the advancement of civilian supremacy entails a reduction in the scope of military participation. In a scheme similar to Colton's, and fittingly applied to transitional contexts, Alfred Stepan introduced the dimensions of military *contestation* and military *prerogatives* for assessing progress, comparatively, in the attainment of civilian control. A situation of civilian control would, in this scheme, result from low levels of contestation and prerogatives.[13]

In the present study, however, a definition of civilian supremacy is needed which can be stated in more positive terms than is obtained from a view of levels of military participation, contestation, or prerogatives. The extent of civilian supremacy ought to be assessed by its concrete manifestations and not merely by determining its compatibility with certain levels of military influence. In addition, an operational definition of civilian supremacy is needed which considers specific prerogatives of civilians in all policy areas.[14]

A Definition of Civilian Supremacy

I define *civilian supremacy* as the ability of a civilian, democratically elected government to conduct general policy without interference from the military, to define the goals and general organization of national defense, to formulate and conduct defense policy, and to monitor the implementation of military policy.[15] Civilian supremacy is reached through a process consisting, first, of the removal of the military from power positions outside the defense area and, second, of the appointment and acknowledgment of civilian political superiors in the defense and military areas. As the military withdraws from non-defense-related policy areas, civilian officials gain authoritative capacity in all policy areas, including defense. Obviously, as the very definition of the boundaries between strictly military and nonmilitary areas is controversial, the assertion of civilian supremacy entails the acceptance of spheres of competence as defined by legitimate civilian authorities and which, in practice, involve a reduction in, but by no means an elimination of, the military's sphere of autonomous action.[16]

Civilian supremacy involves the restriction of military roles to assistance in the formulation and implementation of national defense policy. It also involves acceptance of government decisions in areas that, although customary in long-established democracies, are rather sensitive in new democracies because they entail a new delineation of prerogatives. These areas of decision include the defense budget, force levels, and promotion of officers to the most senior grades and posts. The transfer of prerogatives in these areas takes place gradually during or, more often, after the transition. Civilian supremacy is unlikely to be asserted in one blow, and it does not necessarily imply a civilian imposition; it may well develop through a process in which the military confines itself to a role more restricted to professional matters. Decisions leading to civilian supremacy generally involve more or less overt civil-military negotiations or a tacit bargaining process, before the extent and shape of military participation under the new arrangements are more permanently defined. It should be underscored that, in successful cases, these arrangements balance the expansion of civilian prerogatives with the establishment of appropriate avenues for the expression of military professional concerns and instill confidence in the military that its core institutional interests are being reasonably accommodated.[17]

The attainment of civilian supremacy demands that proper governmental structures already exist or are in the making which allow for a pattern of authority in state agencies such that civilians may effectively exert leadership over the military. Ideally, for the purpose of civilian supremacy, the military should be "subordinate to only one other institution possessing effective final authority." Huntington calls this "ministerial control," since it normally comes "in the form of a civilian departmental minister."[18] In the transition processes that interest us civilians have attempted, though not always successfully, to create such an authority structure. A department of defense helps empower civilian authorities by providing them with a unified structure for the conduct of policy and homogenizes the military with the rest of the state administrative bureaucracy.

My definition of civilian supremacy assumes that the military does not participate in leading positions in spheres deemed civilian and emphasizes, instead, an active presence of civilians in the military and defense spheres. This makes the definition quite demanding if we consider that most Western democratic polities tolerate varying degrees of military influence in politics as normal.[19] We should therefore assume that societies in the process of establishing a democratic regime will find it harder to live up to this definition; it is nonetheless useful, since it makes it easier to compare degrees to which civil supremacy is attained across postauthoritarian regimes.

The definition used here excludes any reference to attitudinal traits within members of the military. While others would appreciate the inclusion of such factors as motivations or ideological consent on the part of military officers toward the new institutions,[20] I do not believe they are necessary components of civilian supremacy. Ideological congruence between civil authorities and the military may eliminate sources of tension in civil-military relations and is certainly desirable for democratic consolidation in the long run. I will argue, however, that democratization and civilian supremacy can be secured without prior voluntary support of the democratic credo by members of the armed forces.[21]

Civilian Supremacy Attained

Finally, it is important to consider the questions: When can the process of asserting civilian supremacy be said to be complete? How do we know that the supremacy of civilians has been set firmly in place? One way to answer these questions is to establish a certain period of time after the end of the transition during which, for instance, the military has abstained from intervening.[22] This, however, would provide only a very limited picture of what is involved in civilian supremacy, which includes much more than nonintervention by the military. More reasonable is to develop operational criteria that combine the time dimension with substantive elements of civilian supremacy. Accordingly, I will argue that civilian supremacy in new democracies is attained when: (1) some habituation—in the sense of repeated practice—has been reached over a number of years in the exercise of civilian leadership as stated in the definition; (2) the prerogatives contemplated in this definition have been formalized in the nation's constitution or other major laws; (3) no overt challenge by the military as institution to civilian authority and the constitution has taken place over a number of years, and (4) the military has manifestly had to accept at least one major decision taken by civilian authorities about which military opposition had been previously voiced. Since most transitions have actually had to face varying levels of military contestation, it should not be hard to pinpoint such an instance.[23]

When all these indicators have been met in a new democracy, one may safely assume that civilian supremacy has been attained, aiding in the consolidation of democracy. A new democracy has become consolidated when democratic procedures and institutions have been set in place, including civilian supremacy, and no politically significant group challenges the principal rules of the new regime.[24]

Civilians and the Military

My focus on the assertion of civilian supremacy highlights two actors: civilians and the military. The military holds the legal monopoly of armed force and includes a variety of organizations and services consisting basically of the forces assigned to national defense: the army, the navy, and the air force.[25] Here the focus is on the officer corps, and, given the hierarchical nature of these organizations, primarily on the superior echelons, in which decisions are made and orders issued: the offices of the commander in chief and chiefs of staff, general staffs, joint staffs, councils of generals and admirals, and, occasionally, influential units such as war colleges and information services.[26]

The term *civilian* is obviously quite vague, as it includes all individuals and organizations that do not belong in the military—that is, most of the state apparatus and civil society at large. I shall focus primarily, however, on those civilian nuclei most relevant for the problem at hand. These nuclei will vary in character as the process of dismantling the outgoing regime and institutionalizing the new one evolves. Initially, the preeminent nucleus is formed by the leadership of the civilian political groups aspiring to become a successor government and the civilian elites from the exiting regime, which hold similar aspirations. In the subsequent phase, when provisional authorities have taken over during the transition or a democratic government has been established, the preeminent nucleus is formed by the head of the government, the cabinet, and those in charge of defense and military affairs.[27] In this and in subsequent stages other nuclei also gain salience: party leaders; leaders of parliamentary groups; defense committees of congress; ad hoc committees such as a constitution drafting committee; the courts; and others. In the case of Spain the king is a critical actor in all stages.

The use of these two major categories—civilian nuclei and the military—does not preclude, however, the analysis of divisions within both civilian and military units and of segmented relations across them.[28] Indeed, during the transition civilian unity and military unity may be less a reality than a goal in attempts by these actors to empower themselves. The process of asserting or resisting civilian supremacy involves efforts by the military to gain civilian allies in support of its interests as well as attempts by civilian democratic leaders to promote and assign critical military posts to those military leaders most congenial to their policies. In this regard civilians may face an important choice: they may help to strengthen military unity with a view to facilitating responsible negotiation, even under hard-line military leadership, or they may promote divisions in the leadership in order to weaken a resilient military stance. Attempts at cross-institutional connections and alliances, however, do not obscure the distinct pursuit of democratization by civilians and the pursuit of institutional-corporate interests by the military, a dynamic that justifies the analytic distinction between these two actors.

Interests, Uncertainty, and Guarantees

The start of the transition finds the military and the civilians holding distinct, often conflicting interests. The military, as with any large complex organization, seeks to advance its institutional interests and prerogatives. These interests are strongly defined by the military's previous partnership in the establishment and maintenance of the authoritarian regime now initiating retreat. This may mean in some cases that the military initially seeks to maintain some of the features of the old regime or to assist in shaping the contours of the new one. In most cases, however, it strives for internal control of the profession and for protection from external political control,[29] fearing and eventually resisting political change if it impinges on the rules of control. Uncertainty over the nature and extent of the impact of regime change leads the military to attempt to maximize its autonomy.

On the other hand, relevant civilian political groups seek the establishment of democracy as an institutional means of solving conflicts.[30] They may hold different postures regarding the extent and specific nature of the democratic rules they would like to see established and the specific policies they would like to see implemented, but, once the transition is started, they all share an interest in democratization. Even if some of them are less than enthusiastic about democratization, no major political group actively and openly seeks military intervention for the advancement of its interests.[31]

Civilians in government will resist veiled or overt military pressures on policy in civilian areas and will attempt to impose greater control in military domains. This creates tension in relations with the military, which will worsen if there develop uncontrolled social mobilization, widespread violence and armed groups, or autonomous movements in society which, for instance, seek accountability for past abuses by military officers.

The military will make preemptive or reactive moves to maximize its autonomy and resist civilian "encroachments." The most extreme reaction is the attempt to block political change altogether, in the hope of an authoritarian re-equilibration.[32] More often, however, the military tries to steer the course of change toward positions closer to its own preferences or attempts obstructive measures, such as maintenance of a veto power or strong oversight capacity over government policies; threats of use of force to stop specific policies, such as an expansion of political pluralism or the transfer of human rights violators to court; control over intelligence agencies; rejection of governmental or congressional "interference" with matters deemed internal. In diverse combinations such military maneuvers were observed in all the cases of concern here, and they were invariably aimed at gaining reassurances and decreasing uncertainty about the armed forces' institutional future.

Guarantees, reassurances, and certainty form the crux of the dynamics of change involving the military in transitions and are critical to understanding military acquiescence to democracy. The military normally operationalizes its core interests in terms of "minimal conditions" that are made explicit in order to test the reaction of political actors, influence the policies they have outlined for the transition, and specify an eventual bargaining position. This will have the effect of moderating the policies of reformists by imposing a "military ceiling" to reforms, even if this ceiling may eventually be pushed up.[33] The military attempts, in this way, to reduce the area of uncertainty which democratization brings about.

The notion of uncertainty has been at the center of the literature on democratization. Adam Przeworski, for instance, viewed democracy as a "system of rule open-endedness, or organized uncertainty," and democratization as the "act of subjecting all interests to competition, of institutionalizing uncertainty."[34] Uncertainty results from the inability of participants to control the outcomes of the political process, and this inability, in turn, is what leads all groups to consent to and comply with democratic rule as a compromise. Compliance is made possible, however, by institutional reassurance that the core interests of participants in the competitive process will not only be salvaged but that they stand a fair chance of actually being realized, if not sooner then later.[35]

Since the military is not a participant in the competitive process, this core part in the institional framework of democracy cannot, in itself, be offered as a guarantee. For the military, guarantees are those that secure its autonomy and protect it from external control. Furthermore, institutional guarantees for the military are those that prevent outcomes in the political process which are deemed threatening to the military institution and to its views of national security. Obviously, not all these guarantees may be obtained, and their nature and extent will vary from case to case according to resources, perceived threat, and the institutional context itself.

In some cases specific guarantees have been demanded and offered regarding immunity from prosecution for past abuses or the preservation of autonomy. More general guarantees have included the formalization of a monitoring role. Guarantees may take the form of constitutional provisions that allow for direct representation of military interests, the continuity of institutions from the authoritarian past, or the continuity in power of formerly authoritarian elites who manage to mobilize enough popular support to play an important role under competitive institutions. Guarantees do not remain fixed, however, after the original bargain leading to the establishment of democracy is struck. Actors continue to attempt to redefine the appropriate extent of areas of uncertainty or to change the content of guarantees. These areas may expand or shrink and will subsequently induce changes in the military's willingness to acquiesce, or, at least, they will affect the opportunity structure of alternative strategies. The point is that, to varying extents, the assertion of civilian supremacy demands that guarantees initially given the military be reduced, replaced, or reformulated.

Guarantees may be withdrawn, or they may simply evaporate. For instance, political groups most congenial to military interests may fail to garner enough popular support in the competitive process, or they may grow increasingly distant from military interests. Whichever way guarantees disappear or weaken, they will cause substantial frustration, such as was experienced by the military in Spain. The Franquist Right was never able to muster enough electoral strength to present itself as a workable guarantee, and more moderate politicians, who the military initially held as allies — the governments formed by the monarchy — pursued policies that struck the core of military interests. The legalization of the Communist Party and the stance taken by these politicians during the drafting of the Constitution destroyed a bond of trust that had initially provided an informal guarantee to the military.

In situations like this the military may attempt a forceful restatement of guarantees, in which case it may win or lose. If it loses, it may be forced to acquiesce peacefully to the new regime and also, it is hoped, to redefine its goals at some later point toward the establishment of professional roles more compatible with democratization. Accumulated frustration, however, may orient goal redefinition in the direction of greater contestation, reawakening a temporarily dormant assertive stance. In any case, changes in the structure of guarantees will renew and increase uncertainty, and civilians and the military will initiate reassessments about the extent to which they regard each other as a continuing source of uncertainty. Ultimately, however, democratization entails a gradual and sensible elimination of this kind of uncertainty on both sides.

Bargaining, Resources, and Empowerment

The acts of offering and withdrawing guarantees, reassurance, and threats during democratization are decided on when they lead to desired outcomes that seem attainable in the light of a given set of constraints.[36] In gauging attainability, these actors assess the resources they can muster and develop expectations and calculations about the resources of others. These actors thus relate to one another in situations in which decisions are interdependent. Actions within this interdependent relationship may be seen as a form of communication and bargaining.

Bargaining does not necessarily entail a formalized situation in which actors explicitly exchange agendas and mutual claims and demands, although it may very well take this form, and it often has. Bargaining is, rather, a constant process in which actors signal intentions and brandish resources with a view to producing reactions and responses, which are in turn taken as signals for renewed interaction. The military, for instance, will resort to "voice" or to various attempts at veto and will play with the fear induced by the powerful threat of a coup or will spread the notion of a military ceiling to reforms.[37] Civilians may also use the threat of a coup by the military to induce moderation and coalescence across the spectrum of political forces. They also may try to upgrade their bargaining capacities with the use of various resources such as mass mobilization, pacts, constitution making, issuance of policy packages, and legitimation via elections and referenda. Compromises or any kind of outcomes reached in a succession of bargaining exchanges institutionalize a new set of opportunities and constraints which unevenly empowers the actors involved, modifying the basis for strategic calculus for the subsequent series of exchanges.

Success in these exchanges is a matter of relative strengths. It is thus critical, for a proper understanding of different outcomes, to focus on the various resource settings, the kind of resources available to different actors, and the ways these actors gain access to them, use them, and deny them to their opponents.

Approaches to Relative Strengths

Studies of civil-military relations and specifically of military intervention in politics also have utilized a focus on relative strengths. Can the study of civilian supremacy profit from these other studies, especially if the factors leading to intervention are the same as those that operate in forcing withdrawals, as some authors maintain?[38] No, these studies are of little use if the factors used to account for intervention are not referred to in the specific and changing institutional context of transitions.

Most of the shortcomings of this literature come from its basis on a "comparative strength" model that tried to balance diverse perspectives within a comprehensive "systems" approach. Scholars with this perspective argued that the key to the military's inclination toward intervention was found in societal factors such as the strength of political institutions, the nature of the dominant political culture, the strength of the social system, or the degree of political institutionalization.[39] A few authors wanted to balance this emphasis on societal factors with an approach that also included elements related to internal characteristics of the military. The result was a systematic contrast between weak social and political systems and purportedly modern, strong, and cohesive military institutions. The contrast yielded a military that was seen as functional in correcting basic societal imbalances that stemmed from the inability of civilian institutions to cope with social development. The military's connection to politics could thus best be seen within a focus on "the comparative strengths of civilian and military organizations."[40]

If we accept this model and its view that military intervention fills a vacuum left by weak civilian structures, we should expect military withdrawal to result from a reversal in the relative strengths of military and civilian structures. Even if, however, military withdrawal were the consequence of a severe weakening of the military, a corresponding strengthening of civilian institutions would not necessarily be implied.[41] The military may weaken, but this will not immediately inaugurate strong civilian structures. Conversely, a strengthening of civilians does not necessarily preclude the retention of political strength by the military. In fact, among the cases considered here civilians were able to advance their supremacy even in the absence of clear signs of strong civilian institutions during the first postauthoritarian years.

The model of comparative strengths sets the military on one side and the political system on the other. It cannot, therefore, capture situations in which actors unevenly empower themselves within a shared institutional setting, itself changing in a period of regime transition. Instead of searching for the presence or absence of "strong civilian institutions," which are likely not yet in place during the transition, we must allow for the analytical inclusion of resources and strengths with which civilian and military actors appear at the outset as well as those that they actually develop and bring to bear during and after the transition. The establishment of strong civilian institutions will be largely the result of asserting civilian supremacy, not the other way around.[42] The analytical starting point here is thus not civilian versus military institutions but, rather, civilian and military actors developing resources to modify or strengthen institutional settings that bind them and differentially empower them.

Opportunities and Constraints for Civilians and the Military

At the outset of the transition and during the unfolding of the transition and post-transition processes, certain resources and institutions will define the opportunities and constraints facing civilian and military actors. First is who, and to what extent, is in control of the transition. If the predominant elite in control of the transition is formed by civilians, the military assumes a secondary role and finds it harder to influence the process and to steer change in directions closer to its own preferences. If, however, the elite in control is military, then the military is at the forefront of the negotiations leading to its retreat, holding the upper hand in the bargaining process that ensues and imposing protective preconditions for itself.

Whether or not the military plays the dominant role is generally influenced by the *formal position* it occupied *in the power structure of the outgoing authoritarian regime*. According to this position of the military, authoritarian regimes can be classified as civilianized or militarized. *Militarized* regimes are those in which the military participates directly in the formulation of major policy orientations and decides on the succession or rotation of those in executive power. Typically, this is the case of governing juntas or other devices for direct institutional participation, such as military councils or predominantly military cabinets. The authoritarian regimes that existed in Greece, Argentina, Uruguay, Ecuador, Peru, Bolivia, Brazil, and Chile conform, in different ways, to this type. *Civilianized* regimes are those in which the civilians rather than the military make major policy decisions, although the latter may be given representation in the governing institutions. This distinction is commonly grounded in the duration of an authoritarian regime, with civilianization gradually taking over among those regimes that lasted longer. The authoritarian regimes that existed in Spain and Portugal conform to this type.[43] Based on this distinction, it may be argued that *the military is in a better position to monitor change, set the agenda for the transitions and impose guarantees for its interests in cases in which it occupied the core leadership positions in the exiting authoritarian regime.*

Second, the nature of the elite in control of the transition and the extent of its control will be affected by *the transition path*. Transitions may be preceded by a gradual process of liberalization conducted by the authoritarian rulers and proceed according to a relatively planned timetable, and they may even follow, as in Spain, the long-anticipated death of an aging *Caudillo*. In transitions that follow this pattern *the militarized or civilianized nature of the outgoing authoritarian regime is the critical factor in determining who will be in control of the transition.* Transitions may also be launched, however, with no anticipation as a result of the sudden collapse of the authoritarian regime, and the elites formerly in control will be subsequently replaced by new ones.[44]

Regimes may collapse as a result of a mass uprising, a coup by the mil-

itary, or a military defeat. If, for instance, a formerly civilianized authoritarian regime is overthrown by a military intent on some form of liberalization or democratization, then it is the military that will command
a controlling position in the eventual transition, regardless of the civilianized nature of the ousted authoritarian regime. This was clearly the
case in Portugal.[45]

If military defeat, or unbearable international humiliation, leads the
authoritarian regime to collapse (as in the case of Greece or Argentina),
the political strength of the ruling elite will be swiftly eroded and pressured to transfer power. If the elite in control was made up of the military and is replaced by civilians, then these cases should be listed as
civilian-controlled transitions. Such was the case in Greece, where a
militarized regime was swiftly replaced by a civilian elite that initiated
and controlled the transition. In Argentina, however, military defeat led
to regime collapse but not to the immediate transfer of power. The military remained in power for more than a year yet, having been defeated
and severely discredited, it was politically weak. The transition path
thus influences which elite will control the transition as well as the extent
of this control. The military's range of options may be severely limited,
for instance, by the factionalism and divisions that defeat in war or a
coup against the authoritarian regime produce, and civilians may thus
be able to play on military divisions to their advantage. The role of unity
and divisions will be addressed in the following pages and a richer discussion of the consequences of different transition paths in chapter 3.
Here I simply want to underscore the importance of the nature of the
elite in control of the transition.

Third, actors' perceptions about their own relative capacities are
strongly influenced by the extent of their *internal unity,* an extremely powerful resource. The military's inherent power as an armed force is vastly
deflated politically unless it is able to display high levels of unity and
institutional consensus. As a hierarchical organization functioning by
command and discipline, unity among the higher echelons of the officer
corps becomes especially relevant when the military trespasses to areas
outside its professional specialization, from combat preparation to politics. Unity as a political resource is measured in the military by the
extent to which definitions of institutional interests, mission, and role
are shared by the officer corps and particularly by the top hierarchies.

Particular historical experiences, professional practice, international
connections, and generational, or "promotions," cliques all affect mili-

tary unity during the transition. But especially important are the varying assessments that the military develops about its own past performance in government roles and about the performance of successor civilian governments. Unity is enhanced if the evaluation of past performance in government is generally positive. Unity also is enhanced if there develops the generalized perception that core institutional interests of the military are being harmed by the action of successor elites.

A certain level of consensus in the military may suffice to resist civilian attempts at military reform or action in specific areas. But higher levels of consensus will be necessary if the military wants to pursue a more assertive strategy. Consensus around a societal project, viewed as alternative to civilian goals of regime transformation, will be necessary in order to stage an assertive attempt to block civilian-led transformations. The military's capacity to do this is enhanced if it develops internal consensus around an *alternative political project,* its own "political utopia."[46]

If the military unites around an alternative political project, it will be able to face civilians from a position of strength. If, however, the military is unable to recover or develop doctrinal coherence on which to base definitions of institutional interest and strategies, it will weaken and eventually become paralyzed. Another possibility is a dangerous situation of stalemate, in which doctrinal consensus breaks down into competing claims to institutional leadership. Decreasing levels of unity reduces the set of choices available to the military and enhances civilian expectations of success.

Fourth, unity is no less important for civilian forces. The ability of political parties and other organizations to coalesce around formal agreements on institutions and basic rules of governance is a factor of civilian strength. Pacts, accords, or informal but explicit understandings on mutual guarantees lend credibility to the forces that will staff democratic institutions. After the installation of democratically elected authorities, the existence of such agreements will facilitate the emergence of a loyal opposition — that is, one that, even if substantively opposed to the party in power, will maintain its opposition within the boundaries permitted by democratic procedures.[47] *Civilian coalescence on fundamentals will limit the range of resistance strategies available to the military.*

Societal or ideological polarization may present obstacles to civilian unity, but it need not hinder coalescent possibilities. There are cases in which civilians have presented a united front despite ideological polarization, while in other cases ideologically close actors have been unable to achieve formal unity. In Uruguay, for instance, the ideologically close traditional parties were unable to coalesce in the "Club Naval" accords with the military. In Spain, in contrast, ideologically distant forces supported, overtly or tacitly, the reform proposals put forward by Adolfo Suárez and coalesced in the drafting of the new constitution.[48]

Fifth, *manifest citizen support* for emergent civilian structures, leaders, and policies is a deterrent to forceful action by the military against reforms, as it signals increased costs to intervention and reduces the military's bargaining power. Support for successor governments is especially important when their ideological makeup collides with military views or when they embark on reforms strongly disliked by the military. Coup attempts in postauthoritarian Spain and Argentina testify to the possible consequences of diminished support for governments facing aggrieved militaries. The ability of civilian governments to garner visible electoral and mass support, and to take measures to elicit this support when needed, is thus critical. Measures aimed at eliciting mass support serve to preempt or deter the military by signaling increased costs to insubordination. These measures include calls for elections or referenda or the timely publicizing of broad policy platforms that give the initiative to the government.[49]

Sixth, the goal of asserting civilian supremacy demands that the civilian leadership develop its own conception of national defense accompanied with appropriate civilian expertise. Civilian leaders must develop their own general appreciation of the nation's security problems and threats and a concordant definition of the goals of national defense. They must develop, accordingly, a position on the armed forces' role and mission as well as specific views on military organization, professional norms, and education. More specifically, they must develop policies on the allocation of resources for national defense and on the relationships that the military should establish with the rest of the state and society. This is the basis for attempts at reform aimed at adapting the military's mission and position in the state to the general goals of democratization.

The lack of an autonomous civilian conception and policy reinforces the military's claim to corporate autonomy and may facilitate the reconstruction of internal consensus in the military on terms contradictory with the goals of political democratization. Civilian attempts at promoting military unity around professional views consistent with constitutional norms demand that the military perceive the civilian leadership as competent. Therefore, the development of a conception and policy

Introduction

on national defense empowers the civilian leadership in the attempt to overcome corporate resistance and to advance democratic leadership in the defense area.

It is generally the case that civilian leaders have little, if any, command of military and defense affairs when the transition to democracy begins. Delay in the formulation of policies, however, may not be harmful for civilians; it may indeed be beneficial. Untimely civilian effort to initiate military reform may prove counterproductive. The need to reassure the military during the first years may, in fact, demand postponement of reform measures, particularly in those areas deemed most sensitive. Civilian expertise is most effective if put into practice when at least some degree of confidence between the new authorities and the military has already developed.

Contextual International Factors

International factors have played a role secondary to the dynamics of local processes in the transitions in southern Europe and South America, and they can be assessed most productively by focusing on the ways they filtered down to the views of domestic actors in strategic scenarios.[50] External factors have indeed been critical in several instances in triggering or encouraging the transition and in supporting processes of democratic consolidation later on. International armed conflict, for instance, played a critical role in triggering the transitions in Greece and Argentina, as did the colonialist burdens in Portugal. Also, a strongly democratic regional environment attracted the participation of Portuguese, Greek, and Spanish elites in multifaceted European networks, greatly aiding the move toward democratization.[51]

International factors have also been influential as demonstration effects. The fact that regime changes were taking place almost simultaneously in two or three countries in the regions of concern here influenced the perceptions of local actors. Revolutionary events in Portugal, for instance, were followed very closely by Spanish elites and certainly influenced their perceptions as they prepared for the imminent end of the Franquist era.

International pressures for democratization were more ambiguous in South America given the role of changing priorities in the foreign policies of U.S. administrations and the stance of international financial sources. Still, only by signaling moves toward liberalization and democratization, no matter how rhetorical, could authoritarian regimes hope to counter international political delegitimation.

Specifically in regard to the question of civilian supremacy, regional military contexts of South America and southern Europe offered uneven opportunities for civilians. The existence of NATO provided special opportunities for the civilian leadership in Spain, when it finally decided to join the organization. Civilian governments could use this opportunity in their empowerment relative to the military in ways that simply were not available for civilian elites in South America.[52]

Economic Factors

Similarly, the role of economic factors cannot be neglected in a discussion of the transition process. It can be generally expected that more favorable conditions for democratization will exist when successor governments are economically prepared to cope with the difficult legacies of authoritarianism and with the eventually rising demands of a resurrected civil society.[53] Economic prosperity also would provide flexibility in government's dealings with the military and assist in the satisfaction of some of its economic and budgetary demands.

Economic difficulties, however, should not be seen as directly and inevitably stimulating the military's reentry into politics, especially in those cases in which the military, from its own governmental experience, learned about the intractability of problems in this area and of the risks involved in being placed in charge of solving them. Also, military evaluation of civilian competence is done on a broader basis than mere economic performance. For instance, in those cases in which the military plotted against ongoing democratization processes, such as in Spain and Argentina, neither the rebels' motives nor the governments' responses were directly related to economic issues.[54]

Most of the cases of interest here faced severe economic difficulties during the transition, and governments had to decide on different adjustment policies. The economies of Spain, Greece, and Portugal, for instance, were severely hit by the oil shocks of 1973 and 1979 and by the recessionary period experienced by their major trading partners in Europe. Portugal's gross domestic product (GDP) declined by 4.3 percent in 1975 in the midst of a volatile political situation in the year after the ousting of Marcelo Caetano, and fear of leftist upsurge led the United States, Germany, and international lending agencies to engage in extraordinary assistance measures. Greece's GDP growth was − 3.6 percent in 1974, the initial year of transition.[55] In Spain almost exclusive concern with political reform led to postponement of adjustment measures, and growth halted. GDP growth rate dropped from 6.3 percent in the period 1965–74 to 2.3 percent in 1975–77 and then to 1.3 percent in 1978–85, with unemployment steadily rising to reach 14.8 for this latter period.[56] The South American transitions took place under much worse conditions. Argentina and Uruguay, for instance, experienced negative growth during the transition years, while Brazil fought for recovery from the economic downturn in the years preceding the presidential election of 1985. Skyrocketing levels of inflation were accompanied by high unemployment and low wages, all in the context of severe international financial constraints imposed by the debt burden.[57] Economic obstacles in the South American cases were reinforced by the sharp internal inequalities in wealth and income inherited from the previous regimes. Indeed, none of the democratic transitions considered here could ride on the wave of an economic bonanza; instead, with the exception of Chile, most of them were weighted down by economic difficulties. Thus, a focus on the constraining effects of the economy per se does not hold much explanatory power.

Nonetheless, the specific ways in which successor governments handle economic problems and the effects that their policies have on the levels of public support may affect the bargaining position from which governments face the military. Public support for democratic advancement has in most cases prevailed over frustration about economic difficulties.[58] Support for a democratic regime, however, is not the same as support for a specific government. And specific governments, especially in South America, had trouble maintaining sufficient levels of public support to empower themselves in their attempts to advance civilian supremacy.

Opportunity Set and Cases

Civilian reformers are ideally empowered to pursue the assertion of civilian supremacy if, either because the exiting regime was civilianized or because the military abruptly withdrew after collapse, they control the transition and set its agenda; they are able to coalesce around fundamental aspects of democratization, and their governments manage to maintain substantial popular support, both of which give legitimacy to emerging structures; and they are able to develop, in due time, expertise on national defense with which they issue coherent military policies. If, at the same time, the military does not oppose them with an alternative project and its resistance to democratization is weakened by internal disunity, civilian reformers should be able to succeed, especially when, in addition, the international context is propitious.

Conversely, a decidedly less auspicious situation arises for civilian reformers when the military conducts its own extrication, controls the transition's agenda, and further empowers itself by assertively developing institutional consensus around a coherent and alternative political project to that of civilian democratizers. If, in addition, civilian parties fail to coalesce, to obtain popular support, and to devise mechanisms to expand what little support they may have, and they are unable to develop their own program on national defense and military policy, military resistance can be expected, or, at the very least, civilians will not be effective in advancing civilian supremacy.

More likely, however, are situations in which elements of civilian and military empowerment combine, with neither the military nor civil authorities holding clearly preeminent positions. These situations, in which neither actor is consistently strong or weak, are roughly depicted in table 2.1 as they appeared in the cases considered here. The table is a rough approximation because it cannot fully depict changes that occur over time, but it does highlight differences across cases and the influence of the various key factors in accounting for differences in outcome.

Just as actors in real situations combine elements of weakness and strength, their resources and empowerment also vary over time, as they are engaged in a highly dynamic interactive process. For instance, a military in control of an authoritarian regime that collapses following military defeat may overcome its initial devastation, as in Argentina, and turn into a highly assertive institution successfully exacting concessions, only to be partly subdued later on by newly empowered civilians. Or a military that overthrows a civilianized authoritarian regime and takes control of the transition, as in Portugal, may ultimately weaken by, among other factors, inciting factionalism. The extent of military unity, civilian coalescence, or government support may vary during the transition and post-transition processes, and the timing of these changes relative to one another may affect the outcome. Policies and strategies, as

Table 2.1
Set of Opportunities/Constraints for Civilian Elites in Democratic Transitions

	Spain	Greece	Portugal	Argentina	Brazil	Chile	Peru	Uruguay
Authoritarian regime was civilianized	Yes	No	Yes	No	No	No	No	No
Transition substantially controlled by civilians	Yes	Yes	No	No	No	No	No	No
High civilian coalescence[a]	Yes	No	No	No	No	No	No	No
Manifest citizen support[b]	Y-N-Y	Yes	N-Y	N-Y	No	Yes	Y-N	Yes
Civilian defense policies	N-Y	Yes	N-Y	N-Y	No	No	No	No
Substantial divisions in the military	Yes	Yes	Yes	Yes	No	No	Yes	No
Military alternative project[c]	No	No	Yes	No	No	Yes	No	Yes
Favorable international opportunities	Yes	Yes	Yes	No	No	No	No	No
Success in civilian supremacy	High	High	High	Medium	Low	Low	Low	Medium

[a]High levels of civilian coalescence are found in different cases at various points in time. Here only Spain is ranked "yes" because of the high level of cooperation in drafting the new constitution.

[b]Obviously, levels of popular support vary over time. The table focuses on level of support at critical junctures, such as referendums. "N-Y" or "Y-N" indicates change at different junctures.

[c]In cases ranked "yes" the military backed distinctly authoritarian constitutional designs.

will be examined in subsequent chapters, also are likely to have different effects depending on the timing and pace of their implementation.[59]

These variables do not exert their influence simultaneously. The first two given in table 2.1 point to initial conditions, while the rest refer primarily to changing conditions during and after the transition. A basic time demarcation is that which separates the period prior to the end of the transition and the period that follows it. The demarcation line varies across cases; in Spain, for instance, the demarcation line is the approval of the 1978 Constitution and the following national elections; in Peru, the approval of the Constitution and the presidential elections of 1980; in Portugal, the Constitution of 1976 and the following elections; in Argentina, the assumption of power by president Alfonsín, and so on. These *transition outcomes,* I argue, should be viewed as landmark arrangements that set the context—the opportunities and the constraints—for the subsequent bargaining process between the civilians and the military. The analysis will be centered on the factors influencing these outcomes and the ways in which these outcomes, jointly with other factors, influence subsequent processes.

Having laid out the basic conceptual tools and variables guiding this study, let me now briefly recapitulate the argument outlined in the previous chapter. The nature of the first postauthoritarian arrangement—the transition outcome—is strongly affected by the strength of the forces that helped produce it. A transition controlled by a unified military conducting the authoritarian exit is likely to result in a new arrangement in which military prerogatives are larger than in a full-fledged unrestrained democracy. A civilian-controlled transition, in which the military has little influence over the agenda and major decisions, will likely lead to a new, postauthoritarian arrangement that starts out with fewer military prerogatives. Thus, the formal, power position of the military and the level of its unity and assertiveness—part of the set of initial conditions—are determinant in shaping the contours of the first postauthoritarian arrangement.

The *first institutionalized postauthoritarian political arrangement,* then, becomes a factor in itself by *shaping the institutions that differentially empower* the civilians and the military for the ensuing process, within which attempts to attain civilian supremacy and democratic consolidation will take place. The new political regime is often the result of transactions and compromises reached after difficult negotiations and laborious efforts, and, once inaugurated, it becomes very costly to any attempts to introduce changes in it. Unsatisfied actors will attempt changes nonetheless, but it is they who will have to bear the burdens of initiating action and rallying support. For instance, the inauguration of a pristine democracy—although democracies, especially "transacted" postauthoritarian democracies, are seldom pristine—would place heavier burdens upon a military that, critical of the transition outcome, attempts to expand its own prerogatives at the expense of an already accorded distribution of power. Conversely, in an incomplete democracy in which the military, for instance, has entrenched itself with excessive prerogatives, the burdens of initial reformist action are placed on civilian democratizers. This reformist action is costly for a number of reasons and often because it implies questioning more or less formalized guarantees previously given the military in the course of liberalization or during the transition.[60] Thus, an *important effect of initial conditions* on the post-transition process is that *they unevenly empower political actors in their attempts to change or maintain the contours of the first, inaugural postauthoritarian arrangement.*

Yet, however weighty the starting conditions may be, actors who had great power at the outset may gradually be subdued, and initially weak actors may recover and strengthen later in the process. In Spain, for instance, the subordinate position of the military in the transition did not settle the military question once and for all. It did facilitate a clean democratic inauguration, placing the burden of subverting this order on the military, but ultimately it did not prevent the growth of military assertiveness, which severely tested the democracy and postponed the attainment of civilian supremacy and democratic consolidation. In Argentina a transition initiated from the ashes of the armed forces' political and military defeat proved not to be an insurmountable impediment for a later reassertion of the military. In Uruguay, conversely, the controlling position that the military held during the transition and the limitations imposed on the first democratic settlement did not in the end hinder the subsequent advancement of democracy and civilian control. In Greece, with initial conditions roughly similar to those of Argentina, democratization nonetheless proceeded much more smoothly and with greater success. What, then, do these cases suggest regarding the extent to which initial conditions influence the fortunes of the post-transition processes?

It will be argued that initial conditions are critical in shaping the first transition outcome and that this, in turn, becomes a powerful factor influencing the subsequent process. Yet many other elements also come into play. Initial conditions exert considerable influence by helping shape institutions with power-distribution consequences. It is then up to the actors involved to mobilize, garner support, and prepare internally to exert the special effort to change the situation in pursuit of goals they value. They may decide they are not able to do this or that it is not worth the risks or that the alternative does not appear to be so bad after all, or, on the contrary, they may decide to take the risks and bear the consequences. Institutional settings and resources provide the constraints but also the opportunities, and it is up to the actors involved to utilize, exploit, or avoid them.

II

Initial Conditions
and the Transition

3   Transition and Militarization

Initial Conditions in Comparative Perspective

THE NATURE of the authoritarian regime — civilianized or militarized — and the modality of transition strongly influence which elite is in control of the transition. When a gradual process of liberalization conducted by the authoritarian rulers moves according to a relatively planned timetable, the militarized or civilianized nature of the outgoing regime will be the critical factor determining who will be in control. If the previous regime was militarized — that is, the military occupied the core leadership positions in it — then the military will be in a better position to set the agenda and monitor change. But, in transitions that follow a sudden collapse of the authoritarian regime, the elites formerly in control will be replaced subsequently by others, who will in turn monitor regime change.

A comparison of authoritarian regimes in southern Europe and South America shows that the civilianized character of Spain's outgoing Franquist regime, and its mode of transition, gave civilian reformers an early advantage in the goal of advancing democratization and civilian supremacy. Civilian reformers were better positioned vis-à-vis the military to outline the transition's agenda than was the case elsewhere. Other conditions present only in Spain also turned out to play a favorable role. The king, for instance, provided a complex and multifaceted element of continuity which helped to reassure the military in the early stages and to keep it from intervening. The nature of military disunity at the start of the transition played a favorable role as well.

Yet not all conditions played a facilitating role. For instance, the very modality of the transition, which allowed for a break with authoritarianism from within, also bequeathed an untouched military, strongly identified with the past and extremely sensitive to the "surprising" turns of the reform process. Terrorism, nationalism-regionalism, and other factors would later combine to incite this legacy against democratization. Indeed, the initial situation in Spain was more complex than the mere account of the civilianized nature of late Franquism might suggest. Civilianization, for one, did not preclude a considerable military presence in the Franquist state. Although the military started out from a relatively weak position regarding its chances of controlling the transition, still the need to dismantle Franquist institutions and to remove the military's manifold presence magnified the task of civilian reformers. A comparative examination here will help to clarify the impact of the civilianized character of authoritarianism in Spain, even with a respectable military presence in state institutions.

Civilianized versus Militarized Regimes

The distinction between civilianized and militarized regimes has been highlighted by several students of transitions. Guillermo O'Donnell and Philippe Schmitter, for instance, argued that a higher degree of militarization of the authoritarian regime would expose the military more saliently to emerging civilian policies, thus increasing the difficulty of the transition.[1] I will argue that the truly critical impact of this distinction lies principally in the greater or lesser ability of the military to influence the transition's agenda.

A *militarized* regime is one in which either regularly established collective military bodies or a selected group of top military chiefs, closely in touch with their services, participate in the delineation of government policy and partake in its implementation. In these regimes the military also has the power to appoint or dismiss the head of the government and other top officials or, at least, significantly influence the selection process. A *civilianized* regime, instead, is one in which the military may have strong representation in the governing institutions but it is the civilians rather than the military who make major policy decisions.

The degree of militarization or civilianization of an authoritarian regime affects the relative empowerment of the civilians and the military in the bargaining process entailed in the transition. It affects the ability of the military to set, or significantly influence, the transition agenda and to impose protective preconditions for itself meant to outlast the authoritarian regime.[2] The military holds more of this ability when the transition is from a militarized rather than from a civilianized authoritarian regime.

In South America and southern Europe only Spain and Portugal displayed civilianized authoritarian regimes, and, of these two, only Spain remained civilianized throughout the transition. Nonetheless, even in this most civilianized case, levels of military participation during the Franquist regime were not negligible. A comparative examination, however, will allow us to distinguish military participation in visible regime positions from inclusion in the regime's core decision-making sites. This distinction permits a more in-depth consideration of the criteria by which authoritarian regimes may be depicted as militarized or civilianized. This examination will show that, however far from negligible, military participation in the cabinet, the assembly, and other distinct institutions of the Franquist state was not tantamount to inclusion in the regime's core decision making. Thus, military presence in state institutions did not make *franquismo* a militarized regime. This examination also will provide a preliminary description of the basic features of the Franquist state which democratization dismantled.

Military Participation in the Cabinet

In Spain's Franquist regime the military consistently participated in the Council of Ministers — the state's central executive body, appointed and led by the president of the government, in turn appointed by Francisco Franco.[3] As a strong collective organ, it was empowered, for instance, to approve government policy and the general orientations for each department; to issue bills on the basis of ministers' proposals; to submit nominations for the administration's higher offices to the head of state, on the basis of departmental proposals (including the nomination of the captains general in command of the country's military regions); to authorize treaties and international agreements; to declare states of siege or other states of emergency; and to perform a number of other functions.[4]

Each armed service (the army, the navy, and the air force) had its own minister in the council, and, although nowhere was it explicitly estab-

Table 3.1

Military Ministers as Percentage of Total Number of Ministers

Argentina (1976–83)	Brazil (1964–83)	Chile (1973–87)	Spain (1938–75)
44.0	36.7	45.8	32.8

Sources: Spain: José M. Cuenca Toribio and Soledad García Miranda, "La Elite Ministerial Franquista," *Revista de Estudios Políticos,* no. 57 (1987): 139. *Chile and Brazil:* Carlos Huneeus and Jorge Olave, "La Participación de los Militares en los Nuevos Autoritarismos: Chile en una Perspectiva Comparada," *Opciones,* no. 11 (May–August 1987). *Argentina:* Daniel García Delgado and Marcelo Stiletano, "La Participación de los Militares en los Nuevos Autoritarismos: La Argentina del 'Proceso' (1976–1983)," *Opciones,* no. 14 (May–August 1988). In the case of Chile the figure would be 56.2 percent if eleven new positions with ministerial rank created at different times by the military government were included.

Table 3.2

Military Ministers as a Percentage of Total Number of Ministers,
Selected Cabinets in Authoritarian Spain and Portugal

	Spain	Portugal*		
February 1938	41.6	80.0	(48)	1926
May 1941	46.1	70.0	(52)	1926–51
July 1945	50.0	30.0	(54)	
July 1951	37.5	33.3	(55)	
February 1957	44.4	44.4	(56)	
July 1962	42.1	36.4	(56)	1951–58
October 1969	26.3	35.7	(56)	1958–74
March 1975	15.8	21.4	(57)	
December 1975	21.0			

Sources: Spain: Rafael Bañón and José Antonio Olmeda, "Las Fuerzas Armadas en España: Institucionalización y Proceso de Cambio," in *La Institución Militar en el Estado Contemporáneo,* ed. Rafael Bañón and José Antonio Olmeda (Madrid: Alianza Editorial, 1985), 310; and Manuel Tuñón de Lara et al., *Historia de España, Tomo X**: Transición y Democracia (1973–1985)* (Barcelona: Editorial Labor, 1992), 516. *Portugal:* Maria Carrilho, *Forças Armadas e Mudança Política em Portugal no Sec. XX* (Lisbon: Imprensa Nacional, Estudos Gerais, Serie Universitaria, 1985).

*Figures in parentheses indicate number of the cabinet. Years: 1926–51, presidency of Antonio Fragosa Carmona; 1951–58, presidency of Francisco Craveiro Lopes; 1958–74, presidency of Americo Tomaz.

lished that the ministers for the armed services had to be active-duty military officers, this had been the continuous practice since the creation of these ministries in August 1939. Military officers served in other posts as well, especially in the early stages. Indeed, as shown in table 3.1, one-third of all the ministers during Franco's governments were military officers, a proportion almost as high as that found in the Brazilian authoritarian regime.

What most matters for the transition, however, is the extent of military participation in the final stages of authoritarianism, especially in those cases (such as in Spain and Portugal) in which authoritarian

Table 3.3

Military Ministers as Percentage of Total Number of Ministers in Different
Phases of Authoritarian Government in Argentina, Brazil, and Chile

Argentina[a]		Brazil[b]		Chile[c]	
(1976–81)	75.0	(April 1964)	25.0	(1973–78)	67.2
		(March 1967)	44.4		
(1981)	42.9	(February 1974)	42.1	(1978–83)	58.1
		(March 1979)	27.3		
(1981–82)	33.3	(August 1982)	31.8	(1983–87)	31.2

Sources: Argentina: Daniel García Delgado and Marcelo Stiletano, "La Participación de los Militares en los Nuevos Autoritarismos: La Argentina del 'Proceso' (1976–1983)," *Opciones,* no. 14 (May–August 1988); *Brazil:* from various years of *Keesings Contemporary Archives; Chile:* Carlos Huneeus and Jorge Olave, "La Participación de los Militares en los Nuevos Autoritarismos: Chile en una Perspectiva Comparada," *Opciones,* no. 11 (May–August 1987).

[a]First phase corresponds to the presidency of General Videla; the second phase to the presidency of General Viola (March–December 1981); the third phase corresponds to the presidency of General Galtieri.

[b]Selected cabinets corresponding, in order, to the first cabinets of presidents Castelo Branco, Costa e Silva, Geisel, and Figueiredo, respectively. The cabinet of August 1982 also falls in General Figueiredo's period.

[c]First phase: from coup of 11 September 1973 to ousting of junta member General Leigh (air force) on 24 July 1978. Second phase goes until the appointment of Onofre Jarpa on 10 August 1983 as minister of the interior. Third phase goes until appointment of Sergio Fernández as minister in the same department on 7 July 1987. Figures include traditional ministries and the new ones created during the Pinochet government.

regimes lasted longest. Table 3.2 displays the level of military participation in the cabinet at different stages during the long period of authoritarian rule in Spain and Portugal. It shows the steady decline in participation after 1951 in Portugal and after 1962 in Spain, to one-fifth or less of the total number of cabinet members at the end of the period.

The South American cases also experienced a declining trend in cabinet participation by the military. These cases, however, especially Argentina and Chile, started out with extremely high levels, and, despite the ensuing decline, military officers still had about one-third of the cabinet positions in the final stages. Table 3.3 portrays this trend in the cases of Argentina, Brazil, and Chile.

These tables show that, while there was significant ministerial participation of the military in Spain, it declined over time to much lower levels than existed in the final stages of the military-authoritarian regimes of South America.[5] In fact, the last government in Franco's time included military chiefs only in the ministries for the armed services (15.8 percent of all ministries).

Nonetheless, when Franco died, and with him the certainty of his institutional legacy, the guarantor role of the armed forces acquired greater visibility, as did their constitutional powers to oversee the proper functioning of Franquist institutions. When newly crowned King Juan Carlos confirmed Carlos Arias Navarro as president of the government in December 1975, the latter in turn appointed an active-duty lieutenant general in the new post of vice president for defense, hierarchically the first of three government vice presidencies. With the vice presidency for defense, and with a military minister for each of the three armed services, four active-duty military officers sat in the Council of Ministers (21 percent of all ministers). The new appointments, although not unprecedented, demonstrated the current feelings of uncertainty and the need to reassure important players and institutions after the disappearance of *el Caudillo*.

Military Participation in the Assembly

In Spain legislative business was handled in the Cortes. The powers of the Cortes, however, never were substantial: "Elaboration and approval of laws, without prejudice to the sanction reposing in the Head of State."[6] In fact, during the six years of chairmanship of the Cortes by Franco's last appointee, Alejandro Rodríguez de Valcárcel, this body handled only 98 legislative proposals from the executive, the majority of which passed unanimously, while the government itself promulgated 101 decree-laws.[7] The semicorporatist nature of this body was meant to allow for some form of participation, aiding the regime's legitimacy by including a diverse array of groups and social sectors.

A number of deputies (*procuradores*) sat in the Cortes as a result of their holding office in government (that is, all members of the cabinet) or in the national council of "the Movement." Others were selected along corporatist lines as representatives of unions, professional, and other kinds of functional organizations and local government bodies. Approximately one-fifth of the variable total membership (about 500) were elected by universal suffrage in the provinces to serve as representatives of the family institution, which gave the Cortes some representational legitimacy. Franco himself, following approval of the Council of the Realm, could appoint up to twenty-five deputies "by virtue of their ecclesiastical, military or administrative status, or their service to the country."[8]

Military officers gained participation through any of these various paths. By reason of office the military ministers, the president of the

Table 3.4

Military *Procuradores* as Percentage of Total Number of *Procuradores*
Spain's Franquist Cortes and Portugal's Corporative Chamber

	Spain[a]		Portugal[b]	
Session				
I	(1943–46)	19.1	(1934–38)	9.3
II	(1946–49)	19.2	(1938–42)	8.1
III	(1949–52)	19.9	(1942–46)	8.5
IV	(1952–55)	20.2	(1946–49)	7.5
V	(1955–58)	22.9	(1949–53)	9.2
VI	(1958–61)	22.8	(1953–57)	7.5
VII	(1961–64)	22.0	(1957–61)	6.4
VIII	(1964–67)	18.0	(1961–65)	5.7
IX	(1967–71)	14.9	(1965–69)	4.2
X	(1971–76)	11.3		

Sources: Spain: Elaborated from data found in José María Comas and Lucien Mandeville, *Les Militaires et le pouvoir dans l'Espagne contemporaine: De Franco a Felipe Gonzalez* (Toulouse: Presses de l'Institut d'Etudes Politiques, 1986); and in Bernardo Díaz-Nosty, *Las Cortes de Franco: 30 años orgánicos* (Barcelona: DOPESA, 1972). *Portugal:* Philippe C. Schmitter, *Corporatism and Public Policy in Authoritarian Portugal* (London: Sage Publications, 1975), 31–33.

[a]Total number of *procuradores* ranges from 424 in the first legislature to 599 in the eighth.

[b]Total number of *procuradores* ranges from 108 in the first legislature to 232 in the seventh. Portugal had a separate Legislative Assembly, different from the Corporative Chamber. In the assembly military participation dropped to 8.5 percent in the eighth session, down from an almost constant 16 percent in the previous sessions.

Supreme Council of Military Justice, and military members of the National Council held seats in the Cortes. Other military deputies joined this governing body either by appointment by Franco, as did a small number of retired generals, or by inclusion in the various corporatist avenues of representation. Although they did not belong formally as *representatives* of the military institution, some of them maintained their commissions in the military while serving in the Cortes.[9]

Just as in the cabinet, military membership in the Cortes declined over time. Table 3.4 shows that in the 1970s in Spain, the proportion of military *procuradores* had dropped to half the levels observed in the Cortes prior to the early 1960s. Also in absolute numbers military participation had dropped to less than one-half the numbers reached in the fifth, sixth, and seventh legislatures. A similar declining trend developed in the Portuguese Chamber. Of the South American authoritarian regimes only Brazil had a functioning, elected legislature, but it included no military members. In the other cases, in which the previous Congress was shut down by the military, legislative power was held directly by military juntas.

Military officers also participated in all other major state and regime organs: the Council of the Realm, the National Council of the Movement, the National Defense Board, security agencies, and local government.

The Council of the Realm, formed by eighteen councillors, had the function of presenting the head of state with a list of candidates for him to select for the principal offices in the state. On this basis Franco would appoint the presidents of the following organs: the government, the Cortes, the Supreme Court, the Council of State, the Court of Exchequer, and the National Economic Council. The president of the Council of the Realm was, in turn, appointed directly by the head of state. This council also advised the head of state on questions concerning the succession to the headship of state, general legislation, referenda, and exceptional measures,[10] although in practice it basically was limited to its principal role of overseeing the succession of the nation's top leader and other critical appointments to the highest offices, especially immediately after Franco's death.

Military participation on this council included the lieutenant general with highest seniority in the armed services and either the chief of the Supreme Staff or the most senior of the chiefs of staff of the armed services. The chief of the Supreme Staff also was a member of the National Economic Council, the Council of State, and the Superior Council for Military Industries, which it chaired. The most senior military officer would also be one of three members of the Regency Council, which would temporarily assume the powers of the head of state, should the position fall vacant.[11]

The military also participated in the National Movement and its National Council, whose head was a cabinet member, minister secretary general of the Movement. The Movement, initially the Falange, unified several civilian groups — some decidedly fascist — who had fought on the nationalist side in the civil war, but it never developed as the official full-fledged regime party, as in the Nazi and Fascist experiences. It aimed at educating the public on the principles of the Franquist state, channeling support for the regime and providing some form of patronage.

All public authorities and functionaries in the Franquist institutions owed allegiance to the principles of the National Movement and were required to take the appropriate oath prior to assuming office. These principles declared the Spanish political system as "a traditional,

Catholic, social and representative Monarchy." The family, the municipality, and the trade union were made the channels of representation, and "any political organization whatsoever outside this representative system" was deemed illegal. The principles were declared "permanent and unalterable," and any law that defamed or injured them would be declared null and void.[12] The National Council of the Movement was called on to defend the integrity of these principles and to channel within them "the contrast of opinion on political action." Military officers became members of the National Council from appointment by the head of state, who could appoint forty members "from among persons who have rendered services of proven worth."[13] Military officers appointed as civil governors (appointments made by the minister secretary general of the Movement) automatically became provincial chiefs of the Movement. In the regime's early stages as many as 20 percent of the civil governorships were held by military officers.[14]

In addition to participating in the Movement, its mission of ideological stewardship, the military provided its own professional journals for the diffusion of the Franquist creed and the principles of the Movement.[15] Individual officers also took part in other organizations, such as the Association of Ex-Combatants and the Fraternity of Provisional Lieutenants (the Alféreces Provisionales), whose goal was to safeguard the principles of *franquismo* and the legacy of the "Crusade."[16]

Regarding defense and security, the military had almost exclusive participation in the National Defense Board. Chaired by the president of the government, the board was formed by the chief of the Supreme Staff, the ministers of the military departments, and the chiefs of staff of each of the armed services. It offered "the general lines to be taken with respect to security and national defense," and only under special circumstances would the board include ministers from the civilian departments (Articles 38 and 39 of the Organic Law of the State [*Ley Organica del Estado*, LOE]).

The armed forces, which included the forces of public order, also held major responsibility for domestic security. Their mission was to "guarantee the unity and independence of the country, the integrity of her territory, national security and the defense of the institutional system" (LOE, Article 37). The most important of the forces of public order were the Armed Police and the Civil Guard, which were fully militarized, governed by military regulations and procedures, and put under the command of an army general, who was dependent on the minister of the interior. Regional jurisdiction over these forces also belonged to regional army commanders. The Civil Guard's General Staff was formed by army generals. In 1976, as the transition began, both the director general of the Civil Guard and the director general of State Security were active-duty army generals.[17] Military roles in internal security were reinforced by the activities of a large number of officers in intelligence networks in various services in the Interior Department, the Supreme Staff, and the presidency of the government, all of which gathered information on domestic politics, especially on opposition to the regime and on the formation of political groups within the regime itself.[18]

Finally, through the maintenance of legislation of the early Franquist period, military courts had vast jurisdiction over civilian areas. For instance, the Code of Military Law (1945) and the Decree on Banditry and Terrorism (1960) permitted military courts to try civilians for crimes such as disobedience, resistance, or offenses to the armed forces, including the police. Military courts retained discretionary power to decide on their own jurisdiction over crimes by civilians. On the other hand, the existing legislation precluded the intervention of civilian courts for crimes perpetrated by members of the armed forces.[19] Other areas of military participation included control over the merchant marine, meteorological agencies, and civil aviation and the participation of officers in the board and executive positions of several public and private firms.[20]

Participation and Militarization

The extent of military participation in Spain was far from negligible.[21] It is true that many of the officers involved remained permanently removed from command posts or belonged in the Military Juridical Corps, while others were no longer on active duty. Nonetheless, these individuals remained loyal to their institutions of origin and worked closely with them. Admiral Carrero Blanco, for instance, who commanded a destroyer and a submarine during the civil war, and who was later chief of operations in the navy staff before taking on the role of subsecretary of the presidency in 1941 as a captain, always kept close touch with the navy high command.[22] Also, the military connections of these individuals facilitated the operation of networks of military influence in the government, thus enhancing the presence of the armed forces in the Franquist state.[23]

The military, however, participated as only one of many groups and "families" of the regime, which Franco maintained in a constant balance in periodic cabinet shuffles. The Cortes and the councils that filled up the state provided room for the participation of, and limited pluralist exchanges among, all the original members of the nationalist coalition: the military, *Falangistas*, Carlists, Catholics, and other groups, in a manner that followed the typical patterns of an authoritarian regime.[24]

Within this structure the military remained an important pillar of the regime, and Franco appointed officers to influential government positions. Between 1957 and 1969 the all-important ministry of the interior was held by a general and between 1969 and 1973 by a functionary who also held the grade of general in the Military Juridical Corps. The vice presidency of the government, created in 1962, was assigned to Captain General Muñoz Grandes, who simultaneously held the post of chief of the Supreme Staff. Admiral Carrero Blanco was a member of the government for twenty-five years, in the influential ministry of the presidency, and was the first president of the government after Franco relinquished this position by separating the headship of state from the presidency of the government.

Although these officers were powerful players, none of them acted in government on behalf of the military institution. While they influenced government policy by participating in the Council of Ministers and other organs, the military as institution did not engage in debate on this policy, nor did it make any of the critical decisions in the regime. In other words, the high presence and visibility of the military in different areas of the Franquist state did not make Franquism a militarized authoritarian regime.

Indeed, the extent to which significant posts in the public sector are occupied by military officers is not a necessary indication of regime militarization. For instance, during the years of authoritarian rule in Uruguay only one active duty military officer held a cabinet position (the ministry of the interior), and, quite uncharacteristically, the defense portfolio remained in the hands of a civilian. It is well-known, however, that real power and control of the government in Uruguay remained tightly with the military. Control of the government in Peru during the period of authoritarian rule also remained tightly with the military. But, in contrast with Uruguay's civilian cabinets, Peru had an all-military cabinet under the presidency of General Velasco (1968–75), and, after the palace coup of 1975, General Morales Bermúdez introduced only two civilians in the cabinet to handle foreign affairs and the economy.

The different forms of participation in regimes that are otherwise similarly militarized clearly indicate that, in order to assess the militarized or civilianized character of a regime, one must go beyond the analysis of cabinet composition and military presence in public positions to inquire into the critical sites of decision-making.

Franco and the Civilianization of Franquism

In militarized regimes the military decides, or greatly influences, who will head the government and participates in the delineation of government policy. In the forty years of Franquism the armed forces selected the head of government only once, when they gave the post to Franco. The leading group of army chiefs who, upon rebelling against the Republic in July 1936, formed the National Defense Junta, named Francisco Franco "Chief of the Government of the Spanish State" on 29 September and gave him "all the powers of the new State." Franco immediately replaced the Defense Junta with a Technical Junta, composed of various committees to monitor state administration. To head the new group Franco appointed the chief of the Army General Staff, but no other member of the previous junta was invited to join the new government.[25] Then, in January 1938, Franco dissolved the Technical Junta and, instead, organized the first regular cabinet of his government. Although nearly half the cabinet posts were assigned to fellow military officers, Franco was well on his way to further concentrating power in his hands. Shortly before the new government was formed, a law was passed which stipulated that the office of president of the government was "attached to that of Chief of State" and charged the latter office with "the supreme power to dictate juridical norms of a general character."[26] These offices were permanently reserved for Franco, whose concentration of absolute powers was later formalized in the 1947 Succession Law. This law stipulated that "the Head of State is the caudillo of Spain and of the Crusade, Generalissimo of the Armed Forces, Don Francisco Franco Bahamonde." The law declared the Spanish state a monarchy and gave Franco, ruler until death or incapacity, the right to name his royal successor for approval by the Cortes. The military as institution was thus denied a role in general policymaking for the new state and in deciding on the succession to Franco. Indeed, never did the armed forces directly delineate or implement government policy after the civil war ended in 1939.[27]

Initial Conditions and the Transition

Franco's appointment as head of the government of the Spanish state in 1936 was the only corporate decision made by the military. In 1943 a group of army generals again attempted a corporate move, this time to pressure Franco precisely by reminding him of the military-corporate origin of his powers. These generals addressed "the caudillo" in the following terms: "Without claiming representation of the entire armed forces" but as companions who "placed in your hands seven years ago in the Salamanca airdrome the supreme powers of military command and of the state," ask "our Generalissimo, with all loyalty, respect, and affection, if he does not think, as do we, that the moment has arrived to give Spain back . . . the monarchical formula. The hour seems propitious to delay no longer the restoration of this authentically Spanish form of government."[28]

Franco replied by reassuring the generals individually, promising restoration only when it became possible in the future. None of the generals insisted or stood up to Franco and, instead, merely renewed their loyalty and acquiescence. This was the last attempt by the military to exert corporate influence during Franco's life. The next opportunity would not come until thirty-four years later, during the transition to democracy, when the military as institution reacted against the legalization of the Communist Party by the transitional authorities.[29]

The high level of military participation during Franquism remained bounded by the roles assigned other groups in the Franquist family and by the powers that Franco reserved for himself. As caudillo of Spain, *generalísimo* of the Armed Forces, and head of state, Franco was "the supreme representative of the nation; personifie[d] national sovereignty; exercise[d] supreme political and administrative power" and supreme command over the armed forces (Article 6, LOE). The military's constitutional roles were contained within the higher responsibilities assigned to Franco, whose duty was to ensure the observance of the *Fundamental Laws,* the continuity of the state, the regular functioning and proper coordination of its high organs, and the maintenance of public order at home and the security of the state abroad.[30]

Contrasting Authoritarian Regimes in South America

The participation of the military in the South American regimes of the 1960s and 1970s was quite different. These regimes emerged from coali-

tions including technocrats, conservative politicians, and the military—
the basis for O'Donnell's concept of "bureaucratic-authoritarianism."
Intent on curbing popular mobilization and promoting drastic changes
in the general orientations over economic policy, these regimes differed
widely from previous personalistic or populist forms of nondemocratic
regimes. The institutionalized presence of the armed forces in the leadership of these regimes was one the most salient distinguishing features.[31] The military determined government policy, directly managed
its implementation in several areas, and held the power to appoint and
dismiss the head of government. Also, the military in many cases held
the power to make laws and rewrite the Constitution.

In Argentina the military junta that took over in 1976 declared itself
the supreme organ of the state holding constituent powers. Passing the
Act for the Process of National Reorganization, the junta also empowered itself to appoint and dismiss the president, to name members to the
Supreme Court, and to approve the appointment of government ministers. The junta had a legislative advisory committee composed of nine
members, three from each armed service. Except for the economic
ministries, the military held most of the other cabinet positions and all
the administrative positions in the regions. Some of the presidents, all
from the army, remained as chief commanders of their service.[32]

In Uruguay the military developed an articulate system of collegial
rule after the coup of 1973. The Juntas de Oficiales Generales, which
included all chiefs with the grade of general or admiral, appointed the
service branch chiefs. This body also joined the newly created Council
of the Nation, charged with the selection of the president and the members of the Council of State (the legislature, in which members of the military were a majority) and of the Supreme Court and the Electoral
Court. The Advisory Commission for Political Affairs, created in 1979
by the Juntas de Oficiales Generales, composed of representatives of all
the service branches, was charged with engineering and handling a
transition from military rule, a task later undertaken directly by the service commanders.[33]

In Peru the Revolutionary Government of the Armed Forces, established in 1968, directly involved the military in all areas of government
policy-making. The second phase, after the ousting of General Juan
Velasco Alvarado, was headed by former army commander General
Morales Bermúdez, who kept even closer touch with the generals than
had his predecessor. In this second phase the new chief of the army, Gen-

eral Fernández Maldonado, also held the government's premiership and the war ministry.[34]

In Brazil the military government established in 1964 maintained legal party activities, elections, and a functioning Congress, but it was the military that held a grip on the government. The presidents were selected by the high command and then elected by an electoral college, in which, due to manipulation of electoral rules, the official government party managed to hold a majority. The president, always an army general, was more autonomous from the armed forces than was the case in Argentina and Uruguay, and the collegial mechanisms of military input were far less institutionalized. The president remained, nonetheless, quite receptive to a military amply represented in the government. The military held at least six positions in the cabinet: one minister from each of the three armed services (who also commanded the forces), the minister chief of the Military Household, the secretary of the National Security Council, and the director of the National Information System.[35]

In Chile government policy after the military coup of 1973 became early on the exclusive responsibility of the president, who also retained the post of commander-in-chief of the army. General Augusto Pinochet, concentrating powers to an extent unknown in the other South American cases, ultimately gave autonomous basis to his power by having his hold of the presidency ratified for a period of ten years in a plebiscite in 1980. The personalization of power around Pinochet was combined, however, with high levels of military participation in critical decision making, and this is essentially the difference with *franquismo*. Military participation, especially by the army, was substantial. A large number of army generals and colonels sat in the cabinet, in legislative committees and government committees, such as the military household of the presidency, the president's general staff, and the presidential advisory committee, which had substantial input in government policy.[36] The military also headed state enterprises and filled all the top government positions in the regions. Most important, the Military Junta, composed of the chief commanders of the three armed services and Carabineros (the Chilean militarized police) held legislative and constitutional powers until 1990 and, for one time only, the power to nominate the single presidential candidate to be voted in referendum.[37] The junta, as the supreme institutional expression of the armed forces, maintained control of legislation until the end.

Evidently, the structure of military participation in Spain differed from the structure that prevailed in the South American regimes. The large presence of the military within the Franquist structures did not lead it to delineate or closely monitor government policy or control its leaders. When compared to the South American regimes, Spain, jointly with Portugal, falls easily into the category of civilianized authoritarian regime. This diminished the military's capacity in Spain to determine or significantly influence the agenda for the transition. As a consequence, civilian democratizers in Spain faced the transition relatively more empowered than civilian democratic elites in South America.

The Impact of the Transition Path

The impact that the civilianized or militarized character of the previous regime has on the power of different elites during the transition is affected by the modality of the transition itself. The transition path determines which elite is in control and strongly influences the extent of its control over the process of transition. These connections will be explored first by distinguishing between transitions triggered by a deliberate and conscious decision by those in power (transition from within and pacted reform) and transitions triggered by unexpected events that provoke a collapse of the regime and force authoritarian rulers to surrender power (unanticipated regime collapse).

Unanticipated Regime Collapse

Regime collapse may result from misconceived policies that produce unintended and devastating consequences for the incumbents. In these cases forced extrication from government is unanticipated and undesired by the authoritarian rulers. If these regimes are militarized—that is, directly run by the military—the military as institution will find itself in a weak bargaining position to seek protective preconditions or to influence the course of change. In Greece and Argentina the transition from militarized authoritarian rule came about as a result of regime collapse, following defeat in a confrontation with a foreign power. In these countries the civilian governments that subsequently took over moved swiftly to assert their authority over a military that was in no position to resist. It is no coincidence that these are the only two cases in which the former junta leaders were put behind bars.

In Greece, after the government was paralyzed by Turkey's offensive on Cyprus, military commanders forced the resignation of the ruling colonels in 1974. Political leaders were summoned by the military-appointed president, General Ghizikis, and adopted the decision to call old conservative leader Konstantin Karamanlis from exile to head a new government. In a matter of hours a new government was formed, and a new constitution was passed in a few months. The president conducted a controlled but significant purge of the military, numerous officers were forced to retire, and the principal leaders of the dictatorship were tried in court for sedition and sentenced to serve prison terms. Others were tried for responsibilities in the anti-student repression of 1973, although the government moderated its treatment of the military in view of the ongoing military threat from Turkey.[38]

In Argentina the government and the military junta collapsed after the British resumed control of the Falklands/Malvinas a few months after Argentine forces occupied the islands in 1982. A temporary president, retired General Emilio Bignone, was appointed by a weakened military to arrange for competitive elections. In 1983 Raul Alfonsín, the candidate who ran a campaign based on the issue of bringing the military leaders to trial for human rights abuses, won an absolute majority. Despite resistance by a military that had granted itself an amnesty before leaving office, the government proceeded to take former presidents and military chiefs to court, to reform the command levels, to dismiss significant numbers of generals, and to bring levels of military spending down to previous historic levels.[39]

In these cases the magnitude of military collapse canceled the impact that the previously preeminent position of the military might have had during the transition due to its position in the authoritarian regime. Collapse further weakened the military as it led to internal divisions, which developed partly as a consequence of efforts to blame different leaders for past failure. At least during the early phase of the postauthoritarian period, the military remained weak, and the new civilian ruling elite could pursue its policies with fewer restrictions.

A transition undesired and unanticipated by authoritarian rulers, as in Portugal, may also be provoked by a military coup against them. If the coup is against a civilianized authoritarian regime and a new, military-led regime takes over to start a transition to a more liberalized regime, then the military will be stronger, provided it remains cohesive.[40] In this case the new preeminence gained by the military cancels the subordinate position it held in the previous civilianized authoritarian regime. This is evidently the case for Portugal's transition to democracy.[41]

In Portugal the coup of April 1974 led to the installation of a military president and a military government and to the formation of officers' committees (the Assembly of the Armed Forces Movement and its Central Commission; the Council of the Revolution; and COPCON, the Continental Operational Command) to monitor revolutionary changes and to negotiate with civilian leaders on the basic features of the new institutions. The constitutional role that the military was assigned through the Council of the Revolution testified to the strength and bargaining capacities of the military. Yet the highly politicized role that the military played in this period, especially in trying to promote substantive social change, eventually resulted in divisions that weakened the military's bargaining capacities.[42]

Anticipated Transitions from within and Pacted Reform

Transitions from authoritarian rule may also start as the result of a conscious decision by those in ruling positions to move toward some kind of liberalization and, eventually, a democratization of the political regime. For whatever reasons (for example, frictions within the ruling clique, loss of public support combined with increased economic difficulties, or outside pressure), the incumbents make the decision to open up while closely overseeing the unfolding process. This type of transition developed in most of the militarized regimes of South America — in Bolivia, Brazil, Chile, Ecuador, Peru, and Uruguay.

The Brazilian military in government devised and monitored a protracted transition that started in the mid-1970s and culminated in the election of a civilian president a decade later. In Peru the military devised the Tupac Amaru plan in 1977, leading to the election of a constituent assembly in 1978 and the transfer of power to an elected civilian in 1980. In Ecuador the military decided in 1976 to oust General-President Rodríguez Lara and replace him with a military triumvirate in order to initiate a return to democracy. In Bolivia the start of the transition in 1978 was followed by a succession of interim civil and military governments, until democratization resumed in 1982. In Uruguay the military agreed to negotiate the transfer of power to the traditional parties in 1984, after voters rejected, in 1980, a military proposal for a new constitution. In Chile the military went ahead with the constitutional time-table for holding a plebiscite in 1988 and subsequent competitive elections for president and Congress in 1989. In all these cases, whether as a result of internal dynamics or pressures from outside or below, it was the incumbents' decision to embark on some form of transition. In all of them the military managed to set the transition timetable and to determine, or significantly influence, the transition agenda. In these cases proposed reforms went along with some kind of agreement, tacit or explicit, with civilian elites which invariably included protective conditions for the military.[43]

In Spain the decision to embark on a transition also was undertaken by elites in the authoritarian regime. During Franquism's late years many officials devised formulas that, however limited in scope, sought to advance some form of participation and competition. Admiral Carrero Blanco, during his brief presidency of the government, commissioned studies in this direction, and his successor, Carlos Arias Navarro, went further by publicly announcing reforms. Although these never materialized, they at least announced a climate that made debate over reforms possible. Other groups — state officials and business elites that no longer supported Franquism — pressured for reforms as they became aware of the liberalization imperatives of the political, economic, and military integration with Europe, which they favored. The possibility of change had thus gained maturity among the elite when Franco's health deteriorated and his death became imminent. When the caudillo finally died, reform initiatives were unleashed by elites within the Franquist regime.[44]

Despite similarities in initiating transitions from within, Spain differs substantially from the South American cases. In Spain the military did not participate in the elite nucleus that made the core decisions for the transition. And, when Adolfo Suárez initiated the transition by announcing his plan for political reform, the military did not attempt directly to seek guarantees for itself or for its preferred political option. Instead, it thought that the king and the authorities appointed by him would suffice as guarantees. Elite continuity and the role of the king thus became a substitute for the direct pursuit of guarantees, which the military embarked upon elsewhere.[45]

The role of the crown evidently placed Spain quite apart from the other transition cases and is critical in explaining the military's feeling of reassurance. Designated by Franco in 1969 as his successor in the headship of state, young Prince Juan Carlos became a pivotal element in the transition, capable of linking Franquist legitimacy in the eyes of the military with forward-looking liberalizing legitimacy catered toward reformist groups. The ceremonious event of the designation highlighted the efforts to transfer Franco's own legitimacy and charisma to Juan Carlos, especially with a view to the armed forces. Franco praised his proposed successor for his direct link to the centuries-old Spanish dynasty, for his proven loyalty to the principles and institutions of the regime, and for his close connections with the land, sea, and air armies. Entrusting the continuity of his institutional creations to Juan Carlos, Franco proclaimed that "everything remains tied up and tied up tightly for the future."[46] Juan Carlos himself would later, once crowned, play the same cords as Franco's heir to secure military loyalty and help gain its acquiescence for the transition. Upon assuming as head of state and supreme commander of the armed forces, Juan Carlos, expressing "gratitude to our Generalissimo Franco," pointed to the armed forces as "the safeguard and guarantee of the fulfillment of all that is established in our Fundamental Laws."[47] The military's comfort in the royal guarantee helped maintain the military at the periphery of a reform process that civilian elites conducted, at least initially, with little military interference.

The military in Spain — this is another important difference with South America — did not feel especially pressed to seek protection from potential attempts at retribution for past crimes. Much time had passed since the atrocities of the civil war, and human rights problems were not an issue. Rather, the memory of heavy tolls from the civil war on both sides was an incentive for moderation.[48] In contrast, the South American militaries felt the need actively to impose guarantees against attempts at prosecution for the violation of human rights. While this was not an issue in the Spanish transition, it was one of the most contentious issues pitting militaries against civilian officials in South America. In Argentina, for instance, the successor democratic president made this issue the focal point of his electoral campaign. Uruguayans also had to deal with this divisive issue, which also was the cause of civil-military tensions in Brazil. Chile's successor democracy remained clouded by the tensions faced in this area as well. Indeed, in a very recent past the military in the South American regimes had engaged in torture, kidnappings, and, in some cases, the killing of a very large number of opponents.[49] This factor added an element of contention in the South American cases which was not present in Spain or Portugal.

Still, the most important differences between Spain and the other

Table 3.5

Relative Position of the Military according to the Nature
of the Previous Regime and Transition Path

Previous Regime	Transition Path	Position of Military	Cases
	(A) Military Defeat	Weak	Argentina
	Regime Collapse		Greece
Militarized			
			Brazil
	(B) Pacted Reform	Strong	Chile
			Peru
			Uruguay
	(C) Military Coup	Strong	Portugal
Civilianized			
	(D) Pacted Reform	Weak	Spain

cases stem from the combined effects of the nature of the previous regime and the transition path. Table 3.5 summarizes the factors that influence the strength of the military at the outset of the transition.

The military faces the transition in a more powerful bargaining position in situation B: the outgoing authoritarian regime is militarized, and the military influences the transition agenda and timetable and secures guarantees for itself. In situation A the collapse of a militarized regime obviously weakens a previously strong military position. Situation C, a transition triggered by a coup against a civilianized authoritarian regime, sets the military in a position of strength, similar to that found in situation B. In this case, however, the military very likely weakens as a result of eventual factionalism, especially when this results from a breakdown in military hierarchy.[50] If the outgoing authoritarian regime is civilianized and the transition agenda and timetable is determined by civilian reformist elites, the military faces the transition in a weaker bargaining position (situation D). This is the Spanish situation, in which reform is pacted among civilian groups and the military finds guarantees only indirectly, in the crown and the continuity of Franquist elites. From the perspective of civilian reformist elites, situations A and D are the most favorable.

The strength or weakness of the military's position highlights the importance of the nature of the elite in control of the transition. A clear understanding of who the dominant transition elites are, in turn, has enormous consequences for a proper understanding of transition and post-transition processes and outcomes. It is thus useful to propose a classification of regime transitions which highlights the distinction between the civilian or military character of dominant transition elites and the consequences this has for subsequent outcomes.

Classifying Transitions from Authoritarian Regimes

The most useful typologies of transitions to democracy point to the forces that initiate the transition or to the extent of control that authoritarian elites maintain over the process of regime change. O'Donnell and Schmitter, for instance, distinguished between transitions initiated by successful, self-confident regimes, which control the rhythm and scope of liberalization, and transitions initiated by the opposition, in which a regime that has failed is left with little control over the agenda and timing of the transition.[51] Along similar lines Alfred Stepan identified transitions "initiated by the wielders of authoritarian power" from those in which "oppositional forces play the major role" and explicitly distinguished civilian-led from military-led transitions.[52] Scott Mainwaring, in turn, proposed a typology that focused on the extent to which the transition process is influenced by the authoritarian regime. At one extreme he placed transitions through regime defeat, in which the authoritarian regime collapses and ruling elites have little choice but to relinquish office. At the other extreme he placed transitions through transaction: "The authoritarian government initiates the process of liberalization and remains a decisive actor throughout the transition." Finally, a third, intermediate category — transition through extrication — captured situations in which "an authoritarian government . . . is able to negotiate crucial features of the transition, though in a position of less strength than in cases of transition through transaction."[53]

These typologies made useful distinctions, but, because they were each based on a single dimension, they generally failed to incorporate critical distinctions, such as I have emphasized here, and led to misleading classifications. For instance, by focusing only on whether transitions were initiated by successful, self-confident authoritarian governments, the Spanish and Brazilian cases were placed in the same category, which, as Stepan rightly pointed out, failed to acknowledge the critical differences in the position of military and civilian elites in the authoritarian regimes of these countries.[54] On the other hand, when the role of mili-

Table 3.6

Types of Transition from Authoritarian Regimes

Nature of Dominant Elite in Transition	Extent of Influence over the Transition by the Outgoing Authoritarian Regime		
	Very Low (Collapse)	Intermediate (Extrication)	High (Transaction)
Civilian	Greece Venezuela (Czechoslovakia) (East Germany)	(Hungary) (Poland)	Spain (Soviet Union) (Bulgaria) (Romania)
Military	Portugal	Ecuador	Brazil
		Peru	Chile
	Argentina	Uruguay	Paraguay

Note: Transition is the period between the collapse of the regime or the announcement of elections and the inauguration of democratically elected civilian officials. In parentheses are the countries that underwent transition from communist regimes and which I list only for the purpose of illustration. Przeworski argued that Poland became a military dictatorship in 1981, but I place it in the civilianized category because the military's presence in government and core party agencies had declined toward the end and because the influence of the generals was still exercised *within* the party (see Adam Przeworski, *The Democracy and the Market: Political and Economic Reform in Eastern Europe and Latin America* [Cambridge: Cambridge University Press, 1991], 74; and Paul G. Lewis, "The Long Goodbye: Party Rule and Political Change in Poland since Martial Law," *Journal of Communist Studies* 6 [March 1990]). For the other cases, see Ivo Banac, ed., *Eastern Europe in Revolution* (Ithaca: Cornell University Press, 1992); Nancy Bermeo, ed., *Liberalization and Democratization: Change in the Soviet Union and Eastern Europe* (Baltimore: Johns Hopkins University Press, 1992); Gilbert Rozman, ed., *Dismantling Communism: Common Causes and Regional Variations* (Washington, D.C.: Woodrow Wilson Center Press and Johns Hopkins University Press, 1992); and Gyorgy Szoboszlai, ed., *Democracy and Political Transformation: Theories and East-Central European Realities* (Budapest: n.p., 1991).

tary institutions in initiating transitions was underscored, cases such as Greece, Portugal, and Peru were placed in the same category, failing to acknowledge important differences in the role of those militaries during the course of the transition itself.[55]

The classification presented in table 3.6 makes combined use of two dimensions: Mainwaring's distinction of the extent to which elites in the outgoing authoritarian regime influence the transition and the military or civilian character of the elites actually in control during the transition. This classification captures differences that are critical, especially in regard to the problems associated with the military in democratic consolidation.

In the cases of collapse authoritarian rulers were ousted and replaced with new elites, who swiftly initiated the transition. In the cases of transaction, the process was conducted under the auspices of the authoritarian constitution, enabling authoritarian elites to command high levels of influence over the transition. In the cases listed in the intermediate category, the authoritarian elites failed to pass a new authoritarian constitution (as in Uruguay) or let an elected convention create a new one (as in Peru; in Ecuador voters were given a choice of two documents). They were thus forced to negotiate with the opposition before the actual transfer of power to a larger extent, or on more substantive issues, than was the case in Spain, Brazil, Chile, or Paraguay. The table also makes it possible to capture important aspects of the elites in control during the transition. There is a crucial difference in this respect between Spain, on the one hand, and Brazil and Chile, on the other.

Whereas, in the intermediate cases, the military nature of the elites in control during the transition needs no further elaboration, the classification of collapse does. In Greece, and Venezuela in 1958–59, military authoritarian rulers were ousted by military coup, and new civilian elites took over to guide the transition. In Portugal a military elite ousted a civilianized authoritarian regime and thus controlled the transition. Argentina was a less clear-cut case. The government was not overthrown, but the military was in such a state of disarray after defeat in the Falklands/Malvinas that the junta virtually ceased to exist for a few months during the transition under President Bignone, a retired army general appointed by the junta. Yet military elites, although severely wounded, remained in power for over a year after the conclusion of the war, conducting initiatives that had enormous consequences for the subsequent resumption of democracy when power was transferred to democratically elected President Alfonsín.[56] Thus, Argentina belongs with Portugal in the category of military-controlled transitions.

This classification is an improvement over the traditional way of simply clustering Argentina and Greece together as cases of collapse because of the similarities in the military fiascos—in Cyprus and the Falklands/Malvinas—which led to the fall of their military regimes. The fact is that, while the Greek military swiftly extricated itself from power, giving way to a civilian elite, the Argentine military stayed on for over a year and attempted to create favorable conditions for its withdrawal by granting itself amnesty and trying to strike deals with the Peronists. Admittedly, the military failed on both counts, since the Peronists did not win the presidency as expected and Alfonsín swiftly repealed the self-granted military amnesty. Yet, by staying in power during the transition and trying to block the future government's actions, the military created a scenario that demanded costly civilian mobilization by the new administration.[57] Such a confrontational scenario was avoided in Greece by the rapid removal of the colonels from power by the military itself. But in Argentina actions against military officers for human rights offenses helped the military recover much of its lost power by arousing internal solidarity against what it perceived as unfair treatment for its "victory in the counter-subversive war." This recovery ultimately forced the government to limit its actions against criminal offenders in the military and even to pardon the former junta chiefs. In Greece, on the contrary, the political clout of the military was systematically weakened, and the junta leaders sentenced to prison terms for the crimes of high treason and insurrection still remain behind bars. It makes sense, therefore, to place these two cases in different categories.

Table 3.6 highlights differences that have been relevant for the transitions' aftermath. Its usefulness is confirmed by the fact that cases (in southern Europe and South America) falling within the civilian category tended to be more successful in achieving democratic consolidation. This way of viewing transition paths suggests that, whenever the military secures an important position in government policy-making—either as a result of the militarization of the outgoing authoritarian regime or, as in Portugal, as a by-product of the transition—it will complicate the transition to and the consolidation of new democratic regimes. The Portuguese transition, for instance, required eight years (1974–82) before the military was removed from tutelary positions and then several more for the consolidation of civilian supremacy (1989). In Greece and Spain the military was put in a position in which it could only react to policies initiated in civilian quarters, and the swift inauguration of democratic regimes was more clearly attained.

Democratization as Surprise

THREE YEARS after Franco's death Spaniards approved a new constitution, conclusively marking the end of Franquism and the inauguration
of a full-fledged democratic regime. How did reformist elites manage to
navigate three years of transition to such successful accomplishment?
Why did the military, which until the very end had sworn "fidelity to the
Fundamental Laws and Principles," acquiesce to such a fundamental
break?[1] Even if we know that at the start of the transition the military
was at a comparatively weak position, the question still remains: Why
did the military not overcome this weakness, and why, in the course of
three years, did it not react to a transition that, before its very eyes,
unfolded in an undesired direction?

The answer is manifold. First, civilian reformers monopolized the
transition agenda, managing to present the military with a sequence of
choices which left no alternative other than acquiescence. Standing outside the group of agenda setters, the military could produce no more
than failed, late reactions to the reformist initiatives developed by the
civilian democratizing elites. The control of the reform agenda by these
elites helped to preempt stronger military actions against democratization than actually took place.

This reactive position of the Spanish military contrasted sharply with
the South American transitions, in which the military managed to influence the transition agenda significantly and to set the transition time-

table. Manipulation and definition of electoral mechanisms (Brazil and Chile), banning of potential candidates or parties (Ecuador and Uruguay), restriction of assembly deliberations (Peru), constitutional restrictions (Chile), and special guarantees provided the military in South American transitions with the means to protect itself and set the bases for influence during the postauthoritarian period. Even in these cases the results often were far from what the military desired, proving that transitions everywhere were laden with unintended consequences, bitter reassessments, and, occasionally, sheer embarrassment. In Ecuador, for instance, the military impeded Assad Bucaram from running for president, only to see his relative and fellow party member Jaime Roldós elected instead. In Peru reconciliation of the military with Alianza Popular Revolucionaria Americana (APRA) did not yield success for APRA, and Peruvians instead elected Fernando Belaunde in 1980, the president whom the military had ousted in the coup of 1968. In Brazil flagrant manipulation of the rules by the military could not prevent the election of the opposition candidate, Tancredo Neves. In Argentina negotiations between the military and the Peronists were rendered inconsequential when voters elected the Radicals instead. In Chile the 1988 plebiscite conceived to sustain General Pinochet in power through the following decade produced, instead, his defeat. Yet, these setbacks notwithstanding, the military guaranteed areas of influence which were far superior to those that had existed prior to the authoritarian period and certainly much larger than anything the military managed to secure in Spain.

Second, the Spanish military did not find it necessary to upgrade its status during the transition in order to influence the agenda, or to anticipate and eventually preempt reforms, because it trusted the Franquist credentials of the elites in control. The king had been selected by Franco and entrusted with the protection of Franquist legality, and the military felt no reason to ignore Franco's posthumous request—"to extend the same affection, loyalty and continued support that you have given me to the future King of Spain, Don Juan Carlos de Borbón."[2] In addition, the governments appointed by Juan Carlos promoted reforms that relied on mechanisms within Franquist legality itself to move "from the law to the law," covering the transformation of Franquism with a veil of legitimacy from Franquism itself.[3] Behind this veil the military felt it could tolerate reforms without betraying its commitment to Franquist legality and principles.

Reforms, however, went far beyond the military's initial expectations. When the military took full account of the extent of the break with Franquism which the transition was accomplishing, it was already too late. In this regard, from the military's angle, Spain's transition truly was a case of democratization by surprise. Those whom the military trusted would maintain reforms within certain limits ended up striking a full and clean break with *franquismo* altogether. Had the military been an inside player within the agenda-setting elites, there certainly would not have been any major surprises to react to.[4]

Third, military reaction to unpleasant surprises was deterred by two critical factors that strengthened reformist elites. One was coalescence of most civilian elites around the goals of reform, especially as expressed, first, in the vote in the Franquist Cortes in support of the plan for political reform and, second, in the workings of the committee that drafted a new constitution. The other critical element was the ability of the reformist leadership to evoke repeated expressions of public support via referendums and elections. Civilian control of the transition agenda, public support for the emerging democratic institutions, and high levels of civilian coalescence were the factors that combined to tilt the balance in favor of successful democratization.

Uncertainty and Reassurance in the Prelude to the Transition

The first post-Franco government did not go very far in promoting change toward democracy. Still, the flurry of rhetoric and maneuvers displayed by reformists sufficed to arouse the anxieties of a military that had entered the transition with the belief that their caudillo had left things pretty well tied up. The government of Carlos Arias—caught between conflicting internal currents, shaken by an increasingly mobilized opposition, and scrutinized by an expectant European public—succumbed to its own inaction only seven months after inception. During this period diverse groups attempted to seize the agenda, either for reform or continuity, but none succeeded, and no agenda prevailed.

Juan Carlos had chosen to confirm Carlos Arias as president in November 1975 more out of prudence than inner conviction. Arias had first been appointed by Franco to succeed Admiral Carrero after his assassination by the Basque Homeland and Liberty organization (Eus-

Initial Conditions and the Transition

kadi ta Askatasuna [ETA]) in 1973 and had conducted his government in a manner so as to fully please the caudillo. Now, in his absence, Arias pursued a timorous course in which his admitted desire "to persevere and continue the gigantic legacy of Francisco Franco" betrayed his own efforts at liberalization.[5] His cabinet, for instance, accommodated the airs of renovation with which the king wanted to associate his recently inaugurated headship of state, but it also included hard-line Franquists.

Arias believed that the legitimation of the monarchy as Franco's institutional legacy required a modification of the authoritarian structures to allow for greater participation and pluralism. He managed, for instance, to have the Cortes pass a Law of Political Associations that would make legalization easier for political parties that were not "totalitarian." He failed, however, to push for regulations that would permit actual implementation of the bill or to make the executive responsible to the Cortes or specify a timetable for elections. Instead, for instance, he continued to advocate a role for the National Council. By satisfying neither the hard-liners, who wanted no reforms at all, nor the reformists, Arias earned the enmity of most from within the regime, and certainly of the opposition.[6]

The opposition, organized around the Junta Democrática and the Plataforma de Convergencia, led by Communists and Socialists, respectively, increased pressure for a complete break with authoritarianism. Demanding immediate amnesty for political prisoners, the elimination of repressive agencies, the legalization of all parties, and the immediate convocation of elections for a Congress that would elect the government and write a new constitution, these organizations pursued a strategy of "*ruptura*" with the Franquist institutions. Strikes increased during the first months of 1976, hitting essential public services and reaching the highest point ever since Franco came to power. Nationalist mobilization increased dramatically as well, also including labor strikes, especially in the Basque region and Catalonia.[7] The opposition succeeded in further isolating Arias and in augmenting tension between the government's contending factions, but it was unable to actually force the government to initiate democratization. Toward the summer major opposition groups, now unified in the Coordinación Democrática, came to realize that a *ruptura*-oriented strategy would not work and that changes would more likely come about through a strategy of negotiation.

The government, however, and Arias in particular, officially rejected dialogue with the opposition. Reformist members of the cabinet were wary of further polarization between a mobilized opposition and a paralyzed government and pressured the latter to promote more substantial change. José María de Areilza, the foreign affairs minister, did so by traveling in Europe announcing and publicizing a domestic process of democratization, even if it was nowhere to be seen. Minister of the Interior Manuel Fraga, meanwhile, promoted his own reformist agenda, hoping to line up the cabinet behind him. The king, during trips abroad, expounded a set of goals that had little connection with what the government was in fact doing. Clearly, a transition agenda had yet to be seized. Yet what little had been already done, and especially the increasing debate that had developed, was enough to stir growing anxieties within the military.

It will be recalled that the military now had a fourth member in the cabinet, as Arias had created the vice presidency for defense for his first post-Franco cabinet. Intended to reassure the military by providing it with core oversight positions in a period of high uncertainty, the post was given to Lieutenant General Fernando de Santiago. In other positions Arias appointed new generals to head the army and the air force ministries and confirmed admiral Pita da Veiga, a well-regarded professional and important player in the previous government, as navy minister. As devoted Franquists, all four military chiefs in the government had a clear notion of the role of the armed forces as guarantors of the fundamental principles of *franquismo*.

This strong presence in the government, however, did not amount to much in practice. The new vice presidency never fully realized its potential as a powerful position from which the military could coordinate its service branches or oversee government policy. General de Santiago only retained traces of a glorious past and prestigious career but, despite his self-definition as "spokesperson for the Armed Forces in the Government,"[8] did not exert special leadership from this post. The vice presidency gave the armed forces one additional vote in the council of ministers but enhanced their effective presence in the government only symbolically.[9]

Surrounded by reform talk, some reform action, and many hard-to-grasp contradictory stances, the generals seemed puzzled and anxious. There was concern that the bill on political associations prepared by the government would open the way for the reemergence of parties that had been a threat to Franquism.[10] They were especially angered when Manuel Fraga, minister of the interior, publicly admitted that the Communist Party would at some point have to be legalized. They were also perplexed by Areilza's statements abroad in favor of full democratization and by the government's authorization for the Socialist Labor Federation, the Unión General de Trabajadores (UGT), to celebrate a Congress in Madrid.[11] They were bewildered by the king's expressions of discontent with Arias's vacillations in carrying out reforms.[12] In order to calm anxieties individual government officials held special meetings with military ministers and the vice president, to reassure them about the direction of government plans and the real meaning of the reforms envisaged. One such meeting, organized by Admiral Pita da Veiga, gathered the four military members of the government and minister of the interior, Manuel Fraga, who had to explain the reform plans to the ministers to calm the fears of their subordinates in the services.[13]

Military anxiety was compounded by concern with a few specifically military problems, such as demobilization of the forces deployed in the last Spanish colony, the Spanish Sahara, in order to avoid an armed confrontation with Morocco.[14] In addition, the sudden outburst of demonstrations under the visible leadership of socialists and communists — "the reds"—represented for military chiefs the unearthing of old demons that had caused the military so much aggravation in the past.[15] Repression of the demonstrations and military court action against dissenters exposed the military to much more controversy and uncertainty than its chiefs had wanted or anticipated.

The king's dismissal of Arias in July 1976 provided a feeling of relief for the military because it signaled the end of government inaction in the face of a mobilized opposition. The appointment of Adolfo Suárez, by the king, to head the new government was reassuring for the military. Suárez had been a loyal Franquist, who served as head of state television and later as minister secretary general of the Movement in Arias's last cabinet. In the eyes of the military Suárez's credentials looked impeccable.

If Arias's dismissal came as a surprise to no one, the king's decision to appoint Adolfo Suárez as president was, indeed, a great surprise.[16] For most of the civilian groups within the regime, Suárez was a disappointing choice because he obviously was not one of the big names among the various families of Franquism or among the new, more fashionable, reformist groups. For others, mostly in the opposition, his designation also was a disappointment because little in his background suggested that he would push reforms any farther than his predecessor had.

Suárez, however, soon surprised everybody with announcements of far-reaching reform plans. For the first time after Franco's death there emerged a clear agenda for the transition, with a distinct view of its ends and means, and a clear timetable for elections. With such an agenda the government now had the ability to demand support and to uncover those who only rhetorically spoke of reforms. Suárez initiated discreet contacts with the opposition, for whom it now became quite clear that the path to democratization lay in negotiations with the government and that electoral preparations had to substitute for an emphasis on mobilization and *ruptura*. [17]

In a national address on 10 September 1976 Suárez announced that a project on the Law for Political Reform had been submitted to the National Council for later debate in the Cortes. In language respectful of the Franquist past, but with no ambiguities, Suárez stated that elections were the key to the project: free elections for Congress to be held no later than June 1977. With the authority derived from electoral representation, added Suárez, topics such as autonomy for the historic regions, trade union reform, and fiscal and other reforms could then be dealt with properly. The project created institutions with open-ended possibilities for further reform. The new Congress and the government, for instance, would have the power to initiate constitutional revisions. These revisions could, in practice, be expanded to include the drafting of an entirely new constitution. In fact, in his address Suárez explicitly rejected the temptation to offer an already completed revised constitution; instead, the government preferred that a new constitution come from a freely elected Congress. [18]

Two days before his 10 September speech Suárez, in a bold step, called a joint meeting with the high council of the three armed services. Vice president de Santiago tried to have the meeting called off in order to prevent any attempt to associate political reform with the military, but Suárez understood that bowing to de Santiago would have weakened his ascendancy over the military. [19] The meeting, held on 8 September, lasted for more than three hours and was a complete success. Suárez explained the general features of his reform plans and found a somewhat warmer reception than expected. Although the content of the presentation was not made public, the following morning's headlines profusely told of the meeting and generally reported it as a positive success. Suárez could portray the image that he had cleared the toughest obstacles and could now proceed further with the plan. [20]

Displaying a great deal of charisma and verbal mastery, Suárez outlined in this meeting the basic features of his plans for reforms and presented the challenges facing Spain in its efforts to adapt to a new period. Speaking for the entire three hours, while the generals and admirals listened, Suárez said almost nothing about plans or policies affecting the military, and nobody among the audience asked. Only toward the end of the meeting, once Suárez had ended his presentation, Army Minister Félix Álvarez-Arenas read a statement with some of the army's concerns, especially those related to the unity of Spain, and then went on to wish Suárez success. The statement had been agreed to by a group of fourteen senior generals and was mostly aimed at preventing other generals from speaking out. A few did, nonetheless, but no one spoke in ways that broke with the general aura of satisfaction with the president which had developed in the course of his presentation. One general insisted on concerns about the unity of Spain, another hailed the president in colloquial terms, and another one asked specifically about the place of the Communist Party in the new institutions advocated by the reform plans. Suárez, who had avoided the latter issue in his presentation, replied that the Communists could not meet the requirements of legalization of political parties in general. The meeting adjourned, the generals stayed for cocktails, and Suárez had succeeded in getting the military's approval for his reforms, without ever formally asking for it.[21]

The government then submitted the project to the Cortes in what was a daring step, as it made the entire reform plan contingent on the ability of the government successfully to lobby the *procuradores*. It was, however, the only path to democratization consistent with the existing Franquist legality, and this was indispensable for obtaining the military's cooperation. When members of the Cortes were called to vote on the reform bill on 18 November, old military *procuradores* stood out among those who voted against the bill. Military ministers, however, had to vote with their president. The reasons were plainly explained by Admiral Pita da Veiga, navy minister and member of the National Council, right after the vote: "My conscience is at peace, because democratic reforms will proceed from Franquist legality."[22]

Following a careful orchestration of speeches and displays of support from important personalities, and intense lobbying by the government and the king's entourage, the Cortes passed the Law for Political Reform with 425 votes in favor, 59 votes against, and 13 abstentions.[23] With a few concessions, mostly concerning limits to proportional representation in the forthcoming elections, the government was now empowered to attempt the transformation of Franquism from within.

By getting the Cortes and the military ministers to support the reform plan, the government had successfully passed the first test. Key to this success was respect for Franquist legality and the perception that Suárez and associates in the regime could command substantial popular support by cashing in on the recently recovered political initiative. Suárez's success was thus based on what Giuseppe Di Palma called "forward-backward legitimation," obtained by respecting both Franquist procedures and the prospects for democratic ratification. Both dimensions were also embodied in the fact that the reformist government was, indeed, the king's government. While emphasizing reforms, Suárez's discourse also stressed that they aimed at providing fertile grounds for the implantation of the monarchy and that restoration of democratic procedures was the mechanism to implement the king's desire to "gain deep knowledge of the aspirations of the Spanish people."[24] The not so distant memory of Franco's political will requesting support for Juan Carlos, which a tearful Arias had read before television cameras to the country upon announcing the caudillo's death, must have resounded insistently in the conscience of loyal, militant Franquists torn between blind allegiance to the old institutions and support for the reinstated monarchy and reformist Franquist heirs. But, in their baffling support of the king's reformist government, the generals could find relief and understanding in the caudillo's posthumous communication.

The Transition Unleashed: Coping with Surprises and Eroding Guarantees

After approval by the Cortes the Law for Political Reform was submitted to referendum on 15 December 1976, winning overwhelming support. With 77.7 percent turnout, 94.2 percent voted in favor of the government's reform plan. Suárez now had a mandate to embark on the preparations required for the first competitive, democratic elections, convoked for 15 June 1977. The referendum gave Suárez electoral legitimacy, allowing him to act independently of support groups that linked him to the past. With the Cortes vote and the referendum behind, Suárez no longer had to concentrate on securing the support of regime groups as much as on making certain that the opposition would participate in the process.[25] Up until this point the military had been continuously reassured about the meaning and extent of the reforms. Although it had not been formally consulted, it at least had been informed about the transition agenda when one was finally put forth. The military was not itself making the agenda, but it was very much part of the government that proposed it. And, because it felt wooed by reformists within the regime who sought its support or neutrality to counteract the constant public reminders that hard-line Franquists made of the role that the *Fundamental Laws* assigned the armed forces, the military could see itself at the center of events that it thought it could influence, even if passively.

The military felt it could rely on its own presence in the government to protect its institutional interests. Despite anxieties rooted in the uncertainties unleashed by the reform plans, military officers would rest assured as long as the service ministers were there to make certain that nothing fundamental went wrong. The generals also thought that the Franquist inclinations of the military, well-known to everybody, guaranteed that reformists within and outside the regime would remain within acceptable limits. In addition, there was the protective role of the king, still holding great powers inherited from Franco. And, finally, there were the civilian officials in the government, whose impeccable credentials were guarantee enough that unavoidable reforms would be steered in the right direction.

Admiral Pita da Veiga had, in October 1975, shortly before Franco's death, admirably summarized the military's position: "We stand firm so that politicians can conduct their business. We watch over the security of the Nation and remain vigilant so that its essence, of which we are the trustees, remains unchanged."[26] Behind this confidence and clarity about division of roles was the military's belief that nothing substantial would change soon after Franco's death. Military chiefs knew that things would have to change eventually, that Spain would have to move closer to the political realities of Europe, but not so soon, at least not within the five or so years following Franco's disappearance.[27] Later, with the knowledge of Suárez's plans after the meeting of 8 September 1976, the military's first impressions during the prelude to the transition—that no great changes would take place for a few years—were greatly shaken. They realized now that Spain's serene transition would be proceeding at a faster pace than previously anticipated. But, still, the military believed that changes and the "politicians' business" would remain within limits tacitly shared by a successor elite with a similar background in Franquism.

Belief in limits *tacitly* shared is important because it meant that the military did not have to specify what those limits were. It never requested or imposed formal guarantees to protect its institutional interests and political preferences in the manner in which the military did in Portugal or in most of the South American cases. In addition, the military relied on the deterrent effect that fear of a reaction by the armed forces would have on politicians should they become wooed by the benefits of pursuing unlimited reforms. In fact, politicians were wary of such a possibility, as they knew about the military's anticommunism and its tough stance on regional and national demands, views that were publicized in military journals and newspaper interviews. It wasn't a mystery, and everybody knew, accordingly, that the military would be a major hurdle in the attempt to pursue democratic reforms that included unrestricted pluralism and recognition of basic regional demands. But no one knew exactly at what point conflict would arise if these reforms were implemented eventually, because the military never had specified any such point. Not once did the military formally and officially warn civilian authorities about its opposition to admitting the Communists in the political system; or about its opposition to granting some kind of autonomy to the historic nationalities; or even about the boundaries of military autonomy which civilians should respect.[28] Never, therefore, were civilian officials impelled to give the military formal assurances on these matters.

When civilian authorities began to implement reformist initiatives and policies, the military experienced them as a succession of surprises. The military began to learn about the practical implications of the reform agenda only as it unfolded through specific measures, to which the military reacted perplexed, always a bit late, unable to reverse the authorities' decisions. After the first bitter surprises brought about by the transition, the military no longer considered having former Franquists in the government to be a guarantor of its interests. All of a sudden, in the eyes of the military, these politicians had turned into expeditious reformers with no sense of the limits that the military thought they all shared. And the king, whom the military considered its last resort, could not, because of his rank, be pressured into interfering with the daily business of politics to defend the military's preferred options. Besides, he was evidently backing the reformists.

When military chiefs realized that politicians were conducting their business way too fast and in unexpected directions, they also found that the military's presence in the institutions had been severely trimmed. The Cortes elected democratically in 1977 no longer included military officers, except for a few senators appointed by the king.[29] The creation of a single defense ministry in the summer of 1977 eliminated the separate service ministries and, with them, the strong presence the military had had in the council of ministers of the first post-Franco governments.[30] Reduction of military participation was further envisaged in the constitution-drafting work initiated by the new Cortes, which started to dismantle old Franquist institutions and military participation in them. Having initially thought to have plentiful guarantees, the military was instead gradually brought to rely more and more on direct, non–legally prescribed pressure to attempt to protect its interests and preferences.

The military's position and perplexed views toward the unfolding transition can best be seen through a series of critical episodes in which decisions advanced by civilian officials were contested by the military, for the most part unsuccessfully. With each one of these decisions the transition advanced farther from military preferences and closer to the goal of inaugurating a full-fledged democracy. At each one of these points the military was left with no alternative other than to accept, however grudgingly, the civilians' decisions. At the end, with the formal inauguration of democracy in 1978, the military found itself in the midst of an outcome that looked quite different from the institutions and principles that it had sworn it would defend.

The First Surprise: The Return of the Unions

The first surprise for the military came only two weeks after the otherwise promising encounter of Adolfo Suárez with the generals on 8 September 1976. It concerned legislation prepared by the government which would remove barriers for the legalization of the nonofficial trade unions aligned with Socialists and Communists. Vice President de Santiago, who had earlier voiced strong protests about the congress of the UGT, was not prepared to compromise the army's position on such a measure and, on 22 September, submitted his resignation from his post in the government.[31]

The episode would have remained low-key had it not been for the use that hard-line Franquists made of it, elevating it as the first significant confrontation between reformist elites and recalcitrant military sectors. De Santiago sent personal letters to army chiefs explaining his resignation, in which he pointed to his unsuccessful opposition to an eventual decree-law that would legalize trade unions that were "responsible for the violence perpetrated in the red zone." Neither his conscience nor his honor, he concluded, would let him compromise the armed forces, which had given him their trust. General Iniesta Cano, former director general of the Civil Guard, a close friend of de Santiago and a well-known hard-liner, replied with a public letter full of adulation for de Santiago and his resignation, which, he added, had come at a time when staying in the government was incompatible with the sacred pledge made when sworn in.[32] The implication was that no military officer with a sense of honor could serve in that government. President Suárez swiftly decided to transfer de Santiago and Iniesta to the reserve and welcomed the opportunity to rid the government of General de Santiago.[33]

The incident was a first warning for both the government and the military. For the military it was a sign that the process was not exactly headed in their preferred direction. For the governing reformists it was the first attempt by hard-liners actually to demarcate positions and limits. The net result, however, was that the government decision to legalize the unions prevailed.

The incident also served to bring divisions in the military closer to the surface. Although most of the generals felt sympathy for de Santiago, most also found Iniesta too extreme and understood that Suárez could not have as vice president someone who opposed his views. The appointment, however, of a more sympathetic officer, Lieutenant General Manuel Gutiérrez Mellado, army chief of staff, to the vice presidency, aroused the opposition of important sectors in the military. Gutiérrez Mellado, known to support political and military reforms, had already aroused opposition from influential military chiefs when his name was considered for the vice presidency by Arias instead of de Santiago. This time his designation in the Suárez government was opposed by the three military ministers, who asked Suárez and the king to stop the appointment, with no success.[34]

The Second Surprise: The Return of the Communists

The issue of the legalization of political parties had been on the top of the agenda ever since the referendum had authorized competitive

elections. In February 1977 the government replaced existing requirements for party registration with a simple administrative procedure. All
significant parties applied for legalization, which they got right away,
except for the Communists, whose application the government referred
to the Supreme Court. The government, aware of the military hurdle,
had hoped that a favorable resolution by the Court would have exempted it from having to face a political decision on the matter. Contrary to
these wishes, however, the Court refused to rule on the case and returned it to the government a month later.

Meanwhile, the Communists were trying to force a quick decision.
Santiago Carrillo, the legendary secretary general of the party, still in
the underground, was caught, detained, and charged with illegal association. His release on bail a week after his arrest, in December 1976,
brought relief to an otherwise difficult situation for the government.
The leader of the "red threat," until then in exile or clandestine, was now
legally in Spain, and hard-liners could do nothing about it.[35] But
Carrillo's legal presence in the country added pressure on the pending
question of the party's legalization. At this point a critical event took
place: on 24 January 1977 an ultrarightist commando broke in on a meeting of four well-known Communist union lawyers in their downtown
office and machine-gunned them to death. Public outrage with the killing convinced the government to authorize a party demonstration to
mourn the victims, a demonstration in which the Communists excelled
in moderation and self-discipline, gaining public support in their quest
for legalization.[36] The party further pressed its case in March by holding a Eurocommunist summit in Madrid, hosted by Carrillo and attended by Georges Marchais and Enrico Berlinguer. With the rest of the
opposition favoring legalization before the elections for parliament, the
credibility of Suárez's plan for the opposition rested on his handling of
this issue.

Suárez could have chosen to have the new Cortes, which was to be
elected in July, to decide on the matter. But, without the Communists
officially in the race, they would be likely to maintain high levels of
mobilization, which the government would then have had to repress,
damaging the democratic credibility of the process. Suárez gradually
became convinced that the benefits of legalization would outweigh any
costs it would entail and devised a strategy for legalization. He had
already met secretly with Carrillo in February to obtain assurances that
the party would respect the monarchy and its symbols and support the

unity of the state against separatist demands from the Basque provinces.[37] He also made sure that reticent members in the government knew that the king supported his initiative. To appease Vice President Osorio's reservations and fears of damage to the crown which could stem from a swift legalization, Suárez told him that "the king . . . agrees because he thinks there is no other solution."[38] Suárez also sought reassurances that the military's discontent would stay within limits. He requested a special report from Colonel Cassinello, head of the information service of the presidency, about the situation in the military. Cassinello informed Suárez that opposition to legalization was quite widespread in the armed forces. His assessment, however, led him to support such a measure.[39] Suárez also believed that periodic informal meetings he had been holding with various groups of generals would serve him well on this occasion. He knew, from what the ministers of the army and the navy had told him, that legalization would create serious problems in their services, but he trusted that Vice President Gutiérrez Mellado, who was in favor of legalization, would be able to prepare the right mood among the top brass.[40] Finally, enthused by polls showing increasing public support for legalization, Suárez convened the two vice presidents and three ministers and decided to go ahead with legalization. They arranged to request, on the eve of Easter holidays, a report from the Consejo de Fiscales del Reino on whether the penal code presented impediments to the registration of the Communist Party. This step would give legal legitimacy to any decision on the matter. Gutiérrez Mellado informed the military ministers about the request to the Consejo, warned them that the report could be favorable to the Communists, and that the president would be available should they want to see him.[41]

The military ministers were understandably concerned, but they felt assured by the specific commitment that Suárez had made before them in the meeting of 8 September. Also, they felt certain that, in keeping with normal procedures, the Consejo's report and whatever decisions were made upon it would first have to be debated in the Council of Ministers. Spared from any feeling of urgency, the military ministers, just as everybody else, took off for the holidays.[42] Never did it cross their minds that, by the evening of Easter Saturday, 9 April 1977, the government would have the Communist Party officially registered, following a positive report that the Consejo de Fiscales had turned in that same day. The generals, as well as the rest of the government and the Communist leaders themselves, would learn about the decisive measure from television news that evening.

Most of the military chiefs felt betrayed by the president. In their eyes, and in those of almost the entire officer corps, the president had broken a commitment made in the course of a solemn occasion.[43] In addition, they felt it an offense that the president should bypass them so blatantly on such a critical matter. The military, particularly the navy and the army, reacted indignantly to the legalization of the Communist Party.

On 11 April Admiral Pita da Veiga submitted his irrevocable resignation as minister of the navy. The following day, in a five-hour meeting of the army's superior council, the generals aired their deep resentment toward Suárez and Gutiérrez Mellado and considered requesting that the king disavow the authority of the president and vice president. Yet the conciliatory attitudes of the chief of staff, the captain general of Madrid, and the director general of the Civil Guard—Generals José Vega Rodríguez, Federico Gómez de Salazar, and Antonio Ibáñez Freire, respectively—managed to cool tempers and focus on the consideration of a more sensible course of action. Debate centered on whether or not to have the minister of the army join Pita da Veiga in his resignation. They realized, however, that not one of them would want to accept the ministerial post if Alvarez-Arenas resigned. As this would leave the possibility open for the government to appoint a civilian, a possibility that they found even worse, they decided to keep their minister in the government. This decision gave the government some relief by leaving the navy as an isolated case, especially since the air force minister was not considering resignation. The government would have otherwise had to risk further confrontation by appointing civilians in the three posts or to make significant concessions to get the military back in the cabinet, including the resignation of the entire cabinet so that the king could form a new government. Any of these alternatives would have stalled the transition and made its future extremely uncertain.

The generals kept their minister in the cabinet but decided to issue a strong statement repudiating the legalization and warned the government about other issues dear to the military. A draft version of the communiqué was leaked by the press office of the army ministry and published in the right-wing newspaper *El Alcázar* on 14 April. The draft stated that the Superior Council demanded from the government the adoption of firm measures to guarantee the unity of the fatherland, honor and due respect to its flag, firm standing of the monarchy, and the prestige and dignity of the armed forces. On 16 April the army minister disavowed the statement, disciplined those responsible for the leak, and offered a softer version of the official final communiqué:

> The Superior Council of the Army unanimously agreed to inform the minister of the following statements according to the respective minutes:
>
> —The legalization of the communist party has provoked general repulsion in all Units of the Army.
>
> —However, attending to the highest national interests, it submits with discipline to a *fait accompli*.
>
> —The Council feels the government must be informed that the Army, unanimously united, considers it its undeclinable duty to defend the unity of the Fatherland, its Flag, the integrity of the monarchic institutions and the reputation of the Armed Forces.

The minister's note added: "We shall know how to fulfil our duty of remaining united, with discipline, fully trusting our chiefs, unconditionally under the orders of our King and Supreme Chief of the Armed Forces, as well as in the service of Spain, within the deepest respect and compliance with the decisions of our Government, which has no other interest than to work ceaselessly for the Fatherland's welfare and with the most absolute loyalty to the Crown, and at the same time with the highest regard and esteem for the Armed Forces."[44]

The "general repulsion in army units" which the communiqué noted was far from being hyperbole. In several units army generals had indeed gone out of their way to stop mobilization orders issued by junior officers.[45] Nonetheless, the publication of the final communiqué ended the crisis in the army.

The government still had to find a new navy minister to replace Pita da Veiga. Clearly, none of the admirals would accept the appointment. In solidarity with the outgoing minister, they felt they could not participate in a cabinet tainted by the legalization of the Communists. Of all the armed services the navy was the one that had been hit the hardest by the Communists in the civil war and which kept alive the memories of large numbers of officers killed during insurrections aboard navy ships. After a few days the government finally found a retired admiral, Pascual Pery Junquera, who was willing to head the ministry, putting an end to the April crisis.[46]

The military's emphasis on its duties regarding the unity of Spain, the crown, and the flag were soon matched by conciliatory statements by the Communists, which helped end the crisis. In their first legal press conference, a week after legalization, when the military crisis was over, the leaders appeared surrounded by the Spanish flag (with the emblem of the monarchy) and pledged not to oppose the monarchy or the unity of Spain.[47]

With the Communist issue and the military crisis behind, the government and the opposition could look forward to the first democratic elections. Yet the episode with the Communists had lasting legacies: a sharp decline in Suárez's and Gutiérrez Mellado's rating in the military, which eventually undermined their ability to subject the forces to effective discipline. Suárez would never again recover the sympathy among the military which had been given him until Easter Saturday.[48] Also, the king's standing in the army would suffer; the high army council had sent a reserved note to the king warning him about the negative effects that the episode had produced on his reputation.[49] For the first time the military had formally and officially stated its views on the limits of reform. Luckily for the reform process, this came after full political pluralism had been adopted.

Confronting the Elected Cortes:
The Issue of the Unión Militar Democrática

On 15 June 1977 Spaniards elected a new Cortes in the first competitive, democratic elections after Franco. The Unión de Centro Democrático (UCD), the reformist party formed by the government, came out first with 34 percent of the vote, followed by the Partido Socialista Obrero Español (PSOE), with 28.9 percent. The Communists ended in third place (9.2 percent), followed by Alianza Popular (AP) (8 percent), a party organized by Manuel Fraga and a group of former Franquists. The tallies confirmed the trend toward moderation which opinion polls had already detected among the Spanish public: the extremes combined could not get more than 17 percent. Although the combined votes of the Left surpassed 40 percent, a figure indeed alarming for those who had feared the eventuality of Socialists in Congress, it was nonetheless reassuring for them that the Communists gained less than 10 percent of the vote.

The military soon became concerned with the reformist thrust of the Cortes, and especially with reforms concerning a political amnesty law which most parties wanted to extend to include the members of the Unión Militar Democrática (UMD), a former clandestine organization in the army, who had been sentenced and expelled from the army in 1975. The deputies wanted to do justice to a group of well-inspired officers, whose crime had been to organize preemptively against any move that hard-line generals might have wanted to try to stop democratization after Franco's death.[50] Amnesty for this group of officers, however, would have legally empowered them to reenter the army. The generals had expressed firm opposition to this possibility; one of the few issues on which all of them agreed. Most generals rejected the UMD on ideological grounds, but their broad consensus was based on the principled view that no precedent of leniency should be established with regard to clandestine organizations within the army.[51] Consenting to the reentry of these former UMD members amounted, in their view, to blatant toleration of institutionalized undiscipline.

The dilemma was swiftly resolved by the generals by putting direct pressure on the deputies. Vice President Gutiérrez Mellado, who had by then been appointed to head the recently created ministry of defense, summoned the deputy who was chairing the congressional meeting while the law was being debated, to warn him, before a group of some twelve generals, about his inability to control the state of undiscipline which would be unleashed in the army if the amnesty was extended to include members of the UMD. Congress acknowledged the warning and dropped the UMD from the amnesty law that was passed in mid-October.[52]

This episode went unnoticed by the public but was indeed quite significant. First, it was one of only two episodes of the transition in which the army acted institutionally against political reforms (the other episode being the reaction against the legalization of the Communist Party). Second, this was the only one in which direct pressure was exercised in anticipation of a decision by a sovereign elected body. Having learned from the experience of legalization of the Communists six months earlier, the generals decided not to wait until a law was passed, which would have again forced them to accept an ex post facto situation. Third, consensus in the army around this issue was of such magnitude and endurance that civilian authorities did not again attempt an amnesty until nine years later, in 1986, and then only through very ad hoc procedures.

Facing the New Constitution

Work on the new constitution presented the military with major uncertainties. A new constitution would be elaborated in the Cortes by representatives of parties that the military had no reason to trust. Suárez, whom the king had confirmed as president right after the elections, was not deemed trustworthy by the military anymore. His party had a plurality in the Cortes and, jointly with the Left and the nationalists, completely dominated it. Since these groups were bound by no previous agreements on the matter, the new constitution would really result from negotiations in an open-ended process.

The open-ended nature of the constitutional debate was especially worrisome in the light of the divisive issues that had to be addressed. For instance, the preference of important sectors for republican forms of government stood against Franco's monarchic legacy. The monarchy itself and its prerogatives would be subject to congressional debate. A redefinition of the constitutional place of the church threatened the resurgence of cleavages that had ravaged the republic prior to Franquism. Debate on the role of the state and private property could not be dismissed in the presence of strong parties that still claimed Marxist inspirations. Finally, the suppressed center-periphery cleavage was expected to reemerge in full force from the claims for autonomy of the Catalans and especially from the Basques.[53] All these were issues that could easily arouse the military's sensitivity.

The decision taken by the Cortes's constitutional committee to keep deliberations secret certainly did little to mollify the military's concerns. In the government only a small group close to Adolfo Suárez, rather than the cabinet at large, decided on the positions of the UCD. And, even if the cabinet had had a say, the military no longer participated in it, since the military ministries had been replaced in the summer of 1977 by a single defense ministry. As a consequence, the military was not on top of the deliberations and agreements and was not fully informed about them, at least not until a draft was leaked in November 1977 and a complete text was submitted for public congressional debate in May of 1978.[54] But the military was not kept fully in the dark. Via Vice President Gutiérrez Mellado, the government inquired about the generals' views on some of the most sensitive issues, and the constitution makers had to adopt language and formulas that were receptive to perceived military concerns. This gave the military much less influence, however, than would have resulted from formal consultation or direct, official military monitoring.

The marginalization of the military from such an open-ended constitutional process contrasts sharply with the position of the military in other transitions that faced broad changes to the constitution. The Portuguese Constitution, for instance, was drafted directly under the shadow of the Armed Forces Movement. In Peru a permanent liaison was established between the majority parties in the constituent assembly and the outgoing military government. In Brazil the military lobbied the assembly with a sizable professional staff. In Chile the junta approved the 1980 Constitution and the 1989 reforms and maintained the power to pass interpretative organic laws on the amended authoritarian constitution until the very end. In Spain, instead, the military stayed at the margins and did not participate in the constitutional debate, a position only shared by the collapsed and defeated military in Greece.

The draft Spanish constitution introduced new clauses in a number of areas which did not please the military: the abolition of the death penalty and the recognition of the right to conscientious objection to military service. Gutiérrez Mellado, expressing the feelings of the military, requested that recognition of the right to conscientious objection be toned down. As a result, the final version indicated merely that the law would later regulate this right. Also, the military opposed the abolition of the death penalty and attempted to save it at least for military crimes. The Cortes conceded to the military on this issue, but the Senate insisted on and approved total abolition. The military was also concerned about what it saw as diminished prerogatives for the king.[55]

What the military disliked most, however, was the recognition of different nationalities, with their own officially sanctioned languages and flags and their right to autonomy. For the military this evidently recalled the warning that the army had earlier made about its fundamental duty to defend the unity of the fatherland.[56] Admiral Marcial Gamboa, for instance, complained against the "recognition of the nationalities" and "the excessive powers given the so-called autonomous communities." In his view "the existence of different nationalities . . . implies leaving an open door for the possible dismemberment of national unity." Lieutenant General Luis Diez Alegría, who thought this was "unnecessary, dangerous and contradictory," warned: "We shall try to suppress the term 'nationalities' in the Senate."[57]

Yet, for the representatives of Euskadi and Catalonia, the inclusion of the term *nationalities* in the constitutional text was not negotiable. They were backed on this by all other groups that sought the active support of the historic regions for the new constitution and were willing to risk military discontent. The military ended up accepting this terminology, but it nevertheless managed to influence the constitutional outcome. Fearing military resentment, most groups consented to rewrite the crude reference to the "nationalities" in the draft version and to wrap it up in more palatable language. Article 2 still recognized and guaranteed the right to autonomy of the nationalities, but in the final version this article was preceded by the affirmation of "the indissoluble unity of the Spanish Nation, common and indivisible fatherland of all Spaniards."[58] In addition, no other mention of nationalities was made in the 169 articles of the constitution; all other relevant sections spoke, instead, of "autonomous communities." And, partly to compensate for the inclusion of the term *nationalities,* the final version upgraded the status of the armed forces in the constitutional text by dedicating a special article to them (Article 8) in the *Título Preliminar* of the Constitution.

Parties on the Right maintained that inclusion of the military in the *Título Preliminar* adequately singled out its special importance, whereas parties of the Left believed that all references to the military should have been included more appropriately in Title IV, "On Government and Administration."[59] Nonetheless, the substance of Article 8 marked a critical break with the definition of the armed forces contained in the previous Franquist Fundamental Laws, by distinguishing between the "armed forces" and the "forces of public order." The Constitution now established police forces apart from the legendary Civil Guard; in the Fundamental Laws they were both included under the rubric armed forces. And the new Constitution deprived the latter of some major domestic functions previously under its control. Thus, while the placement of Article 8 in the *Título Preliminar* was a concession, the substance of this article broke with the fundamental way in which Franquism had conceived of the armed forces. This was a clear expression of the negotiated and consensual character of the Constitution. Socialists and Communists, for instance, favored the withdrawal of public order responsibilities from the armed forces and opposed the placement of this article in the *Título Preliminar.* Alianza Popular, on the other hand, favored this location but opposed the demilitarization of the Civil Guard. Both sides got only part of what they wanted, although enough to support the final result.

Other references to the military were postponed for later treatment in specific legislation. Article 8 stated, for instance, that more specific definitions should be the subject of an organic law on the military and defense. Until then the military would in practice remain within an area of calculated ambiguity delineated by Articles 62 and 97: Article 62 assigned the king the supreme command of the armed forces, while Article 97 charged the government with the defense of the state and the direction of civil and military administration. Later, military leaders played these ambiguities to their advantage, by trying to bypass the government in order to establish a direct hierarchical link with the king. For a period of time, as shall become clear, this ambiguity helped sustain military contestation in the post-transition period. With the benefit of hindsight, however, it is also clear that this ambiguity postponed definitions that otherwise might have either created unnecessary confrontation with uncertain consequences or constitutionally sanctioned solutions that were less than optimal from the angle of civilian supremacy. Instead, the postponement of key definitions left wide open the possibility for substantial reforms in the military and defense when times were more propitious.

The Military in the Clean Ruptura with Franquism

In December 1978 Spaniards overwhelmingly approved in referendum a new democratic Constitution, which all political sectors, with the abstention of the major Basque party and the opposition of few conservative deputies, had previously approved in the Cortes. The Constitution proclaimed a democratic form of government, specified individual freedoms and rights, and incorporated quite diverse interests, which had previously been unable to coexist peacefully. The Constitution's provisions for a parliamentary monarchy legitimated the crown and ended state-church association, although granting special recognition and privileges to the Catholic church. Private property was guaranteed, as were workers' rights, and the historic claims of Basques and Catalans also were officially recognized in the declaration of Spain as a state of autonomies. Franquist heirs and foes had coalesced on the fundamental principles that would regulate their political coexistence.

A clean break with the authoritarian past had been fully accomplished — only three years after Franco's death — in what was much more a *ruptura* than the encapsulation of the Spanish democratization in the dilemma *"reforma o ruptura"* suggests. Its *reforma* dimension rightly emphasizes its negotiated character, because the process was initiated from within Franquism by elites who had seized power following Franquist principles and rules and who reformed the system without significant breaks with Franquist legality. Yet the new regime that replaced Franquism was cleanly democratic. The Constitution, which encompassed these features, was adopted by a democratically elected assembly in a process that, from the very start, envisaged popular ratification of its final product. Reforms certainly achieved a much cleaner rupture than was the case, for instance, in the also negotiated South American transitions, and a much cleaner democracy than was attained in the early phase of the Portuguese *ruptura*. [60]

Democratization in Spain was indeed accomplished via a negotiated *ruptura,* in two phases. In the first phase negotiation took place between reformists and hard-liners within the regime in order to permit the legal abandonment of Franquist legality. In the second phase reformists negotiated with the opposition in order to seek its participation in government-led reforms and then to create a new legality.

The military was surprised with the *ruptura* brought about by the transition. Changes came much quicker and went much farther than it had initially anticipated and thought it would tolerate. The "business" that "politicians" had been allowed to conduct led to outcomes the military had failed to anticipate, to preempt, or to reverse. One of the few instances of success which the military could exhibit after these three years was to have stopped the Cortes from granting amnesty to former UMD members. The military could fare no better, given that it had only reacted, and belatedly, to decisions with which it had strongly disagreed.

It is much harder to reverse a decision already taken than to prevent it altogether. The former takes more strength, unity, and determination than is demanded when trying to prevent a decision from being made. In this latter case anticipation is indispensable, and this is precisely where the initial conditions of democratization hurt the Spanish military, by leaving it outside the critical agenda-setting sites.

The critical episodes and issues previously described and summarized in table 4.1 depict a military facing choices that left it only with the least harmful rather than its preferred options. For instance, on the matter of the legalization of the Communist Party, the army generals assembled in the high army council could have upgraded their reaction by

Table 4.1

Critical Civilian Decisions and Military Reactions

Civilian Initiative	Impact	Military Reaction	Result
Law for Political Reform	Opens door for replacement of Franquist institutions via elections	Military ministers support; opposition by military *procuradores*	Passes
Legalization of Unions	Opens door for legal return of militant Communists and Socialists	Resignation of military vice president with accompanying warnings	Passes
Legalization of Communist Party	Official return of Republican "reds"	Strong rejection by majority in the army; strong statement by High Army Council	Passes
Full Amnesty Law including former UMD members	Possible reincorporation of UMD members into the army	Strong consensual rejection with preemptive action	Does not Pass
Recognition of "Nationalities" in Constitution	Autonomy of historic nationalities	Opposition by majority and announcement of action by military senators	Passes

going ahead with the option of submitting the resignation of the army minister, creating a difficult situation for the government and the king. They decided against this option because they feared that the government could then appoint a civilian minister and create a precedent in which the army would end up worse off.

One may speculate, however, about a hypothetical course of events in which the army decided to have its minister resign. In this course, in order to prevent the undesired outcome of ending up with a civilian minister, the army would have had to take the additional step of announcing that it would reject a civilian appointment. It could then have offered the maintenance of the incumbent army minister if the government took back its decision about the Communist Party. Yet the implementation of either course — rejecting the appointment of a civilian minister or forcing the government to reverse its ruling about the Party — would have pitted the army against the king.

At this point the king could either accede to the military's demands by disavowing the president (a request that the generals actually entertained during their meeting), or the king could reject military pressure and, resorting to his supreme command, call for immediate military subordination and acceptance of the government's decision. The army could then decide that it had gone too far and accept the decision of its supreme commander, in which case it would be weakened by failure, or it would have to remove the king, in which case it would have to take over the government. Or, one step before, if the king had bent to military demands, the king would have been weakened, and so would the chances of consolidating the monarchy.

Either one of the previous scenarios was undesirable for the military, because it weakened or eliminated the best guarantee or protection it would have in the long run — the monarchy — and because Franco's still very fresh request of support for the monarchy made it hard for the army to oppose the king overtly. On the other hand, the previous scenarios would most likely lead to severe internal factionalism, if not outright armed confrontation. Even milder moves that would merely challenge the king could stir divisions in the military, thus weakening it. The military was already divided and could not afford to step beyond its own safe near-consensus on a negative issue: it is one thing to agree to oppose a decision by the president and quite another to agree on what to do without him.

Sensing the enormous risks for itself involved in an escalation course, the army then took the best choice under the circumstances: a strong statement against the government decision, which cleared its conscience—just as Admiral Pita da Veiga's resignation cleared his—and raised warning signs for the future, both for the government and the king. This course of action was the most consistent with the existing state of unity in the military.

The only episode in which the military anticipated a decision by elected representatives and acted promptly to prevent it had to do with the one issue that brought together all different groups of generals: opposition to the reincorporation into the army of former members of the UMD. Unity around this issue was easier because it dealt with matters deemed internal, which is also why blatant pressure on elected representatives was regarded as justified and feasible. On broader constitutional issues the generals could voice their concerns to the government through regular channels or present their grievances before the king, as they quite often did. But it was harder to pressure the Cortes directly because no other issue could be claimed to have the status of an internal military matter. To have put stronger pressure on these broader issues would have required a higher degree of substantive consensus in the military than was actually found.

The extent and reach of opposition to the changes outlined above was, at each juncture, limited by the military's perception of existing alternatives. This was, in turn, influenced by the assessment of its own state of unity and that of civilian reformers as well as of the extent of public support given these reformers. Unified civilian positions on critical subjects and expressions of massive support for these positions were a powerful deterrent to hard-line militaries seeking to block the unfolding transition.

Civilian Coalescence and Public Support

Reformers were able to generate a broad consensus among the Spanish elite and to elicit visible expressions of public support. Suárez's plan for political reform seized the agenda for the transition, setting a clear timetable for a series of elections. This gave the government an edge over the opposition, whose members had then to adjust their strategies and react to this new situation. The commitment to hold elections, as Juan Linz has argued, deflates oppositional mobilization and generates support around the implementation of a reform timetable.[61] Suárez's plan included, in succession, approval of a reform law in the Cortes, a referendum on the law, and democratic elections for Cortes; approval of a new constitution by the Cortes, referendum on the constitution, and elections for a new constitutional Cortes. Carrying out such an agenda in the course of less than three years obviously kept everybody on their toes, the military included.

The referendums and elections included in the timetable elicited expressions of public preference which resulted in enormous support for the government and the reform process. Table 4.2 shows referendums and elections, held at short intervals during this period, which empowered the government with electoral legitimacy.

The referendums expressed widespread and unequivocal public support for reforms, which the elections for Cortes confirmed. Elections also showed the moderate leanings of the electorate: more than 60 percent of the vote went to the UCD and the Socialists in the two Cortes elections, to the detriment of Communists and of parties more closely identified with Franquism.[62] The skillful use of elections and referendums by the government and the moderate platforms presented by the major parties resulted in widespread expressions of support. These legitimated emerging democratic structures and raised the costs of forceful opposition for military hard-liners.[63]

In tune with the public mood, and anxious to avoid the polarization that had prevailed in the past, political elites coalesced. The Communists, who made the most dramatic overtures in promoting "national reconciliation" and consensus, restrained conflictual mobilization, and consented to the monarchy and to arrangements with the church. The church, under the leadership of Bishop Tarancón, had distanced itself from its previous Franquist alignment and adopted a posture of neutrality during the transition.[64] The Socialists, during their Twenty-seventh Congress in 1976, had called for a "constitutional compromise." And, as the government, which could have formed a majority with the right to impose a partisan constitution, also opted for a consensual solution, the spirit of coalescence pervaded the entire political landscape, with the sole exception of the Basque parties. Even Manuel Fraga, who had fiercely repressed Communists in 1976, cordially introduced Communist leader Santiago Carrillo in a public lecture that the latter gave in October 1977.[65] This spirit was fully expressed in the workings of the Cortes's constitutional committee.

Table 4.2

Elections and Referendums during the Spanish Transition to Democracy, as Percentage of Valid Votes

	Referendum December 1976	Congress July 1977	Referendum December 1978	Congress March 1979
Yes	94.2		87.8	
No	2.6		7.9	
UCD		34.0		35.1
PSOE		28.9		30.5
PSP-US		4.4		
PSA				1.8
PCE-PSUC		9.2		10.8
AP-CD		8.0		6.1
PDC-CIU		2.8		2.7
ERC		0.8		0.7
PNV		1.7		1.7
EE		0.3		0.4
HB				1.0
Others		10.0		9.2
Turnout	77.7	78.3	67.7	68.0

Sources: For congressional elections, see Richard Gunther, Giacomo Sani, and Goldie Shabad, *Spain after Franco: The Making of a Competitive Party System* (Berkeley: University of California Press, 1986), 179. For referendum results, see John F. Coverdale, *The Political Transformation of Spain after Franco* (New York: Praeger, 1979), 53 and 119.

UCD	Unión de Centro Democrático and Centristes de Catalunya (CC-UCD)
PSOE	Partido Socialista Obrero Español and Socialistes de Catalunya
PSP-US	Partido Socialista Popular–Unidad Socialista
PSA	Partido Socialista Andaluz
PCE-PSUC	Partido Comunista de España and Partit Socialista Unificat de Catalunya
AP-CD	Alianza Popular and Coalición Democrática
PDC-CiU	Pacte Democràtic per Catalunya and Convergència i Unió
ERC	Esquerra de Catalunya
PNV	Partido Nacionalista Vasco
EE	Euskadiko Ezkerra
HB	Herri Batasuna

The Moncloa Pacts of October 1977 were another important expression of coalescence. They brought together the government and all parties with representation in Cortes to agree on fiscal, tax, monetary, and wage policies that would help face economic hardship and decrease the levels of industrial conflict. The parties also agreed to initiate reforms of the penal code, the police, the code of military justice, and other areas related to the defense of individual freedoms and rights. The pacts were solemnly signed at the government palace and then symbolically commended in resolutions of the Cortes and the Senate.[66]

The press also became, occasionally, a powerful carrier of civilian coalescence. On 29 January 1977 seven newspapers published a joint editorial article in response to the assassination of a group of Communist lawyers and the kidnapping of General Villaescusa. On 16 April 1977, in another joint editorial, the newspapers strongly condemned the public statement issued by the high army council on the legalization of the Communist Party and indicated: "The Spanish army is the armed branch of our society, serving the state and its government. The Spanish army is formed by all Spaniards and has been assigned missions established in the laws; missions which do not include utterance of views about political decisions by the governments of the nation."[67]

Important parties did not participate in the consensus, however, such as the Nationalist Basque Party, which refused to attend the session in Congress which voted on the Constitution and then campaigned for abstention in the referendum. Also, dissidents in Manuel Fraga's Alianza Popular disapproved of the Constitution and voted against it in the Cortes. These groups, however, chose abstention rather than outright opposition on the constitutional referendum and, especially those on the Right, never sought support for their views in the military and did not take advantage of military discontent.[68]

Institutionalized civilian accord and frequent expressions of substantial public support for reforms were a discouraging factor for hard-line military leaders, who thus found it hard to garner active support in the barracks for moves against democratization. When one such move — later known as the Operación Galaxia — was attempted by a small group of mid-level officers shortly before the constitutional referendum, it was uncovered by skeptical fellow officers, who themselves promptly informed the government. The failure of this attempt, which never really took off, and the constitutional referendum that followed marked the successful completion of the transition to democracy. They also marked the inability of the military to prevent, slow down, or limit the extent of the clean break with Franquism which the inauguration of the new regime achieved.

The combination of civilian coalescence and public support in the process leading to the inauguration of democracy appears to have been quite unique to Spain. In Greece, which is the closest to Spain in this regard, high levels of support were not matched with coalescence. After the collapse of the colonels' regime in July 1974, the Karamanlis government engaged voters in a quick succession of elections and referendums, obtaining overwhelming levels of support. The Assembly, elected on 17 November 1974, gave Karamanlis's party (New Democracy) 54.4 percent of the votes and 72 percent of the seats. A referendum on the choice of republic or monarchy was held on December 1974, with over two-thirds supporting the republic (69.2 percent), in the first referendum in Greece which was not contested by the losing side. Work on the constitution stumbled on the issue of presidential prerogatives, however, leading to a major clash, which ended with approval of the Constitution in June 1975 with the substantial but exclusive vote of the majority party.[69] Yet, in light of the substantial levels of support for the government and the weakness of the collapsed military, this failure to coalesce was no impediment for the affirmation of civilian authority over the military.

The Portuguese transition from the regime ousted in April 1974 to a new constitution in April 1976 was marked by divisions and shifting alignments and, especially, by the coexistence of competing electoral and revolutionary legitimacies. The Armed Forces Movement, supported by the Marxist Left, stood against the assembly of parties until after the first elections, for a constituent assembly, in April 1975. The elections did not yield a conclusive majority to any of the competing parties, and coalitions became unstable and minority government the rule. Factionalism in the military led to defeat of the most radical sector, allowing for a change in February 1976 of the terms of agreement with the parties, but the military still was able to force a tutelary role for its Council of the Revolution.[70]

In Argentina the united front of political parties which had formed to fight the dictatorship — the *multipartidaria* — fell apart as soon as the military called for elections after the Falkland Islands / Islas Malvinas debacle. These parties then splintered around the issue of how to treat the atrocities perpetrated by the military: while Peronist unions secretly negotiated with the military, Alfonsín built a platform on democratization and military accountability on human rights crimes. It was, in fact, this strategy that allowed for the unprecedented triumph of the Radicals over the Peronists in 1983. Alfonsín's initially high levels of support led him to succeed in his policies toward the military and on economic stabilization and reform. But when both the military and the economy, and also the unions, turned against him halfway through his term, the absence of civilian coalescence hurt his own standing just as much as the firmness of the policies initially conducted regarding the military.[71]

Brazil's first postmilitary government became the confusing site of major clashes between conflicting groups. José Sarney, whose ascent to the presidency in 1985 was unexpectedly cleared by Tancredo Neves's death right before the transfer of power, was assailed from the start by

Initial Conditions and the Transition

attempts from partners in the government coalition to limit his powers and shorten his term. Sarney protected himself by resorting to the support of the military, whose large presence in the government remained unchanged. The very weakness of Brazilian parties and the subsistence of previous cleavages in successor elites hindered the emergence of coherent and stable political formations and congressional blocs, which might have sustained attempts to check military power.[72]

In Peru elections for a constituent assembly in 1978 yielded a polarized set of parties which initiated a divisive debate for a new constitution, also influenced by agreements between APRA, the largest party, and the ruling military. After approval of the new constitution voters elected as president, in 1980, Fernando Belaunde, whose party had refused to participate in the constituent assembly. Belaunde won only a plurality and failed to get a majority of seats in the Senate, where he was opposed with intolerance and strong-arm tactics by APRA.[73] The military benefited from Belaunde's conciliatory attitude toward it and from the need to respond to the emergence of Shining Path's armed rebellion.

In Ecuador the extricating military, after getting its way in the 1978 plebiscite over the constitution, introduced distortions in the civilian opposition by banning one of the party formations from participating in the first elections.[74] Similarly in Uruguay, the military affected the chances of unity in the civilian opposition by keeping the potentially most popular civilian candidate (of the Blancos) from running for the presidency.[75]

In Chile the opposition, the military, and its civilian partners faced the transition with remarkable pragmatism, which allowed them to reach accord on a limited set of issues and partially reform the regime's 1980 constitution. With the support of its civilian allies, however, the military did not yield on demands from the opposition to include reforms that fully restored democratic prerogatives of the president over the military. After the inauguration of a civilian president and congress in 1990, the two parties on the Right and the senators appointed by General Pinochet continued to block reforms in those areas. Despite consensus across the political spectrum on a number of important subjects, the fact remained that the successor regime dwelled on Pinochet's fundamentally unaltered constitution and that no agreement had developed among parties on this critical aspect of democratization.[76]

Thus, Spain and Greece were the only cases whose transitions culminated in new constitutions adopted freely in unencumbered assemblies, and only in Spain was the new constitution worked out consensually with representatives from across the political spectrum (with the sole exclusion of the Basque parties). This coalescence, in conjunction with visible manifestations of public support, deterred military hard-liners in Spain and kept them from overcoming the weaknesses with which the military's position at the start of the transition endowed them. In Spain success in the clean inauguration of a democratic regime resulted from a distinct combination: a publicly supported and coalescent civilian leadership and a military structurally unprepared to oppose change effectively. As we shall see, the military's difficulties in erecting an effective opposition were further complicated by the presence of important divisions.

Hard-line Failures, Reformist Alliances, and Military Modernization

MILITARY INSTITUTIONS never are fully free of internal rifts and tensions. If this is true for normal times, it is much more so in times of regime transition, when major players find that much is at stake. One should therefore expect that, even within hierarchic, disciplined organizations such as the military, differing and often clashing views will develop about courses of action and ways of countering challenges from without.

Severe internal clashes, however, deflate the political power of a military. Unity—widely shared definitions of institutional interests, mission, and role—is necessary if the military wants to resist civilian attempts at military reform. And even more unity is needed if the military seeks to trespass to areas outside its professional specialization and engage in political concerns. An attempt by the military to block civilian-led transformation of a political regime, for instance, will require consensus around a societal project of its own, viewed as an alternative to civilian goals of regime transformation.

In Spain military leaders displayed some level of unity around very specific issues: denial of amnesty to former members of the Unión Militar Democrática (UMD), a clandestine organization that had formed within the army in 1974, and opposition to certain aspects of the constitution draft. But they could not oppose other reforms with the same level of unity and stamina, at least to limit their scope and reach, nor could they exert greater and more focused pressure to extract some form of compensation for outcomes they had been forced to accept. The oppositional capacity of military leaders was, in fact, severely impaired by internal divisions that prevented the erection of a single, unified military voice and the organization of a coherent institutional response to political reforms. Military divisions inhibited the development of military opposition by affecting the calculations of military leaders at critical junctures in the transition, leading them to restrain opposition to the unfolding transition.

The importance of divisions in the military for the advancement of democratization in Spain has been overlooked. This neglect results partly from a comparison with neighboring Portugal, in which the military featured "periodic garrison-type revolts" during authoritarianism, faced the crisis of a colonial war, and made its fractures more visible as a result of its prominent role in the transition.[1] The implausibility of a Portuguese-type split in the Spanish military, however, should not obscure the fact that significant divisions existed at the top of the military establishment during the transition.

Not only did the existence of these divisions inhibit a more effective military opposition to the transition; their very nature, in fact, facilitated reforms. The existence of a group within the military which favored professional reforms that were highly compatible with political democratization provided the transition governments with sympathetic elements in the armed forces. Reformist civilian elites could count on this group to neutralize the conservative opposition while military reforms, indispensable for the overall democratization project, were pursued. The alliance between this military group and civilian reformers proved to be central to the success of the transition. Although other cases were also characterized by visibly fractured militaries facing transitions from authoritarian rule, it was the particular nature and sources of military divisions in Spain which provided civilian reformers with opportunities that were not available elsewhere.

Certainly, military disunity is not a required ingredient of a successful transition. In other circumstances it might prove disruptive for the normalization of favorable civil-military relations. If the bulk of the military appears to favor reforms or is at least neutral, then divisions will be harmful for civilian reformers, who are better off with strengthened unity around the hierarchic line of command. But, if the bulk of the military stands against reforms, divisions will weaken this oppositional stance. In Spain divisions played this favorable role, and their specific nature helped strengthen the hand of civilian reformers.

The Military's Concern with Unity at the Outset of the Transition

The armed forces had not remained immune to the fragmentation that developed within the Franquist regime starting in the mid-1960s in regard to views about its future, views that later sharpened into the opposing positions of *aperturismo* (interested in political liberalization) and *inmovilismo* (concerned with prolonging the regime). Divisions within the regime were reinforced by opposition movements that developed in the early 1970s in institutions such as the church and the judiciary, which previously had been pillars of Franquism.[2] The assassination of the head of the government, Admiral Carrero Blanco, by ETA in 1973 and the advancing age of Franco raised questions about the future of the regime. These questions were posed at a time when uncertainties had grown as a result of increasing pressures from social and regional conflict. Strongly associated with Franquism, the armed forces were subject to the tensions stemming from outside opposition, the regime's factionalization, and its impending crisis.[3]

The military was quite aware of the threats posed by disunity and outside pressure, and senior officers reflected this concern by, more and more frequently, invoking the need for unity and discipline. For instance, in his inaugural speech as captain general of the Seventh Military Region in Valladolid, in April 1976, Lieutenant General Gutiérrez Mellado insisted on the need to maintain discipline, by appropriately invoking Franco's old definition, which the king, too, frequently recalled later: "Discipline . . . acquires its true character when reason advises us to act contrary to orders that we are given, when our hearts seek to rise in rebellion, or when arbitrariness and error cloud the action of command. This is the discipline we teach you. This is the discipline we practice. This is the best example we can offer."[4]

Later, in September 1976, in his first general report as army chief of staff, Gutiérrez Mellado devoted a special section to "unity among commanding officers" and warned about the various causes of disunity, especially "the most dangerous one, which has already produced internal splits and which has to be made to disappear at all costs: the political cause."[5] The various calls to unity were themselves an expression of fissures, for they strongly disagreed on the sources of divisions. For most, the tendency toward secularization of society was seen as exerting a negative influence upon the soldier. Threats were also specifically identified as originating in democratic Europe, such as Eurocommunism, new forms of subversion, and the debate about unionism in the army.[6] For others, threats to unity came from the politicization of many officers who outspokenly participated in Franquist organizations and in the dissemination of Franquist goals and ideals. For the professional high command, threats to unity came from politicization on all sides.

Cliques within the Military and the Unión Militar Democrática

Much of the military's concern arose from events in neighboring Portugal. Fearing contagious effects from the 1974 revolution of the captains against the old authoritarian regime of Antonio Salazar and Marcelo Caetano, the Spanish military leadership decided to intensify internal vigilance. Army intelligence carefully investigated internal dissent and reported on the evolution of the "state of opinion" in units across the country. Laborious efforts led by the information section of the army general staff soon came to be fully rewarded with the discovery of leading cells of the Unión Militar Democrática. Composed primarily of captains and constituting one to two hundred officers, the UMD sought to organize large numbers of officers throughout the army with the purpose of resisting any possible moves by the high command against democratization in the aftermath of Franco's anticipated death.

The organization grew out of meetings held early in 1974 by about a dozen officers led by Majors Julio Busquets in Barcelona and José Otero in Madrid. The Portuguese Revolution of April that year, whose junior leaders met with Otero and Busquets in Lisbon, sparked such enthusiasm among groups of junior officers in Spain that the organization expanded dramatically. The UMD carefully approached young officers in selected units and disseminated written documents by mail to large numbers of officers. In these documents UMD leaders criticized the dictatorship and were especially critical of the military hierarchy for letting the army fall into levels of extreme backwardness. Very much in line with opposition parties, whose major leaders they had met several times, the UMD leaders favored a strategy of *ruptura democrática* after Franco died. They urged a quick restoration of civil and political liberties and workers' rights, the formation of a coalition government, and the election of a Constituent Assembly to design the country's institutional future. In the thought that this would, in fact, be the most likely course of events, they defined the organization's purpose to be the neutralization of any attempts by the military leadership to get in the way of the process of *ruptura democrática*. By the time some of its most visible leaders were arrested, the UMD had begun the organization of "tactical committees" in critical units to plan the boycott of an eventual anti-*ruptura* move by the army high command.

The activities of UMD—holding national and regional assemblies, meetings with national opposition leaders, production and distribution of documents—soon made it noticeable to the press, and several reports appeared in foreign newspapers and weeklies. Their activities also made the organization well-known to army intelligence. Colonel José Sáenz de Tejada, who had led the information section in the army general staff in 1974, was reassigned to the position in the summer of 1975 with specific instructions to deal with the UMD question. Initially, the high command had decided to monitor UMD movements carefully but without closing in. There was disagreement among lieutenant generals on ways of dealing with the issue. A few felt that, with the impending death of Franco, open repression of fellow officers was not worthwhile. Gutiérrez Mellado, then captain general in Ceuta, an enclave in Morocco, opposed repression of UMD on the grounds that it could result in strengthening the organization. If anything, he argued, only internal warnings and disciplinary action were advisable. Sáenz de Tejada, however, preferred swift action to terminate with the UMD. He believed that, with Franco's deteriorating health in the background, no room for uncertainty should be allowed. Also, he thought, swift action and judicial procedures were the only means to prevent infuriated commanders from conducting witch-hunts of their own. Sáenz de Tejada then supplied information about UMD members to his former chief in the División Acorazada, General Milans del Bosch, a well-known hard-liner, who requested that the captain general of the First Military Region in Madrid, General Campano, have them arrested and tried by military courts. This request was accepted and swiftly implemented in July 1975, when the president of the government was abroad.[7]

In March 1976 the court sentenced nine officers to terms ranging from three to eight years for the crime of conspiracy for military rebellion. They were all set free following a general amnesty issued by Adolfo Suárez upon his swearing in as president later that year. The amnesty, however, upheld the restriction that prohibited their reintegration into the army, an issue that would remain divisive and unresolved for another decade.

The post-Franquist political process did not unfold in the manner foreseen by UMD. Thus, the role that UMD had envisioned for itself was never implemented, and the organization gradually dissolved. Nonetheless, the visibility that it had reached at the time of the detention of its leaders worked to reinforce the feeling—as much outside as within the army—that the military was far from being a monolithic entity.

The UMD was the only group within the army which was truly an organized movement. Other identifiable factions in the military operated more like tendencies and were most discernible in the army. The navy and the air force, smaller in size and more technically oriented, had more homogeneous outlooks and were more fully dedicated to professional concerns. Consequently, my attention will focus on factions existing primarily within the army.

Conservatives and Hard-liners: Problems for an Effective Opposition

Apart from the UMD, three main tendencies could be identified in the army leadership at the beginning of the transition: a hard-line group committed to a strict continuation of the institutions and values of the Franquist state; a conservative group similarly committed to Franquism but more tolerant of transformations, which it was prepared to accept as inevitable as long as the new institutions gave recognition to the autonomy and special role of the military; and, finally, a considerably smaller "liberal" tendency prepared to facilitate the accommodation of the armed forces to a pluralist, democratic regime and to promote modernization in the army. Beyond these groups and among middle-level and lower-level officers lay an uncommitted mass, generally conservative and extremely sensitive to threats against the military's most dearly held values.[8]

Conservatives and hard-liners felt strongly committed to a set of values—the "essences"—of which they saw the military as trustee. These essences were variously defined but basically included: the territorial unity of Spain, the unity of flag and language; anticommunism; and a respect for the past, its institutional order, and many of its values, vaguely, often religiously, defined. These groups saw it as their mission to guarantee the principles of the Movement and generally to protect the religious ethos surrounding Franquism.

Conservatives proudly considered themselves part of the victor army, built upon the violent destruction and surrender of at least half the previous professional army in the opposite ideological camp during the civil war. The army thus stood upon the memories of heroic warfare, which, besides the domestic Crusade, also included war on the Russian Front during World War II. Many of the army generals on active duty during the transition had, in fact, served as volunteers in the División Azul between 1941 and 1943.[9] Also, many of the commanding posts of the victor Franquist army were filled with former partisan civilians—the *alféreces provisionales*—who had hurriedly joined the Franquist army during the civil war passionately proclaiming loyalty to the principles of the Crusade. By the start of the transition many of them had reached the top army posts,[10] occupied exclusively by generals who had joined the army before or during the civil war. Thus, during the transition and early democratic years the army was controlled by the "founding fathers" of the very regime that was being dismantled.[11]

Conservatives and hard-liners were quite wary of democratization and of the impending secularization of Spanish society. They shared a grim view of what post-Franquist society could offer: the gradual return of that "other Spain," defeated in the civil war, and with it the return of subversion disguised as materialistic values, terrorism, drugs, pornography, and challenges to authority. These views generally prevailed in the navy and the air force as well but were most distinctive of the army. Minister of the army, General Félix Álvarez-Arenas, expressed them well in his speech to a new promotion of lieutenants in the *Alcázar de Toledo* in July 1976:

> I want to remind you that, even if officially we are at peace, the truth is that . . . we are immersed in a war that is neither fought nor won with classical weapons but with spiritual resources and moral weapons. . . . I am talking about subversive war, the first phase of revolutionary war, which seeks to weaken our morale and destroy our national ideals and the principle of authority in order to prepare its assault on power. Its weapons are: propaganda, drugs, pornography and terrorism among others.[12]

Conservatives formed the largest group and, jointly with the hard-liners, dominated the highest army administrative and command positions. For most of the year following Franco's death, they controlled the vice presidency for defense (until de Santiago's resignation in September) and the army ministry, the general staff (until Gutiérrez Mellado's appointment in June), the major intelligence services, the direction of the Civil Guard, the highest command positions in most of the military regions, and the command of the Brunete Armoured Division, and with all this came, of course, their control of the supreme army council. Also, they dominated a multitude of critical command positions in units across the country.

Although conservatives and hard-liners shared much of their world and political views, an important difference set these groups apart: the readiness with which hard-liners were willing to challenge decisions by government officials and to overstep both the boundaries imposed by discipline and by the law. The idea of a coup, for instance, or of some form of forceful military intervention was conceivable among hard-liners but not among conservatives.[13] Conservatives were more respectful of authority and hierarchy, and, although very aware of their prerogatives and pressure power, they also were more mindful of the limits imposed by the law and held discipline and obedience in higher esteem than hard-liners. They regarded the transition with great apprehension and were outspoken about their concerns, but they realized that some changes were inevitable. A good example of this position was General Álvarez-Arenas's statement: "We all agree that, in the benefit of Spaniards, change is necessary and therefore we accept it well"—a position qualified, however, with a warning: "It took a lot of blood and pain to defeat them [subversives and separatists] once, and their reappearance in Spain might again be cause of blood and pain."[14] Hard-liners, however, went beyond tough remarks and tolerated or even undertook actions that constituted open defiance of civil authorities.[15] These differences ultimately hurt conservatives, who, forced to disassociate themselves from the continuous action of hard-liners, were hindered from developing an efficient institutional opposition.

The fundamental limitation on the ability of conservatives to exert forceful leadership lay, however, in their lack of an alternative project to guide a credible and coherent opposition to political reforms. No matter how often they praised the "national essences" and their Franquist embodiments or how passionately they presented the army as the quintessential school of national virtues, the fact remained that they did not put forth any agenda more concrete than symbolic references to the past or the goal of its prolongation. This was aggravated by the absence of unifying leaders among conservatives and hard-liners. No single leader stood out to counter fragmentation with the unifying force of undisputed charisma. Carrero Blanco might have served as the leader who expressed the views of large portions of the Franquist civilian and military "families," but his assassination in 1973 left a void that was never filled. Any other alternative leadership had been overshadowed and suppressed by the overwhelming presence of the caudillo. The absence of war operations since the civil war and the División Azul era, which had produced the leadership personified by Franco, gave no new opportunities for the emergence of natural, heroic leaders, especially in the unexciting bureaucratic atmosphere in which military life proceeded. The navy did have a leader in their conservative minister Pita da Veiga, but a national military leader capable of garnering widespread support could only have come from the army, by far the largest of the armed services. As a result, as Adolfo Suárez noted, there was no single military leader who could speak for the armed forces as a whole.[16]

Numerous other difficulties further stood in the way of unity on the conservative and hard-line side. For instance, the diverse origins of the authoritarian coalition and the pluralism, albeit limited, which had developed under Franco was reflected among the generals, who displayed various loyalties. Some exhibited more roots in the *Falange* or the *División Azul*, actively participating in the brotherhood of Alféreces Provisionales; others had open preference for the monarchy, although not necessarily for Juan Carlos; and still others held no monarchic preferences at all. Generational differences also were important. Younger officers, who had not experienced the horror of the civil war, were less mindful of the violent consequences of "taking it to the streets," while older officers, even the most conservative, were justifiably afraid and thus quite mindful of careless engagements that could unleash a new civil confrontation. Also, personal rivalries coexisted with conflict rooted in a more traditional struggle for bureaucratic turf and career development, such as attempts to balance the share of different specializations (infantry, artillery, cavalry, etc.) in the highest positions. None of these specific differences gave rise to distinct postures and policies or to the formation of factions, but they added up as inhibiting factors to the development of a common outlook for action.[17]

Also, many criticized and despised other officers who had gained what looked like too much power in political pursuits without leaving the force. Resentment against "political" officers extended as well to those who enjoyed special privileges and career tracks in the many intelligence services. The most important of these services were those of the presidency, the High General Staff (HGS), and the Army Staff, in addition to those of the other services and the Civil Guard, and the information service of the Interior Ministry. All these services were run and staffed by military officers, and many of them especially by hard-liners, although they served diverse interests and were very poorly coordinated. Except for parts of the High General Staff intelligence, all these services focused on domestic opposition—civilian and military. These activities, however, occasionally turned a few of these officers into efficient middlemen between the government and different political groups and, sometimes, into transmission belts that helped introduce pluralist and *aperturista* views into the army.[18] Although efficient instruments of repression and safe harbors for the activities of hard-liners, the uncoordinated proliferation of these services impeded them from performing any role in unifying outlooks.

Military Opposition and the "National Security Doctrine" of the South American Armed Forces

The lack of an alternative project made the Spanish military ill prepared to oppose civilian reforms with concrete policy alternatives. The disempowering effect of this lack of vision is most noticeable when contrasted with the South American militaries. The militaries of Peru, Brazil, Uruguay, or Chile, for instance, offered reforms and counter-reforms that paralleled civilian initiatives at almost every turn during the democratic transitions in their countries. With ideas about the shape of the political, the party, and the electoral systems and about regional development and other issues, these militaries could sustain an active role during the transition.[19]

Starting in the 1960s, the armies of South American countries had enhanced their capacity for political intervention by developing doctrinal cohesion around a "new professionalism" and postulates of a national security doctrine. This doctrine projected a vision of society divided into various "fronts" whose coordination, for the purpose of facing newly emerging "domestic threats," had to be assigned to those institutions in charge of security. This doctrine led the armed forces to view the entire society through the single, unifying prism of security and prepared them to confront pressures that emanated from a praetorian societal context. With the goal of countering these pressures, militaries expanded their doctrines to include strategies for economic development and restructuration of the political system.[20]

The specific formulation of this doctrine obviously varied from country to country and allowed for different interpretations. For instance, it was relatively more developed in Brazil, where it provided the military with more specific policy guidelines. In Peru it contained political orientations that were quite different from those guiding military dictatorships in the rest of the Southern Cone countries. But, regardless of differences and specificities, these doctrinal developments helped to empower the armed forces politically and to provide a rationale for authoritarian government.[21]

The thrust and reach of the national security orientations that developed in South America were completely foreign to the Spanish military. Although in both regions the military shared a militant rejection of communism and a profound distrust of liberal politics, in Spain this did not evolve into the kind of programmatic development found in South America. The concept of national security appeared among the South American militaries during the 1950s, with inter-American influences, and developed further in the following decades within well-defined institutional settings. Institutions such as the Centro de Altos Estudios Militares (CAEM) in Peru and the Escola Superior de Guerra (ESG) in Brazil became landmark centers for doctrinal development and for the policies conducted by military-authoritarian regimes there. In Spain, by contrast, the concept of national security simply remained absent from the military lexicon. Although the military had inherited a firm domestic role from the civil war and the Franquist laws, it never really hosted the doctrinal tenets involved in the "new professionalism of internal security and military role expansion" which Stepan found in his studies of the Brazilian military.

Spanish military writings on "national defense" never gave this concept the meaning that South American militaries gave to "national security." The closest the Spanish army came to using such a concept was with the notion of "defense of the community" promoted in army circles in 1975–76 but which was, in fact, no more than a poor and vague substitute and did not become part of official usage.[22] The Spanish Centro Superior de Estudios de la Defensa Nacional (CESEDEN)—the institutional equivalent of the prestigious CAEM in Peru and the ESG in Brazil, all created roughly at the same time—was more a functional bureaucracy for the training of upper-level officers and the performance of public relations roles than truly a leading proponent of doctrine or policy.[23]

Only a rough framework may be advanced here to account for this difference in doctrinal developments, which would otherwise require a lengthier analysis of the role of international factors and domestic conditions in the post–World War II period. In South America inter-American military centers, under the spell of a U.S.-led cold war mystique, urged a security approach for the 1960s which focused on domestic threats ("subversion," "Castroism," "communist-led mobilization"). During this time the military was witnessing the failure of "populist," "developmentalist," or liberal-democratic ruling coalitions to sustain growth, while their political systems simultaneously faced dramatic increases in popular mobilization. The military reacted by creating a rationale that could support a strategy of social control and demobilization, fueling national security doctrines.

In Spain, on the other hand, roughly during the same post–World War II period, the military was a basic pillar supporting the Franquist state and its civilian technocracy, which was succeeding in promoting economic and social modernization.[24] The military was, thus, one might say, "exempted" from the task of elaborating its own doctrine for development and controlled social mobilization and to posit it as an alternative to civilian politicians.[25] The Spanish military remained content in a subordinate position, in which it received permanent tribute for its past heroic role in victory but which left it structurally and programmatically unprepared for the challenges that the transition to post-Franquism would place on it.

In South America years of socialization in doctrinal tenets calling for expanded military roles in society helped the militaries to face civilian reformers during the transition, not only with reinforced convictions about the legitimacy of military prerogatives but also with extensive institutional and policy guidelines to protect them. The militaries of South America were thus prepared to adopt more assertive stances during the transition than were their Spanish counterparts—stances that helped them retain larger prerogatives at the time democracy was inaugurated. In Spain conservatives and hard-liners, although dominant forces in the military at the start of the transition, failed to put forth a unified, consistent, and credible opposition to the creation of a post-Franquist democratic state.

The Liberals and the Promise of Reforms

The "liberals" stood out more for their intellectual than their numeric weight. They consisted of a small, unorganized group of officers who shared the feeling that the army did not have much to fear from a relatively quick process of political liberalization after Franco died. On the contrary, many among them felt that the army was badly in need of modernization and would benefit from a shake-up of the entrenched Franquist structures. Their writings generally revealed a desire to see Spain and the army move closer to the style and values of Western democracies, a desire that appeared quite cosmopolitan when contrasted with the overriding concern of conservatives for the protection of the Franquist ethos in society and the army.

Some of the liberals' views had been expressed in several speeches and essays by the best known among them, Lieutenant General Manuel Diez Alegría, who in 1974 headed the High General Staff. In a 1972 publication of selected writings he argued unequivocally for the modernization and depoliticization of the army and for the subordination of military power to civilian control.[26] His widespread liberal image earned him the uncomfortable nickname of "the Spanish Spínola," which certainly played a role in Franco dismissing him in 1974.[27] Nevertheless, other liberals still remained well positioned — Diez Alegría's closest collaborator in the General Staff, Lieutenant General Manuel Gutiérrez Mellado, and others such as Generals Juan Vega Rodríguez, Juan Cano Hevia, Federico Gómez de Salazar, and Antonio Ibáñez Freire.

The liberals' openness to political change went along with a clear view of the type of modern, professional army which the new situation called for. Put simply, Spain's political Westernization would demand a military more like the modern, efficient armies of Western European countries. More or less implicit in this view was a direct criticism of the effects that Franquism had had on the armed forces. During Franquism the military had been left to fall into a state of backwardness in almost every regard: personnel, organization, training, equipment, deployment, etc.[28] The liberals' concern with this situation led them to emphasize issues of professional improvement to a much larger extent than conservatives, who busied themselves more with worries about Franquist continuity. Improved professionalism and modernization became, therefore, a banner more identified with the liberals and one they used to their advantage but which also made them vulnerable to the criticism of those who would come out losers from the implementation of reforms.

It is a mistake, however, to associate professionalism and modernization exclusively with the liberals. Many conservatives were unanimously regarded as excellent professionals and cared about modernization.[29] Also, the navy, for instance, though it was the most homogeneously conservative of the armed services, was highly professional and, as a whole, more modernized. Liberals did not monopolize aspirations for professional improvement, and across the services many officers in the middle and lower levels were highly motivated professionally, regardless of their political-ideological alignments.

Nonetheless, many officers who felt comfortable in the military bureaucracy felt compelled to oppose reforms and, concomittantly, to oppose the ascent of liberals to leadership positions. Personnel reforms, for instance, would necessarily lead to layoffs, and, as the army had evolved into a large bureaucracy of functionaries, those seeking employment stability over other goals would generally oppose reforms and side with conservatives. Also, reform of the seniority-based promotions system would change the career incentive structure to which the majority had grown quite accustomed. Rejection of reforms associated with the liberals, however, was not always or necessarily based on satisfaction with the bureaucratic status quo. Mostly, it was based on a different concept of what the army ought to be, and there existed a conservative ideal of the army which conflicted with certain kinds of reform.

Opposition to Reforms and Contrasting Ideals of the Army

Charles Moskos has presented two opposing ideals of an army's organizational format: an "institutional" versus an "occupational" model.[30] He placed these models in a continuum ranging from a military organization highly divergent with civilian society (institutional format) to one

Initial Conditions and the Transition

highly convergent with civilian structures (occupational format). The military viewed as *institution* bases its legitimacy on normative values, and its members follow "a calling captured in words like *duty, honor* and *country.*" Enjoying esteem based on notions of service, they commonly "regard themselves as being different or apart from the broader society."[31] Their role commitments are diffuse and generalist, and their reference groups are mostly vertical within the armed forces. The recruitment appeals of a military based on this format point to character qualities and life-style orientations.

The military viewed as *occupation* is, in turn, legitimated in terms of the marketplace, and the prestige of its members is based on levels of compensation. Role commitments are specific, as those of the specialist. Reference groups are horizontal with occupations outside the military. Recruitment appeals emphasize high pay for new recruits and technical training. Evaluation of performance is segmented and quantitative, and the bases of compensation are skill level and manpower shortage.

These ideal types help to place the confrontation of ideals in the Spanish army in the larger context of military establishments of advanced countries. In this larger context strains in the corporate identity of the military organization have been seen as the consequence of a lengthy and gradual process of adaptation of the military to new organizational formats, including especially the greater convergence of the military with civilian professions.[32] In Spain, however, strains were more specifically the result of opposing concepts about the army in the context of perceived threats to the military's corporate identity coming directly from political reform. Tensions about military format were related to the question of military *modernization* and were complicated by the question of military *reform*.

Of Moskos's ideal types only the institutional model reflects well one of the opposing sides in the Spanish army—the view of conservative officers. The occupational view pointed more to some of the logical, future, and often unforeseen consequences of modernization than to any actual posture maintained by the liberals at the time of the transition.[33] In fact, while emphasizing the need for modernization and reforms—including greater specialization, the use of civilian expertise, and a larger role for civilians in defense—the liberals did not renounce a view of the army as a separate entity with its own ethics and code of honor.[34]

In the Spanish conservative view the army was essentially a moral repository, in which the strength of the combatants lay more in a special ethic of honor and service than in the abundance of technical means and expertise. Technical progress was seen as introducing homogenization, which broke with the unique spiritual, moral character of the military man, from which he draws his very military strength. For instance, in a 1975 speech to army staff school students, General Jesús González del Yerro, head of the staff school, warned about the extreme materialism that came along with mass society and observed the tendency of the military man to insulate himself from other socioprofessional groups, given his training and more spiritual values: "This tendency toward isolation may be convenient and even indispensable for the military man to conserve his own value code—so different from the average citizen's in the consumer society of our time— . . . to keep forever fervent the spirituality indispensable to his profession."[35]

General Manuel Cabeza Calahorra complained, also in 1975, about the eclipse of traditional military ethics. In his view:

Materialism, which proclaims its victory over Spirit and which promotes a different and "improved image of the Armed Forces" by frivolously maintaining that we all must be willing to accept better forms of arranging our affairs according to patterns from the economic world: to replace manpower (troops) with capital (weapons, vehicles, equipment); military men with specialized civilians lacking in military mentality; to promise economic retributions to attract recruits; to substitute "standard of living" for living with standards of generosity and dignity.

Another danger for the identity of the military group is the phenomenon of what we could call the ascent of civilians to leadership in the military domain . . . which brings civilian criteria and perspectives that may unexpectedly weaken and undermine our internal communion which gives consistency and longevity to the military group.[36]

It is understandable, then, that conservatives who were true professionals were less inclined to provide leadership for modernization, precisely because their concept of a professional army emphasized other dimensions. They, and hard-liners outside the military, systematically opposed the liberals' quest for modernization during Franquism. The demise of Franquism was thus perceived as full of possibilities for the liberals, who would eventually benefit from a post-Franquist progressive government that gave them the upper hand to initiate long-postponed modernization. Before addressing the full political implications of the existence of this group of liberals, it is first useful to establish the meaning of *modernization* and *reform* in the Spanish transition context and, second, the origin of the ideas that guided action in these areas during the initial stages of the post-Franco period.

The Meanings of Modernization *and* Reform

While the terms *modernization* and *reform* as applied to the Spanish military have been used interchangeably, the selection of one or the other term has often not been arbitrary. Those who wanted to emphasize the elements of continuity in this process—gradual evolution or adaptation to inevitable circumstances—preferred to use the term *modernization*. Military officers generally admitted the need for modernization but referred to it as an ever-present process with which the military had for long been occupied. Outside the military those interested in appeasing its concerns used the term *modernization,* thus deflating the import of the concept in the post-Franquist context. On the other hand, those who wanted to see the process as a stark departure from Franquism—generally the Left—preferred to use the term *reform.* Here I will move away from such polemical uses and argue that these terms should be used to refer to different aspects that evolved simultaneously in the same process.

Military modernization involved the urgent need to propel the military out of the state of backwardness in which it found itself and of turning it into an efficient fighting force. Modernization referred to changes in organizational structure, in personnel structure and policy, in logistics and procurement, and other measures. *Military reform,* on the other hand, pointed to all those changes that were necessary to harmonize the military role with emerging democratic institutions. It pointed, for instance, to limiting the military's domestic coercive role, reducing the scope of military justice, and setting limits to military participation in the government and to the participation of individual members in political activities. In the long run it also pointed to socializing military officers in a post-Franquist democratic ethos.

Military modernization of the armed forces could conceivably have been advanced during Franquism, since it did not threaten the authoritarian nature of the regime. Franco preferred, however, to give priority to national development plans and let the military undergo a gradual decline. Besides, modernization would have required at least one set of reform-like measures — the creation of unified superior command and authority structures, eventually a ministry of defense — against which conservatives in the military and government were firmly set. Modernization was then, in fact, postponed until the demise of Franquism and undertaken, albeit mildly, by the transition governments simultaneously with measures of reform. The substitution of the defense ministry for the separate service ministries broke, in 1977, with the Franquist mode of military participation in the government and facilitated the introduction of the authority of the transition government over the armed forces.

At least during the transition and first post-transition stage, reform was a task for the government, while modernization was left for the military to advance. Liberals in the military and reformers in the government made possible an alliance that would promote those changes in the military demanded by political democratization as well as those sought by military elites intent on professional improvement. In this division of labor defense remained under control of the military, but with a different leadership assertively pursuing change. It is distinctive of the Spanish transition that civilian elites could count on a small group of generals to conduct military policies that would contribute fundamentally to the establishment of democracy.

The Military Origin of Ideas on Modernization and Reform

Military policies conducted during the transition were based on schemes previously developed by groups of officers who had long held ideas about ways of overcoming the dismal state in which Franquism had left the armed forces.[37] The military budget during the last decades of Franquism had declined considerably, for instance, from 24 percent of the state budget in 1960 to 14 percent in 1975.[38] The structure of spending reflected distortions typical of a nonmodernized force: a disproportionate share went to the army to the detriment of the other services, and salaries were favored over operations, equipment, and research. Armament and equipment were quite obsolete, despite the rise in quantity and quality which had gradually taken place following military pacts with the United States in 1953. Territorial organization of the forces was designed more to face domestic threats than to procure an efficient defensive deployment against external attack.

The areas most in need of modernization, however, were personnel and organization. The number of officers was excessive, as was the time they remained stagnant in the same grade. The army had 328 generals in 1975, and the age limits set for retirement were quite high: 70 years for lieutenant generals, 68 years for major generals, and 66 years for brigadier generals.[39] This obviously affected the structure of spending, with personnel accounting for approximately 62 percent of total military spending in 1976–78.[40] Also, the professional quality of upper-level officers suffered from the absolute reliance on seniority as a basis for promotions.[41]

As far as the organization of the military was concerned, there was a lack of central, joint structures for the coordination of the forces. This was a major hindrance. The High General Staff, which Franco had created in 1939 after the elimination of a short-lived defense ministry during the civil war, responded to changing demands of the caudillo and had no real authority or coordination functions. Its chief, as well as the chiefs of staff of each armed service, lacked authority over the respective service ministers, who were in fact first in the chain of command. But also among the military ministers there was no coordinating structure, and over time this resulted in a very uneven development of the services. The "establishment" within each armed service, however, preferred the absence of an overarching unified coordinating structure so as to maintain its independent means of access to power.

Nonetheless, starting in the 1960s, deeply dissatisfied officers started to react against the dismal state of their army by conceiving ideas for modernization. This was facilitated by the atmosphere provided in military schools for the exchange of experiences by officers from different services. One of the sources for the inspiration of modernization schemes in the army came from efforts that the navy had made to improve its organization, personnel, and overall planning capabilities. The advantages obtained from the 1953 accords with the United States, and a closer connection with NATO member navies, had demanded an earlier modernization in the navy than in the rest of the forces.

In the mid-1960s the navy's Superior Council approved a number of projects, from which a far-reaching naval program for acquisitions and constructions later evolved. Also, in the same period the navy created study commissions to deal with problems of personnel (Comisión de Estudios de Personal [COMESPER]) and planning (Comisión de Estudios y Planes [COMESPLAN]). From these emerged the rudiments for a law on rank and promotions — *Ley de Escalas y Ascensos de la Armada* (1969) —

which incorporated criteria for selection and promotions which went beyond a strict reliance on seniority. The 1970 Organic Law of the Navy also resulted from these developments. This law separated the command structure for the fighting force from the command of administrative and auxiliary services and reinforced the former. For instance, the law specified the role of the navy chief of staff as the head of the naval chain of command, thereby lessening the powers of the navy minister.[42] In the other service branches the chiefs of staff remained subordinate to their respective ministers. The distinctions introduced in this law would later guide similar reforms in the air force, the army, and the general organization of defense.

Simultaneously, the HGS had begun to promote joint study activities among the service branches, activities that were invigorated with the creation of CESEDEN in 1964 under the supervision of the chief of the HGS. The center integrated existing organs of higher military training and created the Spanish Institute of Strategic Studies, which organized workshops for upper-level civilian and military bureaucrats. Incipient interservice ties developed which helped propagate a shared view on the need for greater coordination. Studies on problems of military coordination, personnel, command structure, and territorial and overall organization proliferated along with the development of critical views on the existing structures of Spanish defense organization. Ideas on the need for a ministry of defense or some higher body of coordination, such as the vice presidency for defense affairs, arose from these studies and was reflected in the work of students attending the Joint Staff School, as shown in table 5.1. Presentations made in the early academic years of the Joint Staff School straightforwardly criticized the inadequacy of defense organization and proposed the creation of a ministry of defense and other radical changes in personnel and education.[43] CESEDEN, as previously noted, never became comparable to the ESG in Brazil or the CAEM in Peru; nonetheless, it provided the institutional milieu for the sprouting of reform and modernization ideas.

These ideas circulated mostly among small numbers of officers and only within military educational centers. Beyond these small circles many within the army feared that the creation of a central structure would ultimately weaken the army's preeminence among the service branches as well as its direct access to the highest power positions. They also feared that the chances of having a civilian appointed to head a central defense structure would increase dramatically with a single defense ministry. Among many officers the existing structure best represented their idea

Table 5.1

Theses Submitted by Students Attending the Joint Staff School

I Course 1965–66	
Lieut. Col. Fernández-Manrique	The Need for New Officer Recruitment and Education Structures in the Armed Forces
Lieut. Col. Martín González	Possible Logistical Coordination of Spain with NATO
Lieut. Col. Dávila	Structure of National Defense Organs
III Course 1967–68	
Lieut. Col. Gavarrón Zambrano	Structuration of High Levels of National Defense
Major Jesús María Costa Furtiá	Ideas for a Doctrine of Unified Action
IV Course 1968–69	
Lieut. Col. Vallespín	Basis for the Organization of High-Level Joint Logistical Services
Lieut. Col. Clavería Semente	Ideas on a Mobilization System Adjusted to Current Times
Lieut. Col. Calvo Peribáñez	A General Academy for the Armed Forces
Major Carreras Mata	Planning in Higher National Defense Organs
Major Gómez Esteban	Study on the Unification of the Armed Forces
Major Mesa Mesa	Different Degrees of Integration Which May Be Considered in the Armed Forces
V Course 1969–70	
Major Cabrero Torres-Quevedo	On the Creation of a Ministry of Defense
Lieut. Col. Losantos Comas	Convenience of Logistical Coordination with NATO
VI Course 1971–72	
Col. Tercero	Interservice Military Logistics
VII Course 1973–74	
Licut. Col. Pastor	Professional Armies: Draft or Mixed System?
Major Martín Bilbatua	Common Logistical Needs of the Three Services
VIII Course 1975–76	
Lieut. Commander Aguirre	An Integrated Management System for the Armed Forces
Lieut. Col. Delgado Sánchez	A Personnel Policy for the Armed Forces
Major Vicente Martínez	A National Defense Structure Which Permits Unified Conduct of War
IX Course 1976–77	
Lieut. Col. Ortiz de la Cruz	Advantages of a Unified Command for Matériel
Lieut. Col. Giraldez Dávila	A Personnel Policy for the Armed Services
X Course 1977–78	
Lieut. Col. Santos Rodríguez	Unification of Higher Military Education in the Armed Forces
Lieut. Col. Revilla Melero	Toward the Unification of the Jurisdictions of the Army, Navy, and Air Force

Source: Centro Superior de Estudios de la Defensa Nacional (CESEDEN), Madrid.

of the military as a power within the state, maintaining direct connections with the head of state, connections that a ministry of defense would eventually threaten. The idea of creating such a ministry did not excite much enthusiasm from the other services either, because they feared that it could lead to an even stronger, more institutionalized dominance by the army. In light of these obstacles military reformers faced an uphill battle during Franquism.

Failed Attempts to Promote Change
in the Twilight of Franquism

In 1967–68 CESEDEN organized a committee to study problems of national defense which included participants from the military and other government ministries, the High General Staff, and university professors. This committee, profiting from earlier work within CESEDEN, proposed the creation of the post of general secretary for defense affairs with ministerial rank under the direction of the president of the government. Further development of the proposal was killed, however, when debate started on the question of the structure of military command.[44]

The promise contained in these initiatives was reinitiated in 1970 when Lieutenant General Manuel Diez Alegría became chief of the High General Staff. Working with CESEDEN, Diez Alegría resolutely sought to transform ideas into realities, but the obstacles placed by military and Franquist bureaucracies slowed down a project he drafted in 1971. This project dropped the idea of a general secretary for defense affairs and offered, instead, the creation of a Joint Chiefs and an enhanced role for the chief of the High General Staff. The project scaled down the role of military ministers to administration alone, while command of the services was fully transferred to the chiefs of staff. Opposition by military ministers delayed the project until Carrero Blanco assumed the presidency of the government in 1973. On April 1974 the project was finally submitted to the Cortes by the government as the Organic Law of National Defense.[45] This was the first project formally to address the need for a unified command structure. Committee work in the Cortes introduced a few modifications, but the core aspects were maintained: the chief of staff became the top authority in each armed service; together they formed the joint chiefs to advise the president and were led by the chief of the High General Staff, who also would assume direction of war operations.

The proposal, however, did not get very far. Under fire from conservative and hard-line military factions, its chances of making any progress diminished further with the assassination of Carrero Blanco, which eliminated government support for the bill, and disappeared completely with the ouster of Diez Alegría himself by Franco.[46] In December 1974 the government decided to withdraw the bill from the Cortes. It became clear that no project so unequivocally aimed at the modernization of the central command structure would pass against the wishes of influential people within Franquism who were complacent with existing structures.[47]

Frustration among liberal modernizers was evident. Major General José Gabeiras, for instance, addressing students at the Joint Staff School in 1975, complained about the years wasted in trying to reform the central structure of defense. Presenting a doctrine for joint action, he declared it tentative—"only God knows for how long given that it also depends on a law on national defense."[48] But frustration also turned into hope that a post-Franquist government would invigorate reform initiatives accumulated in military circles. It was a good sign that ideas developed in military circles had been taken up by civilian political groups, which integrated them into their own more global reform projects. By 1976, for instance, the platforms of the major political parties included proposals for the creation of a ministry of defense.[49] In addition, for civilian reformist elites the group of military reformers were a promise of support within an institution that otherwise, to use Diez Alegría's words, produced in them "reverential fear."

Reformists in Government and the Military:
Coalitional Opportunities in the Transition

Reformist initiatives in the military resumed during the post-Franco government of Adolfo Suárez when, in July 1976, Lieutenant General Manuel Gutiérrez Mellado was appointed to head the army staff. These initiatives gained further impetus with the resignation of Lieutenant General de Santiago, the conservative vice president for defense inherited from the Arias government. This resignation provided Suárez with the opportunity to give the job to Gutiérrez Mellado in September 1976. Less than a year later Gutiérrez Mellado was appointed to head the defense ministry, created in July 1977. The collaboration between the general and the president, with the support of the king, permitted the initiation of a reform agenda for the military and greatly eased efforts to try and tilt military appointments toward the liberals.

In fact, liberals in the military provided the government of Adolfo Suárez with indispensable allies for neutralizing opposition in the armed forces. In turn, the appointment of reformist civilians to the government benefited liberals in the military, because it facilitated their ascent to critical commanding positions and opened the way for modernization, which they deemed urgent for the armed forces.

In his short tenure as army chief of staff Gutiérrez Mellado assumed a much more active role than the army minister in the government. In the first report to the army in his new position Gutiérrez Mellado outlined a number of measures for immediate implementation and guidelines for future action. He put forth a policy to promote exclusive dedication to military employment, ending *pluriempleo,* the practice of holding parallel civilian employment, and he also ended the corrupt practice of using enlisted men for the provision of private services. Such elementary calls to professionalism were complemented with a rigorous regulation of political activities for members of the armed forces with a view to promoting political neutrality or respect toward ranking governmental and military authorities. These regulations, formalized in a strict royal decree, were meant primarily to end the participation of numerous officers in Franquist civil organizations and their appearance in public acts of a political character and came to balance previous measures taken against UMD members.[50] The report also committed the high command to a reorganization of the central staff, to the formulation of plans to end the use of seniority as the exclusive criterion for promotions and gradually to head toward a rejuvenation of the personnel structure, and to grant recognition to the right of conscientious objection in certain cases.[51]

From the positions he assumed in the government in September 1976, Gutiérrez Mellado was finally able to promote the modernization measures that had been rejected under Franquism in 1974. For instance, the Joint Chiefs was institutionalized as Junta de Jefes de Estado Mayor (JUJEM), and steps were taken for the landmark creation of the ministry of defense in July 1977. Gutiérrez Mellado also announced the preparation of significant projects, such as a national defense law that would delineate the responsibilities of national authorities in military and defense affairs. He also appointed a committee to draft a modernized version of military ordinances and to study reforms in the code of military justice.[52] Finally, he outlined policy goals aimed at promoting joint action and greater coordination of the armed services in areas such as training, operations, logistics, administration, and command.

Suárez's reformist government thus opened significant possibilities for liberal reformers in the army. Appointed to top positions, liberals finally set out to implement previously conceived changes and to elaborate long-term plans for military modernization. Although they constituted a small minority in the army, liberal reformers benefited from the formal-legal power of the new positions they commanded as well as from the legitimacy and charisma that flowed from Suárez and the king. Halfway through 1977, with the elimination of the military ministries, Gutiérrez Mellado monopolized all army presence in the government and appointed in critical positions generals who were sympathetic with the reformist platform. Toward the middle of 1977 the positions of army chief of staff, captain general of the Madrid Military Region, and director of the Civil Guard were assigned to sympathetic officers, all of whom played a critical role in limiting the army's reaction to the legalization of the Communist Party.[53] Also important was the replacement in 1977 of General Luis Cano Portal by General Juan Cano Hevia as director of the journal *Ejército*. Cano Portal had played a role in killing Diez Alegría's modernization project in 1974 and had later made the journal an outlet for laudatory articles on Franco, the Crusade, and others which criticized the changes under way. Cano Hevia ended the publication of this kind of article and turned the journal into an outlet for professional concerns.[54]

Appointments in intelligence also received priority. Suárez assigned Colonel Cassinello to head the new information office of the presidency, which had merged the previous government information service and the one from the now near-defunct HGS. Despite Cassinello's intelligence role in the previous regime and his previous concern with the expansion of communism and subversion, Suárez had had a special relationship with him and could fully trust him on the grounds of personal loyalty. With vast experience in Spanish intelligence Cassinello could keep the government well informed about the military's mood on critical issues.[55]

The government's use of appointment opportunities in the army to expand its basis of support had very clear limitations: there was just not a large enough pool of sympathetic generals to select from, or, as Gutiérrez Mellado put it, you could not get apples out of a strawberry basket (si usted tiene una cesta de fresas es muy difícil que saque una manzana).[56] Besides, hard-liners also had to be appeased by providing them with important posts. Moving with prudence to prevent the strengthening of hard-liners while at the same time appeasing them with important posts was a very fine line to walk and one that inevitably made Gutiérrez Mellado the object of criticism from all sides, either for giving too little or giving too much.

Unable to rely on large numbers, Gutiérrez Mellado emphasized discipline, political neutrality, and commitment of the army to the king: "Sir, we do not want to be anything more than good soldiers" (Señor, no queremos ser más que buenos soldados).[57] In addition, Gutiérrez Mellado actively sought support for the government in the army by implying that, through its position in the government, the military was maintaining a watchful eye.[58]

Yet the leading position that liberal reformers gained in the army as a result of the support received from President Suárez was not without costs. Gutiérrez Mellado's ascendancy over the army gradually eroded, harmed by his association with Suárez, whose reputation had suffered irretrievably from his role in the legalization of the Communist Party. Gutiérrez Mellado began to be seen more as a man of the government than of the army, and his appointments policy, though within legal procedures, was seen as politically motivated.[59] Also, his pursuit of reforms started to hurt established interests within military bureaucracy as well as the ideals of conservatives. The success of the transition owed much to the efforts of the liberal leadership of Gutiérrez Mellado, but for this success he was made to pay dearly by an army that remained massively and staunchly anchored in Franquist loyalty. The full consequences of this experience emerged after the inauguration of democracy under the new constitution.

Divisions and Coalitional Opportunities: A Comparative Outlook

Major differences existed among southern European and South American militaries regarding the depth and nature of divisions, the availability of countervailing factors, and the coalitional opportunities that these divisions presented to civilian democratic reformers. For instance, divisions in the South American militaries, which played important roles in the transitions from authoritarianism, were of a quite different nature from those in Spain and certainly not as helpful for democratization. The coalitional opportunities that the small group of liberals in the Spanish army opened for democratic reformers during the transition were, in fact, rather unique.

In the South American cases divisions within the military partly were rooted in the diverse outlooks that the different armed services had developed over time. Some service branches traditionally had advanced more conservative orientations than others, influencing the positions outlined for the transition and post-transition periods. But, specifically in contrast with Spain, other sources of division in South America came from the militarized character of the authoritarian regimes. Because the military-as-institution held important roles in government, it fell prey to the inevitable divisions inherent in the task of making major decisions on policy, regime orientation, and leadership succession.

In Brazil, for instance, the struggle between hard-line and soft-line postures, embodied in the clash between the intelligence community and the military-as-government, became especially intense during periods of presidential succession.[60] In Argentina rifts between the armed services, each one in charge of a different area of state administration, were reflected in frequent policy changes and, most dramatically, in removals of the president.[61] In Peru and Ecuador removal of the top military leadership at some point during the authoritarian regime instilled major changes in regime orientation and kept different factions alive. Such was also the case in Uruguay.[62] In Chile divisions were evident in the removal of founding junta leaders (generals Gustavo Leigh and César Mendoza) at different points in time, in views over the transition and in the campaign for, and handling of, the 1988 plebiscite.[63]

Such divisions undoubtedly helped advance democratization in these countries and often were the decisive factor in triggering liberalization and a movement toward democracy. The burdens of governance in combination with failures in handling economic or international crises convinced many military leaders in the 1970s and 1980s of the virtues of extrication from direct rule. The continuity of these divisions throughout the transitions allowed new civilian governments to count on a few leaders among the military to help neutralize hard-line elements, just as military chiefs would use support from the government to pursue their own policies. For instance, in Argentina President Alfonsín and a weakened high command supported each other in resisting several challenges from rebel colonels; in Peru President Alan García used support from the army to pursue reforms resisted by the other services; in Uruguay President Sanguinetti and General Medina, leader of the former junta, converged and supported each other in the new democratic government; in Chile President Aylwin often relied on various military chiefs to duck out of difficult episodes, especially challenges from the army, during his successor administration. These alliances, however, served limited, and rather defensive, objectives for both sides. They did not represent shared interests in reform and democratization, as did the alliance between liberal military leaders and the transition governments in Spain. None of the successor democratic governments in South America got the kind of support which, for instance, Adolfo Suárez got from General Gutiérrez Mellado.

The existence of a group of liberals within the Spanish military elite gave civilian reformers an advantage that was not available to the democratic elites in the South American transitions. In Spain liberal military officers, placed in leadership roles by the governments of the transition, not only helped to weaken military hard-line opposition; they also set out to initiate the reform and modernization of the armed forces to which they had long aspired. The pursuit of these changes in the military was, in itself, an act of support to the democratic transition. These orientations among liberal officers, and the convergence of interests it created with civilian reformers, did not exist in the South American cases.

No group within the South American militaries held the preoccupation with reform and modernization as Spanish liberal officers did, because none of these militaries experienced during authoritarianism the kind of decline which the Spanish army experienced during Franquism. The share of the military in government budgets during authoritarianism in South America remained high or increased, with the sole exception of Brazil.[64] In all of these countries — Brazil included — sophisticated weapons were introduced from purchases abroad or local production, and officers could live more than comfortably on their military jobs exclusively, never being forced into the practice of *pluriempleo,* (that is, having to take on more than one job). Whatever decline in military professionalism took place under authoritarianism in South America, it was rather the consequence of involvement in direct rule and domestic repression,[65] which detracted concentration on military preparation and tended to produce divisive effects among the generals and down the hierarchy.

The return of civilian rule offered the military the possibility of refocusing on the professional enhancement of the forces. Once driven to arrange for their own extrication from government, the militaries realized that professional gains and improvements could be attained, and often more easily, from outside government positions.[66] With the exception of the collapsed Argentine military, the armed forces could more or less directly ascertain, plan, and implement, with the use of prerogatives safeguarded during the transition, the improvements deemed necessary, with little need for civilian help. These improvements, in fact, were confined to each service branch separately and never contemplated reforms that could provide avenues for a larger civilian role. Modernization was never seen to require deep institutional reforms or reorganization in the central structure of defense.[67] A return to enhanced professionalism after the experience of military rule meant, in practice, a more focused emphasis on the appropriate ways, institutionally, to deploy the military in the context of elected civilian governments, in order to deal with a broad, self-defined security mission encompassing both external and internal roles. No liberal group existed within these militaries which sought radical professional reforms for which government help was needed to counter the influence of other military sectors, as was the case in Spain. A concern in the military with enhancing professionalism did not translate into the same kind of coalitional opportunities that opened up in Spain between liberal military leaders and democratic reformers in the government.

In addition, several factors were present in South America to temper whatever rifts existed in the military. One was the successful institutional arrangements set in several cases purposely to deflect or minimize the divisive impact of governance on military unity. In Brazil and Chile, for instance, the enhanced institutional role of the presidency and other measures helped to preempt or significantly lessen the impact of divisions.[68] Another factor was the national security tenets developed among the South American militaries. National security doctrines did not prevent the emergence of internal friction and clashes. Still, as noted earlier, years of socialization in doctrinal tenets that called for expanded military roles in society, helped the militaries to face civilian reformers more cohesively during the transition (especially in Brazil, Chile, and Uruguay), not only with reinforced convictions about the legitimacy of military prerogatives but also with institutional and policy guidelines to protect them. But, perhaps the single most important factor in lessening the impact of existing divisions — especially in Argentina, Chile, and

Uruguay—was the way in which the military closed ranks in response to charges of human rights violations.

In Argentina this was the single issue the different services could agree upon during the interim period that followed the Falklands/Malvinas debacle. This agreement led the military to pass an amnesty law for itself against the wishes of most of the civilian leadership. After the restoration of democracy the highest military court adopted a unified stance in rejecting attempts by the government to prosecute human rights crimes committed by members of the armed forces. In an attitude of corporate defense the military challenged the government, which ultimately was forced to promote the *Ley de obediencia debida* and *Ley de punto final*. In Uruguay agreement not to prosecute was the result of unified military pressure, further galvanized in response to the plebiscite on the subject put forth by civilian groups. In Chile absolute defense of the amnesty law passed by the Pinochet government brought all military leaders together during the transition and during subsequent encounters in which the military felt challenged on the subject.[69] This element of contention, which brought different military factions together, was not present in the Spanish transition.[70]

In the other southern European cases—Greece and Portugal—the nonhierarchical nature of the militaries during authoritarianism or the transition was, in itself, an expression of deep divisions.[71] In Greece it was the reaction of senior military leaders against the ruling colonels following the fiasco in Cyprus which opened the way to swift democratization. Then, indispensable changes—in order to reaccommodate the military under the new democratic circumstances and to place it back in its outward role in NATO and vis-à-vis Turkey—were undertaken under the leadership of successor democratic governments, with significant public support and with the help of senior military leaders. The collapse of the colonels' regime made it less urgent for the successor civilian leadership to rely on strong allies in the military, as the Spanish transition governments had. In comparison with South America, the nonhierarchic nature of the military in the colonels' regime made it easier, for instance, to prosecute the junta leaders without arousing the solidarity of the military as a whole.[72]

In Portugal rifts in the military led to the ouster of the authoritarian regime, but persisting divisions ultimately got in the way of a rapid transition to democracy. Raucous divisions following the coup of April 1974 badly hurt the military. Only the emergence of a moderate leadership in the army, personified in General Eanes, and its convergence with elected civilian leaders managed gradually to return the military to discipline and professionalism. In contrast with Spain, however, the military, until the constitutional reforms of 1982, held a tutelary role, which it nurtured with a somewhat generalized feeling of sympathy for the "spirit" of the revolution, in turn manifested in the socialist overtones given the Constitution, which remained in place until 1989.[73]

Everywhere in the transitions of the 1970s and 1980s in southern Europe and South America the military presented serious internal rifts. These were countered, in cases such as Brazil, Chile, and Uruguay, with institutional arrangements, doctrinal developments, or attitudes of corporate defense against external challenges which lessened the impact of divisions, occasionally cementing levels of cohesion important enough to enable the military to face bargaining situations from a position of strength. In most of the other cases the military was deeply divided, with no significant countervailing factors. Only in Spain, however, did the nature of divisions present an opportunity for the collaboration of civilian and military leaders in pursuit of democratization and military modernization and reform.

III The Post-Transition

6

Obstacles to
Regime Consolidation
after the Transition

THE SUCCESSFUL completion of inaugural elections is not tantamount to the consolidation of democracy. The introduction of democracy only means that democratically elected authorities have taken over the reins of government for a specified term within a context of guaranteed individual rights and party competition. The secure delineation of democracy's necessary supporting institutions (that is, parties, parliament, organizations of intermediation), which initially are only roughly sketched, is, however, uncertain. In Spain, for instance, March 1979, the date of the first elections conducted under the new constitution, was still too early a date for democrats to relax.[1]

During the years following the inauguration of democracy military hardliners became increasingly assertive. This rising assertiveness reached its peak in the coup attempt of 23 February 1981, in which a heavily armed unit of the Civil Guard took over the Palace of the Cortes, while Congress deliberated with the president of the government and the whole cabinet inside. A few important army units in Madrid and outside the capital mobilized in support of the uprising, while the army's deputy chief of staff maneuvered in the hope of coaxing the kidnapped Congress to appoint him head of a new government. The coup failed, and its major leaders ended up in prison, but the episode nonetheless highlighted the vulnerability of the new democracy, which could not be considered consolidated as long as the "military problem" remained unsolved.

There evidently had been a change in the tide of military acquiescence. In the period between the constitutional referendum and the coup attempt, instances of indiscipline within the ranks occurred more frequently, hard-line figures became boisterous in their discontent, and the stature and respect for both the president and the minister of defense diminished considerably within the armed forces. What had caused this change? Why could the successful inauguration of democracy not pave the way for a smooth consolidation of the new regime? What led hard-line military leaders to revert from disgruntled consent to forceful, violent opposition?

New political developments affected the military's calculus. In the eyes of hard-line leaders the costs of toleration increased with dramatic escalation in terrorist activities, whose brunt was borne by the army, and the unleashing of nationalist demands from some of the major regions.[2] Intervention, again in the eyes of military leaders, was also made less costly by the weakening of civilian consensus and public support for the government. Internecine factional battles, often related to the enormous challenge of promoting the new territorial organization of the state (the *comunidades autónomas*), crippled the government, while the opposition intensified its challenges. In this context — and reassured by the realization that, despite their overt criticisms and contestation, they continued to be assigned to important posts — hard-line military leaders felt imbued with renewed strength.

Constitutional and legal changes during the transition had little effect on the military's actual power. Moreover, some of these changes paradoxically enhanced it. For instance, the creation of the Joint Chiefs gave the armed forces a collective voice it had previously lacked. Perceiving themselves stronger, powerful leaders in the military thought that their major and accumulated grievances could be forcefully and successfully redressed.

In Spain the subordinate position of the military in the transition did not settle the military question once and for all. It did facilitate a clean democratic inauguration, placing the burden of subverting this order on the military, but, ultimately, it did not prevent the growth of military assertiveness, which severely tested the democracy and postponed the attainment of civilian supremacy and democratic consolidation.

Civilian Institutions at the Outset of Democracy

At inauguration the new regime featured basic democratic institutions of representation, arranged in parliamentary form, plus a monarch as head of state and the incipient organization of regional governments in Euskadi and Catalonia.[3] In crucial respects, however, the new democratic state involved plans rather than actualized feats. The Constitution had set guidelines for the development of norms and institutions in specific areas, but their implementation remained pending. Such was the case with the judiciary and the court system, the system of autonomous communities, and the military, for which major definitions were left unresolved, to be developed later in an organic law.

Spain faced the demise of authoritarianism with a double transformative challenge: political democratization and rearrangement of the territorial and administrative structure of the state in response to the demands of the historic nationalities. During Franquism nationalist demands had been severely repressed, and whatever autonomy had existed before was abolished. As the only state among those considered here which is made up of distinct nationalities, Spain was the only one to face this compound challenge.[4]

Although the Constitution included a recognition of the right to autonomy of the diverse nationalities integrated in the Spanish nation, the major Basque parties refused to support the Constitution in the referendum because it did not recognize the *fueros* (historic rights) of Euskadi. Nonetheless, as soon as the new Constitution was in place, leaders from Euskadi and Catalonia, in accordance with constitutional guidelines, submitted draft proposals of autonomy statutes for discussion with the national government. Suárez, who, following the elections of March 1979, had been reappointed head of the government,[5] spent most of that year in negotiations with Catalan and Basque leaders. Autonomy statutes were approved that year, and regional elections for parliament of the new Comunidades Autónomas were held in 1980. The implementation of a state based on autonomous communities,via the negotiation of statutes with leaders of these and other regions practically monopolized the agenda of the Suárez government and became a continuous source of difficulty, tension, and quarrel among civilian elites.

Political parties, essential organizations in democracies, also were, for the most part, in a development and growth phase. Only two parties that preceded Franquism were in existence at the start of the transition, and both were from the Left: Socialists and Communists. Although there were plenty of informal political associations of notables, Center and Right parties did not exist until the transition. Unión de Centro Democrático (UCD), the center party, was formed by Suárez and his associates in the government initially as a coalition to contest the first elections and only then as a unified party. On the Right, Manuel Fraga formed a party (the Alianza Popular–Coalición Democrática) whose leaders were all former Franquist ministers, who, however, deserted the party during the constitutional agreement that Fraga supported. This party got much less electoral support than expected, surprising its leaders as well as hopeful members of the military.[6] The initial weakness of most parties was further expressed in factionalism, which especially affected the UCD, and in electoral setbacks, which were a consequence of public disenchantment with the centralized and quasi-consociational style of elite decision making during the transition, particularly in the drafting of the Constitution. In fact, coalescent behavior on the part of elites engaged in the founding of a new regime often conflicted with the demands of building their own parties.[7]

With undeveloped parties and institutions the post-transition process faced its own uncertainties.[8] The civilian leadership was burdened with the challenge of implementing new institutions, consolidating new or reemerged political parties, and confronting the growing assertiveness of military hard-liners. If initial conditions had provided comparative advantages to the Spanish transition, the post-transition process commenced with no such blessings.

The Military at the Inauguration of Democracy

By dismantling Franquist structures, the inauguration of democracy in 1978–79 eliminated channels for the military's political expression while simultaneously allowing more voice and participation for parties, the "nationalities," and other groups that had been suppressed during Franquism. This had not been the outcome of choice for the military, and the fact that it was brought about precisely by ignoring the military's preferences created in the military sentiments of hostility toward the new system, even if under the facade of formal subordination. This resentment, combined with the fact that the military as an institution remained basically unchanged and that its identification with the ideological tenets of

Franquism had not receded an inch, did not bode well for democratic consolidation. The exclusion of the military from the elite consensus that characterized the Spanish transition implied that the military could emerge as the most potent threat to democracy.

Democracy was supported, however, by all major parties and through the reiterated expressions of the electorate. The very fact that this new arrangement was institutionalized raised the costs for the military to attempt to redress the situation in which it found itself. Moreover, the military still faced severe limitations from its own disunity. Divisions, in fact, continued to be a major impediment to conservative and hard-line mobilization against the democratic regime.

Sharply different evaluations of the transition and its difficulties sprang up within the military. For some, such as Lieutenant General Ignacio Alfaro Arregui, chair of the Joint Chiefs, the transition phase had "been complex and hard," but "in general the armed forces are adapting themselves to change and to the new directives in good spirit and disposition."[9] With constructive resignation his brother, Lieutenant General Emilio Alfaro Arregui, air force chief of staff, affirmed: "There is no doubt that the Spanish people democratically decided a political reform which, also democratically, has been turned into a Constitution. We now face the inevitable difficulties brought about by its implementation."[10]

In the army, generals in the liberal group insisted on neutrality and subordination. In his inaugural speech as Captain General of Madrid, Guillermo Quintana Lacaci argued: "The neutrality of military commanders in political struggle is indispensable; otherwise internal security and the army's internal cohesion are threatened. . . . In democratic societies the armies must be inspired by absolute respect of the Constitution which demands from them a firmly non-partisan attitude. . . . The military, in accordance with the Constitution and the Laws must, at all times, obey [the government's] orders."[11]

These views contrasted with the completely different evaluations of the transition coming from the opposite camp in the military. For instance, Jesús González del Yerro, captain general of the Canary Islands, affirmed in September 1979: "[The problems of Spain] coincide with those of the overwhelming majority of Spaniards: separatism, terrorism, moral decline, economic crisis, personal insecurity, etc., etc."[12] Along the same lines Jaime Miláns del Bosch, captain general of Valencia, concluded in a public interview that, "objectively speaking, the transition thus far does not seem to throw a positive balance: terrorism, insecurity, inflation, economic crisis, unemployment, pornography and, above all, crisis of authority."[13]

But even within the conservative and hard-line camp there remained important strains. A vivid proof of its difficulties was the inability to agree on a leader to fill the top army post when the opportunity presented itself in May 1979. A meeting of the High Army Council, which in practice had at this time the power to decide on the designation of the chief of staff, was unable to reach agreement on the subject, despite the fact that at least four contestants were considered who would have been genuine representatives of an alliance between conservatives and hard-liners. These contestants, however, refused to accept the nomination either because they failed to get the unanimous endorsement that they had requested of the council or because they rejected the possibility of being put in a position of having to collaborate with Vice President Gutiérrez Mellado. The council made no proposals, and hard-liners wasted in this way a splendid opportunity to put one of their own in the top position.[14]

Defense Minister Gutiérrez Mellado, forced to pick someone of his own choosing, and with "no apples in the strawberry basket," had to reach deep down to appoint Major General José Gabeiras in May 1979. In order for Gabeiras to be able to take over as chief of staff, he had, simultaneously with his appointment, to be promoted to the grade of lieutenant general. Needless to say, the appointment of Gabeiras, who held only the eighteenth position in the seniority ranking in the High Army Council, was taken as yet another affront by the council, and the new chief had a rough time trying to exercise his command effectively.[15]

The difficulties encountered by conservatives and hard-liners to promote an assertive opposition were matched, however, by an increase in the costs of toleration. This increase resulted from dissatisfaction with the new democracy, in part due to the notable increase in acts of terrorism by ETA specifically targeted against the military. The first year in which the number of persons killed by ETA surpassed the number of ETA members killed by security forces was 1978.[16]

The result was that, toward the end of 1978, opposition by hard-liners took on a more active and aggressive line. Vice President Gutiérrez Mellado was met with several acts of indiscipline when he traveled around the country to explain government policy and the draft constitution in massive meetings with officers and noncomissioned officers (NCOs). Much more threatening, however, was the first military plot uncovered on 16 November 1978, shortly before the referendum on the constitution. Two mid-level officers, Lieutenant Colonel Antonio Tejero and Captain Ricardo Sáenz de Ynestrillas, were arrested and charged with planning Operation Galaxia, named after the bar in which they met and which aimed at capturing the cabinet in La Moncloa Palace.[17] In a blunt expression of the military's power, a martial court sentenced these officers only to seven and six months of "mitigated prison" in their homes, respectively, and both were allowed to return immediately to active service upon completion of their sentences. Shortly after the Galaxia episode, on 3 January 1979, ETA assassinated Madrid's military governor, General Ortín, and his funeral ceremonies turned into a tumultuous antigovernment demonstration. High-ranking officers interfered with the official funeral plans, and, disobeying orders shouted at them on-site, walked out of the army headquarters and into the street, carrying the coffin on their shoulders all the way to the cemetery, surrounded by groups of civilians chanting "Ejército al Poder" (Power to the Army).[18] Evidently, the government and the chief of staff had trouble maintaining discipline in the army, whose hard-line sectors had been aroused by the unexpected rise of terrorist activities during 1979 and 1980.

The Impact of Terrorism

Several small active terrorist groups from the Left and the Right were responsible for the rise of terrorist acts, but the main contributor was ETA, the largest and most effective organization. ETA had formed in the late 1960s out of a splinter of the Partido Nacionalista Vasco (PNV), the old catholic and conservative Basque Nationalist Party, and had risen to prominence with the dramatic assassination of Admiral Carrero Blanco in 1973. In the final days of Franquism, ETA was active mostly in the Basque country against the Franquist police. During the transition it had gained the sympathies of most anti-Franquists, still lured by the heroism of young combatants whose death sentences an ailing Franco, challenging world opinion, had refused to repeal.[19]

Very few would have predicted ETA's dramatic escalation of terrorism against the nascent democracy. Terrorist actions in fact escalated to coincide with the inaugural years of democracy (see table 6.1). In the view of ETA's leadership the constitution drafted by the 1977 elected assembly

Table 6.1

Victims of ETA Terrorism in Spain

	Total	Wounded	Kidnapped	Killed	Killed (including non-ETA victims)
1977	23	10	1	12	28
1978	159	91	4	64	85
1979	252	161	13	78	118
1980	174	72	9	93	124
1981	98	58	10	30	38
1982	112	68	7	37	44

Sources: José María Maravall and Julián Santamaría, "Crisis del Franquismo, Transición Política y Consolidación de la Democracia en España," *Sistema,* no. 68–69 (November 1985): 105. For the killing of non-ETA members, see *El País,* 4 May 1986, 30.

and the ensuing autonomy statutes betrayed the ultimate goal of total independence for Euskadi. ETA rejected autonomy within the Spanish state and stood for outright separatism. In ETA's views these goals would be best served by promoting a military takeover in Madrid, that is, by placing in La Moncloa whom they saw as the real power behind the throne. Blunt repression, which, they hoped, the military would conduct from the center, would then create the conditions for a massive uprising in Euskadi and eventually for a negotiated path toward independence. Terrorism, especially targeted against the army, was the strategy conceived for this program. Although the ultimate goals were not achieved, the strategy did succeed in straining the new democracy and provoking antigovernment feelings in the armed forces.[20]

Most of the casualties of terrorism in this period are attributable to ETA, and a majority of ETA's targets were police or professional military men (see table 6.2). The most numerous group of victims were privates of the Civil Guard or the national police, but the most symbolically significant actions, that is, those scheduled for special occasions, involved upper-level army officers.

ETA killed an army general for the first time on 21 July 1978, the day Congress approved the Constitution. It gunned down Madrid's military governor, General Ortín, on 3 January 1979, shortly after the Constitution referendum. Next were army chief of personnel, Lieutenant General Gómez Hortigüela, and two accompanying colonels, shot on 25 May 1979, the eve of the celebration of Armed Forces' Day. On the same day a bomb exploded in a Madrid cafe, killing eight and injuring forty

Table 6.2
Affiliation of Victims of Terrorism, 1976–1986

Affiliation	Number of Persons Killed[a]		Percentage Killed by ETA
Police[b]	132		87.9
Civil Guard	140		90.7
Military Officers and NCOs	36		97.2
Generals/Admirals	13		76.9
Total Police and Professional Military	321	(52.6 %)	89.7
Total Civilians and Nonprofessional Military	289	(47.4 %)	58.5
Total	610		74.9

Source: Arranged from a table that appeared in El País, 4 May 1986, 30.

[a]Figures cover the period until 25 April 1986.

[b]Includes Police Superior Corps, National Police, municipal police, and Ertzantza (police of Euskadi).

civilians. On 3 October that year the deputy chief in the navy's post in Bilbao was shot to death.[21]

Army officers found it hard not to link ETA's terrorism to the numerous anti-Spanish actions that took place regularly in the Basque country and the support that the public voiced for ETA in street demonstrations there.[22] Also of concern was the electoral support in Euskadi for organizations that stood for separatism and the sympathies in public opinion for separatism and independence. In Euskadi one-fourth of total valid votes in 1979 went to Herri Batasuna and Euskadiko Ezkerra, both parties that rejected the Constitution outrightly. Twenty-seven percent of the votes went to the Basque Nationalist Party, which had called for abstention in the referendum. In the regional elections of 1980 the combined turnout for these parties reached 64 percent of valid votes.[23] It did not escape the military that the democratic Spanish government negotiated the autonomy statute with leaders who had not supported the Constitution, who refused to give explicit commitments to the unity of Spain, and who had decided to withdraw their representatives from Congress between January and September of 1980, at a time when ETA's actions intensified.[24] In addition, the attitudes of Basque leaders toward the central authorities were often hostile and disrespectful, and, despite public statements, their stance toward ETA was ambivalent.[25]

Trying to convey feelings among those in the army, Minister of Defense Gutiérrez Mellado vehemently stated in a speech before the king in 1978: "Sir: Spain is one and Spaniards will not tolerate that it be broken."[26] In 1979 the chairman of the Joint Chiefs, Air Force General Ignacio Alfaro Arregui, admitted that the Basque problem "is the topic that most troubles the Armed Forces," a statement confirmed by his brother Emilio, air force chief of staff, who insisted a few months later that "this is the issue that worries me the most."[27] Hard-liners profited from this generalized feeling in the armed forces and carried it further, overtly blaming the government for the escalation both of terrorist violence and of nationalist demands.

The military, which faced the transition in an initially weak position, recuperated lost capacities as its most recalcitrant sectors regrouped and expanded their internal influence as a result of the emergence of a visible threat to the institution and its mission. Hard-liners utilized the perception of a terrorist and nationalist threat to activate and reunite opposition forces within the army. Hard-liners' self-confidence was certainly stronger in January 1981 than it had been two or three years before. Thus empowered, they moved to try to exact higher costs for reform attempts.

Hard-liners, Discipline, and the King

Expressions of opposition in the military often carried no real consequences and were, in practice, allowed to occur frequently. Discipline in the army suffered partly from the fact that the army chief of staff, Tomás De Liniers, who had succeeded José Vega Rodríguez in May 1978, did not have the military and professional stature of his resigned predecessor, and his succession in May 1979 by General José Gabeiras had not helped to reassert discipline and leadership, given the circumstances of his appointment. In this context of escalating terrorism, distrust of the government's negotiations with representatives of the nationalities, and diminished internal legitimacy of the defense minister and the army chief of staff, the assertiveness of military hard-liners kept rising.

Hard-line attitudes reinforced themselves by the realization that challenging postures and daring indiscipline carried no major negative consequences for individuals. General Juan Atarés Peña's insults to the defense minister earned him only a light disciplinary measure.[28] The Civil Guard director, General Fontenla, who was removed from his post for announcing in April 1980 that "we will do everything possible to have the Senate reject the [national defense] bill passed in Congress," suffered no further disciplinary measures.[29] General Luis Torres Rojas, commander of the Brunete Armoured Division (DAC), the country's most powerful military installation stationed in the close vicinity of Madrid, was removed from his post in January 1980 and transferred to the military governorship of La Coruña, after the discovery of conspiratorial meetings held in divisional headquarters, but no further investigations or disciplinary or legal actions followed. And the highest military tribunal rejected an appeal by the Captain General of Madrid, Guillermo Quintana Lacaci, to review the extremely light sentences to the conspirators of the Galaxia plot of 1978.[30]

The laissez-faire policy with which hard-liners were apparently treated contrasted starkly with legal and disciplinary measures taken against officers who had overtly voiced support for democracy or denounced military opposition. While generals, with total impunity, overtly blamed civil authorities for what they saw as failures of the transition, others were imprisoned for much lesser faults. For instance, while General Torres Rojas was "punished" only with the transfer to a lesser post, the director of the daily *Diario* 16 was indicted by military courts for reporting on the seditious activities in which the general was involved. And, while the plotters of Operation Galaxia, who had sought to overthrow the government, were allowed to return to active service, UMD officers, who had organized precisely to prevent such moves, were consistently denied that possibility, despite continued attempts to do so in Congress.[31]

The king was understandably concerned with the malaise and unruliness that pervaded the army. As a key initiator of the transition, the king was fully aware of his unique ability, and responsibility, to bridge the military's past allegiances with evolving democratic institutions. In frequent speeches at military ceremonies he never ceased to portray himself as a soldier, going to great lengths to insist on how much he knew of the aspirations of fellow military men and how much he understood and shared their concerns. An address to the generals in 1980 vividly conveys this effort:

I do not feel a stranger in your company, and my functions are not limited to being your King and to holding the Supreme Command of the Armed Forces. I am also your companion. . . . I feel one more among you . . . because my youth has been formed, as yours and with many of you, in military academies where virtues are praised and qualities infused which are not modified by time or by the changes that may occur in society . . .

In my heart, in all my being, side by side with my love for the country, palpitates military spirit, and I feel always identified with my companions in the Army, with your concerns, your sorrows, your satisfactions and your hopes. So, when I see you joyful, I get joyful. When I feel you sad, I get sad. And all, absolutely all your worries; all, absolutely all your problems gravitate on your King and Captain General—your companion—with the same intensity that is felt by you.[32]

Yet from this sympathetic position the king would remind his comrades in arms of the duties of discipline and of the dangers of politicization. The occasion of the Pascua Militar, the solemn celebration of Kings' Day in the Palacio de Oriente, with top-ranking generals and admirals, provided a propitious opportunity every 6 January to convey his views. In 1979, only days after the shameful incidents at the funeral ceremony of General Ortín, Juan Carlos emphatically advised a return to discipline:

A soldier, an army that has lost discipline, cannot be saved. He is no longer a soldier, it is no longer an army. The spectacle of undisciplined, disrespectful attitudes born in passing emotions which unleash passions that fully disregard the poise demanded of every military, is frankly shameful.

What an impaired discipline is that which, for survival, demands explanations or permits objections based on fragmentary knowledge, subjective judgments or personal interpretations.[33]

During the same occasion the following year, the king stressed how much he shared the military's feelings of sorrow and indignation in the face of terrorism. And he issued a series of warnings aimed as much to recalcitrant sectors in the military as to outside groups inciting the army to action:

Let nobody identify you with their own interests or incite you to inopportune leading roles. . . . Let nobody forget that discipline inspires prudent abstention as much as it may propel resolute action if it is determined—by whom legally and constitutionally must do so and not by subjective interpretations—that the essential values, the defense of which is constitutionally entrusted to you, are threatened.[34]

While the king's statements helped deter recalcitrant sectors, they also reflected how much the tide had turned in a direction that continued to strengthen the military's self-confidence and to stunt allegiance to civil authorities. During 1980 it had become customary in the civilian and the military press to discuss military intervention: who wanted it, how it would proceed, were the conditions ripe, what demands the threat imposed on democrats, whether the situation called for a *"gobierno de concentración,"*[35] and so on. Former vice president General de Santiago ominously pleaded for the "rescue of Spain if we have the spirit of Spaniards and believers."[36] In response to this, Army Chief of Staff José Gabeiras declared in March 1980 during a visit to Burgos: "We cannot play into the game of an insidious enemy that only seeks to incite among us an uncontrolled desire to intervene dauntlessly against our own people."[37] Clearly, there had developed a climate in the army in which intervention was openly spoken about.

The Military in the New Institutions: A Power within the State?

Side by side with the criticism and contestation of hard-liners there developed another kind of corporate resistance: the military's defense of corporate boundaries and interests in the specific area of defense. Essentially, corporate defense took two closely related dimensions: one in regard to the defense ministry, the other in connection with the nature of the military's relations with the king. In and of themselves these corporative positions had no direct connection with the threat to democracy which was germinating in other quarters of the military. This corporate resistance, however, did help the military tighten its grip over institutional domains in dispute with civilian authority, further adding to its newfound sense of self-confidence and empowerment.

The first Suárez government had put an end to institutionalized military participation in government by substituting a single defense ministry for the previous ministries of each of the armed services. The dismantling of other Franquist institutions further removed the military from participatory positions, and the Constitution introduced further constraints by formulating clauses that excluded the maintenance of public order as a function of the armed forces, placing it instead in the hands of a now separate Civil Guard. These measures were accompanied by specific regulations that banned individual participation of officers in political organizations or acts and by regulations that made internal rules more compatible with principles of the new Constitution, as did the new general ordinances.

The removal of the military from participatory positions had not, however, automatically led to a substantial increase in the power of the government over the armed forces. The military had lost its ministries, but, since they never amounted to much, this was not seen as a major loss. Besides, the military had been equipped with new agencies, such as the Joint Chiefs. In essence, after these changes civilians and those in the military were facing each other anew, each zealously defending their own prerogatives, many of which were yet to be institutionally defined. And, of concern to the military, the new ministry of defense, in the context of a cabinet that was now accountable to an elected parliament, augured changes that might eventually affect the civil-military balance.

For the most sagacious defenders of the military's corporate power, it was important to prevent the growth of the defense ministry. The latter was perceived as an encroachment of the civilian democratic government in military affairs and as an interference in the "natural" connections between the armed forces and their supreme commander. In the period examined here the military did succeed in its goal of preventing the government from making substantial inroads via the defense ministry and in positioning itself as a strong corporate actor and a tough bargainer.

Paradoxes in Organizational Reform:
The Defense Ministry and the Joint Chiefs

The defense ministry, created in July 1977, was charged with "the ordering and coordination of government policy concerning national defense, and the execution of the corresponding military policy."[38] The creation of the ministry, however, had come after a strengthening of the role of the chiefs of staff, who were consequently the organs best positioned to benefit from the dismantling of the previous separate service ministries.

The strengthening of the chiefs of staff had started even before the creation of the Joint Chiefs in February 1977. In 1976 new regulations had instructed the army and the air force to adopt the organizational principle that distinguished "the force" from "force support" and, accordingly, to assign direct command of all military forces to the chief of staff while the service minister maintained only administrative support functions. This distinction had been originally adopted by the navy in 1970 in its landmark organic law, and its major consequence was the significant empowerment of its chief of staff over its service minister.[39]

The distinction between force and force support, which had guided the strengthening of the chiefs of staff vis-à-vis the service ministers, was interpreted in such a way that, when the defense ministry was created, almost all functions and dependencies from the eliminated ministries were transferred to the respective armed service staff rather than the defense ministry. The most important agencies of the old ministries — those dealing with infrastructure, personnel, and logistics, for instance — were transferred to the army and air force staffs. The new defense ministry, on the other hand, initially only absorbed secondary agencies such as social services and the health and retirement benefits office.[40] The new ministry was supposed to unify and centralize all that, which was previously unnecessarily dispersed and repeated in each one of the service ministries. Instead, it now presided over the same structure, the most important parts of which were not under its domain but, rather, under the domain of the empowered chiefs of staff. Thus, instead of directly absorbing agencies from the old ministries, the new defense ministry was faced with the challenge of having to try to win them over from their new "owners."

In truth, the defense ministry also was given authority over the Center for Defense Information and the Agency for Armament and Matériel, both of which became critical cornerstones of the later development of the ministry. But in this phase the ministry was assigned only a handful of staff personnel and remained only the weak tip of deep, military-controlled service icebergs. Until Agustín Rodríguez Sahagún was appointed minister on 5 April 1979, there was not a single civilian in the ministry, and for two more years he remained the only one.[41] The defense ministry's initial weakness was also all too clearly made evident in the fact that it did not even have a physical plant of its own, being assigned to a few offices in a wing of the air force headquarters, where it remained for six years.

This weakness was partly due to the approach imposed by the first minister, General Gutiérrez Mellado. Aware of corporate fears — the navy and the air force feared even larger, more institutionalized army dominance, and the army feared government encroachment — he wisely devised a gradual strategy in which officers from all services in the ministry staff would patiently persuade the service staffs slowly to move toward greater coordination of similar services and functions, until they could be transferred to the central organ. In the long run this approach helped persuade many skeptics about the advantages of promoting centralization and greater coordination, especially when they came with no special harms to anybody.[42] Gutiérrez Mellado's caution, however, responded to the resolve of the services' corporate defense, led by an empowered set of chiefs, now organized as Joint Chiefs, with important prerogatives of their own.

The Joint Chiefs came to replace the old and ineffectual High General Staff. While the latter had existed separate from the service branches, the new body was formed by the chiefs of staff of each service and was chaired by a fourth member, who rotated among the services. The Joint Chiefs was designated as the "highest collegiate body in the military chain of command," formally placed under the political authority of the president of the government and charged with the joint determination of force levels and the formulation of the joint strategic plan for government approval.[43] This set of changes was formalized in 1978 in a broader law specifying that it was the government that determined and oversaw defense and military policy, assisted by the National Defense Board, which was in turn assisted by the Joint Chiefs.[44]

Despite political-administrative subordination to the minister of defense, as established in the law, the Joint Chiefs liked to see itself more on equal footing with the ministry. Admiral Luis Arévalo Pelluz, the navy chief of staff, put it clearly: "We have got our mission and the Defense Minister has got his, and each one accepts the one he has. We, in the military, what we like is that everybody is in his right place . . . and that we have enough liberty of action and, of course, that we do not interfere in each other's roles."[45]

The defense ministry and the service staffs of the services were, in fact, forced to coexist in stalemate, with the ministry having "to harmonize" its functions with those of the Joint Chiefs.[46] The distinct prerogatives of each were not yet well clarified and were the subject of negotiated definitions or simply of inaction. Military chiefs preferred to emphasize a view of the ministry more as a provider of military needs than as a superior. On this point the military had the support of Alianza Popular, the party of the Right, which generally recommended a restricted role for the government in line with its view favoring an autonomous military power.[47] Coincidence on this issue with a respectable parliamentary party added legitimacy to the military's position.

In 1980, fulfilling the Constitution's mandate that an organic law be elaborated on the mission and administration of the armed forces, Congress passed the Organic Law on Basic Principles of National Defense and Military Organization. It gave higher status to legal dispositions that had thus far ruled in these matters but introduced no substantial advances, and the Joint Chiefs was left as the highest collegiate body in the military chain of command. By the end of 1980 the Joint Chiefs clearly had the upper hand over the young defense ministry. On Minister Rodriguez Sahagún's own admission the ministry of defense was a "preschooler" still facing the much more adult military quarters.[48]

The Joint Chiefs and the King

The competition between the ministry and the Joint Chiefs was compounded by a larger issue. In the view of military chiefs the Joint Chiefs was entitled to have a direct, regular connection with the king, the supreme commander, without the ministry acting as an intermediary. The military wanted to prevent government intrusion in a line of authority that had the king at the apex and which the military saw as essential to defending its autonomy.

Although this position was not maintained officially or openly, it was the preferred position of many at the top.[49] Behind it converged different groups with different goals. Some generals were only intent on defending institutional autonomy or the enhancement of institutional prestige. Others, instead, found it a profitable avenue to widen the gap between the government and the armed forces and to induce further military opposition.[50]

The views that supported a direct organic relation between the king and the Joint Chiefs was, in fact, not without legal grounding, since there had been much ambiguity in the official definition of prerogatives for the government and the king. The Constitution assigned supreme command to the king, while the government was charged with the political and military administration of the state. That there was confusion and bias in the interpretation of these clauses must have been evident to the king when he thought it necessary to remind the military of the prerogatives of defense minister Gutiérrez Mellado in the Pascua Militar of 1979: "[With] support and understanding it will be necessary to continue the task of military reorganization. . . . It was not easy to merge into one the missions previously entrusted to three ministerial departments, and for this reason I congratulate Lieutenant General Gutiérrez Mellado, who, with the firm collaboration of the Government — *constitutionally empowered to conduct the Civil and Military Administration of the State* — and with the support of the Cortes, has worked so hard to attain this goal."[51]

Diverse interpretations on the subject were aired in the constitutional assembly, some of which portrayed the military as a special power in the state. With a special deference for the armed forces, the Constitution included the definition of their mission in the preamble rather than in the sections concerning organs of the state. This gave the military a special symbolic status, precedent to other state powers and, for instance, political parties. In the debate Manuel Fraga, leader of the right-wing Alianza Popular and leading figure in the drafting of the Constitution, argued: "The Armed Forces are not the same as the Treasury." Miguel Herrero Rodríguez de Miñón, a leading figure in the government party and on the constitution-drafting committee who later, in 1982, joined Fraga in AP, maintained: "The Armed Forces cannot simply be reduced to merely another element in the state administration because they constitute, if not the very backbone of the state, at least its right hand."[52] Similarly, Frederico Trillo Figueroa argued in a respectable academic journal that the armed forces "are something more than the three armed services . . . they are, ultimately, a state institution for National Defense, in which people and Army converge under the leadership of the Crown."[53] The perceived ambiguities in the Constitution and the ensuing debate helped to make legitimate the position that sought a closer formalized relation between the king and the armed forces and which portrayed the military as *Poder Militar*.

The creation of the Joint Chiefs and the debate over its role and position reflected, in fact, a military that had suffered no substantial and permanent damage during the transition. In contrast to other transitions in southern Europe, the military in Spain remained institutionally intact and resurfaced now with renewed vigor to press its corporate claims. Even though it did not have the capacity to oppose successfully those aspects of political reform which it did not approve of, it at least remained strong enough to present tough corporate resistance to changes in defense and military organization.

Toward the end of 1980 the ministry of defense remained undeveloped, and the initiation of other critical modernizing reforms had a very hard time taking off. Projects on the reduction and rejuvenation of personnel, which initially had been a priority, were entangled in bureaucratic consultations, and the minister spent a great deal of effort trying to appease the services.[54] The reincorporation of UMD officers remained indefinitely blocked, and the initiation of reforms in the military justice system, which had been part of the 1977 Moncloa Pact, only took effect in 1980. The growing assertiveness of hard-liners and the enhancement of military self-confidence which grew out of the perception of the army as *Poder Militar* contrasted starkly with evidence of weakness in the government.

Declining Government Support
and Party Factionalism

The transition to democracy initiated by Suárez had rallied the support of all the major parties, which joined in the politics of consensus, especially during the constituent assembly. Immediately after the constitution referendum Suárez himself proclaimed the era of consensus over, opening the way for unbounded interparty competition.[55] All parties were eager to resume competition in order to retrieve or develop distinct party profiles. This predicament guided the campaign for the 1979 elections and helped to produce a competitive outcome in which the Socialists came only 4.6 percentage points behind UCD's plurality. Suárez then formed UCD minority governments, with the support of the Right and regional parties in Congress. From this point onward the initially large support that Suárez had commanded since the referendums began to suffer a steady decline.

The first clear indication came in the elections for regional parliament in Euskadi and Catalonia in March 1980, in which UCD lost more than 50 percent of the votes it had gotten in national elections a year earlier.[56] Later, following a vote of no confidence submitted by the Partido Socialista Obrero Español (PSOE) in May 1980, opinion polls showed that UCD's approval rate had fallen behind that of the Socialists, and Suárez's approval rate had fallen to 26 percent, from an all-time high of 79 percent in April 1977. By January 1981, shortly before his resignation, Suárez was less popular than both Felipe González and Manuel Fraga.[57]

Coupled with decline in support for Suárez and the UCD, there developed a general loss of enthusiasm (*el desencanto*) for politics among the public and the electorate,[58] reflected in a steady decline in voter turnout. In the referenda on the autonomy statutes in Catalonia, Euskadi, and Andalusia in 1979 and 1980, abstention had reached about 40 percent and even an extraordinary 71.7 percent in the 1980 referendum in Galicia. Abstention had also progressed steadily from 22.3 percent in the national referendum of December 1976 to 33.6 percent in the elections of

March 1979 and to 40 percent in the municipal elections of April 1979.[59] Inaugurating democracy at all levels had demanded a succession of numerous elections from voters confused by the recent politics of consensus. The initial enthusiasm for political change was also being eroded by increasing concern with terrorism and the economy.

During the transition the economy had been severely hit by an international economic crisis, and the high growth rates experienced in the last years of Franquism had dramatically slowed down. Unemployment had risen to over one million persons in 1978, and by 1981 almost two million (15 percent of the active population) were out of work. On the other hand, however, the high inflation rates of the transition years were reduced to an annual average rate of about 15 percent in 1979 through 1981. The high strike levels that had prevailed during the transition also were brought down as a result of the moderating impact of parties and elite accords, which brought an increase in wage levels. Still, unemployment, terrorism, and inflation were perceived in opinion polls as the most important problems facing Spain, and the political and economic situation was viewed with pessimism.[60]

For the military, especially hard-liners, terrorism, economic crisis, and pornography were all seen as an assortment of evils produced by the politics of democratization, for which the politically ailing Suárez was to blame. Suárez, it should be remembered, had depleted, very early on, the reservoir of trust among a majority in the military, as a result of the legalization of the Communist Party in 1977, and the armed forces were not willing to extend him new blank checks.[61]

Suárez's weakness came from the loss of popularity typical of most incumbents after some time in office but also from an increased isolation from the ruling elite and the party "barons." Suárez's isolation had much to do with his leadership style, but it was more deeply related to the very nature of UCD as a party and to the magnitude of the problems it had to face as a government party. The first post-Franquist governments, as a distinct feature of the Spanish process, not only had to establish democracy but also to initiate the construction of "a state of autonomies." Whoever took charge of this task would clearly face much heavier wear and tear than an incumbent under normal circumstances. The construction of the autonomies implied a series of negotiations with a diversified set of regional elites, not only the most demanding and linguistically distinct of Euskadi, Catalonia, and Galicia but also of Valencia, Aragón, Canarias, Andalucía, Baleares, Extremadura, Asturias,

Old Castile, New Castile, Madrid, Navarra, Leon, and Murcia. These negotiations not only had to avoid "comparative offenses"—that is, the perception that some regions were getting a better deal—but they also had to consider the entangling alliances and patronage connections of regional elites with factions within the party, all this under the heavy atmosphere created by the terrorist actions of ETA. Nothing comparable to the magnitude of this task was found in the South American or the other southern European transitions.

As a party, the UCD proved capable of organizing centrist politics to muddle through the various obstacles of initial democratization, but it ultimately proved ill-suited to survive challenges of such magnitude. The party was formed, from above, as a result of Suárez's decision in 1977 to continue in charge but now in a democratic government and of the realization by diverse elite groups that they stood to benefit from associating with Suárez for the first elections in 1977. The coalition that resulted from this convergence of interests rallied groups that had come from Franquism, as had Suárez himself, from its moderate opposition and from other positions, and included Christian Democrats, Liberals, Social Democrats, and Independents. Leaders of these groups—the "barons," who later became ministers—formed the successful electoral machine that won the first elections and then transformed UCD from a loose coalition into a single party, with a regular structure at mass and national levels, leading it successfully in the general elections of 1979. The party's ability to absorb smaller groups and different currents in the electorate was facilitated by the diversity of its founding groups and the eclecticism of its programmatic tenets. But this was also its major weakness at the time of governing. It soon became clear that deep ideological differences within the party pitted, for instance, Christian Democratic groups that sought greater assurances for the church against Social Democratic groups seeking the legalization of divorce or the latter against the more individualistic views held by liberal groups. Suárez himself had shown inclinations toward social democratic ideas and engaged in politics that, like some of his pro–Third World foreign policy moves, enraged the more conservative and Christian wings of the party. The president, however, was held in check by the enormous bargaining power of each group, since the votes of their members in Congress were needed to pass legislation. Ideological differences, regional patronage connections, and barons' ambitions for higher office combined to make it increasingly difficult for Suárez to maintain any ascendancy over the party's barons and the factions they commanded. Naked ambitions in and around the government became so apparent that the king felt it necessary, in the Christmas speech of December 1980, to remind politicians that "politics is not an end in itself," that efforts had to be made "to protect and consolidate the essential," and that "we cannot lose, in useless swings, compromises and disputes, the commitment to transform and stabilize Spain."[62]

Suárez's isolation from the barons, which ultimately led to his resignation in January 1981, was only comparable to that suffered by Gutiérrez Mellado among the military. Gutiérrez Mellado had done an excellent job in winning support and overt sympathies across the political spectrum in parliament and in lessening the gap between the non-Franquist civilians and the military.[63] But he was badly abused by hard-liners and their civilian allies, who made him pay dearly for his association with the government and its reformist policies. He also made mistakes, by maintaining in practice a dual role as army chief and government figure. Although he had resigned his commission in the army upon assuming his government post, he still was perceived as an operating army chief. Removed from the ministry of defense in April 1979, he was not fully isolated from controversy. Remaining in government as vice president for defense affairs, "el señor Gutiérrez," or "el Guti," as he was disdainfully referred to by the media on the extreme Right, continued to suffer from the charges of hard-liners. The heroic image of Suárez and Gutiérrez Mellado assisting each other while being shoved by armed guards who stormed the Congress on 23 February 1981 reflected both their close association as well as their failure to put the military problem to rest.

The Coup and Its Precipitating Factors

With the abstention of parties of the Right and the regions, Suárez survived the vote of no confidence in May 1980 but came out of it seriously wounded. While the oratorically gifted Manuel Fraga and Felipe González ceaselessly hammered on the president's image during the five days preceding the vote, Suárez inexplicably refused to stand in his own defense, delegating the government's response to cabinet members. Demoralized by the tenor of the attacks—"Suárez does not tolerate democracy just as democracy cannot any longer tolerate Suárez"—Suárez appeared weak, cornered, and silent, while the Socialists' candidate for president, Felipe González, offered a coherent platform and appeared credible and "presidential" before a vast number of viewers.[64]

The debilitating effects of the censure vote against Suárez, combined with other factors, was soon felt within the UCD. During the summer major factional leaders — the barons — as well as the powerful leaders of the major business association, the Confederación Española de Organizaciones Empresariales (CEOE), came to the conclusion that Suárez had to be replaced. From then on leaders of these factions and groups and of the opposition parties, along with innumerable rumors, would be heard more and more frequently, more or less explicitly, voicing formulas for an alternative government: a government of the "natural majority" (Fraga's Center-Right dream government), or a *"gobierno de gestión"* (a caretaker government), *"de concentración,"* or *"de coalición"* proposed by leaders in UCD and the Left.[65]

In addition to the pressure from all political quarters, his own party included, there also was the tense atmosphere that clouded Suárez's relations with the military. Light sentences were handed down by the Supreme Council of Military Justice to the Galaxia conspirators that summer. Also, military pressure to prevent legislation on the UMD members and on the demilitarization of the Civil Guard was strongly felt in the government. Military discontent continued to be heightened by terrorism and anti-Spanish demonstrations in the regions, which surfaced again in January 1981 during a visit by the king to Guernica. Suárez himself had personally witnessed the deteriorated state in government-military relations during a visit to Ceuta and Melilla, the Spanish enclaves in northern Africa, where, in massive meetings with officers and NCOs, he was given a direct and crude message of military discontent. Isolated from all sides, Suárez announced his resignation on 29 January 1981, declaring his desire to avoid a situation in which "the democratic system of coexistence be, yet again, a parenthesis in the history of Spain."[66]

In this context of government weakness, military empowerment, and the assertiveness of hard-liners, General Alfonso Armada's return to a prominent position in the army gained significance.[67] General Alfonso Armada Comyn, with strong aristocratic family traditions in the army and himself a staunch pro-monarchist, had served earlier as tutor of young Prince Juan Carlos, and later, when Juan Carlos moved to the Zarzuela Palace after marrying Princess Sofía, he became secretary of the Royal House. Already at this stage Armada had earned Adolfo Suárez's distrust. As head of the state television network under Franco, Adolfo Suárez, interested in promoting the prince's image, maintained relations with the Zarzuela and had noticed Armada's effort to influence Juan Carlos under the guise of a "protective" zeal. Later, right before the first elections in 1977, when Juan Carlos was king and Suárez president, it was discovered that Armada was using Royal House stationery personally to support his son, who was running for Congress among the list of Manuel Fraga's Alianza Popular. Adolfo Suárez succeeded then in having Armada removed from the king's quarters and assigned to the Mountain Division and the Military Governorship in Lérida.[68]

When Suárez's prestige and support plummeted toward the end of 1980, however, General Armada started promoting himself for the post of deputy army chief of staff. The chief of staff, General Gabeiras, badly discredited among his fellow subordinate lieutenant generals, welcomed the possibility of enriching his staff with a prestigious general with monarchic connections and, upon the post becoming vacant, proposed the appointment of Alfonso Armada. Suárez opposed it, but after his resignation and following Gabeira's insistence, Minister of Defense Agustín Rodríguez Sahagún signed the decree for Armada's appointment in the first week of February, 1981.[69]

At the same time as he pursued the post in the general staff, Armada initiated two interrelated activities. On one hand, he contributed to the chorus, recommending the formation of a *gobierno de concentración,* and cautiously but unequivocally spread the message in political circles that he would be willing to assume the presidency of such a government.[70] As part of these activities, he conducted meetings with leading figures of different parties, including a publicized meeting with PSOE leaders Enrique Múgica and Joan Raventós in October 1980.[71] On the other hand, he visited several military leaders, announcing to them that he would soon see the king at the winter resort of Baqueira Beret and that he wanted to transmit to him the real concerns of the army.[72] With these activities Armada, in fact, spread the impression among many army officers that a *gobierno de concentración* with military leadership could count on the support of the major parties and the acquiescence of the king. His success in getting the promotion to deputy chief of staff, over the opposition of politically ailing Adolfo Suárez and Gutiérrez Mellado, corroborated the impression that he had clout with a diversity of political leaders and expanded the perception that the king, in an unspecified way, stood behind Armada. In addition, the uncontested publication in the press of numerous articles making reference to the "Armada Solution" (meaning both the solution of General Armada and the "armed solution"); of demands by a group of military men calling itself *Colectivo Almendros;* and, on the front page of *El Alcázar*'s edition of 8 February 1981, of Lieutenant General de Santiago's article recalling that, "always in the past, in situations similar to this, there were Spaniards who rescued and saved Spain,"[73] corroborated the general impression of military support for a "legal" coup.[74] The combination of all these elements enhanced the significance of Armada's promotion and gave the diverse plans for government replacement a definite aura of plausibility.

The first post-constitution democratic period in Spain reveals the difficulties that face democratic advancement if a military that has transited intact from the previous regime is led to reassess the costs and opportunities involved in acquiescence to the new regime. This reassessment is encouraged by what military leaders perceive to be persistent attacks on the military institution or its "sacred" mission. Nationalism and terrorism played this role in Spain (as the investigation of human rights violations and subsequent prosecutions did, for instance, in Argentina).

In Spain the successful inauguration of democracy gave way to the increasing assertiveness of military hard-liners, which paralleled the decline in support for the government and the president. This decline, coupled with the government's excessively mild exercise of authority to discipline the military, gradually led the military to visualize reduced costs of intervention. This effect was reinforced by the apparent decline in civilian coalescence: the substitution of overt and aggressive opposition for the previous politics of consensus. Competition from outside as much as from within the government paralyzed its president and his initiative and reduced his popularity.[75] In the face of this changed context the most conservative and hard-line sectors in the military actually started thinking in terms of intervention.

In a separate but not unrelated track the chances of institutionalization of a *Poder Militar* were reflected in the bureaucratic struggle between the services and the ministry, under the military's hopeful view of an aggrandized role for itself and the king. Progress made by the military in these areas added to its increasing levels of self-confidence. In a context in which toleration and intervention are debated as actual alternatives, enhanced military self-confidence does not bode well for toleration. Toleration had become more costly in the post-transition process than it had been at the time of democratic inauguration, and the intersection with the declining costs of intervention made the situation dangerously explosive at the time Suárez resigned and Armada landed in the army staff.

7

The 1981 Coup Attempt
and the End of the
Military Threat to Democracy

THE PROSPECTS of military reaction which had haunted democratization since Franco's death finally materialized in the coup attempt of 23 February 1981. As Congress debated the formation of a new government, a heavily armed unit of the Civil Guard occupied the Palace of Congress with President Suárez and the whole cabinet inside. With the government hostage, large army units in important regions mobilized in support of the conspiracy, shaking the foundations of Spain's brittle new democracy.

But the coup failed, and, just as the attempt had marked the climax of hard-line contestation, it also marked the beginning of the end of military opposition to democratization. The coup attempt was a critical turning point that unclogged the advancement of democratization, unintentionally helping to disarm a significant threat that otherwise may have lingered on and continued to haunt the democratic process.

Grand processes of change, riding on the wave of large structural factors and weighty conditions, sometimes get funneled into small spaces, confined quarters, wee hours, at the end of which they reappear propelled in quite unexpected directions. Such kind of unintended change surfaced in several recent cases to strengthen or weaken the democratic endeavor.[1] The failed hard-line coup against Mikhail Gorbachev in August 1991, for instance, ultimately led to Gorbachev's displacement and, quite unintentionally, to the crumbling of the Soviet Union. The failed military rebellion in Argentina in 1990 ended the sequel of conspiracies with which the military had seemed to have successfully reasserted itself under Alfonsín's administration. In Spain the congressional floor in the early hours of 24 February 1981 almost became the platform for a general with a shadow government to catapult himself to power. Unable, however, to get past the lobby to reach and talk to the deputies confined in rear quarters, the coup failed, leading to the gradual evaporation of the hard-line zeal.

The inauguration of democracy had not settled the military problem. Hard-line military contestation had picked up in the period following the approval of the Constitution, testing democratic institutions and challenging their very survival. The failure of the coup, however, created conditions that led to the dismantling of hard-line opposition. The most conspicuous hard-liners were detained and imprisoned, and discussions among the hard-liners during subsequent trials irretrievably diluted the fervor of hard-line contestation. Twenty months later the election of a stable government majority permitted the firm advocacy and implementation of civilian supremacy.

The failure of the coup, however, did not immediately or automatically end hard-line contestation. The "long" twenty-one months of Calvo Sotelo's government were, in fact, mostly devoted to finally terminating the hard-line threat that had, paradoxically, refused to die with the failure of the coup. The longevity of the hard-line threat, even after the wounds of the coup, was vivid proof of the magnitude of the challenges that the advancement of democracy had to overcome. This longevity was made possible by the continuation of some of the trends started under the Suárez government: terrorism and extraordinary weakening of the government party, to the point of its almost disappearing in the elections of October 1982. In turn, the final defeat of the hard-line challenge was aided by its internal disunity, a resumption of a coalescence among the civilian leadership, the position of the king, and the emergence of a coherent and widely popular government following the 1982 elections.

The Coup

On 23 February Congress had convened to give another try to the election of a new head of the government. In previous votes UCD's candidate Leopoldo Calvo Sotelo had failed to get a majority. That day,

The Post-Transition

however, at 6:30 P.M., debate was interrupted by the violent and vociferous intrusion of Colonel Tejero and a heavily armed company of civil guards. After ordering the deputies to lie under their seats, following a machine-gunning of the ceiling and the TV cameras, Tejero officially announced the coup: they should all wait for the arrival of a superior military authority.[2]

The kidnapping of Congress and the entire cabinet, broadcast live on the radio, gave the signal for other conspirators to make their move. Even before Tejero arrived in Congress, however, the captain general of Valencia, Jaime Milans del Bosch, had already initiated operations "Red Alert" and "Turia," which would promptly lead to the occupation of Valencia and other urban centers and his taking command of the regional government. Milans then informed other captains general of his actions in the hope that they would be encouraged to do likewise. In an edict Milans justified the mobilization of troops under his command as a response to the power vacuum created by the takeover of Congress in Madrid and declared that the measures taken were in support of the king and Spain.

In the vicinity of Madrid deliberation among the staff of the powerful División Acorazada Brunete (DAC) (the Brunete Armoured Division) had also anticipated the events unleashed by Tejero. In fact, when the Congress was taken, officers in the division's general staff were already attempting to convince the division's chief, General Juste, to order a mobilization and take control of strategic sites in Madrid. General Juste was told by his staff and by former DAC chief, General Luis Torres Rojas, inexplicably present in his former unit and dressed in combat gear, that actions were going to be initiated, under the coordination of General Armada from the Zarzuela Palace (the king's headquarters). General Juste, suspicious, called the Zarzuela, asking for Armada, and was told by the king's chief military assistant that Armada was neither there nor was he expected ("No está ni se le espera"). This call convinced General Juste that the military actions planned did not have the support of the king; the call also confirmed suspicion in the Zarzuela that Armada was up to something.

In fact, since the news of Tejero's takeover broke out, Armada had been calling the Zarzuela, offering his aid and his willingness to present himself personally in the palace. Armada had hoped that his presence there, and his handling of military communications from the palace, would send a signal that the king stood behind the insurrection. Yet

Armada's offer was rejected, and he was told instead to stay at army headquarters. Here, however, where he had recently been installed as deputy chief of staff, Armada took control of headquarters. From this critical position he maintained official communication with Milans in Valencia and handled talks with other captains general, conveying to each one of them the impression that military chiefs in other regions generally supported the insurrection.

Meanwhile, army chief of staff, General Gabeiras, was away from headquarters in meetings with the Joint Chiefs. The king had formed an emergency government with the cabinet subsecretaries and ordered that all military actions be approved by the Joint Chiefs.[3] The Joint Chiefs, in session, were interrupted by instructions from the Zarzuela for General Gabeiras to return to army headquarters and take over from Armada, whose behavior had by then become clearly suspect.[4]

Back in army headquarters General Gabeiras, in a flurry of communications with captains general and important unit commanders, gave instructions to loyal generals to arrest Milans. It was apparent that Milans was the only one of eleven captains general of military regions who had overtly rebelled, although only three appeared unequivocally and resolutely loyal to the Constitution from the start; the rest had, one way or the other, expressed hesitation.[5] In addition, a few important unit commanders were unwilling to take orders not to mobilize in support of the plotters.

In the Brunete Armoured Division, General Juste maintained an ambiguous position, in the hope—according to his own version—of preventing his arrest by his subordinates and his replacement by General Torres Rojas. Juste ultimately succeeded in persuading the division to stay put, except for a small unit that decided to go ahead with the takeover of a few broadcasting stations and to reinforce Tejero's forces in Congress. The tenacious efforts by Captain General Guillermo Quintana Lacaci, chief of the Madrid military region, were critical in keeping other forces near Madrid under control and in preparing special units to deter a rebel mobilization of the armoured division should the situation there worsen.

The king, and his military entourage, kept themselves busy on the phone, dispelling any impression that the military action had any royal support. Personal communication by Juan Carlos convinced vacillating chiefs, and all doubts were decisively dismissed by a short statement issued by the king and broadcast nationally on television at 1:14 in the morning of 24 February. Juan Carlos appeared on the screen dressed in his uniform of captain general and said:

> I have issued the following order to all captains general of military regions, naval zones and air regions: in the face of the situation created by the events in the Palace of Congress, and to avoid any possible confusion, I confirm that I have ordered civilian authorities and the Joint Chiefs to take necessary measures to maintain the constitutional order within the existing laws. . . . The Crown, symbol of the unity and permanence of the Fatherland, cannot in any way tolerate actions or attitudes of persons which attempt to interrupt by force the democratic process which the Constitution approved by the Spanish people determined in referendum.[6]

After this Tejero's action appeared to be more and more isolated. He had continued to announce the imminent arrival of a "military authority," but it soon became clear that he was having trouble delivering. Milans del Bosch, after several instructions from the king, and realizing that no other captain general had overtly followed his steps, decided to revoke his earlier edict and recalled his troops. Army headquarters circulated among the captains general a written copy of Milans's new orders, in the hope of halting any further "vacillation." Tejero refused to surrender, however. The director of the Civil Guard, General Aramburu Topete failed to obtain Tejero's surrender in a personal encounter in which Tejero threatened to shoot his visitor in Congress. There was fear among acting government officials that Tejero, in a desperate situation and refusing to give in, but still holding the Congress hostage, might have been planning a bloody end to his failed adventure.

Earlier General Armada had made an attempt to save the rebellion. He convinced the Zarzuela, Gabeiras, and the Joint Chiefs that he should go and talk to Tejero to reach a negotiated solution. Part of his plan included his election as president of a new government by the kidnapped Cortes, an idea, he implied, advanced earlier by Milans. Armada had wrapped up the need for his appearance in Congress by disseminating the alarming information that four other captains general were, in fact, leaning toward supporting Milans. While harboring concerns about his ultimate intent, Armada nevertheless received authorization from General Gabeiras and the Zarzuela to go and talk to Tejero and to offer him and his fellow conspirators free passage to exile abroad. And, in the most inexplicable part of this episode, Armada was not expressly forbidden from making other proposals, such as the "Armada solution." He was only warned that any other proposition that he might want to make would have to be entirely personal and that neither the king nor any other official representation could be invoked in support of it.

In Congress, Armada presented himself with the code word *Duque de Ahumada,* signaling to Tejero that this was the "higher military authority" he was supposed to greet in Congress and whom he had been so anxiously awaiting. Once inside Armada demanded from Tejero that all deputies be congregated in the main chamber because he was going to offer them a solution and propose a coalition government. Tejero inquired about the specifics of the offer, to which Armada replied that he would head the government and be its only military member and that personalities from across the political spectrum, including the Left, would also participate. Then, in one of the most critical episodes that night, an infuriated Tejero replied that he never knew the plot included such a solution and that he had not kidnapped Congress just to return to the same old thing. He decided to escort Armada out of the building and, completely deflating the chances of the coup, gave instructions not to allow him back in. Only later, after the retreat of Milans's forces in Valencia, Tejero called Armada again, this time to negotiate his surrender. He partially succeeded in getting immunity for the members of the forces under his command, and, shortly after noon on 24 February, the deputies were freed, Tejero and his troops turned themselves in, and the coup attempt was over.

Twenty-four February was a busy day. Milans del Bosch and other major military chiefs were arrested, the National Defense Board met to exchange information and determine responsibilities, and the king summoned leaders of the major parties to read them a statement on the importance of the recent events. The king expressed the hope that the reaction of political leaders against the participants in the conspiracy would not be excessively harsh and that the armed forces would not be made responsible as a whole for what had happened. In fact, the king hinted at the responsibilities of political leaders in the coup, called on them to mend their ways, and emphasized the need for unity:

> I invite all to reflection and to the reconsideration of positions that may lead to greater unity and concord of Spain and the Spaniards.
>
> The Crown feels proud of having served Spain with firmness, in the conviction that democracy and the strict respect to the constitutional principles is the majoritarian will of the Spanish people. However, everybody must be aware, from their own responsibilities, that the King can-

not and must not repeatedly face, with his direct responsibility, circumstances of such considerable tension and gravity.[7]

Although the coup attempt was short-lived, a large majority of discontented officers had intensely hoped, in one way or another, for the success of the insurrection. Indeed, many officers, overtly demoralized by the failure of the coup yet later promoted, nonetheless, to the rank of general, laid bare their sympathies and openly admitted: "*We* have failed."[8] The fact that a good number of captains general hesitated the night of the coup is a good indication of the uncertainty with which the outcome was perceived that night.[9]

The coup had failed as a result of deep divisions among hard-liners and conspirators. Hard-liners had progressed to a point at which a coup was actually possible, but they still remained without an alternative political vision, let alone a blueprint for government policy. These divisions surfaced most clearly in the verbal exchanges between Armada and Tejero in the Congress the night of the coup. It is ironic, after all, that Tejero's hard-line stance and his intransigent goals ultimately undermined the chances of a successful coup, by denying his co-conspirator, Armada, entry to Congress the night he had intended to emerge as president of a new government.

Official investigations following the failed coup reported that different conspiracies, encompassing different army sectors and political goals, converged, albeit with poor coordination, in the assault on Congress.[10] One conspiratorial thread came from a network of colonels and lieutenant colonels, who shared a previous experience in intelligence work during the final years of Franquism and who now controlled important positions in powerful units across the country. Inspired by the hard-line military coup in Turkey in September 1980, this group sought the complete replacement of democracy and its major accomplishments. Another group, made up of more loosely coordinated lieutenant generals in retirement, with connections to those still on active duty and to extreme right-wing civilians and newspapers, vaguely sought the formation of a military junta. This group strongly resented democracy but held no clear platform and proclaimed allegiance to the monarchy. A third group, belonging to the Armada operation, was more widely connected across the political spectrum and sought not to destroy the parliamentary monarchy but, rather, under monarchic institutions, to "reconduct" the process à la de Gaulle in order to instill a greater sense of government authority, to limit the excesses of the process of state decentralization, to harden the counterterrorist struggle, and to enhance the institutional position of the armed forces. This diversity of movements and goals was embodied in the competing attempts of a "soft-line coup" and a "hard-line coup," ultimately personified in the figures of Armada and Tejero, respectively, in the dramatic stage in Congress the night of 23 February. This diversity reflected the extent to which conspiracy was a widespread engagement in the army but also the depths of internal divisions.

Continued Military Challenge

While blocking the steady ascent of assertiveness among military hard-liners, the failure of the coup did not fully terminate the threat they posed. Large sectors of the army continued to harbor an overt repudiation of democratic institutions, and contestation and indiscipline continued to challenge civilian authority. The new UCD administration of Leopoldo Calvo Sotelo — inaugurated only hours after the rebels vacated the congressional palace — was forced to spend much of its energies on putting out the fires of military unruliness. Clearly, even after the failure of the coup, the time for democrats to relax had not yet arrived.

The hard-liners' goal of maintaining a contestational mood among army officers was aided by the tensions generated by unrelenting terrorist activities, mostly by ETA. Although the number of ETA's terrorist acts decreased slightly in 1981–82 in comparison with previous years, they now targeted military chiefs. At the same time, other terrorist organizations on the Left and the Right joined in with the evident purpose of inciting military intervention. Leftist terrorists assassinated General González de Suso in Barcelona on 4 May 1981, and, three days later, ETA killed three officers directly in the service of the king, severely wounding Lieutenant General Joaquín de Valenzuela. On 23 May an extreme-right-wing armed group of twenty-five assaulted the Central Bank in Barcelona, and on 3 October an act of sabotage was discovered aboard a navy destroyer. The following year, only a week after the general elections, ETA assassinated General Víctor Lago Román, chief of the Brunete Armoured Division.[11]

The continuous challenge from hard-liners was also facilitated by the steady decline in support for the government among both the public and important leaders who started abandoning the governing party. In October 1981 UCD obtained only 27.4 percent of the vote in regional elections in Galicia, down from 48.3 percent, which it had obtained in Galicia in the national elections of 1979. Most of the gains were made by Alianza Popular. In November the social democratic "barons" of UCD quit the party, including nine deputies and six senators, most of whom would later join the PSOE. In January 1982 leading figure Miguel Herrero left to join Alianza Popular. In May 1982 the PSOE won an absolute majority in elections for the regional parliament in Andalusia, while UCD got only 12.9 percent of the valid votes, below Alianza Popular's share.[12] The exodus of party founders continued again in July 1982, when twelve deputies and eight senators left to establish a party that would later form a coalition with Alianza Popular. In August Adolfo Suárez himself abandoned UCD to found a new party. With the dismemberment of the party, the loss of critical support from the church and business associations, and facing outright ingovernability Leopoldo Calvo Sotelo had no choice but to dissolve the Cortes and call for elections for October 1982.[13]

The continuous decline of UCD had given the chances of the PSOE gaining control of government an air of inevitability. The PSOE had for some time been moderating much of its platform, and its leaders had been pursuing a rapport with all sectors of Spanish society, the military included. The prospects of its triumph, however, still raised anxiety among business groups, the church, and the military. Thus, in the context of a likely PSOE victory, conspiratorial activities that had been going on after the failed coup attempt of February 1981 gained a renewed sense of urgency.

In the period following the coup attempt, military hard-liners never appeared to be a force in retreat, as they continued to challenge, and even ridicule, government authority. In July 1981, for instance, the traditional army speech in remembrance of the Apostle Santiago, given by the captain general of Galicia, Lieutenant General Fernández Posse, purportedly as a representative of the king, contained statements overtly at odds with the government and democratic views. Fernández Posse warned about the "tenacious enemy" infiltrating in "the press, radio and television, in the church, schools and universities, film, arts and culture," which was undermining the "moral and spiritual values" of Western civilization. He described the "gloomy world situation," the hedonism invading Europe, and the "times of confusion and disrepair" in Spain and attacked "totalitarian" parties.[14] At no point in his speech, however, did he condemn the events of 23 February. Later, on 2 November 1981, a publication in the daily army records officialized the award of a medal to Lieutenant General Milans del Bosch—in jail—in recognition of his sufferings for the fatherland: a few minor injuries he had gotten during a rough helicopter landing in 1980.[15]

An accurate summary of the hard-liners' grievances was provided on 5 December 1981, when Europa Press distributed a manifesto signed by one hundred military men (twenty-five captains, twenty-one lieutenants, and the rest NCOs from the Madrid military region) which again challenged civil authority and military discipline. The document condemned politicians and the press for distorting the image of the armed forces, for issuing pejorative judgments about them, for "deprecating national and military values and symbols . . . such as honor and heroism," and for renaming streets and demolishing other monuments to heroes of the past. The statement also rejected "attacks, insults, offenses and slander against members of the armed forces with an illustrious and irreproachable military past" who were awaiting trial and stated that these attacks were to be considered as attacks against the military as a whole. The manifesto rejected demands for "professionalization, democratization and purge" of the armed forces as well as the "antinational partisan politicization" of the grand topics of defense and of internal matters of the armed forces, such as the policy on promotions and appointments. The proclamation concluded by saying that, for the better fulfillment of its mission, the armed forces "do not have to be professionalized, democratized or purged but, rather, they simply must be properly considered and respected. . . . Political powers must respect the necessary autonomy of the army."[16] Fearing a wave of support and an escalating number of adherents to the manifesto, the government reacted promptly by emphatically rejecting the substance of the document and the form of its appearance, and the Joint Chiefs forcefully warned against additional adherence to it.[17]

The king's public addresses continued to be instructive about the state of affairs in the military. The tenor of his speeches was, in fact, a good reflection of the fact that, five or six years after the start of the transition, the military still needed to be reminded of the "exigency to observe the laws and the institutions."[18] In these addresses the king revealed his intention to maintain control over the armed forces but also his need constantly to renew and be assured of the allegiance of all sectors of the army.[19] With tactfully equilibrated statements the king sought to portray himself as a spokesman for the armed forces' feelings.

Only a few days after the failed coup, on 1 March 1981, and still within a tense atmosphere, the king presided over the reunion of his class at the Military Academy in Zaragoza. In his speech the king echoed some of the grievances of his classmates, criticizing "political acts . . . [and] press campaigns which foster conditions that create uneasiness, annoyance and concern in the Armed Forces . . ."[20] Then, in the *Pascua Militar* of January 1982, the king thanked the armed forces for the discipline with which they witnessed the social and political transformations "to which they must inevitably accommodate" and added:

It is often natural that the contrast between the past and the present give rise to tensions . . . or be the cause of surprises. . . . The Armed Forces did not receive notable benefits [after victory in the civil war but they] were used to getting more respect, more distinguished consideration, and protection of its dignity by official and all other sectors of the Nation.

The indispensable freedom of expression . . . , the changes in the ways of public treatment of military affairs, and the imposition of silence on those who perform this profession . . . have undoubtedly caused great impression and surprise among the men who form the Army of Spain.[21]

But he also reminded the army that it "ought to know how to interpret the Constitution with prudence and accuracy and to understand that the security of the Fatherland is not aided with thoughtless actions which place the Armed Forces and the State in critical situations, for which there can be no dignified way out."[22]

In a special joint meeting with the supreme councils of the three armed services on 24 March 1981 the king insisted:

It may be worthy of praise, in the soldier, the courageous impulse, the passionate decision, sacrifice on behalf of a high and transcendental idea that lead to risky action and to offer his own life if it were necessary. But of necessity one must also think in the results, in the situations with no escape or which might lead to true tragedies . . .

Let us be conscious of what must and of what cannot be done, so as not to condemn her [Spain] to bloody strife, to isolation within a world in which we must live.[23]

The continuation of a military challenge to democracy following the failed coup attempt was best reflected in the tense atmosphere that developed around the lengthy preparation for the hearings and trial of the officers involved in the revolt. Existing legislation still gave military courts jurisdiction over the crimes the rebels were accused of. One of the most demanding tasks for the government was, in fact, to make sure that the trial actually took place, and it became clear during the preparations and later in the hearings that excessive care was taken not to irritate military sensibilities.[24] Indictments were limited to only thirty-three persons, freeing from responsibility a large number of officers and servicemen who had actually taken up arms against the government. No more than a few top leaders had been detained, and the number of those against whom charges could be made was relatively small: one lieutenant general, two major generals, three colonels, a navy captain, two lieutenant colonels, and several other officers of lesser grade. This, however, was only the tip of the iceberg: many more had been involved, but charges could not be proved unless large numbers of officers were brought as witnesses against their fellow officers, and this was out of the question.[25]

The trial started in February 1982, a year after the coup attempt, and numerous incidents revealed the biases of the court in handling the demands of the accused and in maintaining discipline. For instance, the president of the court consented to demands of the defense to deny the director of *Diario* 16 access to the trial. The court also tolerated manifest acts of indiscipline of the indicted generals and colonels when certain witnesses were called to testify.[26] Even toward the end, when the sentences were announced, the president of the court had to order the arrest of two of its own members for contempt of court.[27]

The length of the hearings had given opportunity to the defendants' attorneys to plot their defense strategy in a way that looked more like an indictment of democracy. The defense was based on a presumed "state of need" in which the accused—witnessing terrorism, national disintegration, economic crisis, and social conflict, for which they requested the court to supply documentary evidence—felt that their sense of honor and duty had required their decisive and forceful action. Also, the defense of lower-ranked officers resorted to the principle of "due obedience," which was also used to support the request that the king be called to the witness stand, in an attempt to prove that the conspirators thought they were acting on behalf of the king through the orders of General Armada.[28] Even the Supreme Military Tribunal suggested, in its final sentence, that the acts of the accused were nobly inspired by "beliefs based on a disinterested, albeit exacerbated, love of the fatherland."[29]

The court's sentences, in June 1982, fell well short of the public's expectations. Only Milans del Bosch and Tejero were given appropriate punishment: each was sentenced to thirty years in prison and the loss of military employment. Sentences given to the rest were perceived as very light, especially in the case of General Armada, who only got six years, and of those whose return to active service was left open. President Calvo Sotelo criticized the sentences and decided to appeal to the Supreme Court.[30]

The continuous hard-line challenge reflected the durability of the military's accumulated resentment against democracy. Civilian authorities, aware of the magnitude of this resentment, struggled to maintain their ascendancy by trying to enforce discipline in the military. At the same time, however, they were careful not to arouse further resentment and risk being put in a situation in which they might not be obeyed. In this uncertain situation they often relied on the king, who, especially during this time, emphasized his role of arbiter and moderator: "In my role of arbiter and moderator of the normal functioning of the Institutions, I ask from you who serve in the Armed Forces and the Security Forces . . . to remain aware of the important mission which corresponds to you, as well as of the need of integrating yourselves in the political organization which the Spanish people has given itself and that you are, precisely, to defend."[31]

Emphasis on this role as arbiter and moderator strengthened the desire within the military to favor direct links between the king and the armed forces, bypassing the government. The government itself, reflecting its own weakness, was often led to promote an enhanced role for the king.[32] For instance, trying to dispel confusion about the roles of different powers in the lines of command and authority over the armed forces, the minister of defense, Alberto Oliart, addressing himself to the king in the *Pascua Militar* of 1982, stated: "It is possible that in some cases . . . the borderline between what is command *over* and *in* the Armed Forces raises doubts or problems in its operation; but if the case were to arise, You, Sir, in your constitutional function as arbiter, moderator and supreme commander of the Armed Forces, are the guarantee that these doubts or problems will be well resolved . . . [in this way] there will be neither inopportune political intrusion in what is strictly professional, nor professional intrusions in the political order."[33]

The king, on the other hand, insisted on the role of the government and tried to deflate the pretense of military autonomy or of a relation with the king which bypassed the government: "It is to those State Authorities [which are in charge of military policy and governance of the country] to whom corresponds political direction within which the Armed Forces are included as one more factor."[34]

The state authorities that the king invoked for political direction of the military, however, had continued to weaken. Unemployment and inflation continued to rise, terrorism continued to inflict political damage, the divisive situation in UCD worsened, and public support for the government vanished. Military contestation in this context was not likely to recede. Adolfo Suárez, for instance, pointed in August 1982 to "the growing sensation that there exist real attempts to undermine the supremacy of civilian power."[35] Substantiating these suspicions, the government uncovered, on 1 October, a military putsch planned for 27 October, exactly on the eve of national elections.[36] This, however, was to be the last visible military threat to cloud Spain's democratization.

The End to the Military Challenge to Democracy

How did the protracted survival of military contestation after the failed coup of 1981 come to an end? The failed putsch uncovered in October 1982 highlighted the exhaustion of attempts to pursue military opposition, which now visibly clashed with the overwhelming support for a new government in the elections of 28 October. But the truth is that, even before, despite the strength of military hard-liners during the Calvo Sotelo administration, gradually but steadily a large number of officers realized that democracy was there to stay and that the military ought to accommodate itself within it.

This realization was influenced by several factors. In the first place the hard-liners' leadership problem had become truly unsolvable. The most important hard-line military leaders had failed and faced long prison terms. In addition, the demoralization that this produced in the army was bitterly deepened by the deceitful and unbecoming behavior displayed by the prosecuted officers during the long proceedings and hearings of the trial. For months the public was exposed to the reciprocal accusations, the trifling squabbles, and the denial of responsibilities by the prosecuted senior officers with "illustrious" military careers, whom officers in the army had expected to behave more in line with their own view of military honor. Colonel Tejero's final statement before the military court in 1982 expressed succinctly the despondency with which a large mass of officers now viewed the top rebel leaders: "I want that my last words express my deepest abhorrence to the majority of top Army chiefs for their cowardice and treason."[37] The trial itself had unex-

The Post-Transition

pectedly turned into one of the strongest contributions to deflating the interventionist mystique in the army. Thus, the problems of internal disunity, which had haunted the chances of military contestation all along, became even larger after the failure of the coup attempt, as they were compounded with the imprisonment of major leaders and the demoralization that failure itself and the behavior of these leaders produced.

Second, the king's role in defeating the coup and his subsequent stance finally convinced everybody that a military move against democracy would never be given the legitimacy of monarchic approval, necessary to gain the support of a large sector in the army. The king had asserted his authority over the army unambiguously in favor of civilian democratic government.

Third, the coup attempt had been repudiated by a large majority of Spaniards, who demonstrated massively on 27 February 1981 across Spanish cities in support of democracy. In Madrid demonstrators were led by political figures from across the political divide who jointly carried the lead banner: Manuel Fraga from Alianza Popular, Felipe González of the PSOE, Santiago Carrillo of the Communist Party, and leaders of UCD and the national labor organizations. Only the extreme Right of Blas Piñar and the leading Basque parties refused to join in the demonstrations that sent the military an otherwise unambiguous message of civilian unity behind democracy.[38]

Coalescence went beyond the anti-coup demonstration. Despite the fact that Leopoldo Calvo Sotelo declined offers from Felipe González and Manuel Fraga to form a coalition government with their respective parties—the president thought that democracy was best served by not letting the military episode interfere with "business as usual"—overall civilian coalescence reached higher levels during this period than during the final year of Adolfo Suárez's government. This was partly the result of the working agreements that Calvo Sotelo reached with the PSOE on the need to give national coherence to the policies of implementation of the regional autonomies and which led to the Organic Law on the Harmonization of the Autonomy Process (LOAPA).[39] These agreements gave the government a larger basis of support in dealing with critical issues and improved the PSOE's credibility for a future in government.

The LOAPA was received with suspicion by Basque and Catalan leaders, who thought that the pursuit of a comprehensive model for the autonomies was aimed at curtailing some of the progress already made in their regions. Agreements on the LOAPA were, however, generally well received in military circles, suspicious of all developments regarding the autonomies but appreciative of any attempt to introduce order and control.[40] In addition, in order to appease the military and deflect criticism of its handling of the terrorism problem, the Calvo Sotelo government had granted the army some participation in counter-terrorist surveillance, specifically in the control of Navarra's and Guipúzcoa's mountain paths on the French-Spanish border.[41] This role, plus the LOAPA agreements, provided military leaders with the feeling that some of their major concerns were being attended to and gave moderates in the army something to work with.

Overcoming enormous difficulties the Calvo Sotelo government also managed to accomplish a few positive goals specifically related to the military. First of all, this was the first government since 1939 not to include a single military member in the cabinet, a decision that carried the symbolic determination to promote civilian supremacy.[42] Along the same lines, a few posts in the ministry of defense were given to civilians, and for the first time ever a civilian was appointed subsecretary of defense.[43] The positive impact of the civilian appointments was reflected in legislation that clearly placed an emphasis on modernization. One of the laws passed rationalized the growth of military spending and offered realistic criteria for military development plans, laying the groundwork for long-term planning. Another law, originally advanced by an ad hoc military committee previously under the direction of General Gutiérrez Mellado, created an "active reserve" and fixed retirement ages for all professional military personnel. The law created a formula for reforming the antiquated, overcrowded senior command structure in the army and permitted greater fluidity in promotions by introducing criteria other than strict seniority.[44] Also included in the list of government accomplishments was the invigoration and strengthening of the Centro Superior de Informaciones de la Defensa (CESID)—the state intelligence agency—and the creation within it of units expressly aimed at monitoring internal seditious movement in the armed forces.

The government also defied the hard-liners in a critical and controversial decision that caused widespread uneasiness in the military: President Calvo Sotelo decided to appeal the sentences of the military court on the conspirators of 23 February. In the president's view the central goal of this measure was not to alter the severity of the punishment but, rather, to establish that the last word regarding crimes of such overriding national importance should be left to the Supreme Court — *Tribunal Supremo* — and not to a military court.[45]

Calvo Sotelo's government also went ahead with the decision to join NATO, as promised in UCD's electoral platform. A majority in the army, for different reasons, was reticent about such a move, the air force was mildly supportive, and the navy had for a long time made clear its pro-NATO stance.[46] This decision, its halt by the successor Socialist government, and, finally, its reincorporation under the terms of the 1986 referendum generated a protracted debate that in the long run helped empower the civilians.

The president's decision not to include military officers in the cabinet, to appeal the sentence of the military court, and his defense minister's resolve to appoint more civilians in the ministry and to pursue important modernizing legislation all point to the government's determination to consolidate democracy and end the military challenge. The gains made were relatively modest, however, and additional advances in civilian supremacy were arrested by the magnitude of the continuous hardline challenge, which distracted the government from conducting policy and forced it, instead, to handle innumerable skirmishes with hardliners. Declining support for the government and the disintegration of the governing party damaged the capacity of civilian authorities to overcome military challenges firmly. This civilian weakness was reversed with the elections of 1982, which prevented the repetition of the dangerous feeling of a political vacuum, which had been created with the earlier resignation of Adolfo Suárez in 1981.

The General Elections of 1982

Against military hopes the elections of 28 October 1982 gave a resounding majority to the PSOE. The tension surrounding the elections, already advanced by the uncovering of the military plot on 1 October, was further heightened by a new terrorist strike by ETA, which killed the chief of the Brunete Armoured Division, General Víctor Lago Román, on 4 November, only a week after the Socialists' triumph. Terrorism, once again, aroused the passions in military sectors, which awaited the new government in an overt state of agitation.[47] By this time, however, despite signs of continuous tension and indiscipline, the hard-line challenge had been rendered impotent.

The gradual realization among military officers during the Calvo Sotelo administration that democracy was there to stay was accelerated with the impressive triumph of the PSOE in the elections of October 1982. The resounding victory of a homogeneous party augured the end of the period of weak governments, and the more than ten million votes it received made it impossible to ignore the magnitude of its popular support.[48] The king, on the occasion of the *Pascua Militar* in January 1983, thought it necessary to call the military's attention precisely to the magnitude of this support and the need to respect it: "Important events have taken place which force us to open our eyes to reality and to corroborate the enormous weight of the manifestation of the will of our compatriots; manifestation which is necessary to observe and respect as a demonstration in the exercise of freedom."[49]

A number of generals had already publicly declared their respect for the constitutional norms and the popular verdict and committed themselves to lay to rest the image of a "primitive" and rebellious military. In an internal document that represented this view General Emilio García Conde, air force chief of staff, expressed:

> We have to be a serious and modern country, with a military dedicated to its professional activity, forming an indivisible unit, faithful to the fulfillment of its duties, but without thinking that its duty is to save or to redeem the rest of its compatriots who do not want to be saved or redeemed in this fashion.

> We can not get bogged down in discussions over the predominance of civilian power. . . . It is time to drop this issue and to cease propagating the dichotomy between civilian power and military power.[50]

These statements summarized with remarkable clarity the feeling that became predominant in the military and which offered the government-elect peaceful coexistence and a predisposition to work within the framework of the established democratic regime. They signaled the end of contestation on political issues and a willingness to concentrate on matters of military modernization and professional enhancement and reform.

The importance of the 1982 parliamentary elections cannot be overstated. The magnitude of support for the new government raised the costs for hard-liners. If the elections had resulted in the formation of a minority UCD government, military opposition most likely would have persisted. A continuation of the conditions for weak minority governments of any kind would most likely not have led, for instance, to calls,

Table 7.1

Results of Elections for Congress of Deputies, 1982 and 1986

	October 1982		June 1986	
	Percent of Valid Votes	Seats	Percent of Valid Votes	Seats
Partido Socialista Obrero Español	48.4	202	44.1	184
Coalición Popular	26.6	107	26.0	105
Unión de Centro Democrático	6.3	11		
Partido Comunista/ PSUC/IU*	4.1	4	4.6	7
Convergencia i Unió	3.7	12	5.0	18
Centro Democrático y Social	2.9	2	9.2	19
Partido Nacionalista Vasco	1.8	8	1.5	5
Others	6.2	4	9.6	12

Source: Richard Gunther, Giacomo Sani, and Goldie Shabad, *Spain after Franco: The Making of a Competitive Party System* (Berkeley: University of California Press, 1986), 402.

*In 1982 the Communist Party ran jointly with the Partit Unificat Socialista de Catalunya, in 1986 as Izquierda Unida.

such as General García Conde's, to cease propagating confrontation between civilian and military power. The military's repositioning into a collaborative mood was a response to the overwhelming support given a cohesive party and highlights the importance of popular support for civilian governments when civilians face a recalcitrant military.

The Calvo Sotelo government was an intermediate stage between the climax of military contestation—the coup attempt of 1981—and the end of military political challenges following the general elections of 1982. This period witnessed the unfolding of an ambiguous situation resulting from the confrontation of a weakened military hard-line sector, still attempting to reemerge strong against democratization, and a weakened government. The reemergence of the hard-liners was ultimately halted by their own disunity, as demonstrated in the trials, and the deterrent role of the king and civilian coalescence.

The failure of the coup itself was critical as the element that initiated the beginning of the end for hard-liners: it exposed the main leaders whose failure led to their neutralization by imprisonment. Given the leadership problems exhibited by hard-liners, this was a critical and insurmountable difficulty. The incipient sense of futility for further opposition that developed in the military after the failed coup attempt was finally sealed with the promise of a coherent, majority-supported, and stable government augured by the 1982 elections. In these elections voters, in the face of military threats, appear to have been reawakened, bringing down levels of abstention, and punished the UCD for its internal squabbles and lack of authority.[51] Government was transferred to the Socialists on 1 December 1982. In this new context tension in civil-military relations would now move from a concern about military meddling in politics to a concern with the challenges of military reform and modernization.

8

Civilian Supremacy and
Military Reform

Institutions for Control and Modernization

By 1982 it had become clear to everybody in the military that no auspicious institutional future could be conceived outside the existing democratic regime. Hard-line military opposition, already decadent and demoralized, found an insurmountable barrier in the elections of 1982. For the first time in the post-Franquist era one party, the PSOE, obtained a majority of seats in Congress, permitting the formation of a stable majority under a cohesive leadership that replaced the weakened government of UCD.

No political contestation by the military to the democratic regime would take place after 1982. From this point onward military opposition shifted to more strictly corporate concerns, and attempts at resistance turned into strategies of accommodation. Bureaucratic means of pressure and bargaining substituted for the threat of force, and the avenues for civilian-military bargaining would now be filled with the rather unexciting piles of memos and paperwork accompanying laws and regulations. With the definite displacement of the core sites of civil-military relations to these more subdued terrains, democratization in Spain entered, in 1982–83, its phase of consolidation. The civilians' concern regarding the military was no longer concentrated on the prevention of threats to democracy; it now concentrated on the adaptation of the military establishment to democratic institutions and on its transformation into a modern, efficient, professional force.

Two factors converged felicitously at this time to make possible the firm advancement of civilian supremacy. One was the willingness of the new leadership, the Socialists, to initiate, first, the formulation and then the implementation of reform and modernization of the military. This new leadership did not believe it possible that democracy would be stable without major reforms in the structure of civil-military authority relations. Moreover, it saw itself as having the task of leading Spanish society and polity to modernization and Europeanization. Leaving military backwardness untouched could have ultimately hampered the whole modernization effort.

The other factor was the vast public following, cohesion, and disciplined majority in Congress of the new government party. This would allow the party leadership to concentrate on the advancement of its platform without the distractions confronted by previous governments. Reform proposals could successfully go through Congress and be turned into law. Opponents of military reforms would now be unable to rely on the disruption caused to government by hard-line contestation or by the costs involved in structuring a parliamentary majority on bills dealing with sensitive military issues. Opposition to these reforms would now have to rely exclusively on bureaucratic obstacles and delays.

The Socialist leadership thought reforms were necessary to fully democratize civilian-military authority relations. And they saw military modernization as imperative to bring the military out of the state of postponement inherited from Franquism, to help it catch up with other more advanced institutions in Spanish society, and to keep it from arresting the effort to set Spanish polity more in tune with Western Europe. The decision to join NATO, later in 1986, after the Socialists changed their position on this issue, added impetus to the modernization drive.

Reform and modernization bills, approved following debate and improvements in parliament, were supported by liberal groups in the military and a core of professional modernizers working in the ministry. However, the top military leadership appointed by the government was not necessarily made up of liberals and represented, rather, mainstream orientations in the military. At times collaborating in reforms but often dragging its feet, this military leadership would zealously speak up for its nonetheless fading powers and prerogatives. The process leading to major reforms in the military and the structure of defense organization is accounted for in the following pages, but here I will examine the way the main actors constituted and positioned themselves at this stage.

In the wake of negotiations for political reform in 1976 sectors in the military had expressed concern over the possibility that Socialists would gain seats in an elected parliament. Yet, only six years later, the armed forces were placed under the authority of a Socialist government. At this time, however, the military had exhausted its chances for political contestation and was willing to concentrate on narrower issues such as defense of corporate prerogatives. At the same time, the Socialists had contributed to making themselves more tolerable by substantially moderating the platform with which they had entered the transition.

In the Twenty-seventh Party Congress in December 1976, the first one after Franco's death, the Socialists had introduced an official definition of the party as Marxist and class based and reaffirmed the *ruptura* path, which the previous 1974 Congress held in France had outlined as the strategy for the transition from Franquism. Just emerging from the underground, and skeptical about Suárez's reformist plans, a mobilizational strategy had then seemed most appropriate. But, following Suárez's success in the referendum of December 1976, in which the PSOE had called for abstention, and the PSOE's own good showing in the 1977 elections, the Socialist leadership in practice initiated collaboration with Suárez's reform plans and abandoned, to the chagrin of the party's Left, the radical tenets approved in the party congress. The consensual strategy followed in the constituent assembly opened the way for a more moderate electoral platform in the 1979 elections, in which the party, envisaging a real chance of capturing the government, moved closer to adopting a catch-all model.

The Twenty-eighth Party Congress in May 1979, after the general elections, represented a landmark in the evolution of the party's platform. The party leadership succeeded in rejecting a strategy of alliance with the Communist Left but not in their effort to drop the "Marxist" label from the party's definition. Felipe González refused to run for reelection as general secretary, forcing a crisis and the call for an extraordinary congress in September 1979. González fought for what he called a more mature party, one willing to represent different sectors of Spanish society in their desire for peaceful social change. In this extraordinary congress Felipe González won an overwhelming majority and succeeded in dropping the party's official Marxist definition and in reforming party structures to allow for greater central control. The Twenty-ninth Congress, held in October 1981, reaffirmed support for González's leadership, addressed more specific issues for a government program, and gave the party an image of unity and homogeneity which sharply contrasted with the debacle in the Communist Party and in the UCD. This and the collaboration with President Calvo Sotelo on specific issues greatly enhanced the PSOE's credibility as a party ready for government. The PSOE was thus the main beneficiary of the fear of political regression which the coup attempt and the subsequent hard-line challenges had kept alive and offered itself as the best institutional channel for moderate change and political stability.[1]

The timing of the PSOE's ascent should be viewed as a blessing for the party and, perhaps, for the success of Spanish democratization. The Socialists emerged to power at a time in which military reaction had already exhausted its best possibilities and hard-line leaders were in jail. Also, the party had had the time to evolve and soften the roughest edges of its previous platforms, making itself far more tolerable to the military.[2]

Upon assuming office, the Socialists first worked with the Joint Chiefs that the Calvo Sotelo government had appointed in January 1982. Lieutenant General Alvaro Lacalle Leloup chaired the group, made up of the chiefs of staff of the army, Lieutenant General Ramón de Ascanio y Togores; the navy, Admiral Saturnino Suances; and the air force, Lieutenant General Emilio García Conde. All of them had taken part in the civil war, and General Lacalle had participated also in the Blue Division, with the *Wehrmacht,* in the Eastern Front of Hitler's Russian campaign. General García Conde had been for ten years preceptor of Prince Juan Carlos and, later, had been assigned to work as assistant to Vice President General Gutiérrez Mellado, a position he had refused to take because of his disagreements with the vice president. It was Lieutenant General García Conde who, as host of the ministry's offices in the air force headquarters, welcomed the new Socialist minister, Narcís Serra. In their first meeting the general made it known to the minister, respectfully but unambiguously, that it would serve him well to respect the criteria of the air force and the prerogatives of its chief of staff in making decisions regarding promotions and command assignments and warned him that any action to the contrary would provoke his immediate resignation.[3] This warning by General García Conde, who had earlier issued a supportive statement by calling an end to the dichotomy between civilian and military power, was an apt expression of a widespread feeling among military chiefs, who feared the encroachment of civilians in matters they deemed internal to the military.

Until his ministerial appointment Narcís Serra had been the mayor of Barcelona and had distinguished himself as an excellent administrator and a prominent leader for the Socialists in Catalonia. He had caught the attention of military leaders for the excellent organization of ceremonies and events around the national Armed Forces Day, celebrated in Barcelona in May 1981. Military chiefs, who had feared an apathetic response by Catalans and acts of violence by extreme nationalists, were instead impressed by the tremendous success of the festivities, which included a brilliant military parade and a warm reception by spectators and Catalan officials.[4] Serra's image in the military plus his professional skills in economics and administration made him prevail, for the ministerial post, over other Socialist leaders who had portrayed themselves as more experienced in military affairs but whose record in the eyes of the military (and of Felipe González) were much less attractive.

The Socialists had given early indication that they were prepared to give military and defense issues due consideration. The documents of the party's twenty-seventh congress in 1976, for instance, had included a whole section on defense which emphasized the need for coordination and integration of the armed forces, for their withdrawal from areas of civil administration, and for reforms in their territorial organization. The document expanded on the need for "a total assimilation between the armed forces and society,"[5] but the core of the proposals emphasized organizational reforms:

> The core idea in the organizational scheme of the armed forces is their submission to civilian power. This idea presumes that the armed forces are subject to the control of Parliament. What is needed is the creation of a Ministry of Defense which outlines common doctrine for the armed services and which expresses government thinking on Defense topics, both to the nation and the armed forces. This ministry of Defense must be assisted by a General Staff, the mission of which is technically to implement established defense doctrine.[6]

The Socialists also advanced a diagnosis of the backward state of the armed forces and criticized the state of abandonment in which Franquism had left them. As a consequence, they favored modernization and higher levels of spending in the military.[7] The PSOE's twenty-ninth congress in 1981, the last one before it captured the government, put forth new proposals for the rejuvenation of command positions by lowering the retirement age of upper-level officers and for the improvement of their qualifications by changing promotion criteria. The congress's resolutions also announced that a Socialist government would implement a general plan for the modernization of the armed forces, including the areas of organization and personnel as well as the development of local military industry. The resolutions went on to praise the creation of the ministry of defense and the appointment of a civilian to head it but criticized its evident weakness as a government agency:

> We Socialists believe that the first step is to make it possible that currently existing regulations on the organization of the Ministry of Defense permit the appointment of civilians to leadership positions . . .

> It is urgent that civilians be appointed to facilitate the distribution of prerogatives among the different agencies. Still today the Ministry of Defense merely is the administrative organ of the Joint Chiefs. And this is not the result of demands of the Joint Chiefs; it is, rather, the result of the political ineptitude of successive UCD governments and defense ministers. [8]

Serra expressed similar ideas in his speech at the *Pascua Militar* in January 1983 and in a presentation of policy outlines to Congress in February. In May, in his first statements to the press, Serra succinctly highlighted the core of his initial set of policies: "We have got to create a ministry which really integrates the three armed services and which transforms the armed forces into a coordinated, efficient instrument. . . . Ultimately what I want is to create a potent ministry."[9]

The ideas developed thus far by the Socialists, however, were often quite vague and expressed the personal dedication of a few leaders, assisted by connections with former members of the UMD. In government these ideas proved clearly insufficient, and Serra, who before his appointment to the ministry had been an outsider in military affairs, spent his first year in office studying the problems of his department and setting the basic guidelines for long-term military and defense policy. Toward the end of the summer of 1983, after studying other European experiences, working closely with military aides and meeting weekly with Felipe González for in-depth discussions of defense and military issues, the government came up with basic orientations for action.[10] These orientations maintained some continuity with the policies attempted in the preceding UCD governments, but they went much beyond the original military-conceived modernization plans on which the UCD had based its defense policies.

The government sought to insert the executive unequivocally in the command and authority structure, thereby preventing the resurgence of the autonomy that had traditionally been behind the notion of *Poder Militar*. This goal resembled changes introduced, for instance, in the Federal Republic of Germany (FRG) in the postwar decades. The defense organization of the FRG fully integrated the military into the executive structure and assigned the government with political and military leadership over the armed forces, breaking the autonomy that the military, especially its General Staff, had previously enjoyed.[11] Spanish officials also conceived the figure of the minister of defense following the prerogatives specified for the federal minister of defense in Germany, who "commands, controls and manages the *Bundeswehr*, develops long-term politico-military goals, and defines and delineates the limits and objectives of *Bundeswehr* planning," in a manner not confined to broad security policy but which "also bears on the day-to-day routine of the armed forces."[12]

The goals specified in the Spanish defense reforms initiated by the PSOE government also followed the tendencies toward management centralization and the unification of military command structures which were earlier adopted elsewhere in Europe and the United States. Here such organizational reforms were pursued to meet increasing complexities in management and budget control as well as the requirement of joint action in the employment of military force. In Spain these reforms were both a means of catching up with organizational modernization and of asserting civilian political control, in a double-edged effort that pointed to the interdependence of modernization and reform policies.

The government's announcement of plans to strengthen the ministry augured clashes with military chiefs on the direction, the pace, the scope, and the depth of the reform process. The minister's attempts to expand civilian powers would be pitted against the generals' effort to maintain their own.[13] But this showed that the critical sites for civilian-military tensions had shifted from the publicized political arena to more secluded bureaucratic corridors.

In these clashes the generals could count on the bureaucratic control of their large, complex, organization. On his side the minister had a disciplined party in parliament which could pass reform laws. He also had the generals' expectation that his powers could only increase, a belief that led many of them to assume that their chances of career success improved if they did not get on the minister's bad side. The upper hand was clearly held by the government, but it remained to be seen whether it would be able to back its reform plans with specific policies and expert support and to overcome the military's bureaucratic resistance.

Invigorating Military and Defense Reform: The Organic Law 1/1984

Not much had been accomplished in defense reform and modernization when the Socialists came to power. Most of the initial efforts had been oriented toward elementary measures of de-Francoization of military structures and of basic accommodation with the new democratic regime. Such were, for instance, changes introduced in the Constitution; the new military ordinances;[14] laws that restricted political participation of officers;[15] encouragement of exclusive military employment; inauguration of the Armed Forces Day; and other measures implemented by minister Gutiérrez Mellado. Under his leadership the ministry itself had been created and the Joint Chiefs institutionalized, but the ministry remained more a project than a true policy instrument, and the Joint Chiefs had made very little progress in joint strategic planning and coordination.[16] Minister Agustín Rodríguez Sahagún, who succeeded Gutiérrez Mellado, had enacted partial reforms to the code of military justice and passed the Organic Law on National Defense. This law, however, did not eliminate ambiguity in authority relations between the government and the Joint Chiefs. Minister Alberto Oliart, during the Calvo Sotelo government, also passed important legislation: budget planning, personnel rejuvenation and reduction, and the relative devaluation of seniority as the exclusive criterion for promotions. A sustained effort, however, to tackle in a global, coordinated fashion the combined problems of organization, personnel, planning, armament and infrastructure, supplies, territorial deployment and organization, and training and instruction was evidently lacking.

What was needed was a centralized impetus — political commitment from a truly operational defense ministry — which could push these reforms forward. For minister Serra the strengthening of the ministry and the specification of the individual powers of the president and the minister were indispensable preconditions for further modernization and reform. In his view the post of minister had thus far only "an indeterminate role in his relations with military command," and the fact that the ministry had no physical facilities of its own was symptomatic of its diluted role.[17]

After almost a year in office, in October 1983, the government submitted to Congress a bill to reform the 1980 Organic Law on National Defense, in the first major attempt to firmly insert the authority of the government in military affairs. In essence the reform bill promulgated on 5 January 1984 (Organic Law 1/1984) transformed the Joint Chiefs from a command organ into an advisory body for the president and the defense minister. Along the same lines the National Defense Board, which previously had the king, the government, and the Joint Chiefs sharing in the formulation of military policy, was transformed into an advisory board for the king and the government. The authority and command held by these formerly collective bodies was replaced by the individual powers of the president, the minister, and the chiefs of staff. The latter retained individual command of their respective services, now explicitly under the authority and "direct dependence" on the minister of defense. The minister was charged with the formulation and implementation of military policy, joint strategic planning, as well as with the direction of military administration and the monitoring of military preparedness. The minister also assumed, by delegation, functions of the president, such as the direction of defense policy and the authority to order, coordinate, and direct the action of the armed forces. The president was directly assigned the determination of grand strategic goals, the general distribution of forces, and the direction of war.

This landmark bill significantly empowered the minister vis-à-vis the chiefs of staff of the service branches and specified individual responsibilities in the chain of authority and command, starting with the president and descending through the minister to the chiefs of staff. The constitutional position of the king as supreme commander was respected by leaving him as chair of the National Defense Board, but the bill left no room for ambiguity regarding the exclusive leading role of the government.

A critical innovation was the creation of the new post of chief of defense staff (*Jefe de Estado Mayor de la Defensa* [JEMAD]), who would be the "principal collaborator" of the minister for the formulation and implementation of the operational aspects of military policy and would eventually, in case of war, be appointed chief of the operational command of the armed forces for the conduct of military operations under the authority of the president. The JEMAD was assigned a joint staff for defense as his own working group, and, in the absence of the minister, the JEMAD would chair the Council of the Joint Chiefs.[18]

The chiefs of staff and the minister collaborated in the preparation of this bill. The chairman of the Joint Chiefs, a fourth member with no real powers of his own, also encouraged the reforms in view of the impotence that his post had thus far displayed for effective military coordination.[19] For the military chiefs it had become evident that superior military command, because of its collective nature, was not working. Agreement was rare in the deliberations of the Joint Chiefs, and decisions could not be enforced unless unanimously supported. Real unification in planning had never been seriously pursued, and attempts at formulating a joint strategic plan had resulted in a disparate accumulation of dispersed plans by each service, contained in endless reports and documents. Proposals on force levels simply added up the requests of each service to budget figures completely lacking in realism.[20] It would have thus appeared unfounded for the chiefs of staff not to assist in the minister's initiative to reform this structure and replace it with a single, individual command.

The actual bill, however, expanded the minister's prerogatives beyond the expectations of the military chiefs, who privately commented that the minister had turned into a four-star general by taking too many of the prerogatives previously held by them. In fact, in addition to the powers already mentioned, the bill empowered the minister to direct, coordinate, and control the armed forces' policy on personnel and supervise military education, two very sensitive areas, which military chiefs regarded as internal to the institution.

With the passing of the Organic Law 1/1984 the government appointed new chiefs of staff in January 1984. Lieutenant General José Santos Peralba assumed command of the air force, Admiral Guillermo de Salas Cardenal took command of the navy, and Lieutenant General José María Sáenz de Tejada became chief of staff of the army. Admiral Angel Liberal Lucini was appointed as the first chief of defense staff.[21] In order for these generals and admirals to be able to work in the reforms envisaged, the government approved an extension of their tenure for the entire duration of the legislature. These military chiefs, the minister, and new civilian appointees in the ministry became the principal actors in the reform process initiated with the organic law.

A "Potent Ministry" and a Powerful Minister

The Organic Law 1/1984 empowered the minister further to pursue the goals of central reorganization and of building "a potent ministry." The minister had previously charged Eduardo Serra, subsecretary of defense, who continued from the previous administration, to draft a proposal for the reorganization of the ministry. This reorganization was enacted only three weeks after the promulgation of the organic law, with Royal Decree 135/1984, which regulated the internal structure and functional relations of the ministry.[22] The decree created the secretary of state for defense who would manage, coordinate, and control financial and economic resources and determine policy on armament, matériel, and defense infrastructure. This agency was to absorb the numerous scattered agencies that each armed service had separately for these activities. The subsecretary of defense was charged specifically with the direction of personnel policy, a decision that singled out the importance of reforms in this area. Personnel was at the core of the goals of modernization and professionalization, as it dealt with reductions, promotions criteria, and career structures and paths. The decree also incorporated each armed service and their respective central organizations into the organic structure of the ministry and established a general functional dependency between the *Direcciones Generales* and equivalent agencies in the headquarters of each armed service. The JEMAD was empowered with the creation of various divisions within the joint defense staff and was granted control of the Directorate General for Defense Policy (DIGENPOL).

An important clause in the decree substituted *Direcciones Generales* for the previous *Secretarías Generales,* homogenizing the ministry's administrative structure with the rest of the state administration, a decision aimed at enhancing the status of the top ministry's functionaries over the chiefs of staff of each armed service branch. It will be recalled that, before the creation of the defense ministry in 1977, the top military chiefs held ministerial status. With the elimination of the military ministries the chiefs of staff, at the top of the command structure, descended, in the administrative structure of the Spanish state, to the status of secretaries of state, still above the rank of the civilian subsecretary. With the 1984 reform only the highest-ranked military chief—the chief of defense staff—kept the category of secretary of state, while the chiefs of staff of the armed services were given the administrative rank of subsecretaries, below the JEMAD and the civilian secretary of state.[23]

The intent of the reforms was to unambiguously transfer prerogatives from the military general staffs to the ministry, empower the top civilian officials, and rationalize and simplify the organization of defense via unification and centralization of major agencies. Part of this operation included the installation of the ministry in its own building: in 1985 the ministry took possession of the large building in *Paseo de la Castellana* which had previously housed the ministry of culture.

From intent to execution, however, there was a long stretch. The new organizational charts took form on paper, but the actual operation of the bureaucratic flow of reports, information, requests, and instructions was thwarted or severely slowed down by the recalcitrant service staffs. Royal Decree 135/1984 had, for instance, established a dependency of units in the services' staffs on their functional equivalents in the central units in the ministry. Units in the services' staffs, however, restricted their communications only to superiors within their own services. For instance, a request for information from the ministry's director general of personnel to its equivalent in the army headquarters had to go through the subsecretary, the minister, and the army chief of staff before it reached its destination. In practice this amounted to sabotaging the functioning of the new structures.

After thirteen months of bureaucratic resistance the minister issued an order in April 1985 which authorized officials in equivalent administrative levels reciprocally to request information and transfer pending matters, even if the units under their control did not functionally relate to one another. The carefully worded order only authorized reciprocal requests of information but, reflecting the actual state of affairs, shied away from explicitly authorizing "orders" and "instructions" in the flow of communication from the ministry's to the military agencies.[24]

The only areas in which the new provisos were actually observed were those under the secretary of state for defense—economic resources, armaments and matériel, and infrastructure. Eduardo Serra, the former subsecretary of defense, now appointed secretary of state for defense was, following the reforms, administratively ranked over the chiefs of staff. Before, as subsecretary, Eduardo Serra learned about the joint strategic plan (*Plan Estratégico Conjunto* [PEC]) once it had already been formulated by the Joint Chiefs. Now, as secretary of state, he determined the overall spending ceilings from which the Joint Chiefs would start working on the PEC and on force levels (*Objetivo de Fuerza Conjunto*). The chiefs of staff now had to come to him to request instructions and guidelines, rather than the other way around.[25] Construction and infrastructure development, weapons and supplies' purchases, and budgeting and spending by each one of the armed services were now increasingly managed and controlled by the *Secretaría de Estado,* and military chiefs had no choice but to abide by the new rules.

The success of the secretary of state in enforcing the new authority structure was the result of its enhanced administrative rank, combined with the office's alluring power of the purse. Also, the benefits in increased coordination and efficiency (brought about by the centralization of purchases and negotiations with foreign firms, the long-term planning, and the move toward the standardization of weapons systems within and among the armed services) could not have been contested on professional grounds, even if they diminished the powers of the separate service staffs. Indeed, military chiefs soon began to realize the benefits brought by civilian direction, which sped up a modernization process that could not have been undertaken separately.[26] In addition, air force and navy chiefs witnessed how civilian leadership helped to bring about their long-held hopes of seeing the army's share of the budget gradually reduced. Here, as in other areas, modernization would lead objectively to place civilians and the other armed services in opposition to the army, helping to deter its corporate reaction.

In the other areas of the ministry, however, in which the military had less to gain and much more to lose in terms of corporate prerogatives, progress was much slower, and new regulations had to be issued to clarify the prerogatives of ministry officials. In 1987, nearly two years after the clarifying decree of 1985, the government — with the Socialists already in their second term and still holding a majority in parliament — issued a special decree (RD 1/1987) which organically restructured the ministry.[27] This was a major restructuration that went beyond regulations on functional relations. The decree stated more specifically than previous ones the prerogatives assigned to each position and the authority and functional interrelations that they established. This time the defense ministry's units were explicitly made hierarchically superior to their functional equivalents in the headquarters of the general staffs.

As with previous reform decrees, however, the military's bureaucratic resistance essentially sought to keep the minister from making the new regulations immediately operational. In fact, the 1987 decree did not automatically eliminate the intense struggle between the ministry and the armed services' staffs for actual prerogatives. The legal authority of units in the ministry to provide policy guidelines for, and to ensure their implementation by, the general staffs was only very partially translated into practice. To a large extent, a year after the decree was issued, hierarchical lines still operated more as horizontal lines for protracted consultations on specific measures than as effective lines of authority.[28] Nonetheless, every new decree pushed the line of civilian prerogatives further into the military's secluded domains, pointing to the importance of the formal-legal power of the minister. Civilians complained about bureaucratic resistance, but the generals complained even more strongly about what they saw as an excessive encroachment of civilian officials in military matters. In fact, the formal powers that civilian officials attained with the reorganization of 1987 were quite significant and firmly set in motion the dynamics of transformation and reform.

Figure 8.1 displays the structure that the ministry had secured by 1987, with the armed services integrated in it (in 1990 the subsecretary was upgraded to secretary of state for military administration). Change was quite visible in the steady increase in the number of civilian appointees in top positions. It should be recalled that at the time of the attempted coup of 1981 the minister himself was the only civilian, and when the Socialists took over in 1982 the number of civilians had expanded only to three: the minister, the subsecretary, and the director general for economic affairs. With the 1984 reforms a few more were added in critical posts, such as the secretary of state for defense and the director general for communications, and many more were appointed following the 1987 reorganization. By 1989 the director general of personnel was a civilian, and military officers remained in charge of only armaments and matériel and the critical posts in intelligence and education. Outside the core structure of the ministry the unprecedented appointment of a civilian as director general of the Civil Guard, previously commanded by army generals, broke with a tradition begun with its creation in 1844.[29] Table 8.1 summarizes the progression in the appointment of civilians to the top positions, especially those at the level of director general, since the reforms of 1984.

Figure 8.1 also displays the authority relations formally prescribed for the ministry of defense. In line with the reforms of 1984, which had replaced collective organs of military command with individual command and authority positions, RD 3/1985 restricted the supreme councils of the army, navy, and air force to the performance of advisory functions for the minister and the respective chiefs of staff. The chiefs of staff, assembled in the Joint Chiefs, became advisors to the minister as well.[30] This change in the powers of the supreme councils and the chiefs of staff was reflected critically in the area of promotions. Previously, the supreme councils had had collective authority for decisions on promotions. The 1985 decree authorized them only to provide the ranked classification of upper-level officers to be considered for promotion. A ministerial order

The Post-Transition

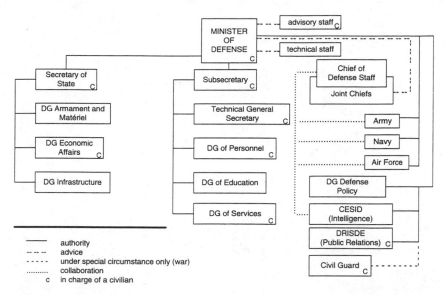

Fig. 8.1. Civilians in top positions in, and structure of, the Ministry of Defense (1987).

in March 1986 further restricted their powers. Instead of proposing a list of three names for a vacant position in the grade of general for the minister to select, the councils now had to submit the entire list of those qualified, and the minister could select anyone from within it.[31]

The minister also acquired the power to appoint officers in the grade of colonel or navy captain to the posts of divisional chiefs of staff, regiment or ship commanders, and directors of military schools as well as their directors of studies. The area of schools and education was extremely sensitive because it touched upon areas related to the internalization of concepts of military morale, personality, and honor, which the military viewed as distinct corporate traits, which should remain insulated from the domain and outlook of civilians. This was an area that would prove extremely resistant to the expansion of civilian powers in the ministry. Nonetheless, the government passed a couple of controversial measures against the firm and express opposition of the three armed services. Ministerial Order 66/1985, for instance, gave the minister a say in the appointment of professors in centers of higher military education, empowering him to consider candidates on the basis of his own evaluations (*destinos de libre designación*) and set a limit of six years for tenure of the

Table 8.1

Civil-Military Status of Top Appointees in the Ministry of Defense
(1984, 1987, 1989, and 1993)

	Civilian		Military		Total
1984					
Director General	2		5		7
Subdirector General	4		25		29
Total	6	(17%)	30	(83%)	36
1987					
Director General	3		6		9
Subdirector General	9		26		35
Total	12	(27%)	32	(73%)	44
1989					
Director General	5		4		9
Subdirector General	9		26		35
Total	14	(32%)	30	(68%)	44
1993					
Director General	11		3		14
Subdirector General	14		27		41
Total	25	(45%)	30	(55%)	55

Source: 1984, 1987 and 1989, based on information provided by memo, Colonel Carlos Gil Muñoz, director of the *Unidad de Estudios Sociales,* Ministry of Defense, Spain; 1993, *Fichero de Altos Cargos de la Administración del Estado.*

Note: Functionaries at the level of secretary general in CESID — the state intelligence agency — are not included.

appointments.[32] The order sought to improve the technical qualities of military education by attracting officers with experience in operational commands to teaching positions. The military, instead, preferred specialization in teaching, favoring the corporate-oriented values of an entrenched professorial corps. Also opposed by military chiefs was RD 2078/ 1985, which unified requirements for admission in all military schools. Military chiefs thought that their service branches were different enough to maintain different requirements for admission and resented the central control in the ministry which unification implied. Ministerial Order 37/1986 expanded the previous royal decree and outlined common subjects to be taught in all schools.[33]

The new ministerial powers pitted ministry officials against military chiefs on a number of other issues. On the draft, for instance, civilian officials were interested in attending to regional-political demands as well as to the need to improve a tarnished image of the military among civilian youths and privates. But military chiefs opposed decisions that, as in the educational area, they perceived as breaking with distinct corporate features and with the essence of the "military character." For instance, it was established in 1987 that 60 percent of all draftees would be allowed to serve in military units located in their regions of origin. The military opposed, for instance, that units in the Basque country were peopled mostly with Basque youths. For the military this entailed obvious risks, but, even worse, the measure hindered the role of military service in the formation of a Spanish national sentiment among the youths. The minister prevailed, and no longer would conscripts be assigned to garrisons in different regions across the country. Also strongly opposed by the military was the authorization given privates to wear civilian clothes outside the regiment.[34] Important, too, was the government's decision in November 1986 finally to grant the former members of the UMD the right of reincorporation in the army, against the opposition of the army leadership.[35]

The empowerment of the ministry and the minister vis-à-vis the armed services and the top military chiefs was indispensable to unequivocally establishing the supremacy of civilian authority. The reforms that made possible this empowerment also helped to centralize and unify military command. This dimension of military modernization reinforced central civilian control, and, insofar as this control led to efficiently promote modernization in other areas in the services, it built legitimacy for civilian leadership among the military.

Much of the modernization scheme had been conceived earlier in military quarters, especially with regard to the advancement of central unified structures, personnel reduction, unification of command and services, and the modernization of matériel. Civilian leadership, however, provided the conditions for the implementation of these measures, removing political and organizational impediments and facilitating the dominance of the most professionally oriented and best-prepared officers in the top positions. Although many of the military-conceived modernization measures were widely perceived as necessary within the services, they required an external impulse and direction because of the internal costs they would exact. Personnel reduction, for instance, would inevitably truncate the career aspirations of many officers, and the services lacked the thrust to pursue these reforms on their own.[36] Civilian leadership, with the advice of a selected group of top-level officers, pushed the modernization and reforms goals beyond their original reach and provided coherence by taking a global view that the individual services could not attain and by connecting modernization with the reforms necessary for the accommodation of the armed forces within the rules of a democratic regime.

Central Military Modernization:
The Role of Chief of the Defense Staff

The creation in 1984 of the position of Chief of the Defense Staff (JEMAD) played a crucial role in the overall modernization effort. Although this chief only controlled a few unified and specified commands[37] and had no direct authority over the service chiefs of staff, he had the senior most ranking in the military and was assigned a mission with potentially vast implications. The reforms of 1984 stipulated that the government could place the JEMAD in charge of wartime operations as general chief of the operational command of the armed forces, in which case the services' chiefs of staff would become his advisors. His principal role was the formulation of directives for joint and combined logistics and operations, the direct or delegated command of unified and specified commands, and the formulation of proposals for the unification of units dispersed in the separate service branches. These reforms thus unleashed a process that empowered both the minister and the JEMAD: the centralizing impetus of the JEMAD's mission had the functional consequence of helping the minister achieve the goal of bringing the armed services to unified and centralized control in the ministry. In this way the minister had the highest military authority working for the purpose of overcoming military resistance to the strengthening of the ministry.

The first JEMAD, Admiral Angel Liberal Lucini, understood that the clause stating the "the government could" place him in command of all military forces meant that his job initially was to do everything necessary to be ready for such an eventuality. His first effort was to promote further specification of the meaning of this clause to enlarge his powers over the service branches. The ministerial reorganization of 1984, for instance, specified his powers to include the development of directives and operational plans derived from the joint strategic plan; the logistical coordination of the three services; the determination of requirements for mobilization; the proposal of doctrine for unified action; the proposal for the creation and composition of unified and specified commands and the exercise of direct command over them; the proposal, planning, and conduct of joint-combined maneuvers; the coordination of intelligence, telecommunications, and electronic warfare systems in all three of the service branches; and the supervision of the state of preparedness of all the armed forces. Admiral Liberal moved swiftly to initiate the implementation of his role, organizing working sessions at the headquarters of each service branch.

The implementation of the new structures and roles brought about greater dynamism in previously dormant central agencies. Contrary to previous practice, the defense minister now regularly attended the meetings of the Council of the Joint Chiefs and the National Defense Board, which, while meeting only once in 1983, held seven meetings in 1984–85, with an active participation of civilian ministers.[38] Initially, these meetings concentrated on the analysis of the failure of previous attempts to produce a workable National Defense Plan and Joint Strategic Plan. More realistic goals were set, especially by providing fixed budgetary ceilings prior to the formulation of the plan instead of planning force levels first and budgeting later. A defense policy cycle and a planning system were established for the operation of the whole defense structure as well as for each service, based on the Planning, Programming and Budgeting System (PPBS), which the U.S. Defense Department had adopted in the 1960s.[39] The first workable joint strategic plan was approved in 1985, and, although it was still far from attaining real unification and coordination, it was the first serious attempt to move in this direction by, for instance, attempting a common definition of threats. Up until then each service branch worked on the basis of very different definitions of threat, with the "internal enemy" still lingering in army documents.[40] Planning for the 1985 joint strategic plan, instead, was based on serious efforts to produce a common view of the threats and, although not explicitly, to define defense and military objectives on the assumption of roles that Spain would presumably be assigned as an eventual NATO member.

The emphasis on reforms and modernization underscored experience in central management as criteria in the appointment of new chiefs of staff in the final months of 1986. The new army chief of staff, Lieutenant General Miguel Iñiguez del Moral, for instance, had been one of the principal collaborators of former minister General Gutiérrez Mellado and had headed the army's planning division charged with the army's modernization plan. The new air force chief of staff, Lieutenant General Federico Michavila, had been director general of personnel in the ministry and, as such, had had central responsibility for the implementation of personnel reductions. Admiral Fernando Nárdiz, navy chief of staff, was previously the director general of defense policy in the ministry. Also, for the first time, the new leadership was formed entirely by officers who had not participated in the civil war, and the same was true for all generals and admirals in the three services by the start of 1987.

The new JEMAD, Air Force General Gonzalo Puigcerver, whose post had been further strengthened in its operational aspects with the ministerial reorganization of January 1987,[41] continued to call for deeper reforms to attain "a command structure for the Armed Forces which adequately responds to the challenge of the peculiar conditions of modern warfare." Aware of the corporate-bureaucratic resistance for further integration, he noted: "A long and respectable tradition sets molds which are hard to break and which hinders the process of adaptation to new situations. . . . In order to attain the necessary and desired integration of the three services into an armed force endowed with a doctrine of unified action which guides the organization of its command structure and its joint action, we will have to obtain the enthusiastic collaboration of the services."[42]

The functional dynamics of the Defense Staff continued to work in the direction of integration and central control. Ministerial Order 7/1989 of 3 February created a new structure for the Operational Command of the Armed Forces, giving new powers to the chief of defense staff to integrate forces from the different services and to command them for the purposes of planning and training.[43] At this point there already existed a core of middle- and upper-level officers with experience in joint staff activities and central defense planning and management which gave impetus to an already self-sustained modernization drive.

Defense Organization: Changes since the End of Franquism

The tenor of the modernization of defense structures which had been attained in the years since the end of Franquism is vividly conveyed in the contrast between figures 8.2 and 8.3. During Franquism the military ministers were at the top of the command structure in the defense estab-

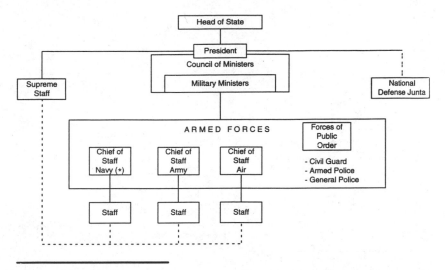

(∗) The Navy was the only service in which the Chief of Staff was not subordinated to the minister

——— authority
- - - - coordination
-- -- -- advice

Fig. 8.2. National defense structure in the Franquist state.

lishment, within the regulations of the council of ministers and under the political leadership of the head of state. By 1987 the role of civilians in military and defense affairs had been vastly expanded and had, in fact, become dominant. The Cortes retained its old powers to authorize the head of state to declare war or peace and to sign military treaties and made effective its powers to approve the budget. It was additionally empowered to authorize the government to declare states of exception and siege and, generally, to pass defense laws and to exercise control over the government and the military administration.

The direction of defense and military policy was assigned explicitly to the government. More specifically, according to the Organic Law of National Defense (LODN), the president determines the basic goals for military policy, directs defense policy, and is responsible for the conduct of war. The National Defense Board (Junta)—only an advisory body to the government and the king—is formed by a majority of civilians.

The king, as head of state, is charged with the supreme command of the armed forces. Authority for definitions of goals and conduct of policies, however, lies entirely with the government. The minister of defense is at the center of the new structure, conducts defense policy, and directs

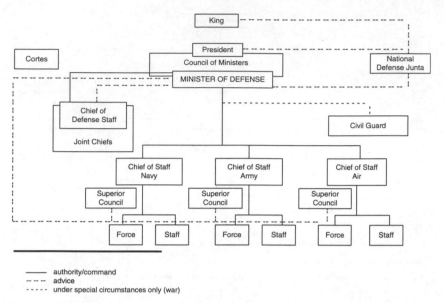

Fig. 8.3. National defense structure in the post-Franquist state (1987).

the armed forces by delegation of the president. The minister formulates and implements defense and military policy, formulates the joint strategic plan for the armed forces and determines force levels, directs and coordinates resource management, conducts and controls personnel policy, and oversees military education.

Decisions are made in the following way: the starting point is a national defense directive issued by the president. This directive initiates a defense policy cycle that aims at the promulgation of a general defense plan, a joint strategic plan for the armed forces, and a determination of force levels. The policy-making cycle includes substantial military input, but the military only plays an advisory role in the final decisions. The highest military echelon to participate in this cycle is the chief of defense staff, who is the principal collaborator of the minister. The Joint Chiefs had ceased in 1984 to be "the top collective body in the military chain of command," a capacity that it had acquired with its creation in 1977.

Figure 8.3 shows no place for the forces of public order in the defense structure. The 1978 Constitution had separated the forces employed for domestic security from the armed forces, stating in Article 8: "The Armed Forces, consisting of the Army, the Navy and the Air Force, guarantee the sovereignty and independence of Spain, and defend her terri-

The Post-Transition

torial integrity and the constitutional order." The Security Corps and Forces, as the old Forces of Public Order were renamed, were now given the mission "to protect the free exercise of rights and liberties and to guarantee citizens' security."[44]

An Organic Law of Security Corps and Forces, passed in 1986, went a long way in promoting the demilitarization of the police and security forces. By 1987 these corps and forces were all led by civilians.[45] The organic law regulated the Civil Guard, and the newly created National Police Corps, which merged the previous Superior Police Corps and the National Police. The National Police Corps was defined as a civilian armed service, and active-duty army officers serving in it were forced to retire from the army in order to be able to remain in the police.[46]

While the new democratic constitution still made the military guarantors of the constitutional order, the performance of this function was made entirely dependent on the initiative and command of the government. A number of provisions, such as Article 116 of the Constitution, the Organic Law on the States of Exception and Siege, and the Organic Law of National Defense (LODN), clarified the role of Congress and the government in the enforcement of measures that would lead the military to mobilize in defense of the constitutional order. This mobilization would proceed only as a result of instructions by civilian authorities.[47]

Finally, the military judicial system was integrated within a single national judicial system. The Supreme Council of Military Justice was eliminated and replaced with a special unit within the Supreme Court, which deals with military affairs. Other reforms eliminated the jurisdiction of military courts over civilians and expanded the jurisdiction of civilian courts over military personnel.[48]

NATO: The Debate and the Incorporation

Spain's incorporation into NATO provided an international impetus for centralization and civilianization of top defense structures. Also, the intense debate prior to the final incorporation helped to expand the participation of diverse civilian sectors in the definition of issues that would have otherwise been left exclusively to military quarters.

Debate in Spain about the advisability of joining NATO was intense and protracted. In 1981 Leopoldo Calvo Sotelo announced the incorporation of Spain into NATO as a core part of his platform, and, during his short tenure in government, the ministry of foreign affairs hurriedly advanced through the process that led to a ceremonious incorporation in 1982. The PSOE strongly opposed UCD's policy on this matter, arguing that Spain's security interests were best served by staying away from the politics of the blocs. The PSOE maintained that such an important policy decision could not be made by simple majority in Congress and offered a referendum on the issue as a central part of its electoral campaign. When the Socialists took over in 1982, participation in NATO was frozen, and all Spanish delegates to the various NATO working groups were withdrawn. Initially, Socialist leaders did not set a date for the referendum, and it soon became obvious that a major change of position was taking place among Felipe González and other leaders on the issue. When it finally became clear that the government officially was in favor of staying in the alliance, the issue for the PSOE and the government became whether to hold a referendum or not. After a painful internal debate Felipe González stuck to his campaign promise of a referendum. This time, however, the Socialists, in a major turnaround, would campaign for the yes vote. The Socialist leadership, risking defeat until the very end, given that opinion polls showed the public rejecting NATO, had to struggle to convince its own recalcitrant followers. In a passionate campaign Manuel Fraga and other opposition leaders indicated that holding the referendum made no sense if the government and the PSOE now favored integration. After all, Spain had already entered the organization, and all the government had to do was stay in. They disliked having to participate in a referendum on the goverment's side which, if won, would be capitalized as a victory for the PSOE. As it turned out, the campaign concluded in March 1986 with a clear victory for the government and those in favor of maintaining Spain as a NATO member.[49]

The debate preceding the referendum contributed to inform and educate the public and to rally the interest of large numbers of civilians in the discussion of alternative courses for Spain on security and defense. All parties and parliamentary groups were forced to develop positions on the subject and to expand them into their own conceptions on security. The media gave expression to protracted and heated exchanges, and all kinds of publications on the subject proliferated in bookstores and newsstands. An open debate ensued by diverse civilian sectors about consequences for defense orientations and mission for the armed forces.

The expansion of this debate reinforced the civilian-political character of a decision with obvious implications for the military. The military had had no influence on the original decision and remained uninfluential on this issue during the whole period culminating in the referendum.

The low profile maintained by the military was determined also by the diversity of views it harbored. The navy had long supported incorporation in NATO, conducted joint exercises with NATO members under NATO guidelines, and, with the help of the Portuguese navy, had adopted and continuously updated operating procedures of NATO navies. The air force was also inclined, although not as unequivocally, in support of NATO. In the army, however, a substantial number of generals had serious reservations. A few did not share the "liberal" ideological features of most NATO members. Others disapproved of the eventual shift in threat definitions which membership would bring about. These generals preferred not to be distracted from their concern with domestic and North African threats and feared that NATO would force a concern with Eastern and Central Europe and endow the Spanish army and territory with missions that would serve European rather than specifically Spanish interests. Still others were simply too aware of the backwardness of the army and the radical changes in standards across the board which NATO membership would require. There also was fear of the implications that modernization — inevitable with membership — would have in diminishing the relative weight of the army.[50] None of these different motives, however, had the necessary substance or the backing to be turned into a positive alternative stance.

Once incorporation was decided upon and later reaffirmed under the new terms of the referendum, civilians gained a new source of empowerment. The nature and structure of NATO, based on unequivocal political civilian leadership by member governments, helped civilian leaders in Spain gain ascendancy over the armed forces. Membership allowed civilian leaders to position themselves as the central, inescapable link between the benefits that the new international connection would provide and its domestic implementation in national defense and the military. NATO membership would facilitate Spanish participation in joint weapons development programs, helping its own industry and technological modernization. It would encourage domestic reforms to bring the military's operational capacity up to NATO standards, and it would force the government to define the specific Spanish military contribution and the forms of participation in the organization.[51] This would provide additional thrust to domestic military reforms, especially in the army. Membership thus reinforced civilian leadership and reform plans as well as civilian military planning and expertise.

Strategic Planning and Army Modernization

Modernization did not only affect the central structures of defense; each service had its own modernization plan, which included reorganization of headquarters and of the general force structure. The modernization effort hit the army much more severely than the navy and the air force. The new definitions of threat behind the joint strategic plan substantially diminished the role of the army. Force mobility in the defense of the areas stretching from the Canary Islands through the Strait of Gibraltar to the Balearic Islands favored naval and air forces as well as high-technology air defense weapons. Political decisions not to allow land forces to be employed outside Spanish territory in the context of NATO further weakened the role of the army.[52] An efficient defense based on unified forces would lead gradually to a new equilibrium between the army and the other services, in which the army would suffer the most. This new balance was reflected in the allocation of expenditures: the share of the army in total defense spending declined from 46 percent in 1982 to 41 percent in 1986 and to an all-time low of 35 percent in 1992. The decline in the army's share, however, was mostly due to larger allocations for joint structures in the ministry rather than directly for the navy or the air force (see table 8.2).

The transformation of the army into a modern, efficient fighting force as defined by the Modernización del Ejército de Tierra (META) plan — the army's own modernization plan — required substantial personnel reduction and reorganization of military regions and units and changes in the career and professional structure, in addition to new equipment and weapons systems.[53] Progress in each one of these areas involved tremendous effort, given the backward state in which the army found itself.

In the area of personnel the army had suffered an endemic inflation of its officer corps in the decades following the civil war, and none of the various partial measures taken during those years could remedy the problem. A special law in 1984 addressed this problem frontally by setting ceilings on staff levels by grade and a planned yearly reduction that

Table 8.2

Share of Armed Services and Personnel in the Military Budget (MB)

	Percentage Share in Military Budget				Total Personnel (as % of total MB)		Army Personnel (as % of total army budget)	
	C.O.*	Army	Navy	Air Force				
1970	0	55	20	25	66.1		80.5	
1980	4	51	25	20	58.1	('79)	65.5	('79)
1985	14	42	25	19	44.5	('86)	62.6	('86)
1990	22	37	22	19	43.6		56.5	('89)
1993	27	36	18	18	54.8			

Sources: José Luis Lancho de León, "El Gasto en Defensa," *Papeles de Economía Española,* no. 37 (1988): 303; *Ministerio de Defensa: Memoria de la Legislatura (1982–1986),* 302–4; *Ministerio de Defensa: Memoria de la Legislatura (1986–1989),* 286 and 289; *Ministerio de Defensa: Memoria de la IV Legislatura (1989–1993),* 297; Jaime Díaz Deus, "El Gasto Público Español: Su Evolución y Principales Características Actuales. El Gasto de Defensa," Ministry of Defense, Madrid, July 1979.

*C.O.: central organ (Ministry of Defense, Defense Staff, and other central organs)

sought to reach those ceilings by 1991. The law established a reduction of 42.8 percent in the number of generals, 27.6 percent in the number of majors, colonels, and lieutenant colonels, 7.6 percent in the rest of the officer corps, and 7.8 percent in the NCOs. Also, army troop levels would descend from 280,000 to 195,000 in the same time period, while total military personnel would decrease from 373,005 in 1984 to 227,096 and further to 180,000 planned for the year 2,000.[54] These reductions were accompanied by reductions in the age limits for each grade in order to reach averages more comparable to those of NATO armies. These changes were also reflected in the declining share of personnel in total spending. While personnel spending in the army, as a percentage of total army spending, increased from 59.3 percent in 1982 to 62.6 percent in 1986—mostly to finance massive retirements in accordance with the laws on personnel reduction—it then declined to 56.5 percent in 1989.[55] Furthermore, changes in the promotions system gradually to substitute election and selection procedures for sheer seniority-based promotions were devised and finally approved in the 1989 comprehensive law on military personnel.[56]

Regarding units and territorial organization, the number of brigades was brought to fifteen, down from twenty-four, and all nine of the territorial brigades (*Defensa Operativa del Territorio*) were eliminated. The number of divisions was maintained at five. The number of Military Regions was reduced from eleven to eight, and there was planning to displace the largest units away from urban areas, in which a previous concern with internal order had located them. The reforms were accompanied by corresponding changes in the organization of logistics and administration. These reforms were an indispensable contribution of the army to the overall modernization effort.[57]

Modernization and the Budget

Military spending increased only slightly during the transition; the only marked changes occurred in internal budgetary allocations that supported the modernization effort. Governments of the transition continued efforts initiated earlier, during the last years of Franquism, to attend to, at least minimally, long-accumulated needs of the military. The first important effort to support modernization, after protracted lobbying by the High General Staff, was undertaken in 1971 with budgetary Law 32/1971 to finance investment and maintenance for a period of eight years. The bill authorized an annual cumulative growth of 19.85 percent in nominal terms for these items (leaving personnel expenses for handling by the national budget every year), but inflation in the following years severely limited the impact of the bill.[58]

Later, during the transition in 1977, allotments for the last two years contemplated in the 1971 bill were raised and extended until 1982 (Royal Decree-Law 5/1977). Then, when the law expired during the Calvo Sotelo government, Minister Alberto Oliart passed a bill for investment and maintenance in the armed forces which sought to maintain the level of expenditure of 1982 in real terms and to guarantee an annual cumulative growth of 4.432 percent for investment and maintenance.[59]

Following the 1971 budget bill and during the transition years, up until 1978–79, the military budget increased its share of the government budget. From then on the military portion of the government budget initiated a gradual but steady decline (see table 8.3). Yet, while experiencing this decline, the military budget increased its share of GDP. The reason for this is that, as military expenditure expanded, government expenditures expanded even more, partly as a result of the Moncloa pacts of 1978 but mostly due to increases in transfers to territorial entities involved in the process of creation and consolidation of autonomous communities.[60] Up until 1985 the military budget kept growing in real terms, but, reflecting the aim of force reduction, it then initiated a period of stagnation

Table 8.3

Military Budget in Spain, 1970–93 (in Million *Pesetas*)

	Current *Pesetas*	1988 *Pesetas*	Percent of National Budget	Percent of GDP
1970	43,255	375,310	14.0	1.7
1971	47,072	379,454	12.7	1.6
1972	54,260	402,685	12.9	1.6
1973	60,699	402,296	12.8	1.5
1974	77,591	442,269	14.1	1.5
1975	93,683	464,369	14.3	1.6
1976	118,354	501,209	15.1	1.7
1977	149,820	513,945	15.5	1.7
1978	188,745	532,090	13.2	1.7
1979	235,433	570,277	13.6	1.8
1980	286,961	603,769	12.5	1.9
1981	337,463	635,635	11.9	1.9
1982	409,283	677,419	11.6	2.1
1983	478,333	709,275	10.6	2.1
1984	552,834	738,939	10.2	2.1
1985	618,631	760,991	10.1	2.1
1986	630,983	699,659	8.8	2.0
1987	704,077	738,531	8.7	2.0
1988	762,061	762,061	8.5	1.9
1989	817,913	765,448	7.7	1.8
1990	836,661	730,342	6.6	1.7
1991	823,180	670,487	6.1	1.5
1992	785,882	605,311	5.0	1.3
1993	757,710	553,559	4.5	1.2

Sources: For 1970–79, Jaime Díaz Deus, "El Gasto Público Español: Su Evolución y Principales Características Actuales. El Gasto de Defensa," Ministerio de Defensa, Madrid, July 1979; for 1980–81, *Información Comercial Española*, no. 592:12; for 1982–93, Ministerio de Defensa, *Memoria de la Legislatura (1982-1986), (1986-1989)*, and *(1989-93)*; and José Luis Lancho de León, "El Gasto en Defensa," *Papeles de Economía Española*, no. 37 (1988): 301.

Note: Budget figures do not include the High General Staff, eliminated in 1980, or the Civil Guard. Also, it does not include extrabudgetary credits such as those provided under the Friendship, Defense and Cooperation Agreements with the United States.

and, with the third Socialist administration in 1989, a period of cutbacks, which also led to lesser shares in national budget and the GDP.

Budget decline affected all major areas except compensation for active and reserve personnel. The continuous importance of personnel expenditures reflected both the difficulties encountered in promoting change in a large organization with a strong corporate identity and the enormous care with which defense authorities conducted reforms and personnel reductions.

Voluntary retirements—the request to be transferred from active-duty status to a situation of "active reserve" or "transitory reserve"—was the principal way to attain personnel reductions, a method that maintained personnel costs high. According to the ad hoc "transitory reserve" situation, for instance, an officer could leave active duty retaining full salary, be promoted to a higher grade, with the corresponding salary raise, and could instantly engage in civilian employment.[61]

Care also was reflected in successive attempts to improve the income situation for officers and NCOs. The salary for military personnel had consistently deteriorated during Franquism, partly as a result of the inability to pursue a policy of personnel reduction. During the transition additional forms of monetary compensation were found to encourage exclusive military professional dedication. Also, the income system was rationalized (Royal Decree-Law 22/77 of 30 March 1977) to make the salary structure of the armed forces homologous with that of state bureaucracy.[62] During the Socialist administrations efforts were made to further rationalize monetary compensations and to establish increases by grade and attain greater homogeneity with civil servants (Law 20/1984). For instance, base-level compensation for the grade of brigadier general was made equivalent to that of subdirector general, and salary increases of 33 percent were set for lieutenant generals (the highest increase) and of 15 percent for lieutenants (the lowest).[63] Further increases were differentially approved in 1989 to support the career restructuring propitiated by the law on military personnel.[64]

Civilian authorities during and after the transition were receptive to the problems that military personnel had suffered under Franquism, and this was partly reflected in serious efforts to face the difficult income situation. In the long run civilian authorities managed to promote modernization with the accompanying personnel reductions while simultaneously attending to the economic demands of officers and NCOs.

The Changing Nature of Military Discontent

Many of the sources of military discontent which had haunted democratization before 1982 continued, however, to exist. ETA, especially its *Comando Madrid,* remained active during the Socialists' first term, taking the life of Generals Quintana Lacaci and Rosón in 1984, of Admiral Escrigas—director general of defense policy—in 1985, and of Admiral Cristóbal Colón in 1986. In numerous other spectacular operations, including a rocket-launched grenade attack on the central building of the defense ministry, many officers and civil guards were killed or wounded.[65] This continued to be a cause for concern among the military, whose members were also worried about the implications of the ETA-government negotiations in the context of ETA's demands of amnesty for its prisoners and of the inclusion of Navarre in the Basque autonomous region.[66] Many officers appeared confused by these negotiations, by the expansion of the prerogatives of the autonomies, and by the growing support within the Socialist party for a federal organization of the state.[67]

There obviously remained small groups in the military which could still engage in seditious activity, and the outgoing secretary of state for defense, Eduardo Serra, pointed to them in 1987: "The problem is over as a whole, but there remain smoldering minorities that should not be overlooked. We have to be cautious as serpents and never forget this possibility."[68] Serra's apprehensions were later confirmed with revelations on a plan to assassinate the king and members of the government during a military parade in La Coruña in 1985, by a group of conspirators angered by the king's behavior during the coup attempt of 1981.[69] Nonetheless, the top military leadership confidently dismissed the chances of overt challenges to civilian authority. When asked what he thought about newspaper stories describing political unrest in the military, air force chief of staff, Lieutenant General Federico Michavila, responded: "[I think] I'm reading a back issue."[70]

The major sources of discontent now came from the very implementation of modernization and reform, which often created strains between the military-as-institution (the corporate interests of each armed service) and the military–as–central defense structure (the outlook developed by those in high positions in the ministry and the Defense Staff), which worked for modernization and the consolidation of civilian control. The functionally modernizing role of the Joint Defense Staff and the top positions in the ministry led the occupants of those positions to assume an outlook that conflicted with the corporate attitudes of each armed service.

The military especially resented the minister's expanded prerogatives in the area of personnel and senior military promotions. In March 1986 the minister decided against the proposal of the army chief of staff to promote Major General Fernando Yrayzoz to the grade of Lieutenant General. Yrayzoz headed the classification list arranged by the supreme army council, but the council of ministers followed the defense minister's suggestion to promote, instead, his close collaborator in the ministry, General Francisco Veguillas. General Yrayzoz aired his discontent and requested his transfer to the reserve. The minister's decision provoked widespread dissatisfaction among the top brass, because it purportedly ignored their criteria and gave the impression that the minister selected those closer to him personally. The event signaled unequivocally that the minister would put his prerogatives to use.[71]

Furthermore, in stark contrast with past lenient attitudes of civilian officials, the minister imposed a policy that prohibited top military officers from airing critical views on controversial political or defense issues and backed this policy by removing those who violated it. In September 1983 Lieutenant General Fernando Soteras was removed from the post of captain general in Valladolid for making statements that lessened the graveness of the 1981 coup attempt and other impertinent statements to the press. In July 1984 the minister ordered the removal of the director of the naval war school, Vice Admiral Salvador Moreno de Alborán, for circulating a critical memo in which he anticipated the rejection of his own promotion. In October that year Lieutenant General Manuel Alvarez Zalba was removed from his command of the Fifth Military Region for criticizing U.S. policy in the Mediterranean. In January 1985 General David Fernández Teijeiro was removed from the military governorship in León following a laudatory speech on Franco. In February 1986 General Abel Barahona was removed from his ministerial post for failing to control an official military publication that contained laudatory references to the 1981 coup attempt. In October 1986 General Andrés Cassinello was removed from the Civil Guard general staff for a newspaper article in which he criticized politicians, judges, and journalists. In June 1987 the minister removed the military governor of Guipúzcoa, General Angel Díaz Losada, for making controversial statements on regional independence and federalism. In October 1987 the minister removed the military governor of Zaragoza, General Joaquín Segura, for criticizing the minister's appointment of captain general in the Fourth Military Region.[72]

Clearly, the situation at the top had changed much since the Socialists had come to power. A defense minister with stable political support and empowered by a number of regulations, actually excercising the full extent of his prerogatives, created a situation that gave incentives to accommodation and collaboration while strongly discouraging contestation. "In the military we are less fearful of AIDS than of speaking out," commented a major assigned in the ministry.[73] Many in the military complained that freedom of expression for military officers had reached an all-time low since the transition, a fact that contrasted starkly with the freedom that existed in other European militaries, where diversity of opinions on international and defense policy was often aired.[74]

Nonetheless, these accumulated grievances led to a major agitation in the military during the debate and approval in 1989 of the general law on military personnel, which dealt comprehensively with previously disperse regulations on reform and modernization in the different services.[75] The law concluded a protracted period of preparation of reforms in career patterns, requirements for promotions, and civil-military prerogatives in each level in a unified fashion for all services. The new regulations specified very well the professional incentives in the military career and encouraged professional dedication, formation, and improvement, by significantly lessening the importance of promotions by seniority. These regulations, however, came at a time in which the number of positions in each grade were being reduced. Thus, the incentive for personal professional improvement and effort was combined with the uncertainty of eventual promotions to higher grades. This was one of the reasons for the unintended and unexpected exit of pilots in the air force and the navy to civilian positions in commercial airlines.[76] In the army numerous sectors protested for the number of personal career implications of the new laws, and, while some groups appealed in courts of law, other groups became involved in street demonstrations.[77]

Again, the spectacle of military indiscipline, about which the king had lectured a decade earlier, reemerged in full visibility. In previous years, throughout the Socialist administrations, the king's speeches in the *Pascua Militar* had ceased to highlight the need to keep the military away from politics, as they had before. Instead, the speeches had become focused on encouraging support and understanding for the reforms underway. In 1984, for instance, the king argued that adaptation to new historical circumstances called for reorganization, which, in turn, required that antiquated criteria be left behind: "It is necessary to cooperate with these reforms, with no doubts or reservations, because the modernization of the armies is only one more aspect of the modernization which the nation requires in other areas."[78] In 1986 the king underscored the importance of "the unconditional acceptance of the reforms in military organization . . . in order to attain the indispensable changes which empower and modernize its capacity for action."[79] In 1990, however, the king returned straightforwardly to the subject of discipline: "All professions have characteristics which cannot be changed or suppressed, because that would lead to a fundamental alteration of the very essence of those activities. And this is the case with discipline in the military."[80]

Indiscipline, always a cause of concern, was not, however, spun this time by dissatisfaction with the direction of the political process or with the right of civilian authorities to decide on military matters. Rather, it emerged from grievances among individuals in the military in response to career dislocations produced by organizational modernization. Thus, protests could be taken, paradoxically, as a measure of the effectiveness of the reforms, which had been expected to hurt the career expectations of many within the forces. The minister himself referred to the "legitimate" character of protests by those affected by the reforms.[81]

Civilian Supremacy

The landmark 1982 general elections generated a stable majority government with a cohesive leadership intent on promoting reform and modernization in the military. It found a military that had neither the sufficient will nor the capacity to oppose democratic institutions but which prepared itself to protect its corporate boundaries and prerogatives. While this corporate defense slowed down reforms, the government nonetheless prevailed. Critical to success were the expanding formal prerogatives of a minister who had full support in Congress to pass legislation that would shape the major contours of reformed institutions for defense. The reorganization of the ministry and the creation of the Defense Staff unleashed functional dynamics through which the military–as–central defense structure helped advance the goals of the civilian leadership against the resistance of the military-as-institution. This centralizing impetus was aided by opportunities provided by the debate around, and integration into, NATO. Also, the economy facilitated levels of spending in the military which helped to support a nonconfrontational strategy for reforms.

During the tenure of the Socialists the scope of military participation was brought down from societal to institutional issues, and bargaining came to replace force as the means by which the military let its preferences be known. After continuous and systematic leadership in the promotion of reform and modernization since the installation of the Socialist government in December of 1982, Narcís Serra ended his appointment as defense minister in March 1991 to become vice president of the government. The ministry was now placed under the direction of the former health minister, signaling that the once feared *Poder Militar* was now, in many respects, one more branch of state administration.

The extent of civilian preeminence reached in the authority structure of defense with the major reforms of 1984–87 was comparable to that found in most of Western Europe. It was clear that, as specified in the criteria outlined in chapter 2, civilian and military officials had reached a level of habituation — repeated practice — in the exercise of civilian leadership. Several national defense directives had been issued by the government, unleashing policy cycles leading to defense and joint strategic plans under civilian leadership. Similar cycles had taken place in areas such as appointments and promotions, budgetary allocations, and military acquisitions.

Civilian powers in defense had been clearly formalized in the Constitution and other major laws. No overt challenges by the military-as-institution to civilian powers took place since 1982. Beyond the protests to specific issues of reform, civilian-military tensions in Spain were confined to service pressures and departmental turf battles in a manner and extent that did not differ much from the bureaucratic intrigues found in the defense establishments of other NATO member countries.[82] Finally, the military had visibly had to accept decisions by the civilian leadership with which it manifestly disagreed, such as the much postponed decision on the UMD members or those on internal or institutional matters, such as the expansion of the minister's powers over promotions and military education. Undoubtedly, during the Socialists' second term in office civilian supremacy had been fully attained.[83]

IV
Conclusion

Outcomes Compared

Southern Europe and South America

THE NEW democracies of South America were less successful in their efforts to attain civilian supremacy than were the new southern European democracies. This difference in outcomes was connected, in parts 1 and 2, to initial conditions of the transition. These conditions influenced the ability of the military and civilian democratic elites to shape initial postauthoritarian arrangements, and these, in turn, unevenly empowered those actors in their ensuing attempts to redress the resulting allocation of prerogatives. A quick glance at tables 2.1 or 3.6, for instance, underscores the influence of initial conditions in the civilianized transition common to Spain and Greece, the two most successful cases of democratization. Civilian authorities there initiated the post-transition with an advantage, primarily because they, rather than the military, had controlled the transition.

Yet, as part 3 revealed, the initial success of Spain's democratization was eclipsed by a mounting military threat, which nearly toppled the new regime. The post-transition route was, in fact, marked by bumps, ditches, and roadblocks that were not fully visible from the starting line at the end of the transition. In Spain, as in the other cases, initial conditions strongly influenced the nature of the power arrangements that ended the transition, but they could not fully confine subsequent developments to their ponderous—positive or negative—spell.

The first transition outcome becomes an important "initial condition" of the ensuing post-transition process. But other factors emerge during this process which either counter or reinforce the impact of the first transition outcome. Former military disunity, for instance, may turn into greater unity in support of hard-liners, as a result of perceived threats to the military's core interests and mission. Civilian coalescence may be strengthened or weakened, as may the magnitude of public support for the successor government. International and economic factors, varying capabilities of civilian elites and successor governments for policy formulation, as well as the timing and pace of policy proposal and implementation all influence the civil-military balance during the post-transition in ways that cannot be predicted merely from knowledge of initial conditions.

Also weighing in are unanticipated events that end up unexpectedly but decisively benefiting one or another set of actors. Coup attempts — such as those in Spain in February 1981, in Argentina in December 1990, and Portugal in November 1975 — are a case in point. In the first two cases hard-line military groups engaged in swift and violent actions that could have led to substantial changes in the nature of the process in which their countries were involved. In Spain, for instance, although it is unlikely that the military could have consolidated a well-entrenched military-authoritarian regime, it nonetheless could have significantly tainted democratization, restrained reforms, repressed the implementation of regional autonomies, established tutelage over the post-Franquist regime, and tarnished the credentials of parties and politicians. In Argentina the rebels could have ousted the civilian government or attained greater concessions for the military. But, because the plotters failed in both countries, those favoring democratization came out more powerful than before, often able to inflict terminal wounds on military opponents of democratic change.

In Portugal it was not the failure but, rather, the success of a mobilization by military moderates which, by ending the supremacy of the more radical Armed Forces Movement, unexpectedly gave the upper hand to civilian democratic reformers after November 1975.

In hindsight these events proved to be decisive for the success of democratization. Nowhere, however, can democrats purposely arrange for these events to take place: not only are they out of their control (they would otherwise preempt them) or found to be morally questionable; mostly, the consequences of such actions are deemed to be much too uncertain.

How do post-transition factors position themselves to influence, jointly with initial conditions, the chances of advancing civilian supremacy? How did they affect results in the southern European and South American cases? I will address these questions but will first provide a descriptive account of the results observed in each case.

Southern Europe

Greece faced no challenges from its military since consolidation of its democratic regime in the early 1980s, and Portugal, whose democracy remained incomplete as a result of military tutelage until the constitutional reforms of 1982, has since achieved civilian supremacy. Let us first look at the case of Greece.

Following the collapse of the colonels' regime in 1974, the Karamanlis government established a firm grip over the armed forces. This was facilitated by the substantial electoral support obtained by the government party in 1974, by the referendum that same year against the reinstatement of the monarchy (which in the past had played an active and mostly deleterious role in civil-military relations), and by the subsequent enactment of a new constitution. The military contested government decisions such as legalization of the Communist Party, redeployment of large regiments away from Athens, and reincorporation into the army of officers who had been dismissed by the junta, but the government prevailed. Subversive plots by army officers in 1975 were crushed, and several hundred officers were dismissed and several others transferred to different posts. Also in 1975 the former junta chiefs, whom the government had taken to court on charges of insurrection and high treason, were sentenced to life imprisonment. Expressions of discontent still surfaced at later stages, but no major challenges from the military took place in Greece beyond 1975.[1]

A decisive step in regard to civilian supremacy was the 1977 reorganization of the armed forces' command structure. The post of chief of the armed forces, conceived by the junta as a permanent buffer between the military and a future civilian government, was eliminated. Instead, a Supreme Council of National Defense was created to assume responsibility for defense policy and for top appointments in the military. This council, formed by the prime minister and five cabinet members, in addition to the chief of defense staff, permitted the government to affirm the subordination of the armed services to civilian authority.[2]

Socialist leader Andreas Papandreou directly assumed the defense portfolio when elected to head the government in 1981. Papandreou, with whom the military had had a history of hostilities prior to the dictatorship, promoted reforms that challenged the lack of pluralism and the strong anticommunist rhetoric in military academies which had persisted since the civil war of the late 1940s. The government granted general amnesty to individuals who fought on the side of the Communists in the civil war and eliminated the requirement of background investigations for eligibility to enter the military. These policies gave occasion to expressions of dissent in military circles, but the government prevailed in carrying out those policies, giving proof of civilian supremacy.[3]

In Portugal the constitutional revisions of 1982 eliminated the tutelage that the military had held over democratic politics since the overthrow of Caetano, and the principles of civilian control were unequivocally asserted in the Armed Forces and the National Defense Law. Both the Council of the Revolution, with its broad prerogatives, and the Armed Forces Movement were dismantled, and the powers of the president, the assembly, and the government were clearly defined. The new High National Defense Council, with a majority of civilians (including the president, the prime minister, and representatives of Congress), was charged with the final approval of military promotions. The armed forces and the conduct of military and defense policy were placed under the supreme command of the president and the political authority of the cabinet. After disputes over the practical implementation of these powers, negotiations led the president and the prime minister to share in the appointment of the chiefs of staff. The cabinet's leading role, however, was enhanced by the incorporation of the armed services into the structure of the ministry of defense.[4]

Although the constitutional changes and legislation of 1982 ended military tutelage and provided the formal framework for the advancement of civilian supremacy, effective implementation was quite slow. Civilian authorities did prevail over military chiefs on controversial appointments and assignments, but the chiefs of staff of the armed services, and especially the Estado Maior Geral das Forças Armadas (the General Staff of the Armed Forces), maintained substantial leverage while the effective leadership of the ministry was hardly visible. Also, military officers remained much more outspoken than anywhere in southern Europe about internal political matters. Only in the early 1990s was the defense ministry effectively strengthened, along lines similar to those developed earlier in Spain, enhancing its capacity to formulate policy and advance reforms and modernization.[5]

South America

The regimes that emerged in South America after the demise of authoritarianism were less successful in the promotion of civilian supremacy. Under a combination of legally formalized and de facto arrangements that varied across countries, the military secured the protection of prerogatives acquired during authoritarian rule and continued to exert influence over civilian institutions and the political process. Civilian authorities formally reigned over government and the administration but actually often faced constraints in many policy areas as a result of a clash of overlapping prerogatives or the fear of military retaliation. Argentina and Uruguay, however, managed to overcome some of these difficulties.

In Argentina, following the resumption of democracy in 1983, the government empowered itself with prerogatives from the pre-authoritarian order and with new ones but often failed in practice to impose its authority over an unyielding military. The administration of President Raúl Alfonsín (1983–89) passed legislation that redefined the military mission, reassigned prerogatives, restructured the central organization of defense, and increased the number of civilians in charge of defense agencies. These reforms were enacted, along with initially impressive attempts to reduce military expenditures and force levels substantially and to hold the military accountable for past crimes—leading to the incarceration of former junta leaders, a feat unprecedented in Latin America. Halfway through the Alfonsín administration, however, the military gradually reasserted its power by reacting against budget cuts, organizational reform, the "hostile media," and legal actions against hundreds of officers for human rights offenses, all of which were seen as part of a concerted "attack." In retaliation middle-level officers staged a series of revolts (in April 1987, December 1987, and December 1988) against both government policy and "obsequent" senior military leaders. President Alfonsín yielded to demands of the rebels by submitting a bill—*ley de punto final*—which set a deadline for the initiation of judicial action against military officers, limiting the number of such actions, and then another bill — *ley de obediencia debida* — which restricted responsibility for human rights crimes to only senior officers, relieving hundreds of officers from court action.[6]

The partial success of the revolts weakened government leadership and encouraged army factions to seek further concessions. In fact, President Carlos Menem, seeking to appease military discontent, started out his term in 1989 by granting pardons to all officers who had participated in military revolts during the Alfonsín administration as well as to senior officers prosecuted for human rights offenses. Then, in 1990, and against the wishes of public opinion, the president went much further and pardoned the former junta members sentenced during Alfonsín's term.

In December 1990 several hundred army men, mostly NCOs, surprised the government with a bloody uprising. This uprising, however, received no support among commissioned officers, who felt satisfied with the government's previous concessions. The rebellion failed, its leaders were repressed by the army leadership, and their failure substantially strengthened the government and reduced the chances of a new rebel plot. From then on the government managed to concentrate on the further civilianization of central defense structures, the privatization of defense industries, the reduction and reallocation of the forces and on efforts to rationalize military policies and budgets. Also, in accordance with foreign policy priorities, projects that had previously been dear to the military, such as the development of intermediate-range ballistic missiles, were arrested. Along the same lines Argentina committed itself to the principles of nuclear nonproliferation and reached agreements on safeguards with Brazil and international agencies. The government also promoted several measures with implications for the military, such as new understandings on pending border issues with Chile, agreements with Brazil and Chile banning chemical weapons, and participation in international peace-keeping operations. Significantly, and breaking with a long tradition, the military ceased to be spoken of as a political resource for domestic disputes and more and more as a service of the national state.[7] In the second half of Menem's administration Argentina was getting close to attaining civilian supremacy, although the concessions on human rights issues, the reversal of legislation on military roles in internal security which had been advanced under the Alfonsín administration, and the persistence of numerous internal military problems still stood in the way.[8]

Conclusion

Uruguay successfully restored traditional civilian prerogatives but not without first overcoming major roadblocks. During the civil-military negotiations of the Naval Club Pact, which opened the way to the first democratic elections in 1984, the military demanded that special prerogatives be incorporated in the constitution. After the inauguration of democracy, however, these demands were given no serious consideration, and President Julio María Sanguinetti (1985–90) succeeded in bringing civil-military relations closer to traditional patterns of civilian control in Uruguay. And, in a rare event in Latin America, President Luis Alberto Lacalle (1990–95) appointed new service commanders in the navy and the air force, against the preferences of top military commanders.[9]

The military, nonetheless, retained autonomy in most internal matters and succeeded in removing defense intelligence from the direct control of the new civilian minister of defense. Later, with the appointment of former junta chief General Hugo Medina as defense minister, the ministry itself became more of a buffer between the military and civilian authorities than the government's instrument for the conduct of military policy. The most sensitive issue facing the ministry involved past human rights violations. In dealing with these matters Minister Medina assumed the role of protector of the armed forces and, in open defiance of judicial authority, instructed military officers not to appear in court to respond to crimes committed during the dictatorship. The situation forced President Sanguinetti to urge Congress to approve the *Ley de Caducidad*, which in practice granted amnesty to human rights violators. Opponents of the amnesty, invoking a clause in the Constitution, succeeded in collecting the required number of signatures (one-fourth of the electorate) to call a national referendum. They were defeated, however, in the referendum held in 1989, and the *Ley de Caducidad* was upheld. The dark spots related to human rights violations, military pressures for the law that exempted officers from legal responsibility, and military concern with domestic political dynamics distinguished this case from the successful European cases. The referendum, however, may well have laid to rest the most sensitive issue in civil-military relations, opening the way for a normalization and progress in civilian control.[10]

In Brazil the accession of a civilian to the presidency in 1985, for the first time in two decades, did not lead to a reduction of the military's political power. During the five-year term of President José Sarney the military participated with six active-duty officers in the cabinet; controlled its own services, the national intelligence, and defense systems;

and held an expanded presence in the presidential and general government bureaucracy. The military continued to act on its own initiative in social and political affairs: it mobilized against workers on strike, for example, without any prior instruction from the appropriate civilian officials. The armed forces also organized the largest and most efficient lobbying team, with officers assigned full-time to Congress, in an effort to influence the debate on a new constitution, which would replace the authoritarian document of 1967. The team successfully influenced the assembly's deliberations over several important matters: it helped oppose legislation on agrarian reform and played a critical role in defeating proposals in favor of a parliamentary form of government and a move to shorten Sarney's presidential term.[11] Although the 1988 Constitution made progress on clauses dealing with the military, the military remained largely autonomous.[12]

Upon assuming the presidency in 1990, however, President Fernando Collor de Mello implemented his campaign promise to reduce the number of military ministers. He appointed a civilian to head national intelligence and disciplined officers who verbally challenged his authority. Collor also took other steps that would have been unthinkable a few years earlier: he denounced a secret military program to build a nuclear bomb, worked with Argentina to set up a system of international safeguards, and created a reserve in the Amazon for imperiled Yanomami Indians. Furthermore, during the protracted political turbulence that led to Collor's removal by Congress in October 1992 on corruption charges, the military, visibly breaking with a long tradition of intervention in crises of this nature, stayed on the sidelines.

Yet, despite the visible relative decline in military influence, the military still had recently challenged decisions by elected officials, prevented the creation of a defense ministry, and kept civilian officials from effectively controlling intelligence and other strategic domains.[13] Also, because salaries remained meager and modernization plans were halted as a result of budgetary constraints imposed by Congress and the poor state of the economy, agitation in military circles resurfaced in the early 1990s. The military publicly disagreed with Congress and civil courts on divisive policies concerning salaries and raises for civil servants, which affected military personnel directly. Declining salaries, constitutional clauses, and presidential lack of restraint in involving the military in disputes among civil powers continued to maintain the military as a strong autonomous domestic political force.[14]

In Chile democratically elected authorities assumed office in 1990 under a constitution that had been originally devised to sustain Pinochet and his authoritarian regime in power. This design was thwarted by Pinochet's defeat in the 1988 plebiscite, which led to partial reforms of the Constitution (agreed upon by the government and the opposition) and to a viable transition. Before leaving the presidency, however, Pinochet used his constitutional powers to appoint members of a partially elected Senate and other official agencies. The designated senators played a critical role, during the successor administration, in hindering reforms in Congress and preventing any chances of major constitutional revisions. The Constitution also granted the military a diffuse oversight capacity through the National Security Council and limited the president's powers to appoint and dismiss military chiefs. General Pinochet, for instance, remained commander in chief of the army (and stayed on after the first successor democratic president ended his term in March 1994) and could choose to keep the post until 1998, with the president having no power to remove him. Legislation passed during the final days of the Pinochet regime placed limits on the power of government to affect the military budget significantly or to appoint senior officers and kept military officers immune from judicial action for crimes against human rights. The inauguration of elected authorities also went along with a massive transfer of state facilities and resources to the army — in particular, those associated with previous intelligence activities — greatly empowering the army and withdrawing resources from the new government. During the first years of the successor democratic government, however, officials were able to affirm some civilian prerogatives and to fend off military noncompliance, although significant reforms remained conditioned by the requirement of securing, as demanded by the Constitution, a large congressional majority, which the government did not have.[15]

In Peru democracy was officially established by a new constitution approved in 1980 by an assembly that, although under military supervision, had been freely elected in 1978. The cohesion of APRA and the plurality it held in the assembly led the military to reconcile with its old foe. It entered into agreements that secured a smooth transfer of power following the two-year coexistence of a military government with an elected assembly whose jurisdiction was restricted to constitution making. Under the skillful leadership of the octogenarian APRA helmsman, Víctor Raúl Haya de la Torre, the assembly managed to resist many pressures from the military, maintain its independence, and produce a demo-cratic constitution, while simultaneously letting the military govern.

In the 1980 presidential elections, however, the electorate favored APRA's adversary Fernando Belaunde, rewarding his refusal to partici-pate in the military-supervised 1978 elections, while punishing APRA's collaboration with the military during the transition. Belaunde, the former president, whom the military had overthrown in 1968, made sure this time that he would preside over a peaceful coexistence by keeping the military appeased, respecting its ample sphere of autonomy, and reward-ing it with a generous increase in military expenditures. Civil-military relations were clouded, however, by the dramatic escalation of violence by the subversive Sendero Luminoso. The role assumed by the army in countersubversion highlighted the significant emergency powers that the military had secured through laws passed in the final days of the military government. These were further expanded in 1985 with the creation of political-military commands in geographical areas placed under states of emergency. In these areas the military's control was total and outside political control. Violations of human rights skyrocketed in this period, and, in contrast to the other South American cases, they became salient only after the termination of military-authoritarian rule.[16]

President Alan García (1985–90) attempted to restrain military auton-omy and enforce presidential prerogatives over the armed forces. Part of this strategy involved creation of a ministry of defense — a move sup-ported by the army but strongly opposed by the air force, whose chiefs staged a mutinous mobilization when, after several postponements, the ministry was actually created. The new ministry, however, confirming the fears of the air force, was placed under the control of an army gen-eral instead of a civilian. The escalation of Sendero Luminoso's war, entangled with the problems of narcotraffic, massive violations of human rights, and the loss of legitimacy of the national government, rendered ineffectual the efforts to enhance civilian control.[17] Finally, President Fujimori's unconstitutional coup against Congress and the parties in February, 1992, with the support of the military, moved this country fur-ther away from the goal of democratization.[18]

A Comparative Assessment

The southern European cases were clearly the most successful. New con-stitutions and ordinances unequivocally established the supremacy of elected civilian officials in all areas of policy, including defense and the military, and these officials showed they could use the powers assigned to them in general policy decisions as well as on specific areas such as promotions and assignments.

In South America, Argentina and Uruguay stood out for their relative accomplishments. In both cases the previous democratic constitutions were restored, including clauses on military subordination to elected officials. None of the "institutional acts" passed by the former juntas remained in place, and new national security legislation specified restricted military roles. In Argentina, after the stormy years of the Alfonsín administration and the first year under Menem, civilianization of the defense ministry and military acquiescence to democracy seemed to start taking hold, at the same time that important reforms in the military were promoted. In Uruguay the military's hope of changes in the Constitution after the transition did not materialize, and, since the referendum on the *Ley de Caducidad* ended the turmoil on the prosecution of human rights' abuses, civilian prerogatives also seemed to have taken hold. In Brazil, Chile, and Peru, on the other hand, survival of institutionalized, or de facto, prerogatives for the military which clashed with and limited the powers of civilian authorities or continuing episodes of military challenge to this authority precluded the advancement of civilian supremacy.

In sum, Greece, Portugal, and Spain were successful in the attainment of civilian supremacy, while Brazil, Chile, and Peru were cases of low or no success. Argentina and Uruguay occupied an intermediate position, displaying many features that resembled civilian supremacy, but could not yet be considered as having successfully attained it (see table 2.1).[19]

Among the southern European cases Greece was fastest in attaining civilian supremacy, marked by the 1977 reforms of the military command structure, only three years after the transition. This success was corroborated with the acceptance by the military of the Socialist electoral triumph in 1981. In Spain success came more slowly: military challenges to democracy did not end until 1982, and the actual attainment of civilian supremacy became visible only in 1984 — nine years after Franco's death — with the reform of the national defense organic law.

Portugal was the most troublesome of the southern European cases. Being the first to break away from authoritarian rule, it was also the one that took the longest in attaining civilian supremacy. For eight years since the start of the transition the military maintained a tutelary role, until the constitutional revisions of 1982. The actual definition of roles between civilian and military officials took several years after these revisions. Further specification of civilian roles in defense did not emerge until the late 1980s, aided by the election of a civilian president in 1986, and actual implementation of these roles did not in fact begin until the 1990s.

The experience of Portugal raises two issues in regard to the South American cases. One is time: the southern European transitions started earlier and had, therefore, more time to develop the conditions and instruments of civilian control. It is certainly possible that the South American cases, which initiated transition later, may succeed in due time. In Chile, for instance, the most recent case, it is easy to see how the passage of time might make a difference, as some of the authoritarian legacies and reserve domains have a set life expectancy specified in the Constitution. Democratically elected presidents will be able, for example, to alter the composition of the Senate and thus create a majority for constitutional reform when the tenure of Pinochet-appointed senators expires in 1998. Yet most of the South American cases have already had as much time (about ten years) as the southern European cases to develop the conditions for civilian supremacy.[20] Attention should thus be paid to the particular conditions surrounding the processes of democratization in these two regions rather than to time differences per se.

The second issue is the different classification of the cases of Portugal, Argentina, and Uruguay. In many regards the latter two appeared to have made more and faster progress than Portugal, and, in all three, civilian governments decided on defense policy, military matters, promotions, and assignments. One essential difference that warrants placing them in distinct categories, however, is the burden of the very recent legacy of human rights crimes in the cases of Argentina and Uruguay. The military in these countries forced amnesties or pressured for pardon without ever admitting wrongdoing, pointing to the conditionality of its acquiescence.[21] Still, assessing Portugal as a case of success relative to the intermediate position of Argentina and Uruguay should not obscure the difficulties that had to be overcome in the former or the chances of success existing in the latter.

Outcomes and the Post-Transition

As argued in chapter 3, the nature of the elite in control of the transition strongly influences institutional outcomes. For instance, a cleanly inaugurated democracy was the transition result only in Greece and Spain, the only two cases in which civilians controlled the transition. All the other cases inherited tutelary powers or special prerogatives for the armed forces or an unusually large number of posts for members of the military in the successor government or legal impediments to legitimate claims to retribution. The starting point after the transition ended was thus very different for civilian elites and the military in these two sets of cases.

Differences between Spain and Greece—namely, the much longer time it took Spain to do away with the military challenge to democracy—point to other important initial factors. In Greece the colonels' regime collapsed, allowing the successor government to purge the military, albeit cautiously, and promote swift changes in it. The successor government could also benefit from the disrepute that covered the former ruling elite following the humiliating international circumstances of its collapse. Although Prime Minister Karamanlis encountered occasionally intimidating opposition in the military, the exiting ruling elite had no support left in the armed forces. The "military problem" was thus made to disappear earlier in Greece. In Spain, on the other hand, a military led by generals who were hailed by the officer corps for their loyalty to the principles of Franquism remained intact throughout and well beyond the transition. The implication was that resistance from the military to democratic change would survive for a longer period of time and that military reforms could be tackled only when that resistance was overcome.

The significance of collapse is also revealed in the case of Argentina. Here, despite collapse, the military still managed to occupy controlling positions in the transition. The only legacy of this control, however, was the staunch refusal to collaborate on the human rights issue by, for instance, decreeing amnesty. Yet, with the inauguration of the successor democratic administration, the previous democratic legality resumed with no special clauses favorable to the military, and the military amnesty was nullified. Without collapse military control of the transition would have had greater and more favorable consequences for the military.

Beyond these initial conditions other factors emerge during the posttransition which influence the position of the military, and its level of unity, in regard to the advancing new democracy. For instance, the intensity of the military's reaction to the policies emerging from new democratic institutions is affected by its perception of threats to the core interests of the organization—including its corporate integrity and its view of the national "essences." In Spain the strengthening of hard-line opposition in the military after the transition was aided by the escalation of terrorism against military targets, coupled with gains made by various regional subgroups in pursuit of the expansion of historic and newly acquired rights. In Argentina military reaction was awakened by the indictments of large numbers of officers for human rights violations. This, jointly with budgetary and force reductions and the civilianization of defense structures, was perceived by the military as a concerted attack from traditional domestic adversaries disguised as democrats. In Chile reactions by the military against civilian authority were also triggered by similar perceptions. In Peru the emergence of a large and violent subversive movement at the time democracy was inaugurated allowed the military to implement rules and procedures inherited from the previous regime which enhanced its autonomy. In all these cases, in different ways and with varying intensity, reaction to perceived threats strengthened the military and severely limited or delayed the reformist initiative of democratic civilian elites.

What factors, then, helped to strengthen or weaken the ability of civilian elites to counter military resistance, develop democratic arrangements, and advance civilian supremacy? Here I will consider briefly those that appeared to have exerted the greatest influence in the different cases of southern Europe and South America.

Civilian Military and Defense Policies

In the successful cases civilian elites during the post-transition aided themselves with the advancement of policies on defense and the military. This provided orientations for restructuring and streamlining the forces and gave substance to civilian claims to leadership.

In Greece the Karamanlis government and the major parties were forced to develop policies in this area as a consequence of the tensions with Turkey, which ended the military government, and the problems it posed for Greece's participation in NATO. Karamanlis advanced a policy that combined depoliticization of the army, withdrawal from NATO's military wing, procurement of weapons to deter the threat from Turkey, and a more friendly approach in the Balkans. When the Socialists assumed power in 1981, they came prepared with a set of policies which included a more specific definition of participation in NATO and a greater emphasis on "the threat from the East," that is, Turkey. Military and defense policies since the transition were developed and decided upon by civilian government and party elites.[22]

In Spain and Portugal civilian elites concerned themselves mostly with problems of disentangling the military from politics and with completing the task of political democratization before they could focus on defense and military policy. In Spain, with no international crisis looming over the transition, this focus did not really emerge until after the assumption of government by the Socialists in 1982. Before this the UCD governments concentrated on military depoliticization and promoted policies advanced by reformist military elites. Later a large part of the orientations on defense became inextricably linked to the issue of NATO membership. With the advent of the Socialists, military and defense policy was advanced in civilian circles, was debated in Parliament, and was more closely linked to foreign policy objectives.

In Portugal, besides the dominant concern with domestic issues for several years after the demise of authoritarianism, critical external developments demanded policies that directly affected the military. The dismantling of the empire, with the gaining of independence by colonies in Africa, led to demobilization and a great reduction in the size of the military. The colonial policies of the corporatist authoritarian regime of Salazar-Caetano had been contested, however, from within the military institution, and decolonization and military demobilization were conducted by the military, although in the context of power-sharing arrangements with political parties that emerged from the transition. It was not until the "normalization" of domestic politics that civilian elites began to develop policies on defense and the military, mostly guided by the redefinition of roles within NATO and the aspiration of closer European ties via accession to the European Economic Community and the Western European Union (which Portugal joined in 1986 and 1988, respectively).[23]

In South America only in Argentina were civilian elites forced to deal with an international crisis as a result of the military-induced Malvinas debacle. With a fully discredited military leadership, the successor civilian government initiated policies aimed at peaceful resolution of controversies, both with England, and also with Chile, as the referendum on the Beagle dispute called by President Alfonsín showed. These policies and the dismal state of the economy led to sharp reductions in military spending and force levels. Military reaction to (indeed, rebellions against) government policies and court action on human rights cases, however, forced authorities to concentrate on the resolution of domestic turmoil. After several concessions and the failure of the last military revolt in December 1990, the Menem administration resumed direction of military and defense policy. Reduction and modernization of the forces, participation in international missions, termination of weapons development projects, institutionalized military cooperation with Brazil, civilianization of the defense ministry and defense industries all provided evidence of incipient policy formulation by civilian elites in these areas.

Brazil, Chile, Peru, and Uruguay fared much worse in this dimension. With no international crisis to encourage the immersion of civilian elites in defense and military matters, and with greater continuity in the military and its prerogatives, civilian elites resumed a long-held tradition of aloofness in this area. In Peru defense and military matters were absorbed by the insurrection of Sendero Luminoso and by narcotraffic, and they did not encourage civilian involvement. In Brazil, during the Sarney administration, civilian leaders did not even attempt to formulate policy in defense areas or dispute the heavy presence of the military in them. On the contrary, it was the military that advanced postures on civilian domains. President Collor did attempt to advance policy in defense and military areas, but his effort was short-lived and was not sustained by the participation of a wider array of civilian elites. In Chile, during President Aylwin's successor administration, the civilian leadership remained mostly preoccupied with episodes of military contestation and, unsuccessfully, with attempts to reform legislation on civilian prerogatives. Only marginally could it begin to address national defense policy, which, except for a few important foreign policy initiatives with military implication, remained mostly within the confines of the military.[24]

The advancement of civilian policy initiative in military and defense areas is essential for the assertion of civilian supremacy. Disengagement of the military from politics is an important condition, but it is not tantamount to civilian supremacy. In Spain, for instance, democrats could have remained perfectly content with terminating military contestation without initiating any major changes in military and defense structures. They could, for example, have exchanged tolerance of an ample sphere of military autonomy for an implicit commitment from the military not to challenge civilian governance. Instead, they deemed changes in the military and defense structures indispensable to guaranteeing long-term democratic stability.

In Spain and Portugal, however, development and implementation of genuinely civilian policies had to wait for the elimination of the problem of military domestic contestation. Problems were thus tackled one at a time. In Spain, in particular, this allowed for time to help lessen distrust between previous foes. At the time the Socialists came to power intent on promoting military reform, fear of them as "reds" had substantially subsided in the army. The Socialists were then promoting more moderate policies and the army had been severed of its most hard-line leaders. Reforms conceived and implemented on this basis were more likely to endure. In Argentina, on the contrary, the Alfonsín administration tried to make progress on several fronts at the same time. Trials for the military on human rights violations were pursued at the same time that numerous reforms were tackled: reduction in budget and force levels, changes in doctrine — elimination of the national security doctrine — and changes in legislation. This policy backfired, however, as the military reacted and mounted an intimidating sequel of rebellions. In the end Alfonsín had to compromise and reverse some of the legislation previously passed which banned the armed forces from dealing with domestic security problems. In hindsight civilian military policies that were implemented more gradually seemed to have attained greater success. [25]

Gradual timing of policy implementation should not be misconstrued as indefinite postponement of civilian initiative, which might lead to "abdication" of civilian responsibility. [26] If civilian governments do not generate policy, then the military has no choice but to develop its own orientations. Civilians then find it harder to try to redirect those policies. In Brazil, for instance, without substantive guidelines provided by the government, the military provided its own goals. With the end of rivalries with Argentina and the lessening of previous domestic threats, the military turned to the protection of sovereignty in the Amazon and redeployed accordingly. Whether or not this is a sensible course of action, civilians are left only to react to policies advanced by the military. [27]

It also is possible that civilians develop and affirm instruments merely for control of the military without providing more substantive guidance in regard to roles and missions for the armed forces. For instance, budget and force reductions may be sensitive instruments of control — brandishing the power of the purse. Yet budgetary and force constrictions that are not accompanied with clear definition of goals and mission contradict the goal of depoliticizing and reprofessionalizing the military. Left with little to work with (no budget for replacing obsolete matériel or for training and military exercises — with pilots not flying, ships not sailing, and tanks rusting in depots) and often with less time devoted to the profession (low salaries, less working hours, and, often, toleration of second, outside jobs for officers), and without clear statement of alternative roles, restlessness in the military is likely to occur and opposition to return.[28] These problems were faced, in South America, by Argentina and Brazil.[29]

Economic capacity to sustain civilian policies on defense and the military is thus helpful in preventing a military reaction. In this regard Spain, for instance, did not have to face the kind of economic difficulties of the post-transition processes of Argentina or Brazil, which affected their own modernization drives and which, more dangerously, affected salary levels downward. In Spain, instead, salaries and compensations systematically improved for the military during democracy, thwarting the emergence of additional sources of discontent.

Support for Civilian Governments

The capacity of governments to promote democratic policies regarding the military is affected by their ability to maintain high levels of public support. A military finds it harder to push for nondemocratic prerogatives and to resist government policies when the government is visibly backed by a wide array of electorally strong political forces. Thus, critical for the advancement of civilian supremacy are governments that, because of their popular backing and the unity of the forces supporting them, can persuade the military to desist from further opposition.

The ability of governments to maintain high levels of public support is often the result of their success in handling the economy. All the cases considered here were put to severe tests by the difficult economic conditions faced especially at the time of regime change and during the first years of democratic government. Overall, governments in southern Europe were able to face these difficulties in relatively better conditions. In the South American cases social demands, which had accumulated over time in the context of greater inequality, presented stiffer challenges to governments facing much more severe economic constraints.[30]

The southern European cases never reached the levels of economic disruption displayed by most of the new South American democracies, in which inflation skyrocketed to three-digit levels. Under circumstances like these, economic hardship and uncertainty nurture the feeling that governments are not really in control, lack a sense of direction, and, essentially, cannot be trusted. While the public may still prefer democracy over a return to military rule, extreme economic hardship may lead the public to withdraw its support from the government, leaving it in a weak position vis-à-vis the military. Lacking popular support, incumbents in the presidential systems of South America are left to sit out the rest of their terms, merely awaiting the inevitable electoral defeat that will throw them out of office. In this scenario governments become incapable of meeting the great challenges posed by the military.[31] The parliamentary systems of government in southern Europe—which in most cases ensure that the government will enjoy majority support in parliament—can avoid the "lame-duck" phenomenon that often afflicts South American presidents.[32]

The cases of Argentina and Peru are quite illustrative of the problems of government support. President Alan García (1985–90), in the second postmilitary administration, started out his term with immense popularity and far-reaching plans. Reversing his predecessor's passive style in military affairs, he pursued reforms to strengthen civilian control and reduced the levels of military spending which President Belaunde (1980–85) had raised substantially. By 1987, however, the situation had dramatically changed. Challenged from within his party and from the Left, he embarked on erratic policies, which included nationalization of all major banks, provoking a reaction from the Right and further increasing his isolation. GDP fell abruptly, inflation skyrocketed to over 1,000 percent, and the president's approval rating fell from over 70 percent in June 1987 to below 30 percent in October of that same year, and then to under 10 percent in 1989.[33] Paralyzed by these economic difficulties and lack of popular support, the initially activist president quickly turned into a lame duck, thereby inhibiting the government's ability to solidify civilian control.

In Argentina President Alfonsín also started out with immense popularity and even more far-reaching plans. The government set out to implement unprecedented policies that would subject the military to civilian control—to restructure labor relations, promote broad constitutional reforms, and even create a new capital city. The government's initial strength and popular support were ratified later, in midterm congressional elections and in a referendum convoked by the president concerning resolution of the Beagle dispute with Chile. Yet failure in the battle against inflation and a sharp decline in the standard of living of most

Argentines led to electoral defeat in the 1987 congressional elections and further failures in economic policy.[34] Optimistic initial plans had to be shelved, and severe military challenges to presidential authority (which a strongly supported government could have eventually overcome) acquired self-sustained impetus for increased military assertiveness.

In both cases significant sectors of the public found ways to express their preference for democracy whenever a serious threat from the armed forces emerged to challenge it. The calculations made by the military, however, considers not the general regime preferences of the public as much as its own assessment of the strengths and weaknesses of a specific administration and its leader.[35] Government leaders with waning support among the elites, the public, and the Congress found it difficult to appease and control discontented militaries in conflict-laden, post-transition situations.

In Brazil President Sarney lost support shortly after his inauguration in 1985, with most members of the coalition that brought him to power shifting to the opposition. Much of his support came, in fact, from the military, which he utilized to pressure Congress on several occasions. His successor, Fernando Collor, supported by an ad hoc party created for his campaign, lacked consistent support in Congress.[36] Despite initial attempts to check military autonomy, his loss of support and his ultimate removal kept the government from making further progress.

In Spain Adolfo Suárez's visible loss of popularity and the steady weakening of his government during 1980 contributed to the arousal of authoritarian illusions among military hard-liners, despite the fact that the public expressed a general preference for democracy. This trend toward weak government was starkly reversed following the failure of the 1981 coup attempt and especially after the 1982 elections, which gave the Socialists a solid majority in Congress. This election provided a homogeneous and stable government majority and a credible institutional vehicle for the affirmation of democracy, thus making it possible for the new government to approach reforms in the military and the general organization of defense confidently.

Postmilitary governments in Greece never had to face problems of government support such as those just mentioned. Large electoral pluralities for the major parties and the system of "reinforced proportional representation" ensured sturdy parliamentary majorities, which were further strengthened by the firm leadership of both party and government under Karamanlis and Papandreou.[37]

Portugal, on the other hand, experienced frequent government turn-over and all kinds of government coalitions—presidentially appointed, coalition, and minority—until the elections of 1987. This very instabil-ity, although far from the ideal of any executive, at least precluded paral-ysis by providing for the expedient removal of ineffective governments. It was not until the formation of an unprecedented parliamentary major-ity and stable government, following the 1987 elections, that government officials enabled themselves to promote military reforms and enhance civilian supremacy.[38]

In sum, problems of government support were better overcome in the new southern European democracies, in which the electoral and govern-ment systems adopted—parliamentary or semipresidential—tended to facilitate the formation of working government majorities. The early UCD and the Socialist governments in Spain and the Conservative and the Socialist governments in Greece, for instance, stood quite apart from the awkward position in which Alan García, Raúl Alfonsín, and José Sarney were placed as lame-duck chief executives in the presiden-tial systems of their countries. With the loss of support in congress, either because of midterm elections or shifting loyalties of undisciplined party members, presidents were unable to implement their policies or recover popularity and were forced to wait out the rest of their terms in minority status, while retaining only formally the powers granted to the executive branch.[39] These institutional rigidities only compounded gov-ernmental weaknesses in dealing with the military.

Civilian Unity

Table 2.1 marked only Spain as a case of high civilian coalescence. As noted, Spain stood out for the high level of concertation in drafting the new Constitution. In Greece important segments of the opposition did not support the new Constitution, and in Portugal that document was drafted under the shadow of military pressure. In South America, Peru and Ecuador adopted new constitutions to inaugurate democracy in processes that did not unify civilian elites and which also were con-ducted under the shadow of military influence. In the rest of the coun-tries the transition resumed competition with no accord (Argentina) or was channeled through agreements that failed to include all players (Uruguay) or to include all relevant domains (Chile and Brazil).

New conditions developed during the post-transition in several of these cases, however, which impacted the ability of government to promote policies on the military. In Spain, after coalescence reached its peak during work on drafting the Constitution and the subsequent negotiations with regional-national leaders, the end of the politics of consensus and the factionalization of the ruling party weakened the government and its stand toward the military. Coalescence was partly resumed only after the failed coup attempt of 1981, at least until the absolute majority obtained by the Socialists in the 1982 elections.

In Greece, despite the persistence of bitter disputes, opposing parties developed converging views on several issues critical to military and defense policy. Breaking with tradition, and prompted by the situation created with Turkey, the Right adopted a critical view of NATO and a closer approach to the Balkans. The socialist Left, in turn, adopted a more pragmatic approach toward NATO relative to its previously intransigent rejection of Greece's participation in it. The shared feeling among those of the Left, Center, and Right about the U.S. position toward the colonels' regime and Turkey's policy on Cyprus "constituted the consensual basis of Greek defense policy."[40]

In Portugal, after the divisive first years of the transition, the Socialist Party, parties of the Right, and the president, General Eanes, collaborated in promoting the return of discipline and depoliticization in the army. Further collaboration between the Right, Center parties, and Socialists in Parliament managed occasionally to defeat resistance by the military to attempts to diminish its autonomy. In 1982, for instance, the government obtained the required two-thirds majority to override General Eanes's veto of the measures creating the ministry of defense.[41] Subsequent constitutional and legal stipulations encouraged the collaboration of different parties in control of the presidency and the government for the appointment of top military chiefs and the promotion of defense policy.

Among the South American cases Argentina's collapse-triggered democratization kept contending political groups from reaching the kind of accords that characterized transitions facing better entrenched militaries.[42] Peronist groups tried, before the elections, to reach accord with the military on guarantees against prosecution and then presented stiff opposition to President Alfonsín's administration. Later, during Menem's administration, the end of major civil-military tensions on human rights issues as well as the end of military contestation opened room for incipient collaboration among political elites on defense and military matters. A similar situation evolved in Uruguay.

In Brazil, beside the troubled circumstances of the emergence of José Sarney to the presidency and the tenure and exit of Fernando Collor, the formation of unified coalitions was made difficult by the very nature of the political system. The combination of presidentialism, multipartism, and federalism, in addition to more specific regulations that discourage party discipline, stood in the way of the promotion of stable coalescent tendencies among the various and shifting sources of political power.[43] Peru did not fare any better, especially given the divisive administration of President Alan García and the confrontational policies pursued by President Fujimori, which combined substantial popular support with deepening divisions among the elite. In Chile, despite the consensus that emerged on numerous areas, particularly on economic and foreign policy, no accord developed on constitutional issues regarding presidential powers over the military.[44]

Military Divisions

In chapter 5 I argued that all militaries faced the transition with internal divisions, although in South America doctrinal developments and a shared concern with the threat of retribution contributed to temper those divisions. I asserted that only in Spain, in which differing views developed in the army from different assessments of the impact of Franquism on the armed forces, could those divisions sustain the possibility of joint efforts with civilian democratic reformers. In the other cases divisions resulted mostly from the experience of military rule or, as in Portugal, from different views on the course that the revolution begun in 1974 should take.

With the end of the transition and the advancement of democracy, divisions subsided in some cases and developed in others. In Spain, for instance, the invigoration of civilian-led military reforms after the definitive defeat of hard-liners led to the blurring of previous divisions. In Greece the initial purges, the irretrievable discredit of the colonels' regime, the resumption of hierarchy and discipline, the concern with foreign threats, and the convergence of views on defense by civilian elites also ended previously existing divisions. In Portugal the extreme factionalization that the policies of the military government unleashed in the armed forces gradually gave way to a convergence around moderate postures as espoused by General Eanes. The most leftist groups lost momentum with the fall of Otelo Saraiva de Carvalho, and the generation of the revolution gave way to moderate officers at the time civilians gained more control over defense affairs.

Argentina's military experienced a more complex path. The interservice divisions that surfaced so visibly during the transition subsided later in reaction to the civilian-led human rights "offensive" during the Alfonsín administration. Vertical divisions developed subsequently, however, as mid-level officers complained that the military leadership gave in too much on the human rights issue and did not assume full responsibility for the disastrous performance in the Malvinas crisis. The top brass was also criticized for tolerating excessive reductions in budget and force which curtailed the professional capacity of the armed forces. Defeat of the last rebellion in 1990, exit of formerly rebel-prone officers to the political electoral arena, and serious though modest attempts to rebuild the military helped to erase the most visible divisions. Whereas in Portugal post-transition divisions meant the gradual strengthening of the moderate groups that favored the resumption of professionalism and discipline, in Argentina divisions after the transition presented severe challenges to the stability of civilian government.

While the Peruvian military became absorbed in the fight against Sendero Luminoso, the rest of the militaries in South America displayed an increasingly uniform interest in modernization. Catching up technologically and enhancing military capacity with appropriate research, organizational change, and weapons procurement characterized Chilean and Brazilian military attempts to accommodate themselves to changed domestic scenarios. Contrary to the Spanish case, the modernization drive did not originate in negative evaluations in military quarters of the authoritarian experience and, except in Argentina, was not accompanied by defense reform. The modernization goal was designed by more autonomous militaries and, contrary to the coalitional opportunities with civilians which it had opened up in Spain, it ran the risk in these cases of developing a dangerous gap between military aspirations and the willingness and ability of civilian political elites to support them.

External factors provided the southern European cases with a regional environment that was strongly democratic and which offered the benefits of economic integration. This type of international influence—"democratization through convergence"[45]—was distinctively southern European. Specifically in the military field, international conditions in southern Europe made it possible for civilian governments to redirect the military to missions away from domestic politics. NATO, for instance, in very specific ways for each of the three southern European cases, provided an opportunity to redirect military missions to external professional concerns.[46]

Although Portugal was a long-standing NATO member at the time of the transition, its military had not engaged in the East-West concerns of the Atlantic alliance as much as sought to hold onto its African dependencies. The ousting of the Caetano regime, however, brought about a swift end to the colonial struggle, and with it thousands of troops were returned to Europe. The extraordinary power that the radical faction of the military then held during most of the transition intensified foreign involvement in support of the moderate groups. Among a number of foreign initiatives undertaken to influence the course of the transition, veiled NATO pressures were brought to bear on the radicals, who were forced to reassure the allies. When the moderates took control of the transition, after the November 1975 showdown with the radicals, General Eanes moved the military closer to NATO perspectives, while military forces were swiftly reduced. The gradual reorientation of the military's mission from colonial and domestic to one more in accordance with NATO's outlook began at this point. Goal reorientation, effective modernization, and command reorganization evolved only very slowly, but it helped that civilian officials had NATO to rely on as a reference point for future reforms.[47]

Greece underwent a different experience with NATO. Successor civilian officials reduced participation in NATO as a result of the inability of the alliance to prevent Turkey's maneuvers in Cyprus. Persistent disputes with Turkey, however, coupled with the problematic implications of this conflict for Greece's self-perceived military role in NATO, were sufficient to redefine a mission for the armed forces outside internal politics. The "Turkish factor" and changing modes of alliance participation thus helped provide the civilian leadership with an opportunity convincingly to redirect military concerns strictly to external defense.[48]

In South America international condemnation of the military regimes and support for the democratic opposition — especially from West
European sources and, more erratically, U.S. administrations — played
an important role in democratization. On the whole, however, the international context of democratization in South America was much less
auspicious than it was in southern Europe, especially in regard to the
military dimension. The Interamerican Treaty of Reciprocal Assistance
created in 1947 was the equivalent, or, rather, the poor relation, of NATO
but had long lost its initial dynamism and was perceived by most of its
members as rather moribund.[49] It was not prepared, therefore, to provide the kind of framework for military renovation which NATO provided for the southern European democratic governments.

In addition, many features of the military component of the inter-
American system were much less unequivocally supportive of the goals
of civilian supremacy than NATO was. NATO had a clear structure of
political and military participation, with preeminence of the political
level, whereas in the inter-American system the political and military
components were parallel. Thus, military participation in inter-American military activities did not presume a prior strengthening of the civilian political connections. For instance, inter-American army conferences often ended with statements on policy orientations, with great
impact on domestic affairs, which had little to do with the stated goals
of national governments. Also, despite the gradually more supportive
stance toward democratization which U.S. administrations took since
President Reagan's second term, U.S. security concerns in the hemisphere led to an emphasis on domestic concerns of the Latin American
countries which did not facilitate a shift away from domestic politics. In
sum, civilians in southern Europe could utilize international structures
to their own advantage in ways that were not available to civilians in
South America.

Civilian supremacy was firmly established in southern Europe, and
reversal of this situation was unlikely. In Greece and Spain, in particular, civilian control of the transition, civilian formulation of policy on
defense and the military, government support, and institutional capacity to conduct policy, and timely civilian coalescence appeared to have
played a decisive role. Also, the collapse and discrediting of the colonels'
regime was as important in Greece as the nature of military divisions
was in Spain.

Conclusion

In Spain the process of attaining success was less straightforward than in Greece. The successful completion of the transition was followed by the reassertion of hard-liners, which peaked in the coup attempt of 1981. Only after failure of this attempt could civilian leaders resume democratization in the military area. Portugal's path was even more complex. Beginning with a situation that came dangerously close to an all-out civil war, several factors operated to work gradually toward a successful outcome. Military divisions and the resumption of the primacy of military moderates, the sharp reduction in the size of the military, and the strength of the "European pull" were significant here.

In South America, Brazil, Chile, and Peru made the least progress, while Argentina and Uruguay moved further ahead. The weight of negative initial conditions was felt in all these cases via the remaining prerogatives of the military or the recent gloomy legacy on the human rights area. Military control of the transition, abruptly shifting levels of government support, lack of civilian policies and coalescence, and, in some cases, institutional incapacity to produce the conditions for stable policy formulation and implementation stood in the way of progress.

Among the South American cases Argentina presented the most complex path. It combined military regime collapse with, nonetheless, a military-controlled transition; impressive early achievements by a successor civilian administration followed by mighty military reaction and civilian concessions; and a succession of military rebellions and their final exhaustion followed by the resumption of progress in civilianization, modernization, and reform. Clearly, both the Argentine and Portuguese cases demand careful monitoring in order to ascertain the factors operating in the complex paths to, it is hoped, success.

That the full impact of initial conditions may change over time bodes well for those that started out with unfavorable conditions. Progress, however, depends on the ability of civilian elites to produce the will, policies, and instruments needed to promote change — all of them exacting and elusive conditions. At the same time, they will be set against the uncertain path of military accommodation to the democratization of the political regimes of their countries and to the momentous recent international political and economic changes.

Notes

All passages originally in Spanish — interviews and publications — have been translated by the author.

Chapter 1: Uncertainty, the Military, and Democratization

1. Whereas many traits of the transition, such as negotiation and compromise, were regarded as benchmarks of success in Spain, similar features in the Eastern European transitions were, instead, deemed as the source of deep dissatisfaction. See Andrzej Tymowski, "The Unwanted Social Revolution: Poland in 1989," *East European Politics and Society* 7, no. 2 (1993): 180. See also Bronislaw Geremek, "Postcommunism and Democracy in Poland," *Washington Quarterly* 13, no. 3 (1990): 130–31; and the references made in Josep M. Colomer, "Transitions by Agreement: Modeling the Spanish Way," *American Political Science Review* 85, no. 4 (December 1991): 1283. Adam Przeworski depicted the path of Spain as the one Eastern Europe would want to follow. In his view Spain's success in "irreversibly consolidating democratic institutions" "is a miracle" (*Democracy and the Market: Political and Economic Reforms in Eastern Europe and Latin America* [Cambridge: Cambridge University Press, 1991], 8). See also Kenneth Maxwell, "Spain's Transition to Democracy: A Model for Eastern Europe?" in *The New Europe: Revolution in East-West Relations,* ed. Nils H. Wessell (New York: Academy of Political Science, 1991).

2. Observers rightly noted, for instance, how reformist Franquist elites accorded all players, old and new, a stake in the emerging democratic regime, securing the interests of the church, business, the military, labor, the Left, and the historic nationalities. Also praised was the way in which elite agreement led to forging the nearly unanimous approval of a new constitution, in the Cortes and the ballot box, despite the persistence of some of the deeply rooted cleavages carried over from the past. See Richard Gunther, "Spain: The Very Model of the Modern Elite Settlement," in *Elites and Democratic Consolidation in Latin America and Southern Europe,* ed. John Higley and Richard Gunther (Cambridge: Cambridge University Press, 1992).

3. This point has been emphasized, for instance, in Juan J. Linz, "La Transición a la Democracia en España en Perspectiva Comparada," in *Transición Política y Consolidación Democrática: España, 1975–1986,* ed. Ramón Cotarelo (Madrid: Centro de Investigaciones Sociológicas, 1992), 435–36 and 456–57.

4. Spain's transition, prompted by Franco's death in 1975 and concluded with a new Constitution in 1978, was in fact preceded by the demise of authoritarianism in

Greece and Portugal. In Greece the political system was redemocratized shortly after the military dictatorship came to an abrupt end in 1974. In Portugal the overthrow of Caetano's regime that same year unleashed a process that led to the inauguration of democracy in 1976. Nearly a decade later some of the staunchest dictatorships in South America also came to an end. A civilian democratically elected government took over in Argentina in 1983, following a year that started with the military's humiliating defeat in the South Atlantic. In Uruguay the elections of November 1984 made possible the installation of a democratic regime. In 1985 Brazilians elected, although indirectly, the first civilian president since the coup of 1964. In 1990 a civilian democratically elected president took over in Chile after nearly seventeen years of military rule. These countries joined Ecuador and Peru, where military dictatorships had been replaced with democratically elected governments in 1979 and 1980, respectively.

5. At the time of their transitions Greece and Portugal were NATO members, and Spain maintained military agreements with the United States. The case of Portugal especially attracted the attention of Western powers as a result of the role of the Communist Party and of Left-leaning militaries in the transition. Western intervention via economic aid lessened the uncertainty that had taken hold of the Portuguese process following the ouster of Marcelo Caetano.

6. Obviously, uncertainty also applies to Eastern European democratization in so far as this kind of domestic variables is concerned. See Valerie Bunce and Mária Csanádi, "Uncertainty in the Transition: Post-Communism in Hungary," *East European Politics and Society* 7, no. 2 (Spring 1993).

7. In Poland, however, the military was more powerful and prominent than in the other Eastern European countries, as shown by the 1981 intervention to arrest anti-regime opposition. For Eastern European militaries, see Zoltan D. Barany, *Soldiers and Politics in Eastern Europe, 1945–1990* (New York: St. Martin's Press, 1993); and Elizabeth Coughlan, "Martial Law in Poland: The Dynamics of Military Intervention in Politics" (Ph.D. diss., Indiana University, 1993).

8. Good bibliographies may be found in José Félix Tezanos, Ramón Cotarelo, and Andrés de Blas, eds., *La Transición Política Española* (Madrid: Editorial Sistema, 1989); Santiago Miguez González, *La Preparación de la Transición a la Democracia en España* (Zaragoza: Universidad de Zaragoza, 1990); Paul Preston, *The Triumph of Democracy in Spain* (London: Methuen, 1986); Robert M. Fishman, *Working Class Organization and the Return to Democracy in Spain* (Ithaca, N.Y.: Cornell University Press, 1990); and Felipe Agüero, "The Assertion of Civilian Supremacy in Post-Authoritarian Contexts: Spain in Comparative Perspective" (Ph.D. diss., Duke University, 1991).

9. A path that has been described as *reforma/ruptura pactada,* pointing to procedural continuities with which, nonetheless, a sharp break with authoritarian rule was accomplished. See Juan J. Linz, "Transitions to Democracy," *Washington Quarterly* 13, no. 3 (Summer 1990); and Charles T. Powell, "Reform versus Ruptura in Spain's Transition to Democracy" (Ph.D. diss., Oxford University, 1989).

10. See Juan J. Linz, "The Transitions from Authoritarian Regimes to Democratic Political Systems and the Problems of Consolidation of Political Democracy" (paper presented at the International Political Science Association, Tokyo Round

Table, 29 March–1 April 1982); Juan J. Linz, "Innovative Leadership in the Transition to Democracy and a New Democracy: The Case of Spain" (paper presented at the conference, Innovative Leadership and International Politics, Leonard Davis Institute for International Relations, Hebrew University, Jerusalem, 8–10 June 1987); Linz, "La Transición a la Democracia"; José María Maravall, *La Política de la Transición* (Madrid: Taurus, 1981); José María Maravall and Julián Santamaría, "Political Change in Spain and the Prospects for Democracy," in *Transitions from Authoritarian Rule: Southern Europe,* ed. Guillermo O'Donnell, Philippe C. Schmitter, and Laurence Whitehead (Baltimore: Johns Hopkins University Press, 1986). For a view that explicitly establishes a relationship between the preceding types of authoritarian regimes and the chances of democratic consolidation, see Juan J. Linz, Alfred Stepan, and Richard Gunther, "Democratic Transitions and Consolidation in Southern Europe (with Reflections on Latin America and Eastern Europe)," in *The Politics of Democratic Consolidation: Southern Europe in Comparative Perspective,* ed. Richard Gunther, P. Nikiforos Diamandouros, and Hans-Jürgen Puhle (Baltimore: Johns Hopkins University Press, 1994).

11. Gunther, "Spain." For a view of the transformations in the socialist elites, see Donald Share, "Two Transitions: Democratisation and the Evolution of the Spanish Socialist Left," *West European Politics* 8, no. 1 (1985); Richard Gunther, "The Spanish Socialist Party: From Clandestine Opposition to Party of Government," in *The Politics of Democratic Spain,* ed. Stanley G. Payne (Chicago: Chicago Council on Foreign Relations, 1986); and Antonio García Santesmases, "Evolución Ideológica del Socialismo en la España Actual," *Sistema,* nos. 68–69 (November 1985). For a thorough historical account with an emphasis on elite interaction and the role of the king, see Charles T. Powell, *El Piloto del Cambio: El rey, la Monarquía y la transición a la democracia* (Barcelona: Editorial Planeta, 1991).

12. See Josep M. Colomer, *El arte de la manipulación política: Votaciones y teoría de juegos en la política española* (Barcelona: Editorial Anagrama, 1990), 30–34; and "Transitions by Agreement," 1295. From a different, non-game-theoretic perspective, see Rafael López Pintor, *La opinión pública Española del Franquismo a la Democracia* (Madrid: Centro de Investigaciones Sociológicas, 1982); and "Mass and Elite Perspectives in the Process of Transition to Democracy," in *Comparing New Democracies: Transition and Consolidation in Mediterranean Europe and the Southern Cone,* ed. Enrique Baloyra (Boulder, Colo.: Westview Press, 1987).

13. Víctor M. Pérez-Díaz, *The Return of Civil Society: The Emergence of Democratic Spain* (Cambridge, Mass.: Harvard University Press, 1993), 26 and 6. In this author's view, liberal democratic traditions consisted, in essence, of the fact that Spain, by the mid-1970s, had become like Western Europe "with regard to both economics and culture" (19).

14. Maravall and Santamaría, for instance, warned us that "obviously, the new regime could be described as a 'fragile' or 'difficult' democracy." See their essay "Political Change in Spain," 71. See also Juan Pablo Fusi, "Spain: The Fragile Democracy," *West European Politics* 5, no. 3 (1982).

15. This is consistent with Alfred Stepan's finding that the military is probably "the least studied of the factors involved in new democratic movements," a neglect he attributed largely to dominant theoretical approaches that overlook the role of

organized force (*Rethinking Military Politics* [Princeton, N.J.: Princeton University Press, 1988], xi and 9). Indicative of this neglect in the case of Spain is, for instance, the fact that, of the twenty-four chapters in the Socialist Party's official publication on the party's successful sectoral policies after ten years in government, none deal with the notable accomplishments in the field of civilian supremacy and defense reform. See Alfonso Guerra and José Félix Tezanos, eds., *La década del Cambio: Diez Años de Gobierno Socialista, 1982–1992* (Madrid: Editorial Sistema, 1992).

16. Pérez-Díaz, *Return of Civil Society,* 34–35, 36–37.

17. This emphasis on the process linking different stages in democratization stands in contrast with Colomer's analysis of the military, which provides only snapshot depictions of preferences and payoffs in specific situations. Although tremendously illuminating of the options available to actors and the strategic calculations that engage them, greater articulation among the parts is, in his own admission, necessary for a fuller understanding of democratization. See Colomer, *El Arte de la Manipulación Política,* 303.

18. This goes along with Huntington's view that "the one prime essential for any system of civilian control is the minimizing of military power" (Samuel P. Huntington, *The Soldier and the State* [New York: Vintage Books, 1957], 84).

19. The end of the transition is identified as the successful holding of a free election which gives way to the installation of new authorities and institutions or the formal inauguration of a new democratically approved constitution. In turn, the start of the transition is marked by indicators such as: (1) a public and official commitment by the ruling authorities to hold free elections and transfer power to newly elected officials within a specified time period; or (2) a forceful removal of authoritarian rulers followed by the commitment to transfer power to democratically elected representatives. These indicators were suggested by Linz in "Transition from Authoritarian Regimes to Democratic Political Systems." A summarized version is Juan J. Linz, "Transitions to Democracy," *Washington Quarterly* 13, no. 3 (Summer 1990): 143–64. For a demarcation of the start of the transition in the process of "liberalization" by authoritarian incumbents, see Guillermo O'Donnell and Philippe C. Schmitter, *Transitions from Authoritarian Rule: Tentative Conclusions about Uncertain Democracies* (Baltimore: Johns Hopkins University Press, 1986), 6–7.

20. The approach taken here is thus consistent with some formulations of the new institutionalism, which, for instance, state that "options at any given time are constrained by available institutional capabilities that are themselves the product of earlier choices" (Paul Cammack, "The New Institutionalism: Predatory Rule, Institutional Persistence, and Macro-Social Change," *Economy and Society* 21, no. 4 [November 1992]: 405). See also Kathleen Thelen and Sven Steinmo, "Historical Institutionalism in Comparative Politics," in *Structuring Politics: Historical Institutionalism in Comparative Analysis,* ed. Sven Steinmo, Kathleen Thelen, and Frank Longstreth (Cambridge: Cambridge University Press, 1992).

21. Felipe Agüero, "The Military in the Processes of Political Democratization in South America and Southern Europe: Outcomes and Initial Conditions" (paper presented to the Fifteenth International Congress of the Latin American Studies Association, Miami, 1989); and "Democratic Consolidation and the Military in Southern Europe and Latin America" (paper presented at the Social Science Re-

search Council [SSRC] conference, "The Politics of Democratic Consolidation in Southern Europe," Rome, 14–15 December 1990). Przeworski first argued that the transitions' "final destination depends on the path" but later concluded that the transitions' institutional traces "can be gradually wiped away." *Democracy and the Market,* 51 and 98. For a view that gives more emphasis to "the institutional legacies of the transitions themselves," see David Stark, "Path Dependence and Privatization Strategies in East-Central Europe," in *Changing Political Economies: Privatization in Post-Communist and Reforming Communist States,* ed. Vedat Milor (Boulder, Colo.: Lynne Rienner Publishers, 1993), 117 and 134–36.

22. See Nancy Bermeo, "Surprise, Surprise: Lessons from 1989 and 1991," in *Liberalization and Democratization: Change in the Soviet Union and Eastern Europe,* ed. Nancy Bermeo (Baltimore: Johns Hopkins University Press, 1992).

Chapter 2: Asserting Civilian Supremacy in Postauthoritarian Regimes

1. Robert Dahl, *Polyarchy: Participation and Opposition* (New Haven, Conn.: Yale University Press, 1971). See also Joseph A. Schumpeter, *Capitalism, Socialism and Democracy,* 3d ed. (New York: Harper and Row, 1975), 269; and Norberto Bobbio, *The Future of Democracy* (Minneapolis: University of Minnesota Press, 1987).

2. Robert A. Dahl, *Democracy and Its Critics* (New Haven, Conn.: Yale University Press, 1989), 221. See also Juan J. Linz, "Totalitarian and Authoritarian Regimes," in *Handbook of Political Science,* ed. Fred I. Greenstein and Nelson W. Polsby (Reading, Mass.: Addison-Wesley, 1975), 3:182–83.

3. The hierarchical and specialized nature of the military institution makes it impossible for military officers in active duty to run for office. Only in noted exceptions has the election of an active-duty military officer to the highest office in free, competitive elections been tolerated. Such was the case in Portugal during the presidency of General Eanes, in a formula conceived, paradoxically, to facilitate the subordination of the military to democratic executive power.

4. Fortunately, many scholars concerned with issues of democratization have recently made explicit connections between notions of democracy, the power of civilian officials, and civilian control over defense and military issues. See, for instance, J. Samuel Fitch, "Toward a Democratic Model of Civil-Military Relations for Latin America" (paper presented to the International Political Science Association, Washington, D.C., 31 August 1988). Robert Dahl added to his previous formulations that "civilian control over the military and police is a necessary condition for polyarchy" (*Democracy and Its Critics,* 250). See also Philippe C. Schmitter and Terry L. Karl, "What Democracy Is . . . and Is Not," in *The Global Resurgence of Democracy,* ed. Larry Diamond and Marc F. Plattner (Baltimore: Johns Hopkins University Press, 1993).

5. Huntington, *Soldier and the State,* 84.

6. Ibid., 83–84.

7. Ibid.

8. J. Samuel Fitch rightly noted that "internal autonomy may indicate a lack of political interference in promotions and assignments, but often implies the abdica-

tion of civilian responsibility for military policy, particularly for changes in military institutions necessary for the long term stability of a democratic model of civil-military relations" ("Toward a Democratic Model").

9. With different emphases this view is found in Bengt Abrahamsson, *Military Professionalization and Political Power* (Beverly Hills, Calif.: Sage Publications, 1972); Samuel Finer, *The Man on the Horseback: The Role of the Military in Politics* (New York: Praeger, 1962); Amos Perlmutter, *The Military and Politics in Modern Times* (New Haven, Conn.: Yale University Press, 1977); Alfred Stepan, "The New Professionalism of Internal Warfare and Military Role Expansion," in *Authoritarian Brazil,* ed. Alfred Stepan (New Haven, Conn.: Yale University Press, 1973); and Guillermo O'Donnell, "Modernization and Military Coups: Theory, Comparisons and the Argentine Case," in *Armies and Politics in Latin America,* ed. Abraham F. Lowenthal and J. Samuel Fitch, rev. ed. (New York: Holmes and Meier, 1986).

10. Timothy J. Colton, *Commisars, Commanders and Civilian Authority: The Structure of Soviet Military Politics* (Cambridge: Harvard University Press, 1979), 233. See also Claude E. Welch, Jr., *No Farewell to Arms?* (Boulder, Colo.: Westview Press, 1987), 13.

11. During the presidency of Jose Sarney (1985–90), the military held a large number of cabinet positions, maintained significant influence in shaping or constraining government projects, remained in control of state intelligence agencies, and influenced the workings of the Constitutional Assembly (Stepan, *Rethinking Military Politics*). See also Eliézer Rizzo de Oliveira, "Constituinte, Forças Armadas e Autonomia Militar," in *As Forças Armadas No Brasil,* ed. Eliézer Rizzo de Oliveira et al. (Rio de Janeiro: Editora Espaço e Tempo, 1987); and Jorge Zaverucha, "The Degree of Military Political Autonomy during the Spanish, Argentine and Brazilian transitions," *Journal of Latin American Studies* 25 (1993): 283–99.

12. Citing the realm of education, Colton exemplified these categories in the following way: "The determination of the overall objectives of the education system would be a *societal* issue; the treatment of military themes in civilian curricula an *intermediate* issue; the nature of officer training an *institutional* issue; and the fixing of responsibility for, say, poor performance by the graduates of a naval school an *internal* issue" (*Commisars, Commanders and Civilian Authority,* 233; my emphases).

13. For the notion of prerogatives, see Stepan, *Rethinking Military Politics,* 93 and 100.

14. Useful in this regard is the development of normative models of democratic civil-military relations which offer various forms of civilian oversight of defense and military policy. These models are a necessary "benchmark for measuring the progress toward a stable democratic system of civil-military relations," in the absence of which "virtually any set of relationships — short of direct military rule — [may] be rationalized as democratic or at least compatible with democracy" (Fitch, "Toward a Democratic Model").

15. Although civilian supremacy may also develop along with authoritarian rule, this definition is offered for a study of civilian supremacy as part of democratization. Authoritarian regimes, founded with high levels of military participation, may give way to "civilianization" as a mechanism for institutionalizing authoritarian rule. The second half of the Franquist regime and Hitler's Nazi regime are examples of civilianized authoritarianism. For the case of Hitler's regime, see Amos Perlmutter, *The Military and Politics in Modern Times* (New Haven, Conn.: Yale University Press,

1977). For the consideration of civilianization as part of authoritarian institutionalization, see Alain Rouquié, "Demilitarization and the Institutionalization of Military-Dominated Polities in Latin America," in *Transitions from Authoritarian Rule: Comparative Perspectives,* ed. Guillermo O'Donnell, Philippe C. Schmitter, and Laurence Whitehead (Baltimore: Johns Hopkins University Press, 1986); Samuel Finer, "The Retreat to the Barracks: Notes on the Practice and the Theory of Military Withdrawal from the Seats of Power," *Third World Quarterly* 7, no. 1 (1985); and Linz, "Totalitarian and Authoritarian Regimes."

16. My definition is in line with previous formulations by Claude E. Welch and J. Samuel Fitch. See Claude E. Welch, "Civilian Control of the Military: Myth and Reality," in *Civilian Control of the Military,* ed. Claude E. Welch (Albany: State University of New York Press, 1976); and J. Samuel Fitch, "The Theoretical Model Underlying the Analysis of Civil-Military Relations in Contemporary Latin American Democracies: Core Assumptions," Inter-American Dialogue, 1987.

17. Civilian leadership should entail more than merely suppressing military discontent or narrowing its prerogatives. As Morris Janowitz put it, "The task of civilian leadership includes not only the political direction of the military, but the prevention of the growth of frustration in the profession, of felt injustice, and inflexibility under the weight of its responsibilities" (*The Professional Soldier* [New York: The Free Press, 1971], lviii).

18. Huntington, *Soldier and the State,* 86–88.

19. Welch, *No Farewell to Arms,* 13.

20. For instance, Finer, *Man on the Horseback.*

21. This has practical implications. Democratic reformers often devise policies based on the desire to make the views and ideologies of the military more democratic. This may be an unnecessarily strenuous effort, and often a counterproductive one. If the military adhered to democracy at the outset of the transitions, democratization or civilian supremacy would be much less of a problem than it actually is. Yet transitions have succeeded without the military becoming committed to democratic values overnight.

22. Welch, for example, defined "long-term military disengagement from politics" as "a minimum period of ten years during which at least one successful regular executive transition has occurred" (*No Farewell to Arms,* 20).

23. Civilian supremacy in emerging democratic regimes should be approached differently than in long-consolidated democracies. When, for instance, there is evidence of a surge in military influence in consolidated democracies, regime stability is not threatened in any real way, whereas similar evidence has greater repercussions for civilian efforts in new democracies. Differences over NATO or related policies, for instance, have often been voiced by top-ranking military officers in countries such as France, Germany, and the Netherlands. This voicing of dissenting views does not threaten or question the routine practice of civilian supremacy in consolidated democracies. Similar events, however, would be seen as a drawback in the effort to assert civilian control in a new democracy. As a result, much less freedom to voice different views may be granted in these cases. For a recent commentary on the muteness forced on the Spanish army, see Jesús Ignacio Martínez Paricio, "Defensa Nacional y Militares en el Umbral del Nuevo Siglo," in *España a debate: La política,* ed. José Vidal Beneyto (Madrid: Editorial Tecnos, 1991), III.

24. For a view of consolidation which emphasizes actual compliance with democratic procedures by all politically significant groups, see Richard Gunther, Hans-Jürgen Puhle, and Nikiforos Diamandouros, "Introduction: The Politics of Democratic Consolidation," in *The Politics of Democratic Consolidation in Southern Europe,* ed. Richard Gunther et al. (Baltimore: Johns Hopkins University Press, 1995). Other views of consolidation emphasize the extension of democratic procedures to all significant political domains, with no groups controlling outcomes ex post. See Juan J. Linz and Alfred Stepan, *Problems of Democratic Transitions and Consolidation: Eastern Europe, Southern Europe and South America* (forthcoming); J. Samuel Valenzuela, "Democratic Consolidation in Post-Transitional Settings: Notion, Process and Facilitating Conditions"; and Guillermo O'Donnell, "Transitions, Continuities and Paradoxes," both in *Issues in Democratic Consolidation: The New South American Democracies in Comparative Perspective,* ed. Scott Mainwaring, Guillermo O'Donnell, and J. Samuel Valenzuela (Notre Dame, Ind.: University of Notre Dame Press, 1992); and Adam Przeworski, *Democracy and the Market: Political and Economic Reforms in Eastern Europe and Latin America* (Cambridge: Cambridge University Press, 1991). Still other notions underscored regularity of interactions, group and regime structuration, and rule formalization. See Philippe C. Schmitter, "The Consolidation of Political Democracy in Southern Europe and Latin America," MS, 3d rev. ed., June 1988. For a minimalist view, see Giuseppe Di Palma, *To Craft Democracies* (Berkeley: University of California Press, 1990), 138–44. However, these views either fail to specify the military dimension, or they provide elements and criteria that simply do not apply or are misleading when applied to the military, although most would agree that this dimension is critical for consolidation, and even "the neuralgic point of democratic consolidation" (Przeworski, *Democracy and the Market,* 29). See also Leonardo Morlino, "Consolidación Democrática: Definición, Modelos, Hipótesis," *Revista Española de Investigaciones Sociológicas* 35 (July–September 1986). Stepan, however, does highlight "the military dimensions to the obstacles to democratic consolidation" and the major issues involved in "articulated military contestation," which inform many of the concepts I develop here. See Stepan, *Rethinking Military Politics,* xiv.

25. In some cases it also includes a militarized police, such as Spain's Civil Guard, Venezuela's Armed Forces of Cooperation, or Chile's Carabineros.

26. We are speaking here of modern professional armies, that is, complex bureaucratic organizations staffed by an officer corps that has expertise in the organization and direction of military forces; maintains a unified training and educational system; and develops a strong sense of corporate identity among its members. See Samuel P. Huntington, *The Soldier and the State* (New York: Vintage Books, 1957), 7–18; and Morris Janowitz, *The Professional Soldier* (New York: The Free Press, 1971), xlviii–liii.

27. With the exception of cases in which the defense ministry, or any equivalent government agency, is placed under the direction of military officers whose policies respond more to the armed forces' orientations than to those of elected representatives.

28. Colton warned that use of the dualistic civil-military category risks ignoring internal differentiation as well as cross-institutional connections and alliances (*Commisars, Commanders and Civilian Authority,* 232–33). Amos Perlmutter argued for "a fusion

model" focused "on the power of the fused military and civilian bureaucracies and their relationship" ("The Military and Politics in Modern Times: A Decade Later," *Journal of Strategic Studies* 9, no. 1 [March 1986]: 6-7). Such a focus may be appropriate for the study of stable regimes, not necessarily democratic, in countries with a large defense sector and a large defense industry.

29. Perlmutter, *Military and Politics in Modern Times,* 2.

30. The terms *political groups* and *civilian groups* refer to conglomerates of influential elites which share political interests and converge in the formulation of strategies for political action. These groups are typical in transition periods, in which more permanent alignments and partisan formations are not yet in place.

31. This is a critical condition for any attempts to promote civilian supremacy. The cases addressed in this study comply with it, with the partial exception of Portugal, where Left-leaning civilian and military groups initially sought to remain in power after the ousting of Caetano's regime. In Brazil formerly authoritarian elites, which remained in power, benefited from the influence that the military exerted in the first successor civilian government but did not overtly favor a military takeover. In Chile elites on the Right who participated in Pinochet's regime supported the military's enhanced constitutional powers during the successor democratic government but did not encourage military contestation. In Spain ETA sought to provoke military intervention in order to ripen conditions for its armed struggle, but it remained a small, minority, regionally based group. Violent opposition by small groups may foster greater cohesion among major groups around the support for democracy — as was the case, for instance, in Venezuela during Betancourt's period. See Felipe Agüero, "The Military and Democracy in Venezuela," in *The Military and Democracy: The Future of Civil-Military Relations in Latin America,* ed. Louis W. Goodman, Johanna S. R. Mendelson, and Juan Rial (Lexington, Mass.: D. C. Heath / Lexington Books, 1990).

32. For reequilibration, see Juan J. Linz, *Crisis, Breakdown and Reequilibration* (Baltimore: Johns Hopkins University Press, 1978); and Adam Przeworski, "Democracy as a Contingent Outcome of Conflicts," in *Constitutionalism and Democracy,* ed. Jon Elster and Rune Slagstad (Cambridge: Cambridge University Press, 1988), 63.

33. For a reference to a "military ceiling" in Spain — "techo militar a las reformas" — see Enrique Gomáriz, "Los Militares ante la Transición," *Zona Abierta* (Madrid), nos. 18-19 (1979).

34. Przeworski, *Democracy and the Market,* 13 and 14. See also Dankwart Rustow, "Transitions to Democracy: Towards a Dynamic Model," *Comparative Politics* 2, no. 3 (April 1970).

35. Przeworski, *Democracy and the Market,* 19. For an emphasis on guarantees provided in democratic arrangements, see Juan J. Linz and Alfred Stepan, "Political Crafting of Democratic Consolidation or Destruction: European and South American Comparisons," in *Democracy in the Americas: The Swing of the Pendulum,* ed. Robert A. Pastor (New York: Holmes and Meier, 1989), 47; Guillermo O'Donnell and Philippe C. Schmitter, *Transitions from Authoritarian Rule: Tentative Conclusions about Uncertain Democracies* (Baltimore: Johns Hopkins University Press, 1986), 67; Giuseppe Di Palma, "Government Performance: An Issue and Three Cases in Search of Theory," *West European Politics* 7, no. 3 (1984).

36. We assume that these actors behave rationally—that is, they can identify goals perceived to maximize their interests and can select from various courses of action that which is deemed best to achieve those goals—within a set of constraints and opportunities.

37. Albert Hirschman, *Exit, Voice and Loyalty: Responses to Decline in Firms, Organizations and States* (Cambridge: Harvard University Press, 1970). O'Donnell and Schmitter pointed to the role of "playing coup poker [with] the coup that doesn't happen" (O'Donnell and Schmitter, *Transitions from Authoritarian Rule,* 23–24).

38. Martin C. Needler, "The Military Withdrawal from Power in South America," *Armed Forces and Society* 6, no. 4 (1980): 622; Needler, "Military Motivations in the Seizure of Power," *Latin American Research Review* 10, no. 3 (1975); Finer, "Retreat to the Barracks," 23–29.

39. See, for instance, Theodore Wyckoff, "The Role of the Military in Latin American Politics," *Western Political Quarterly* 13, no. 3 (1960); Gino Germani and Kalman Silvert, "Politics, Social Structure and Military Intervention in Latin America," *Archives Europeenes de Sociologie* 2, no. 1 (1961); Lyle McAlister, "Recent Research and Writing on the Role of the Military in Latin America," *Latin American Research Review* (Fall 1966); John J. Johnson, ed., *The Role of the Military in the Underdeveloped Countries* (Princeton, N.J.: Princeton University Press, 1962); and Gwyn Harries-Jenkins and Jacques van Doorn, eds., *The Military and the Problem of Legitimacy* (Beverly Hills, Calif.: Sage Publications, 1976).

40. Abraham F. Lowenthal, "Armies and Politics in Latin America," in Lowenthal and Fitch, *Armies and Politics,* 19. See also Perlmutter, *Military and Politics in Modern Times.* Remarkable exceptions to the flaws of this model are O'Donnell, "Modernization and Military Coups"; Alfred Stepan, *The Military in Politics. Changing Patterns in Brazil* (Princeton, N.J.: Princeton University Press, 1971); and J. Samuel Fitch, *The Military Coup d'Etat as a Political Process: Ecuador, 1948–1966* (Baltimore: Johns Hopkins University Press, 1977). For an excellent review of this literature, see Arturo Valenzuela, "The Military and Social Science Theory," *Third World Quarterly* 7, no. 1 (1985).

41. The model, however, does not elucidate the problem of measuring strength or weakness in civilian institutions nor the political strength or weakness of military institutions. Often, it was affirmed ex post, tautologically, that civilian structures must have been weak if the military intervened and took over. On the other hand, in periods of democratization some civilian institutions may strengthen at the expense of others, complicating the problem of measuring their overall strength. For instance, the effort of building a democratic regime may weaken party structures, a critical civilian institution. See Richard Gunther, Giacomo Sani, and Goldie Shabad, *Spain after Franco: The Making of a Competitive Party System* (Berkeley: University of California Press, 1986), 396; and Richard Gunther, "Democratization and Party Building: The Role of Party Elites in the Spanish Transition," in *Spain in the 1980s,* ed. Robert P. Clark and Michael H. Haltzel (Cambridge, Mass.: Ballinger, 1987).

42. As Welch argued, "Whatever the causes for the assertion of civilian control, its maintenance over time endows political institutions with strength and legitimacy" ("Civilian Control of the Military," 27).

43. The importance of the extent of participation of the military in authoritarian regimes was highlighted early on, in Juan J. Linz, "An Authoritarian Regime:

Spain," in *Mass Politics,* ed. Erik Allardt and Stein Rokkan (New York: The Free Press, 1970), 317–19; and Juan J. Linz, "Totalitarian and Authoritarian Regimes," in *Handbook of Political Science,* vol. 3, ed. Fred Greenstein and Nelsom Polsby (Reading, Pa.: Addison-Wesley, 1975). The distinction between civilian and military influence in authoritarian regimes also was addressed in O'Donnell, Schmitter, and Whitehead, *Transitions from Authoritarian Rule;* and Guillermo O'Donnell, "Introduction to the Latin American Cases," in the same volume. Stepan argued that military-led transitions could be disaggregated into transitions led by the military-as-government or transitions led by the military-as-institution. Although these distinctions are useful in highlighting different military dynamics in the transition, the basic contrast to be emphasized here is that between military-led and civilian-led transitions ("Paths toward Democratization: Theoretical and Comparative Considerations," in O'Donnell, Schmitter, and Whitehead, *Transitions from Authoritarian Rule: Comparative Perspectives.*

44. An early discussion of different transition paths is found in Philippe C. Schmitter, "Speculations about the Prospective Demise of Authoritarian Regimes and Its Possible Consequences," *Revista de Ciencia Política* (Lisbon), nos. 1–2 (1985); and Stepan, "Paths toward Redemocratization."

45. This was also the case in Venezuela (1958–59), although civilian participation in the coup against dictator Pérez Jiménez was far greater than it was in the coup that ousted Caetano in Portugal.

46. In the period that preceded the 1966 coup in Argentina, the military succeeded in achieving cohesion and professionalization, which, according to O'Donnell, resulted in a feeling of organizational accomplishment which led the military to believe it "possessed superior capacity to confront the social problems which the civil authorities evidently could not solve." The military empowered itself with a "political utopia" that guided the attempt to restructure the social (national) context ("Modernization and Military Coups," 105, 120, and 121). From a different angle Fitch maintains that these conceptions are influenced by the prior importance of particular doctrines, or "role beliefs" ("Theoretical Model"). Depending on their pervasiveness and specific content, role beliefs operate as opportunities and as constraints for military action.

47. For a discussion of disloyal, semiloyal, and loyal opposition, see Juan J. Linz, *The Breakdown of Democratic Regimes: Crisis Breakdown and Reequilibration* (Baltimore: Johns Hopkins University Press, 1978), 27–38.

48. Charles Gillespie, "Uruguay's Transition from Collegial Military-Technocratic Rule," in O'Donnell, Schmitter, and Whitehead, *Transitions from Authoritarian Rule: Latin America.* In Italy, much earlier, as in Spain, a broad spectrum of forces coalesced after the "svolta di Salerno," which led to the collaboration of all parties with the monarchy (Giuseppe Di Palma, "Italy: Is There a Legacy and Is It Fascist?" in *From Dictatorship to Democracy,* ed. John H. Herz [Westport, Conn.: Greenwood Press, 1982]); and Gianfranco Pasquino, "The Demise of the First Fascist Regime and Italy's Transition to Democracy: 1943–1948," in O'Donnell, Schmitter, and Whitehead, *Transition from Authoritarian Rule: Southern Europe).*

49. Good examples are: Adolfo Suárez's early announcement of a timetable for the series of referendums and elections with which he garnered support for his plan of political reform in Spain; the skillful use of referendums by General de Gaulle in

France, which gave his government the upper hand in dealing with military opposition on the Algerian question; President Alfonsín's submittal to referendum in Argentina of the sensitive Beagle territorial dispute with Chile, an action that helped remove a "national security" concern from exclusive military domains and which helped settle a question otherwise prone to military utilization.

50. Philippe C. Schmitter, "An Introduction to Southern European Transitions," in O'Donnell, Schmitter, and Whitehead, *Transitions from Authoritarian Rule: Southern Europe,* 5. See also Guillermo O'Donnell, "The United States, Latin America, Democracy: Variations on a Very Old Theme," in *The United States and Latin America in the 1980s,* ed. Kevin J. Middlebrook and Carlos Rico (Pittsburgh: University of Pittsburgh Press, 1986); and Abraham F. Lowenthal, ed., *Exporting Democracy: The United States and Latin America* (Baltimore: Johns Hopkins University Press, 1991).

51. Business and other elites sought to benefit from economic and military integration in European organizations that demanded democratization as condition for formal entry. This kind of international influence facilitated what Whitehead called "democratization through convergence" ("Democracy by Convergence and Southern Europe: A Comparative Politics Perspective," in *Encouraging Democracy: The International Context of Regime Transition in Southern Europe,* ed. Geoffrey Pridham [New York: St. Martin's Press, 1991]). Still, in Whitehead's earlier view the international setting "seldom intruded too conspicuously on an essentially domestic drama" ("International Aspects of Democratization," in O'Donnell, Schmitter, and Whitehead, *Transitions from Authoritarian Rule: Comparative Perspectives,* 5).

52. Felipe Agüero. "The Military and the Limits to Democratization in South America," in Mainwaring, O'Donnell, and Valenzuela, *Issues in Democratic Consolidation.*

53. For a discussion of this point, see Guillermo O'Donnell, "Transitions, Continuities and Paradoxes," in ibid.

54. David Pion-Berlin, "Between Confrontation and Accommodation: Military and Government Policy in Democratic Argentina," *Journal of Latin American Studies* 23 (October 1991): 543–71.

55. Alfred Tovias, "The International Context of Democratic Transition," in *The New Mediterranean Democracies: Regime Transition in Spain, Greece and Portugal,* ed. Geoffrey Pridham (London: Frank Cass, 1984); and José María Maravall, "Politics and Policy: Economic Reforms in Southern Europe," in *Economic Reforms in New Democracies: A Social-Democratic Approach,* ed. Luiz Carlos Bresser Pereira, José María Maravall, and Adam Przeworski (Cambridge: Cambridge University Press, 1993), 82. Maravall highlights a decline in GDP growth and a rise in inflation in Greece, Portugal, and Spain in the initial year of transition, compared to the situation in 1970.

56. Miguel A. Fernández Ordóñez and Luis Servén, "Reforma Económica en la Europa del Sur: El Caso de España," *Pensamiento Iberoamericano,* nos. 22–23 (1992–93): 211. GDP growth was 1.4 in 1978; – 0.1 in 1979; 1.2 in 1980; – 0.2 in 1981; and 1.2 in 1982.

57. During the critical transition years Brazil and Argentina had to devote more than half of their earnings from exports of goods and services to interest payments on the debt (United Nations, *Preliminary Overview of the Latin American Economy* [n.p: Economic Commission for Latin America, 1987]). With the exception of Colombia and Chile, all South American countries experienced negative average annual growth rates of their GDP per capita in the period 1981–90 (Paraguay's was zero) (*Economic*

and Social Progress in Latin America: 1992 Report [Washington, D.C.: Inter-American Development Bank, 1992]).

58. Linz and Stepan, "Political Crafting of Democratic Consolidation or Destruction." See also Guillermo de la Dehesa, "Enseñanzas de la transición económica española para los países de Europa central y oriental," *Pensamiento Iberoamericano,* nos. 22–23 (1992–93).

59. For the importance of the time factor, see Juan J. Linz, "Il Fattore Tempo nei Mutamenti di Regime," *Teoria Politica* 2, no. 1 (1986); and Juan J. Linz and Alfred Stepan, "Political Identities and Electoral Sequences: Spain, the Soviet Union and Yugoslavia," *Daedalus* 121, no. 2 (Spring 1992).

60. Inaction also may be costly in the long run because it leads to erosion of popular support for these civilian groups and to the institutionalized fixation of excessive prerogatives for the military.

Chapter 3: Transition and Militarization

1. Guillermo O'Donnell, Philippe C. Schmitter, and Laurence Whitehead, eds., *Transitions from Authoritarian Rule: Latin America* (Baltimore: Johns Hopkins University Press, 1986), 34; and Guillermo O'Donnell, "Introduction to the Latin American Cases," in the same volume, 10–11.

2. For instance, the self-granted amnesty by the Argentine military prior to the elections of 1983 and the passage of the Mobilization Law by the Peruvian military government only days prior to the transfer of power to an elected civilian president in 1980. See Andrés Fontana, *Fuerzas Armadas, Partidos Políticos y Transición a la Democracia en Argentina* (Buenos Aires: CEDES, 1984).

3. As head of state, Franco was entitled to preside over the meetings of the council if he so wished. For a vivid narration of Franco's chair of cabinet meetings only a month before his death, see Juan Pablo Fusi, *Franco: A Biography* (New York: Harper and Row, 1987), 168.

4. See Article 10 of the Law of Juridical Procedure of the Administration of the State (26 July 1957), in Rafael Entrena Cuesta, "El Texto Refundido de la Ley de Régimen Jurídico de la Administración del Estado de 26 de Julio de 1957," *Revista de Administración Pública,* no. 24 (September–December 1957). See also Kenneth N. Medhurst, *Government in Spain* (Oxford: Pergamon Press, 1973). The minister of the Interior appointed civil governors for each province and mayors for every city with a population over ten thousand. The rest of the mayors were designated by the respective civil governor. See Richard Gunther, *Public Policy in a No-Party State* (Berkeley: University of California Press, 1980), 35.

5. In Greece the military occupied nearly 40 percent of the cabinet positions halfway through the colonels' regime in August 1971. Twelve out of 18 ministers in the cabinet of July 1972 were military officers, although they had resigned their commissions. Eleven out of 24 undersecretaries were assigned to officers from the military (*Keesings Contemporary Archives*).

6. Constitutive Law of the Cortes (1942, amended 1967), *Fundamental Laws of the State: The Spanish Constitution* (Madrid: Ministry of Information and Tourism, 1972), 100.

7. Stanley G. Payne, *The Franco Regime: 1936–1975* (Madison: University of Wisconsin Press, 1987), 614.

8. See Article 2 of the Constitutive Law of the Cortes, *Fundamental Laws of the State: The Spanish Constitution*, 102.

9. Such was the case, for instance, of Lieutenant General Angel Campano, a *procurador* and captain general of Madrid.

10. See the Organic Law of the State, in *Fundamental Laws of the State: The Spanish Constitution*. Hereafter I will refer to the Organic Law of the State by its Spanish acronym, LOE (Ley Orgánica del Estado).

11. See LOE (1967) and the Law of Succession in the Headship of State (1947, amended 1967), in *Fundamental Laws of the State: The Spanish Constitution;* and Luis García Arias, "Las Fuerzas Armadas en la Ley Orgánica del Estado," in *Revista de Estudios Políticos*, no. 152 (March–April 1967): 153.

12. See Article 43 of LOE (87) and the Law on the Principles of the National Movement (May 1958), in *Fundamental Laws of the State*, 44, 45, and 46.

13. See Articles 21 and 22 of the LOE, in *Fundamental Laws of the State*, 78–79.

14. Three military officers still were civil governors in 1977. See Julio Busquets, *El Militar de Carrera en España* (Barcelona: Ariel, 1984), 270; and Manuel Ballbé, *Orden Público y Militarismo en la España Constitucional (1812–1983)* (Madrid: Alianza Editorial, 1985), 444.

15. An example is the army journal *Ejército*, which, although it did not officially express the views of the highest army organs, was entirely staffed by army officers and edited by the brigadier general in charge of the Publishing Division of the General Staff. A study conducted on this journal indicated that nearly 12 percent of the articles published in the period 1975–77 were political in nature. See José Antonio Olmeda, *Las Fuerzas Armadas en el Estado Franquista* (Madrid: Ediciones El Arquero, 1988), 332.

16. The *alféreces provisionales* were recruited into the army during the civil war, after a very short training period. Some underwent further training after the war and remained in the army, reaching the top positions. Most of them, inside or outside the army, became strong sources of support for franquism. The term *crusade* referred to the victor mobilization that crushed the republicans in the civil war. See Stanley G. Payne, *Politics and the Military in Modern Spain* (Stanford: Stanford University Press, 1967), 388, 390, 421, and 519. See also Julio Busquets, "Los Alféreces Provisionales Hasta la Creación de la Hermandad (1936–1958)," in *Historia 16* II, no. 119 (March 1986).

17. See the Organic Law of the Civil Guard (15 March 1940) and the Organic Law of the Armed Police (8 March 1941). The Civil Guard also had a General Staff formed by army generals, and many other upper-level positions were filled with army officers. See Diego López Garrido, *El Aparato Policial en España* (Barcelona: Ariel, 1987), 14. Military roles in the maintenance of public order were expanded in 1969 with the Basic Law for National Mobilization, which permitted the subjection of civilians to military authority under special circumstances. On this basis the government placed striking subway workers in Madrid under military jurisdiction in 1970. In January 1976, shortly after Franco's death, a similar procedure was used against postal service and railroad workers. See M. G. García, "The Armed Forces:

Poor Relation of the Franco Regime," in *Spain in Crisis*, ed. Paul Preston (Sussex: Harvester Press, 1976), 30; and Ballbé, *Orden Público y Militarismo*, 455.

18. See José Ignacio San Martín, *Servicio Especial* (Barcelona: Editorial Planeta, 1983). Colonel San Martín was director of SECED (Central Documentation Service), which gathered intelligence for the presidency and the Supreme Staff. See also Jesús Ynfante, *El Ejército de Franco y de Juan Carlos* (Chatillon-sous-Bagneux: Ruedo Ibérico, 1976).

19. See Ballbé, *Orden Público y Militarismo*, 409–49; and Antonio Millán's prologue to *Competencia y Organización de la Jurisdicción Militar* (Madrid: Tecnos, 1987). In 1974 and 1975 military courts tried civilians in 305 cases involving resistance, disobedience or offenses to the armed forces, or crimes against state security (Julio Busquets, "La Justicia Militar ante la Unidad de Jurisdicciones," *Diario* (Madrid) 16 (11 August 1977).

20. The Supreme Staff initially participated in steering programs of the Instituto Nacional de Industrias toward the satisfaction of defense needs, although with no great success. See García, "Armed Forces," 28. Over four hundred individuals from the military were appointed by decree in political posts outside the defense area in the period 1939–73 (12 percent of all those appointed in this way). See "Las Fuerza Armada en España: Institucionalización y Proceso de Cambio (1939–1975)," in *La Institución Militar en el Estado Contemperáneo*, ed. Rafel Bañón and José Antonio Olmeda (Madrid: Alianza Editorial, 1985), 308–14; and Olmeda, *Las Fuerzas Armadas,* 362–66.

21. It certainly was much larger than in Portugal. Marcelo Caetano's last defense minister, for instance, was a civilian. For Portugal, see Maria Carrilho, *Forcas Armadas e Mudanca Politica em Portugal no Sec. XX* (Lisbon: Imprensa Nacional, Estudos Gerais, Serie Universitaria, 1985); Tom Gallagher, *Portugal: A Twentieth-Century Interpretation* (Manchester: Manchester University Press, 1983); Philippe C. Schmitter, *Corporatism and Public Policy in Authoritarian Portugal* (London: Sage Publications, 1975); Schmitter, "Liberation by Golpe: Retrospective Thoughts on the Demise of Authoritarian Rule in Portugal," *Armed Forces and Society* 2, no. 1 (1975); and Schmitter, "The 'Regime d'Exception' That Became the Rule: Forty-Eight Years of Authoritarian Domination in Portugal," in *Contemporary Portugal: The Revolution and Its Antecedents*, ed. Lawrence S. Graham and Harry M. Makler (Austin: University of Texas Press, 1979).

22. Carrero never moved to the special "non-activity situation" that was required of officers in political assignments. See Carlos Fernández, *El Almirante Carrero* (Barcelona: Plaza y Janés, 1985), 258.

23. See Ballbé, *Orden Público y Militarismo*, 418–19.

24. See Juan J. Linz, "An Authoritarian Regime: Spain," in *Mass Politics*, ed. Erik Allardt and Stein Rokkan (New York: Free Press, 1970); and Linz, "Totalitarian and Authoritarian Regimes," in *Handbook of Political Science*, vol. 3, ed. Fred I. Greenstein and Nelson W. Polsby (Reading, Mass.: Addison-Wesley, 1975). See also C. Viver Pi-Sunyer, *El Personal Político de Franco (1936–1945)* (Barcelona: Editorial Vicens-Vives, 1978); Julio Busquets, *El Militar de Carrera en España* (Barcelona: Editorial Ariel, 1984); Amando de Miguel, *Sociología del Franquismo* (Barcelona: Editorial Euros, 1975); Miguel Jerez Mir, *Elites Políticas y Centros de Extracción en España* (Madrid: Centro de Investigaciones Sociológicas, 1982); José Antonio Olmeda Gómez, "The Armed Forces in the Francoist Political System," in *Armed Forces and Society in Spain: Past and Present*, ed. Rafael Bañón and Thomas M. Barker (New York: Columbia University

Press, 1988); Miguel Angel Aguilar, *Las Ultimas Cortes del Franquismo* (Barcelona: Editorial Avance, 1976).

25. Payne, *Franco Regime,* 107–19.

26. The law established that resolutions by the chief of state were to be subjected to prior deliberation of the Council of Government. The Council of Ministers became in this way the core power nucleus in the Franquist state. For references to this law, see ibid., 180.

27. See Law of Succession in the Headship of State, in *Fundamental Laws of the State.* Franco's concentration of power vis-à-vis the military was aided by the creation of the Movement, which automatically included the military, under Franco's perennial leadership. Another factor was the availability of a vast, however vastly purged, cadre of state functionaries, on which Franco relied for recruitment of political personnel. See Pi-Sunyer, *El Personal Político de Franco,* 72–73. On the other hand, however, the army in Spain was important in preventing the development of separate armed militias like the organizations that developed in Nazi Germany or in Fascist Italy. See Stanley G. Payne, *Falange: A History of Spanish Fascism* (Stanford: Stanford University Press, 1961).

28. Taken from Payne, *Politics and the Military,* 433–34.

29. The formal significance of the military's participation in the Council of Ministers became apparent during this episode. As then minister of the army, Lieutenant General Félix Alvarez-Arenas y Pacheco admitted: "You should not forget that all members of the government are co-responsible [*solidariamente responsables*] for decisions made in the Council of Ministers." See María Mérida, *Mis Conversaciones con los Generales,* 3d ed. (Barcelona: Plaza y Janés Editores, 1980), 49. This participation, in fact, helped to arouse the military's institutional response.

30. The military's constitutional role of defending the institutional order could not be activated autonomously, without leadership from the head of state. Other mechanisms of defense of the institutional order, specified in the appeal of *contrafuero,* assigned special roles to the National Council of the Movement, the Standing Committee of the Cortes, and the Council of the Realm (Title X of the LOE). See Luis García Arias, "Las Fuerzas Armadas en la Ley Orgánica del Estado"; and Diego Sevilla Andrés, "La Defensa de la Constitución en la Ley Orgánica Española," both in *Revista de Estudios Políticos,* no. 152 (March–April 1967).

31. However, the concept of bureaucratic authoritarianism as put forth by O'Donnell, which highlights an active government role for the military as institution and civilian technocrats, may in fact encompass either civilianized or militarized regimes. See Guillermo O'Donnell, *Modernization and Bureaucratic-Authoritarianism: Studies in South American Politics* (Berkeley: Institute of International Studies, University of California, 1973); and *Bureaucratic Authoritarianism: Argentina 1966–1973 in Comparative Perspective* (Berkeley: University of California Press, 1988). See also David Collier, ed., *The New Authoritarianism in Latin America* (Princeton, N.J.: Princeton University Press, 1979).

32. The *Proceso,* as this period (1976–83) was called, differed in this regard from the previous dictatorship (1966–73), in which its first president, General Onganía, retired from active duty and appointed civilians to all cabinet positions, requesting independence from the military to govern. He, nonetheless, succumbed to military

pressure and was replaced by General Levingston and, later, by General Lanusse. During the *Proceso* a succession of military juntas and of presidents revealed that the top chiefs were also accountable to their respective council of generals or admirals. See Daniel García Delgado and Marcelo Stiletano, "La Participación de los Militares en los Nuevos Autoritarismos: La Argentina del 'Proceso' (1976–1983)," *Opciones,* no. 14 (May–August 1988); and Felipe Agüero, "La Constitución y las Fuerzas Armadas en Algunos Países de América del Sur y España," *Revista de Ciencia Política* (Santiago) 7, nos. 1–2 (1986). A distinct feature of the Argentine *Proceso* also was the extent to which the regular structure of the armed forces was employed in the extermination of opponents. See Paul G. Buchanan, "The Varied Faces of Domination: State Terror, Economic Policy, and Social Rupture during the Argentine 'Proceso,' 1976–81," *American Journal of Political Science* 31, no. 2 (May 1987).

33. See Juan Rial, *Las Fuerzas Armadas en los años 90* (Montevideo: Peitho, 1990).

34. See Julio Cotler, "Military Interventions and 'Transfer of Power to Civilians' in Peru," in *Transitions from Authoritarian Rule: Latin America,* ed. Guillermo O'Donnell, Philippe C. Schmitter, and Laurence Whitehead (Baltimore: Johns Hopkins University Press, 1986); and Peter S. Cleaves and Henry Paese García, "State Autonomy and Military Policy Making," in *The Peruvian Experiment Reconsidered,* ed. Cynthia McClintock and Abraham F. Lowenthal (Princeton, N.J.: Princeton University Press, 1983).

35. See Stepan, *Rethinking Military Politics.*

36. In 1983 all the president's advisory committees were merged under the post of minister secretary-general of the presidency. See Carlos Huneeus and Jorge Olave, "La Participación de los Militares en los Nuevos Autoritarismos: Chile en una Perspectiva Comparada," *Opciones* (Santiago), no. 11 (1987); and Carlos Huneeus, "El Ejército y la Política en el Chile de Pinochet: Su Magnitud y Alcances," *Opciones,* no. 14 (1988). See also Genaro Arriagada, *Pinochet: The Politics of Power* (Boston: Unwin and Hyman, 1988); Augusto Varas, *Los Militares en el Poder: Régimen y Gobierno Militar en Chile, 1973–1986* (Santiago: FLACSO and Pehuén Editores, 1987); Karen L. Remmer, "Neopatrimonialism: The Politics of Military Rule in Chile, 1973–1987," *Comparative Politics* (January 1989); and Felipe Agüero, "La Autonomía de las Fuerzas Armadas," in *Chile en el Umbral de los Noventa,* ed. Jaime Gazmuri (Santiago: Editorial Planeta, Espejo de Chile, 1988).

37. After a new constitution was promulgated in 1980 the junta retained the power to initiate constitutional reforms, but these would have to be approved in referendum. Regarding the appointment of the president, the junta designated its own president—General Pinochet—officially to the post of president of the republic and supreme chief of the nation in 1974. The referendum of 1980 on the Constitution prolonged Pinochet's mandate until 1990. For the presidential plebiscite that the Constitution prescribed for 1989, the junta had to nominate a single candidate. Pinochet, the junta's nominee, was defeated in the referendum of October 1988, opening the way for competitive elections in December 1989 and the inauguration of a civilian government in March 1990.

38. See Harry J. Psomiades, "Greece: From the Colonels' Rule to Democracy," in *From Dictatorship to Democracy,* ed. John H. Herz (Westport, Conn.: Greenwood Press, 1982).

39. See Aldo Vacs, "Authoritarian Breakdown and Redemocratization in Argentina," in *Authoritarians and Democrats: Regime Transition in Latin America,* ed. James M. Malloy and Mitchell A. Seligson (Pittsburgh: University of Pittsburgh Press, 1987).

40. If the coup overthrows a previously militarized regime, the strength of the new military clique will be largely determined by its ability to garner institutional unity around its tenets. Lack of cohesion will weaken the military's position. Whether alternative civilian elites benefit or not from these developments depends, among other factors, on their own leadership structure and coalescence and their ability to demonstrate public support.

41. The 1958–59 democratic transition in Venezuela also originated from a military coup against a military dictator. The dictatorship here was less civilianized than Portugal's, however, and the ruling junta that temporarily took over included an influential civilian presence at the outset. See Felipe Agüero, "The Military and Democracy in Venezuela," in *The Military and Democracy: The Future of Civil-Military Relations in Latin America,* ed. Louis W. Goodman, Johanna S. R. Mendelson, and Juan Rial (Lexington, Mass.: Lexington / D. C. Heath, 1990).

42. For a description of factional splits in the Portuguese military leadership prior to Caetano's overthrow, see Schmitter, "Liberation by Golpe," 24–25; and Lawrence S. Graham, "The Military in Politics: The Politicization of the Portuguese Armed Forces," in *Contemporary Portugal: The Revolution and its Antecedents,* ed. Lawrence S. Graham and Harry M. Makler (Austin: University of Texas Press, 1979).

43. In Uruguay these conditions were formalized in the "Club Naval" pact; in Peru, in military mobilization laws; in Brazil, in dealings by the president-elect Tancredo Neves and by the appointment of six military chiefs in the cabinet; in Chile, in agreements to special requirements for the modification of the constitutional clauses dealing with the military and by consenting to a future role for Pinochet. For the case of Peru, see Víctor Villanueva, "Peru's 'New' Military Professionalism: The Failure of the Technocratic Approach," in *Post-Revolutionary Peru: The Politics of Transformation,* ed. Stephen M. Gorman (Boulder, Colo.: Westview Press, 1982).

44. See Edward Malefakis, "Spain and Its Francoist Heritage," in *From Dictatorship to Democracy,* ed. John H. Herz (Westport, Conn.: Greenwood Press, 1982).

45. It must be noted, however, that the military also relied on its belief that it instilled enough fear among the civilian elites and population so as to deter any attempt at radical changes that might trespass the limits of military tolerance, however unclear these might have been. The minister of the army maintained in 1976 that "it is possible that, inadvertently, the Army does indeed attain that goal [of acting like a moderating power] for the simple fact that it abides by the laws and our duties" (María Mérida, *Mis Conversaciones con los Generales,* 3d ed. [Barcelona: Plaza y Janés, 1980], 53). This view about the deterrent role of fear of the army was also expressed in interviews with Lieutenant General José María Sáenz de Tejada and Admiral Angel Liberal Lucini, Madrid, 24 September and 10 November 1987, respectively.

46. During the ceremony on the Act of Succession in the Zarzuela Palace, attended by high military chiefs, Juan Carlos wore the uniform of navy lieutenant. Hours later, before the Cortes, the Prince was dressed in the uniform of an army captain. See Fernando Rodrigo, "El Papel de las Fuerzas Armadas Españolas Durante la Transición Política: Algunas Hipótesis Básicas," *Revista Internacional de Sociología* 43, no. 2 (April–June 1985): 355.

47. See Mérida, *Mis Conversaciones*. Along similar symbolic lines Juan Carlos issued on 5 December 1975 a royal decree on the military's promotions lists, disposing that they be preceded, in perpetuity, by the line: "His excellency Don Francisco Franco Bahamonde, Generalissimo and Captain General of the Armies, followed by the phrase 'Caudillo of Spain.'" See Carlos Fernández, *Los Militares en la Transición Política* (Barcelona: Argos Vergara, 1982), 53.

48. During the civil war 268,500 persons died as a result of combat, military action, or executions. During the postwar period (to December 1961) 23,000 Republicans were executed (see Payne, *Franco Regime*, 219).

49. In Argentina the National Commission on the Disappeared established the disappearance of 8,960 persons during the authoritarian period. See *Nunca Más: Informe de la Comisión Nacional sobre la Desaparición de Personas* (Barcelona: Seix Barral, 1985); and Marysa Navarro, "The Personal Is Political: Las Madres de la Plaza de Mayo," in *Power and Popular Protest,* ed. Susan Eckstein (Berkeley: University of California Press, 1989). In Brazil 125 persons disappeared during military authoritarian rule, besides numerous other cases of detention and torture (*Brasil: Nunca Mais* [Petropolis: Editora Vozes, 1985]). In Chile extrajudicial executions and disappearances leading to presumed death during the Pinochet regime numbered close to 2,000. See *Informe Rettig: Informe de la Comisión Nacional de Verdad y Reconciliación* (Santiago: Talleres La Nación, 1991). Peru and Ecuador were exceptions to the repressive legacy of military authoritarian regimes.

50. Linz and Stepan introduced a useful distinction—hierarchically and nonhierarchically led militaries—which might capture situations of this kind. In transitions controlled by nonhierarchically led militaries, the military is less able to retain superior strength over civilian elites than is the case in transitions conducted by hierarchically led militaries. See Juan J. Linz and Alfred Stepan, *Problems of Democratic Transition and Consolidation: Eastern Europe, Southern Europe and South America* (Baltimore: Johns Hopkins University Press, forthcoming).

51. Guillermo O'Donnell and Philippe C. Schmitter, *Transitions from Authoritative Rule: Tentative Conclusions about Uncertain Democracies* (Baltimore: Johns Hopkins University Press, 1986), 17–21.

52. Stepan, "Paths toward Redemocratization: Theoretical and Comparative Considerations," in *Transitions from Authoritarian Rule: Comparative Perspectives,* ed. Guillermo O'Donnell, Philippe C. Schmitter, and Laurence Whitehead (Baltimore: Johns Hopkins University Press, 1986), 65.

53. Scott Mainwaring, "Transitions to Democracy and Democratic Consolidation: Theoretical and Comparative Issues," in *Issues in Democratic Consolidation: The New South American Democracies in Comparative Perspective,* ed. Scott Mainwaring, Guillermo O'Donnell, and J. Samuel Valenzuela (Notre Dame, Ind.: University of Notre Dame Press, 1992), 322. Also see Scott Mainwaring and Donald Share, "Transitions through Transaction: Democratization in Brazil and Spain," in *Political Liberalization in Brazil,* ed. Wayne A. Selcher (Boulder, Colo.: Westview Press, 1986); Donald Share, "Transitions to Democracy and Transition through Transaction," *Comparative Political Studies* 19 (January 1987). The substance of the distinctions made by Mainwaring influenced subsequent classifications, such as offered in Samuel P. Huntington, *The Third Wave: Democratization in the Late Twentieth Century* (Norman: University of

Oklahoma Press, 1991), 113. For an excellent discussion of criteria employed in the classification of transitions, see James W. McGuire, "Interim Government and Democratic Consolidation: Argentina in Comparative Perspective," in *Interim Governments in Transitions to Democracy*, ed. Juan J. Linz and Yossi Shain (Cambridge: Cambridge University Press, 1994).

54. Stepan, "Paths toward Redemocratization," 74–75.

55. See, for instance, Stepan's treatment of these cases in "Paths toward Redemocratization," 76–78.

56. That a very weakened military stayed in power in Argentina for so long after the collapse of the regime speaks also of the weaknesses of the civilian leadership, which did not effectively become organized until the final stages of the presidential race. In this regard Argentina clearly differs from the Venezuelan experience. The latter is placed here under the category of civilian control during the transition, despite the fact that the transition junta was presided over by Admiral Wolfgang Larrazábal, who had conducted the coup against the dictator. However, this junta included civilians appointed in agreement with the major parties, and they were most influential in conducting transition policies guided by the terms of the pact which party leaders had previously reached. Also W. Larrazábal was running as presidential candidate of one of the major parties. Indeed, the Venezuelan case distinguished itself for the leading role of political parties, which reached broad consensus from the outset. See Terry Lynn Karl, "Petroleum and Political Pacts: The Transition to Democracy in Venezuela," *Latin American Research Review* 22, no. 1 (1987).

57. James McGuire, in fact, argues that Argentina is more a "medium-to-low" than a "very low" case of military-authoritarian control of the transition and maintains that, had the Peronists won the elections, as expected, "Argentina's transition would have been interpreted as a carefully-staged, incumbent controlled [transition] on the Brazilian, Chilean or Spanish model, not as a case of 'regime collapse' as in Greece or Portugal" ("Interim Government"). See also Gary W. Wynia, "The Military's Attempts to Manage the Transition," in *Authoritarian Regimes in Transition*, ed. Hans Binnendijk (Washington, D.C.: Center for the Study of Foreign Affairs, Foreign Service Institute, Department of State Publications, 1987). Linz and Shain, however, highlight the role of leaders of the major parties in influencing the transition and refer to the situation of Argentina's interim government as "power-sharing from without" (Linz and Shain, *Interim Governments*).

Chapter 4: Democratization as Surprise

1. Speech by the minister of the navy, Gabriel Pita da Veiga, on 6 January 1976, *Revista General de Marina* (February 1976): 198.

2. Quoted in E. Ramón Arango, *The Spanish Political System: Franco's Legacy* (Boulder, Colo.: Westview Press, 1978), 246.

3. Numerous transitions from authoritarianism have later followed a similar pattern of transformation based on the existing legality, such as in Poland, Hungary, the former Soviet Union, South Korea, and South Africa. Spain, however, was the first case of "third-wave" democratization to follow this path.

4. If, for instance, as Juan Linz suggested, the armed forces had had a stronger say in the transition's agenda, they most certainly would have made the negotiation of the autonomy statutes—critical for the nationalities' support for democratization—much more difficult, if not entirely impossible ("Some Comparative Thoughts on the Transition to Democracy in Portugal and Spain," in *Portugal since the Revolution: Economic and Political Perspectives,* ed. Jorge Braga de Macedo and Simon Serfaty (Boulder, Colo.: Westview Press, 1981), 32. Similarly, Lieutenant General José María Sáenz de Tejada, chief of army intelligence at the time the transition started and army chief of staff in the 1980s, admitted that if there had existed a so-called *poder militar,* the transition would have probably taken a very different course (Madrid, recorded interview at the Fundación Ortega y Gasset, 24 September 1987).

5. Speech by Carlos Arias on 13 December 1975, quoted in José Oneto, *Anatomía de un Cambio de Régimen* (Barcelona: Plaza y Janés, 1985), 142.

6. See Charles T. Powell, "El Primer Gobierno de la Monarquía y la Reforma Suárez", *Revista de Occidente,* no. 54 (November 1985).

7. There were 17,731 labor strikes during the first three months of 1976, whereas in 1975, the year of greatest worker militancy under *franquism,* there were 3,156. See José María Maravall and Julián Santamaría, "Crisis del Franquismo, Transición Política y Consolidación de la Democracia en España," *Sistema,* nos. 68–69 (November 1985): 92. Strikes during the twelve months of 1976 reached a total of 40,179. See Sebastian Balfour, *Dictatorship, Workers and the City* (Oxford: Clarendon Press, 1989), 143.

8. See his personal letter to army friends following his resignation of the vice presidency in September 1976, in Carlos Fernández, *Los Militares en la Transición Política* (Barcelona: Argos Vergara, 1982), 111.

9. The generals did not bring any projects of their own to the council. Debate of some of the initially important projects took place in outside bodies in which the generals were not included, such as the joint National Council-Government Committee formed to work on a proposal for political reform.

10. Manuel Gutiérrez Mellado, *Recorded Interview,* Fundación Ortega y Gasset, Madrid, 9 May 1985.

11. Manuel Fraga, *En Busca del Tiempo Servido* (Barcelona: Planeta, 1987), 50 and 43. See also General Federico Gómez de Salazar, *Recorded Interview,* Madrid, 3 July 1986.

12. An article in *Newsweek* (26 April 1976) by correspondent Arnaud de Borchgrave, which told of the king's exasperation with Arias's inability to proceed with reforms, was widely circulated and commented on in Madrid.

13. Between January and June 1976 Fraga recorded five meetings like this (held 8 March 1976) in his diaries. See Manuel Fraga, *En Busca del Tiempo Servido,* 38–40; José María de Areilza, *Diario de un Ministro de la Monarquía* (Barcelona: Planeta, 1977), 110 and 126; and, for meetings on the issue of trade union reforms, see Rodolfo Martín Villa, *Al Servicio del Estado* (Barcelona: Planeta, 1984), 31 and 61.

14. On 26 February 1976 the Spanish flag was officially replaced by the Moroccan flag (see Diario 16, *Historia de la Transición,* chap. 10). See also the statements before the Foreign Affairs Committee of Congress by former governor-general of Sahara, Lieutenant General Federico Gómez de Salazar, in *Diario de Sesiones del Congreso de los Diputados,* no. 30 (1978): 25–36. Also the negotiations with the United States for the renewal of the Hispanic-American Friendship and Cooperation Agreement required

the participation of top military chiefs, who were, in addition, suffering the tensions brought about by the uncovering of the clandestine Unión de Militares Demócratas.

15. The military was insensitive to the more moderate positions adopted by the communists and rejected them flatly. This rejection also extended initially to the socialists, who were still admittedly Marxists and republicans. "It took hard work to discover that the Socialists were no longer Reds," admitted Lieutenant General Federico Gómez de Salazar (*Recorded Interview*, Madrid, 3 July 1986). "We thought the Socialists had not changed; that if they became too powerful we would have to migrate" (General García Conde, *Personal Interview*, Madrid, 24 May 1988).

16. When the king confirmed Arias in November 1975, he had also made sure that chairmanship of the Cortes and the Council of the Realm be assigned to someone he trusted personally. The Cortes became an essential piece because reform legislation would have to be handled there, and the Council of the Realm was crucial as well because the king's appointment of a new president of the government could only come from a list of three proposed by this council. By placing Torcuato Fernández Miranda in these core positions, the king had adequately prepared the terrain for change. It was he who managed to place Suárez in the Council of the Realm's list of three, and his selection by the king was so unexpected that he was not even in the lists of possible choices speculated about in the media. See, for instance, *El País*, 2 July 1976. See also Charles T. Powell, *El Piloto del Cambio: El rey, la monarquía y la transición a la democracia* (Barcelona: Editorial Planeta, 1991), 168–75.

17. A secret meeting between Adolfo Suárez and Felipe González, the leader of the Spanish Socialist Workers Party (PSOE), took place in August 1976. In December, Santiago Carrillo, leader of the Communist Party, held a clandestine press conference in Madrid and managed to legalize his personal situation after a very brief detention. Also in December, right before the referendum on political reform, the Socialists, not yet officially legalized, held their first party congress in Spain since 1932, widely attended by European socialist figures.

18. This was the distinctive feature of Suárez's reform plans, as opposed to previous reform plans that had been harbored during Arias's government, especially by Fraga. Fraga's plans contemplated the gradual institutionalization of reforms but never considered granting constitutional powers to a freely elected body. See Charles T. Powell, "El Primer Gobierno de la Monarquía," *El Piloto del Cambio*, 10. For Suárez's address and the text of the law, see *Un Nuevo Horizonte Para España: Discursos del Presidente del Gobierno, 1976–1978*, Colección Informe no. 21 (Madrid: Servicio Central de Publicaciones, Presidencia del Gobierno, 1978).

19. Alfonso Osorio, *Trayectoria Política de un Ministro de la Corona* (Barcelona: Planeta, 1980), 183–84.

20. The meeting was obviously quite unusual, as Suárez chose to address directly in a single meeting all generals with command of army and air regions and all admirals with command of naval zones, instead of simply meeting with the ministers and chiefs of staff, who also attended. Also attending were the president of the Supreme Military Court, the director general of the Civil Guard, and the general chief of the king's military quarter. See *El País*, 9 September 1976.

21. Information on the meeting is based on the previously cited interviews with generals Federico Gómez de Salazar and Manuel Gutiérrez Mellado and with Lieu-

tenant General José Vega Rodríguez (*Recorded Interview,* Madrid, Fundación Ortega y Gasset). See also Charles T. Powell, "Reform versus Ruptura in Spain's Transition to Democracy" (Ph.D. diss., Oxford University, 1989; and *El Piloto del Cambio,* 192–94.

22. Quoted in Powell, *El Piloto del Cambio,* 204.

23. Among the votes against were those of seven military chiefs. Three of them were members by direct appointment by Franco (a former minister of the army among them), and three others derived their membership from their seats in the National Council of the Movement, to which they also had been appointed by Franco. Admiral Pita da Veiga, also with the National Council by Franco's appointment, was a minister and had to vote with the government. The seventh, a former director general of the Civil Guard, was *procurador* elected by Ceuta (see Diario 16, *Historia de la Transición,* chap. 23, pp. 352 and 356; and Aguilar, *Las Ultimas Cortes del Franquismo,* 144–46.

24. See *Un Nuevo Horizonte para España,* 18.

25. Communists, socialists, regional nationalists, and other groups campaigned in favor of abstention. In a joint declaration the unified opposition had called for the immediate formation, on 23 October, of a provisional government including all democratic groups. This provisional government would be called upon to legalize all parties and unions and all democratic liberties, grant complete amnesty for political prisoners, and reestablish the autonomy statutes for Catalonia, Euskadi, and Galicia. Only then could the new government call elections for a constitutional convention. This *"ruptura"* strategy contrasted with Suárez's plan, which first contemplated election of an assembly during a period of continuity of the king's government (see "Programa Político de la Plataforma de Organismos Democráticos," in Diario 16, *Historia de la Transición,* chap. 22, p. 344). The opposition's call for abstention rather than rejection, however, signaled its recognition of the inevitability of compromise and the futility of *ruptura.* Indeed, while calling for abstention — at that point only a face-saving strategy — the opposition innerly desired the approval of Suárez's plan. Luckily, the call for abstention was received only halfheartedly. Abstentions only reached 22.3 percent and the highest levels concentrated in areas with strong nationalist movements, such as provinces in Euskadi, Catalonia, and Galicia. See John F. Coverdale, *The Political Transformation of Spain after Franco* (New York: Praeger, 1979), 51–53.

26. Quoted in Jesús Ynfante, *El Ejército de Franco y de Juan Carlos* (Chatillon-sous-Bagneux: Ruedo Ibérico, 1976), 137.

27. Admiral Angel Liberal, for instance, while serving in Spain's naval mission in Washington, D.C., between 1971 and 1974, was convinced that, "when Franco dies, nothing will happen for five years; after that, whatever the Spanish people want. . . ." It was a widespread impression among his colleagues that there would be enough time after Franco's death "to do things right" (*Recorded Interview,* Fundación Ortega y Gasset, 10 November 1987). This impression was later well stated by Admiral Pita da Veiga in a newspaper interview on 14 April 1976: "Today the transition is logical, natural, it had to come; calmly, however, and within regular conduits that are compatible with our history, with our traditions; perfectly compatible with progress and social advancement, that is, we move from a regime of consent to a regime of participation" (qtd. in Fernández, *Los Militares en la Transición Política,* 87).

28. Informally stating concerns, as the military many times did, is not the same

as stating a position formally and officially. The closest the military ever got to making a formal statement on its opposition to the legalization of the Communist Party was the reaction of the military ministers to Manuel Fraga's statements that the Communists would at some point, after the first elections, have to be legalized. Fraga's statements, when he was minister of the interior under Arias, were published in the *New York Times,* 19 June 1976. Vice President de Santiago and the military ministers made their views known to the king and demanded from Arias that Fraga recant his statements. Fraga, however, did not recant (see Fraga, *En Busca del Tiempo Servido,* 50). According to Alfonso Osorio, then minister of the presidency, Admiral Pita da Veiga told him that "under no circumstance can the legalization of the Communist Party be conceived of and that, as minister of the navy, he knows that it would cause great commotion in the navy and, therefore, could greatly harm an otherwise desirable political evolution of the regime and even the monarchy" (*Trayectoria Política,* 124).

29. The law for political reform empowered the king to appoint a number of senators equal to one-fifth the number of elected members (207). Among the 41 senators appointed by the king were: Lieutenant General (r) Luis Diez Alegría, former chief of the general staff and former director general of the Civil Guard; Admiral Marcial Gamboa, captain general of the Cartagena Naval Department; and air force General Angel Salas Larrazábal, also member of the Council of the Realm by virtue of seniority (see Diario 16, *Historia de la Transición,* chap. 31, pp. 466–70).

30. Vice President Gutiérrez Mellado became the only military man in the government when he assumed the ministry of defense in July 1977. He had already resigned his commission in the army, however, when accepting his appointment to the vice presidency in September 1976.

31. De Santiago had met with Suárez the day before to express his view that the trade unions, more than political parties, had been the source of the gravest problems in Spain and that changes in trade union legislation should not be made to coincide with political reforms (see Osorio, *Trayectoria Política,* 185).

32. Quoted in Fernández, *Los Militares,* 110–12. Iniesta's letter appeared in *El Alcázar,* 27 September 1976.

33. As the respective press release was about to be aired on television, Suárez was informed that he was not legally empowered to pass them to the reserve. De Santiago and Iniesta stayed in the army, although holding no posts, until their retirement.

34. Powell, *El Piloto del Cambio,* 194–95.

35. Suárez seemed genuinely troubled by Carrillo's forcing the issue and wanted to have him expelled from the country, but his advisors convinced him of the legal difficulties in doing so. Nonetheless, some in the military suspected that it was all part of Suárez's machinations to disguise his real intention of normalizing Carrillo's legal status in Spain (interview with General Emilio García Conde, Madrid, 24 May 1988). See also Osorio, *Trayectoria Política,* 256; and Villa, *Al Servicio del Estado,* 60.

36. The party was widely praised in the media for its moderation. *Ya,* for instance, editorialized that the Communist Party's legalization was well deserved (28 April 1977). The day after, eight newspapers published a joint editorial page rejecting violence and calling for unity, democracy, and pluralism, in reaction to the killing of Communist lawyers and the kidnappings of the president of the Supreme Military Court and the president of the Council of State by extreme leftist groups, all of which had taken place on the same day.

37. Villa, *Al Servicio de la Corona,* 62. The Communists had been shifting to moderate positions on these issues for some time. See Eusebio Mujal-León, *Communism and Political Change in Spain* (Bloomington: Indiana University Press, 1983), especially chapter 6.

38. Osorio, *Trayectoria Política,* 287.

39. Andrés Cassinello, *Recorded Interview,* Madrid, Fundación Ortega y Gasset, 2 October 1986.

40. The minister of the air force, Franco Iribarnegaray, had told Suárez that there would be no problems in his service (Powell, *El Piloto del Cambio,* 219–20).

41. Osorio, *Trayectoria Política,* 286–89; Villa, *Al Servicio de la Corona,* 57–67; Manuel Gutiérrez Mellado, *Recorded Interview,* Fundación Ortega y Gasset, Madrid, 9 May 1985. A poll conducted by the Centro de Investigaciones Sociológicas (CIS) in January 1977 showed that 25 percent opposed legalization while 29 percent favored it with no conditions. Osorio tells of a poll that was made available to Suárez in mid-March showing no changes in the percentage of those who were opposed but a significant increase of those in favor: 40 percent. Right after legalization a poll by CIS showed that 45 percent approved, while only 17 percent disapproved.

42. According to Charles T. Powell, army minister Alvarez-Arenas knew of the Consejo's resolution on 7 April, but, confident that nothing would be done without a prior decision by the Council of Ministers, he called a meeting of the High Army Council for right after the Easter holidays (*El Piloto del Cambio,* 220).

43. Regardless of the exact words used by the president in reference to the Communist question during the meeting of 8 September the previous year, what mattered was that he had left the clear impression of a commitment not to proceed with the legalization of the party. Three army generals present in the meeting (Manuel Gutiérrez Mellado, José Vega Rodríguez, and Federico Gómez de Salazar) clearly agree, in previously cited interviews, that the prevailing impression among the military participants was that the president promised not to legalize the party. The impact of the legalization was sharpened by the fact that only a few days earlier the Franquist "Movimiento Nacional" had been officially dissolved.

44. Both notes are found in María Mérida, *Mis Conversaciones con los Generales,* 3d ed. (Barcelona: Plaza y Janes Editores, 1980), 56–58.

45. Interview with General Ricardo Arozarena, Madrid, 19 October 1987.

46. See Osorio, *Trayectoria Política,* 289–90; Fernández, *Los Militares,* 155–64; Manuel Gutiérrez Mellado, *Un Soldado de España* (Barcelona: Argos Vergara, 1983); and Diario 16, *Historia de la Transición,* chapter 28.

47. Mujal-León, *Communism and Political Change,* 154.

48. Gutiérrez Mellado put it unequivocally: "The anti-Suárez campaign in the Armed Forces starts with the legalization of the Communist party. A slogan takes off from here: 'We Cannot trust Adolfo Suárez.'. . . The campaign extends, good people in isolated places are led to doubt, some commanders act with excessive tolerance, the tendency is nurtured that the best that can be expected is the failure of the situation and since Suárez is in charge, well, let's take him on" (*Un Soldado de España,* 155–56).

49. Powell, *El Piloto del Cambio,* 222.

50. See Francisco Caparrós, *La UMD: Militares Rebeldes* (Barcelona: Argos Vergara, 1983).

51. Gutiérrez Mellado had been critical of the way in which the detention of UMD officers had been handled during the Arias Navarro administration and of the treatment given the detainees, but he shared the generalized position in the army that the readmission of these officers was not acceptable. In his first general report as army chief of staff he had emphasized: "The recent amnesty has reached the sentenced officers with regard to regaining freedom. But it must remain clear—in the face of so many unjustified speculations—that their readmission is not possible" (*Al Servicio de la Corona* [Madrid: Ibérico Europea de Ediciones, 1981], 52).

52. According to Rafael Arias Salgado, secretary of the ministry for government-Congress coordination, he was suddenly called out to attend an urgent call from vice president Fernando Abril, who instructed him to report at once in La Moncloa, the government palace. Upon arriving, Abril showed Arias to the president, who, in turn, told him that Vice President Gutiérrez Mellado was awaiting him in an adjacent room. To Arias's surprise Gutiérrez Mellado was surrounded by some twelve army generals in their uniforms who, with somber expressions on their faces, stared at Arias as the vice president issued the warning. Gutiérrez Mellado told Arias that, should Congress persist in the attempt to grant amnesty to the former UMD members, he could not guarantee his capacity to control the strong reaction that, with unforeseeable consequences, would undoubtedly develop in the army. Rafael Arias acknowledged receipt of the general's concern and rushed back to inform the committee, whose members had been anxiously waiting for him. The UMD members were dropped instantly from the amnesty law (interview with Rafael Arias Salgado, Madrid, 23 November 1987). Gutiérrez Mellado has given a different version: "I had to oppose the full amnesty because, with or without justification, it would produce grave commotion and strong rejection. . . . Two leaders of UCD, not in the government, came to me to explain that they planned to include the UMD members in a full amnesty. I told them that in such a case I would submit my resignation. They transmitted my position and I guess they must have thought about the powerful reasons I must have had to announce my reaction" (*Un Soldado de España,* 136).

53. See Richard Gunther, "Constitutional Change in Contemporary Spain," in *Redesigning the State: The Politics of Constitutional Change,* ed. Keith Banting and Richard Simeon (Toronto: University of Toronto Press, 1985); and Richard Gunther and Roger Blough, "Religious Conflict and Consensus in Spain: A Tale of Two Constitutions," *World Affairs* 143 (Spring 1981).

54. The special drafting committee was formed by seven members: three from UCD, one from AP, one Communist, one Socialist, and one from the major Catalan party. A first draft was leaked in November 1977 and published in major newspapers. See Bonifacio de la Cuadra and Soledad Gallego-Díaz, *Del Consenso al Desencanto* (Madrid: Editorial Saltés, 1981).

55. See Julio Busquets, "Tres Presiones Militares sobre los Constituyentes," Diario 16, *Historia de la Transición,* chapter 37, pp. 553–54.

56. The army journal, in its editorial page, could not have put it more clearly: "In a single principle of the Movement are defined both the untouchable nature of the unity of Spain and its guarantee assigned to the Armed Forces" ("Relevo de Mandos en Nuestro Ministerio," *Ejército,* no. 432 [January 1976]: 5). The editorial article was reprinted with slight changes in the November 1976 issue (no. 442: 71).

57. Similar statements were made by Lieutenant General Angel Salas Larrazá-bal. All three of them were senators by royal designation (see *Reconquista,* no. 342 [September 1978]: 4). It should be noted that the issue of "the unity of Spain" was compounded in 1978 with the questioning by the Organization of African Unity of the Spanish character of Canary Islands. This gave place to a special meeting, conducted by President Suárez on 22 April in Tenerife, of the joint chiefs and the Unified Military Command of Canary Islands.

58. At a meeting on 16 March 1978 the constitutional committee agreed to this formula, suggested by Communist representative Jordi Solé Tura. According to Manuel Fraga, who opposed the use of the term, José Pedro Pérez Llorca, chief representative of the government team, informed the group that the formula could be accepted because it had the necessary approval of the military (see Fraga, *En Busca del Tiempo Servido,* 113). Military concern with this matter remained very much alive, especially as the autonomous communities gradually became a reality, with their own languages, flags, and symbols (see Francisco Ríos García, "Repercusión del Desarrollo Autonómico en la Defensa Nacional y en las Fuerzas Armadas," in *Las Autonomías en España,* Ciclo de Conferencias, Centro Superior de Estudios de la Defensa Nacional, Madrid, October 1982).

59. See Félix Arteaga Martín, "Reflexiones sobre el Artículo Octavo de la Constitución Española de 1978" (paper presented to the First Iberoamerican Congress of Military Sociology, Madrid, September 1985); and Federico Trillo Figueroa, "Las Fuerzas Armadas en la Constitución Española: Esbozo de una Construcción Institucional," *Revista de Estudios Políticos,* no. 12 (November–December 1979).

60. Catalan deputy Miquel Roca explained this well: "We have not obtained a constitution through some breach in the status quo, but rather, through a constitutional process we have achieved a *reform* and, in a certain sense, a *revolution* — all at the same time" (qtd. in Antonio López Piña, "Shaping the Constitution," in *Spain at the Polls: 1977, 1979, and 1982,* ed. Howard R. Penniman and Eusebio Mujal-León [Durham, N.C.: Duke University Press, 1985], 31; my emphasis). Obviously, use of the terms *reforma* or *ruptura* was politically charged: *reforma* gave a leading role to regime groups, whereas *ruptura* singled out the role of opposition groups. Opposition groups added that it was *"ruptura pactada,"* to account for the adjustments made to their purely rupturist previous strategies. For a view of *"reforma-ruptura"* as a false dilemma, see Juan Linz, "The Transition from Authoritarian Regimes to Democratic Political Systems and the Problems of Consolidation of Political Democracy" (paper presented at the International Political Science Association Tokyo Round Table, 29 March–1 April 1982).

61. Linz, "Transition from Authoritarian Regimes."

62. See José Ignacio Wert Ortega, "The Transition from Below: Public Opinion among the Spanish Population from 1977 to 1979," in Penniman and Mujal-León, *Spain at the Polls,* 74–75; and Richard Gunther, Giacomo Sani, and Goldie Shabad, eds., *Spain after Franco: The Making of a Competitive Party System* (Berkeley: University of California Press, 1986), 55–58. However, the high level of support for UCD and PSOE was for many observers a clear move to the left. Two days before the 1977 elections *El País* reported the findings of a poll predicting elections results that came quite close to the actual tallies, under the title: "A Strong Move toward the Left" (see

Juan Roldán Ros, "The Media and the Elections," in Penniman and Eusebio Mujal-León, *Spain at the Polls,* 264). Also the military, which had felt relief after the Communists' poor showing, still saw electoral trends as rather left leaning. For public opinion studies during this period, see Juan Linz, Manuel Gómez-Reino, Francisco Andrés Orizo, and Darío Vila, *Informe Sociológico Sobre el Cambio Político en España, 1975-1981,* IV Informe, FOESSA (Madrid: Editorial Euroamérica, 1981); and Rafael López Pintor, *La Opinión Pública Española del Franquismo a la Democracia* (Madrid: Centro de Investigaciones Sociológicas, 1982).

63. Charles de Gaulle had previously used similar means with great success in France in dealing with a rebellious military on the Algerian question. In a short period of time he elicited public support for his plans via elections and referendums that empowered the president and raised the costs of rebellion by the military. See George A. Kelly, *Lost Soldiers: The French Army and Empire in Crisis, 1947-1962* (Cambridge: MIT Press, 1965); Orville Menard, *The Army and the Fifth Republic* (Lincoln: University of Nebraska Press, 1965); and Ronald J. Stupak, "The Military's Ideological Challenge to Civilian Authority in Post World War II France," *Orbis* 12, no. 2 (1968). For the difficulties that the Spanish armed forces had historically had in successfully resisting political change, see Stanley Payne, "Modernization of the Armed Forces," in *The Politics of Democratic Spain,* ed. Stanley Payne (Chicago: Chicago Council on Foreign Relations, 1986).

64. On the role of the Catholic church, see Juan J. Linz, "Church and State in Spain from the Civil War to the Return to Democracy," *Daedalus* 120 (Summer 1991).

65. Fraga, *En Busca del Tiempo Servido,* 97.

66. See *Los Pactos de La Moncloa* (Madrid: Servicio Central de Publicaciones, Presidencia del Gobierno, 1977); and Diario 16, *Historia de la Transición,* chapter 33.

67. This second editorial, however, did not include *ABC* and *El Alcázar,* clearly identified with the Right. See José María García Escudero, *YA: Medio Siglo de Historia, 1935-1985* (Madrid: Biblioteca de Autores Cristianos de la Editorial Católica, 1984), 281-82 and 287-88.

68. Right-wing extremists who overtly favored military intervention remained marginal, as did small paramilitary groups on the Left and the Right. However, armed groups held the capacity to stage disruptive terrorist acts. Left-wingers had kidnapped the president of the Supreme Council of Military Justice, and right-wingers had assassinated a group of Communist lawyers. ETA was emerging as a larger threat, escalating terrorist acts during this period. On 28 July 1978 the first army general was assassinated by ETA.

69. See Roy C. Macridis, "Elections and Political Modernization in Greece," in *Greece at the Polls: The National Elections of 1974 and 1977,* ed. Howard R. Penniman (Washington, D.C.: American Enterprise Institute for Public Policy Research, 1981), 14-15; and Nikos Alivizatos, "The Difficulties of 'Rationalization' in a Polarized Political System: The Greek Chamber of Deputies," in *Parliament and Democratic Consolidation in Southern Europe: Greece, Italy, Portugal, Spain and Turkey,* ed. Ulrike Liebert and Maurizio Cota (London: Pinter Publishers, 1990), 133-34.

70. See Kenneth Maxwell, "Regime Overthrow and Prospects for Democratic Transition in Portugal," in O'Donnell, Schmitter, and Whitehead, *Transitions from Authoritarian Rule: Southern Europe;* and Lawrence S. Graham, "Redefining the Portu-

guese Transition to Democracy," in *Elites and Democratic Consolidation in Latin America and Southern Europe,* ed. John Higley and Richard Gunther (Cambridge: Cambridge University Press, 1992); and J. R. Lewis and A. M. Williams, "Social Cleavages and Electoral Performance: The Social Basis of Portuguese Political Parties, 1976-1983," *West European Politics* 7, no. 2 (1984).

71. Alfonsín's Radical Party obtained 52 percent of the votes in the 1983 elections and a majority of seats in the Chamber of Deputies but not in the Senate. See Manuel Mora y Araujo, "The Nature of the Alfonsín Coalition"; and Marcelo Cavarozzi, "Peronism and Radicalism: Argentina's Transition in Perspective," both in in *Elections and Democratization in Latin America,* 1980-85, ed. Paul W. Drake and Eduardo Silva (San Diego: Center for Iberian and Latin American Studies, Center for U.S.-Mexican Studies, Institute for the Americas, University of California, San Diego, 1986). For an account of this process, see Luigi Manzetti, *Institutions, Parties and Distributional Coalitions in Argentine Politics* (Pittsburgh: Pittsburgh University Press, 1994), especially chapters 1 and 3.

72. Frances Hagopian, "The Compromised Consolidation: The Political Class in the Brazilian Transition," in Mainwaring, O'Donnell, and Valenzuela, *Issues in Democratic Consolidation;* and Scott Mainwaring, "Politicians, Parties and Electoral Systems: Brazil in Comparative Perspective," *Comparative Politics* 24, no. 1 (1991).

73. Ronald H. McDonald and J. Mark Ruhl, *Party Politics and Elections in Latin America* (Boulder, Colo.: Westview Press, 1989), 218-19.

74. See Anita Isaacs, *Military Rule and Transition in Ecuador* (Pittsburgh: University of Pittsburgh Press, 1993).

75. The Blancos had previously refrained from participation in the Naval Club agreement with the military which opened the way to the transition. See Charles Guy Gillespie, *Negotiating Democracy: Politicians and Generals in Uruguay* (Cambridge: Cambridge University Press, 1991); and Juan Rial, "The Uruguayan Elections of 1984: A Triumph of the Center," in Drake and Silva, *Elections and Democratization in Latin America.*

76. See Felipe Agüero, "Brechas en la Democratización: Visiones de la Elite Política sobre las Fuerzas Armadas en Chile," in *Democratización y Reforma Política en Iberoamérica: Los Casos de Chile, Uruguay y Brasil,* ed. Manuel Alcántara and José Ramón Montero (Madrid: Centro de Investigaciones Sociológicas, 1994). For election results, see Alan Angell and Benny Pollack, "The Chilean Elections of 1989 and the Politics of the Transition to Democracy," *Bulletin of Latin American Research* 9, no. 1 (1990).

Chapter 5: Hard-line Failures, Reformist Alliances, and Military Modernization

1. Philippe C. Schmitter, "Liberation by Golpe: Retrospective Thoughts on the Demise of Authoritarian Rule in Portugal," *Armed Forces and Society* 2, no. 1 (1975): 23. See also Juan Linz, "Some Comparative Thoughts on the Transition to Democracy in Spain and Portugal," in *Portugal since the Revolution: Economic and Political Perspectives,* ed. Jorge Braga de Macedo and Simon Serfaty (Boulder, Colo.: Westview Press, 1981), 28; and José María Maravall and Julián Santamaría, "Political Change in

Spain and the Prospects for Democracy," in *Transitions from Authoritarian Rule: Southern Europe,* ed. Guillermo O'Donnell, Philippe C. Schmitter, and Laurence Whitehead (Baltimore: Johns Hopkins University Press, 1986), 90. For accounts that did point to diverse positions in the Spanish military, see Joaquín Romero Maura, "After Franco, Franquismo? The Armed Forces, the Crown and Democracy," *Government and Opposition* 11, no. 1 (Winter 1976): 45; Enrique Gomáriz, "Los Militares ante la Transición," *Zona Abierta* 18 and 19 (1979); and Kenneth Medhurst, "The Military and the Prospects for Spanish Democracy," *West European Politics* 1, no. 1 (1978): 55.

2. On the judiciary, see Justicia Democrática, *Los Jueces Contra la Dictadura (Justicia y Política en el Franquismo)* (Madrid: Tucar Ediciones, 1978). On the evolution of the church in the twilight of the Franco regime, see E. J. Heubel, "Church and State in Spain: Transition toward Independence and Liberty," *Western Political Quarterly* 30, no. 1 (March 1977); Alfred Fierro Bardaji, "Political Positions and Opposition in the Spanish Catholic Church," *Government and Opposition* 11, no. 2 (Spring 1976); and Leslie Mackenzie, "The Political Ideas of the Opus Dei in Spain," *Government and Opposition* 8, no. 1 (1973).

3. See José María Maravall, *Dictatorship and Political Dissent* (London: Tavistock, 1978); and Kenneth Medhurst, "The Prospects of Federalism: The Regional Problem after Franco," *Government and Opposition* 11, no.2 (Spring 1976). On the military prior to the transition, see Joaquim Lleixà, *Cien Años de Militarismo en España* (Barcelona: Anagrama, 1986); and Carlos Seco Serrano, *Militarismo y Civilismo en la España Contemporánea* (Madrid: Instituto de Estudios Económicos, 1984).

4. Franco's passionate farewell address at the Zaragoza Military Academy, shut down by the Republican government in 1931, when he was its director and Gutiérrez Mellado an attending student (Francisco Caparrós, *La UMD: Militares Rebeldes* [Barcelona: Argos Vergara, 1983], 21).

5. See Manuel Gutiérrez Mellado, *Al Servicio de la Corona* (Madrid: Ibérico Europea de Ediciones, 1981), 48 and 50. Numerous editorials in the army journal *Ejército* between 1974 and 1976 addressed the theme of unity.

6. From May 1977 through April 1978 all but one of the monthly issues of *Boletín de Informaciones* (CESEDEN [Center for High National Defense Studies]) included articles on Eurocommunism or subversion. See also the speech by Lieutenant General Fernando de Santiago, at the conclusion of the academic year, in CESEDEN in July 1975 (*Ejército,* no. 427 [August 1975]); and the speeches by General Manuel Cabeza Calahorra, director of the High Army School, and General José Martínez Jimenez, head of the Army Staff School, on graduation day, 4 May 1977 (*Ejército,* no. 449 [June 1977]).

7. *Recorded Interview,* with General José Sáenz de Tejada, Fundación Ortega y Gasset, Madrid, 24 September 1987. Also see Caparrós, *La UMD;* and José Fortes and Luis Otero, *Proceso a Nueve Militares Demócratas* (Barcelona: Argos Vergara, 1983). A selection of documents with an introduction by UMD appears in *UMD* (n.d., n.p.). Also an excellent source is Ministerio del Ejército, Estado Mayor Central, *La "UMD", y la Causa 250/75* (Madrid: Talleres del Servicio Geográfico del Ejército, 1976).

8. "In the army there has always been a very small minority of liberals, a larger minority of right-wing extremism, and a large mass rather sedate, although concerned with things such as terrorism" (Manuel Gutiérrez Mellado, *Recorded Interview,*

Fundación Ortega y Gasset, Madrid, 9 May 1985). See also Manuel Gutiérrez Mellado, *Un Soldado de España (Conversaciones con Jesús Picatoste)* (Barcelona: Argos Vergara, 1983).

9. The División Azul (Blue Division) was the Spanish contribution of volunteers for the Wehrmacht's Russian front during World War II. Spanish officials encouraged this participation as a natural continuation of the Crusade. Seventy percent of the volunteers, and all of the officers, came from the army. In all, 47,000 Spaniards served on the eastern front, suffering about 22,000 casualties, 4,500 of whom died. The Spanish forces were commanded by General Muñoz Grandes, who later was the first vice president in the government, while keeping his post as chief of the high general staff (Stanley G. Payne, *Franco Regime: 1936-1975* [Madison: University of Wisconsin Press, 1987], 281-83 and 333-34).

10. In the army's active promotion list (those eligible for command posts) in 1969, the following officers had started out as *alféreces provisionales:* 37.1 percent of the colonels; 97.9 percent of the lieutenant colonels; 85 percent of the majors; in all, 34.4 percent of all officers in the grades between lieutenant and colonel (from figures contained in Julio Busquets, "Los Alféreces Provisionales hasta la Creación de la Hermandad (1936-1958)," *Historia* 16 II, no. 119 (March 1986): 47.

11. All the generals in the Spanish army in 1976 had joined the service before or during the civil war. Sixty-eight out of 95 major generals in 1976 had joined the army between 1936 and 1939 (71.2 percent). In 1980, 85.1 percent of the major generals had joined the army during the civil war years, and only one did after the war (calculated from *Escalafones de Oficiales Generales y Asimilados,* Madrid, 1 July 1976 and 1 January 1980). Until 1980 all admirals, vice admirals, and rear admirals in the navy had joined the service during or before the civil war (see *Estado General de la Armada:* 1980 [Madrid: Servicio de Publicaciones del Cuartel General de la Armada, n.d.]).

12. *Ejército,* no. 440 (September 1976): 6. Lieutenant General de Santiago, vice president for defense, announced that the armed forces rejected "the wave of materialism and pornography, of attacks to the family and its spiritual values and so much neglect of God that reaches us because it hits the world" (*Ejército,* no. 438 [July 1976]: 5). Colonel Juan Manuel Sancho Sopranis y Fauraud warned against the disruption of "the sanctity of the Family, the Militia, the Fatherland and Religion, with the instruments of pornography, drugs, generational conflicts, divorce, abortion, conscientious objection, strikes, terrorism, separatism, hedonism, materialism and nihilism" (*Ejército,* no.446 [March 1977]: 4).

13. A factor in this propensity to intervene was Spain's copious prior history of military intervention in politics. Between the end of the war of independence in 1814 and the dictatorship of Primo de Rivera in 1923 there were forty-three military *pronunciamientos,* ten of which were successful (see the appendix in Julio Busquets, *Pronunciamientos y Golpes de Estado en España* [Barcelona: Editorial Planeta, 1982]). Interventionism had left a tradition of autonomous military prerogatives, and, despite the "taming" of the military which franquism brought about, especially in comparison with Portugal, there remained a tolerance for political input by military officers who participated in the Franquist structures and political associations (see Antonio Porras Nadales, "Ordenamiento de la Defensa, Poder Militar y Régimen Constitucional en España," *Revista de Estudios Políticos,* no. 35 [September–October 1983]). See also

Miguel Alonso Baquer, "The Age of Pronunciamientos"; and Fernando Fernández Bastarreche, "The Spanish Military from the Age of Disasters to the Civil War," both in *Armed Forces and Society in Spain: Past and Present,* ed. Rafael Bañón and Thomas M. Barker (New York: Columbia University Press, 1988); Miguel Alonso Baquer, *El Ejercito en la Sociedad Española* (Madrid: Ediciones del Movimiento, 1971); Jorge Cachinero, "Intervencionismo y Reformas Militares en España a Comienzos del Siglo XX," *Zona Abierta,* nos. 39-40 (April–September 1986); and Gabriel Cardona, *El Poder Militar en la España Contemporánea hasta la Guerra Civil* (Madrid: Siglo XXI, 1983).

14. María Mérida, *Mis Conversaciones con los Generales,* 3d ed. (Barcelona: Plaza y Janes Editores, 1980), 47.

15. General Iniesta Cano, for instance, director general of the Civil Guard at the time of the assassination of Admiral Carrero Blanco in 1973, ordered his forces, without previous government approval, to set up checkpoints in major cities and not to hesitate to use their firearms. General Campano, head of the Civil Guard in December, 1976, acted leniently toward a major and dangerous demonstration of some one thousand members of the Civil Guard and police in front of the interior ministry, which ended up injuring a general who tried to order them away. Campano, removed from the Civil Guard, was nonetheless assigned later to command the Madrid Military Region (Carlos Fernández, *Los Militares en la Transición Política* [Barcelona: Argos Vergara, 1982], 21-22).

16. "No había un líder militar que representara el pensamiento del conjunto de las Fuerzas Armadas . . . había posiciones más duras y más blandas que las de los ministros militares" (Charles T. Powell, "Reform versus Ruptura in Spain's Transition to Democracy" [Ph.D. diss., Oxford University, 1989]).

17. Based on recorded interviews with Lieutenant General José María Sáenz de Tejada (Madrid, 17 November 1987) and Lieutenant General José Gabeiras (Madrid, 11 December 1987) and an interview with Lieutenant General Juan Cano Hevia (Madrid, 5 October 1987).

18. Interviews with Colonel Manuel Monzón Altolaguirre, Madrid, 23 November 1987, and Lieutenant General Ricardo Arozarena, Madrid, 19 October 1987. See also *Recorded Interviews,* Fundación Ortega y Gasset, with General Andrés Cassinello (2 October 1986) and Lieutenant General José Sáenz de Tejada (24 September 1987). See also Jesús Ynfante, *El Ejército de Franco y de Juan Carlos* (Chatillon-sous-Bagneux: Ruedo Ibérico, 1976); Gutiérrez Mellado, *Un Soldado de España;* and José Ignacio San Martín, *Servicio Especial* (Barcelona: Editorial Planeta, 1983).

19. See Felipe Agüero, "The Military and the Limits to Democratization in South America," in Mainwaring, O'Donnell, and Valenzuela, *Issues in Democratic Consolidation;* and Alfred Stepan, *Rethinking Military Politics* (Princeton, N.J.: Princeton University Press, 1988).

20. The best presentation of this argument appears in Guillermo O'Donnell, "Modernization and Military Coups: Theory, Comparisons and the Argentine Case," in *Armies and Politics in Latin America,* ed. Abraham Lowenthal and J. Samuel Fitch (New York: Holmes and Meier, 1986). For the concept of praetorianism, see Samuel P. Huntington, *Political Order in Changing Societies* (New Haven, Conn.: Yale University Press, 1968), 195-96.

21. See Genaro Arriagada, *El Pensamiento Político de los Militares (Estudios Sobre Chile,*

Argentina, Brasil y Uruguay) (Santiago: CISEC, n.d.); Liisa North, "Ideological Orientations of Peru's Military Leaders," in *The Peruvian Experiment Reconsidered,* ed. Cynthia McClintock and Abraham Lowenthal (Princeton, N.J.: Princeton University Press, 1983); Jorge Chateau, "Antecedentes Teóricos para el Estudio de la Geopolítica y Doctrinas Castrenses," FLACSO, Santiago, Documento de Trabajo, January 1977; Alfred Stepan, "The New Professionalism of Internal Warfare and Military Role Expansion," in *Authoritarian Brazil,* ed. Alfred Stepan (New Haven, Conn.: Yale University Press, 1973); David Pion-Berlin, "Latin American National Security Doctrines: Hard- and Softline Themes," *Armed Forces and Society* 15, no. 3 (Spring 1989); and Brian Loveman and Thomas M. Davies, Jr., *The Politics of Antipolitics,* 2d rev. ed. (Lincoln: University of Nebraska Press, 1989).

22. In the 184 issues of CESEDEN's (see following note) information bulletin (*Boletín de Información*), which go from 1966 through 1985, there is only one article that used the term *national security* in the title ("Cambio en el Concepto de Defensa de la Seguridad Nacional," *Boletín de Información,* no. 182 [April 1985]). Among the academic activities conducted by CESEDEN, only one seminar contained the term *national security* in the title: "Política de Defensa y Seguridad Nacional" (Quinto Ciclo de Defensa Nacional [ALEMI]). On "defense of the community," see "Clausura del Seminario 'Amenazas a la Comunidad,'" *Boletín de Información,* no. 97 (January 1976).

23. CESEDEN was created in 1964 and given the mission to conduct studies of general relevance for national defense; to study and propose general doctrine for joint action; to complete the formation of general officers of the three armed services; and to provide joint staff instruction (see *Breve Información Sobre el Centro Superior de Estudios de la Defensa Nacional [CESEDEN],* Madrid, October 1985).

24. See Juan Pablo Fusi, "La Década Desarrollista," in *Historia de España,* no. 13; *Historia* 16 8, no. 25 (February 1983); and Jacint Ros Hombravella and Josep Oliver, "Los Planes de Desarrollo," in Siglo XX, Historia Universal no. 29, *Historia* 16, n.d.

25. In 184 issues of the *Boletín de Información* of CESEDEN between 1966 and 1985, only seventeen articles (10.8 percent) contain titles that include references to "communism" or "subversion," fourteen of which appeared between 1974 and 1978. The number of conferences on subversion in the Joint Staff School and in the High Military Studies cycle was very small as well.

26. Manuel Diez-Alegría, *Ejército y Sociedad* (Madrid: Alianza Editorial, 1972), 50–69.

27. In reference to General António de Spínola who led the overthrow of Marcelo Cactano in Portugal in 1974. Although there was no official version about the ouster of Diez-Alegría, the pretext was a meeting he held with Nicolae Ceausescu during a visit to Romania, wrongly portrayed in Spain as unauthorized. Hard-line civilian and military personalities spread the rumor that he had also met with Spanish Communist leader Santiago Carrillo.

28. Upon assuming the position as army chief of staff on 9 July 1976, Lieutenant General Manuel Gutiérrez Mellado pointed to "the sacrifice which our Army has made in the last decades in favor of the development of the nation." In September 1976, in his first general report, he again emphasized that "the military was left aside in the allocations which were made in the context of the Development Plans" (see Manuel Gutiérrez Mellado, *Al Servicio de la Corona* [Madrid: Ibérico Europea de Edi-

ciones, 1981], 33 and 55). Conservatives were opposed to having these complaints aired and criticized Gutiérrez Mellado when in the early 1970s he had spoken in a military conference in CESEDEN about the operational insufficiencies of the Spanish army (see Gutiérrez Mellado, *Un Soldado de España,* 56 and 51; and *Recorded Interview,* Fundación Ortega y Gasset, Madrid, 8 September 1987). General Gabeiras, who in 1975 was director of studies of the Joint Staff School in CESEDEN and then director of Industry and Matériel in the army ministry, later commented that his view of franquism was tainted by "the enormous degradation which the army had reached during Franco's lifetime." This view, he said, was not predominant in the army (José Gabeiras, *Recorded Interview,* Fundación Ortega y Gasset, Madrid, 11 December 1987). For a critique of the failure of the development plans to incorporate the armed forces, see the presentation by Lieutenant Colonel Poyato, "El Plan de Desarrollo y la Defensa Nacional," V Course 1969–1970, Joint Staff School, CESEDEN.

29. Conservatives as well had made a few attempts at modernization and reform in the past, albeit not very successfully. Jointly with the efforts and initiatives of liberal officers who gained notoriety later, they promoted in the mid-1960s the organizational distinction between territorial defense forces and rapid deployment forces, created the CESEDEN, and encouraged studies for further organizational reforms (see Gomáriz, "Los Militares," 20–30; and César Ruiz Ocaña, *Los Ejércitos Españoles* (Madrid: Editorial San Martín, 1980), 63–69.

30. Moskos's typology takes off from an examination of trends in the U.S. army (see Charles C. Moskos, "From Institution to Occupation: Trends in Military Organization," *Armed Forces and Society* 4, no. 1 [November 1977]; and Charles C. Moskos, "Institutional and Occupational Trends in Armed Forces," in *The Military: More Than Just a Job?* ed. Charles C. Moskos and Frank R. Wood [Washington, D.C.: Pergamon-Brassey's, 1988]). For a critique, see Morris Janowitz, "From Institutional to Occupational: The Need for Conceptual Continuity," *Armed Forces and Society* 4, no. 1 (November 1977).

31. Moskos, "Institutional and Occupational Trends," 15 and 16.

32. Morris Janowitz referred to "powerful strains and even signs of decisive cleavages in the military officer corps," partly related to the fact that "the military profession [was] undergoing long-term transformation which involve[d] increased penetration by other professions and institutions." Janowitz "described these trends as those of the civilianization of the military, as they converged more and more with civilian professions" ("From Institutional to Occupational," 52 and 53).

33. Some of these consequences surfaced later, for instance, in the massive exit of air force and navy pilots to higher-paying jobs in commercial airlines (see *El País,* 1 December 1987, 17).

34. See, for instance, Colonel Juan de la Lama Cereceda, "De la Instrucción en el Ejército," *Ejército,* no. 441 (October 1976); and no. 446 (March 1977). For a discussion of different postures in the Spanish military with reference to Moskos's categories, see Miguel Alonso Baquer, "Los Problemas de la Defensa," in *España: Un Presente Para el Futuro (2), Las Instituciones,* ed. E. García de Enterría et al. (Madrid: Instituto de Estudios Económicos, 1984).

35. *Ejército,* no. 426 (July 1975): 9.

36. Manuel Cabeza Calahorra, "Nuestras Responsabilidades Primeras," *Ejército,* no. 429 (October 1975): 34–35. Promoted to lieutenant general, Cabeza Calahorra became director of the High Army School in 1977.

37. Admiral Liberal, for instance, maintained that "the reforms are one hundred per cent military" (recorded interview, Madrid, 4 December 1987). Also Gutiérrez Mellado commented that the creation of the defense ministry was cherished in military circles long ago and that, therefore, when people "talk of 'military reform,'" the term seems to me an exaggeration" (*Un Soldado de España,* 83).

38. José Luis Lancho de León, "El Gasto en Defensa," *Papeles de Economía Española,* no. 37 (1988): 299.

39. Ministerio de Defensa, *Memoria de la Legislatura (1982–1986),* 181.

40. Gregory Treverton, "Spain: Domestic Politics and Security Policy," *Adelphi Papers,* no. 204 (Spring 1986).

41. Gutiérrez Mellado, *Al Servicio de la Corona,* 44.

42. *Ley Orgánica de la Armada* (Madrid: Ministerio de Marina, E.M.A.-Reglamentos).

43. See especially the presentations by Fernández-Manrique, Gavarrón Zambrano, Dávila, and Cabrero Torres-Quevedo, listed in table 5.1.

44. Interviews with Lieutenant General Juan Cano Hevia, Madrid, 17 September and 5 October 1987. Also see César Ruiz Ocaña, *Los Ejércitos Españoles* (Madrid: Editorial San Martín, 1982), 67.

45. *Boletín de las Cortes Españolas,* no. 1340 (23 April 1974): 32614.

46. A strong attack on the bill appeared in the article "La Defensa Nacional" published in the right-wing newspaper *El Alcázar* (10 June 1974). The article was signed by Jerjes, a pseudonym used by General Luis Cano Portal, who at the time was director of the journal *Ejército.* Diez Alegría officially left the High General Staff on 14 June 1974.

47. Addressing the Royal Academy of Moral and Political Sciences on 4 March 1975, Manuel Diez Alegría listed the obstacles to defense reform: "the characteristic inertia of the Armed Forces . . . and its permanent resistance to change; the aversion to a Ministry of Defense . . . ; the resistance of the [armed services'] ministries to what they believe is loss of independence; the fact that the [military] ministers . . . exercise command of the armies; the 'reverential fear' with which politicians and in general all civilians consider military affairs, which they prefer to leave aside; the jealousy between the different services, and other motives of a personal nature . . . personal rivalries inherent in any reform" (qtd. in Ruiz Ocaña, *Los Ejércitos Españoles,* 66).

48. This doctrine (for joint logistics) had been approved internally in the HGS as part of the larger reform package. Since this failed to pass, the HGS decided to go ahead anyway and make the doctrine a required course material for the Joint Staff School and the High Military Studies courses. But, as air force General Rafael·López-Sáez Rodríguez commented to his student officers, "This situation creates organizational difficulties which must be overcome with the good will of all." Interestingly, he added: "You will find that [the doctrine of joint action] has a marked American accent . . . which may give rise to misgivings on your part, but this should disappear with an in-depth knowledge of the doctrine" (CESEDEN, *Boletín de Información,* no. 89 [February 1975]).

49. See, for instance, chapter 5, "Defensa Nacional," in *Libro Blanco para la Reforma Democrática* (Madrid: Imprenta Cervantes, 1976), which represented the views of the group led by Manuel Fraga. A more general and vague treatment of national defense issues appears in the documents of the 27th Congress of the PSOE (Socialist Party) held in 1976.

50. Royal Decree-Law no. 10/1977 regulated the exercise of political and union activities by members of the armed forces (*Diario Oficial del Ministerio del Ejército* 88, no. 34 [11 February 1977]: 577–78).

51. "Informe General 1–76 del Ejército de Tierra," in Gutiérrez Mellado, *Al Servicio de la Corona,* 41–58.

52. The approval of new military ordinances almost simultaneously with the new constitution was an important accomplishment as it successfully dealt with sensitive issues in the military such as questions of "duty" and "honor." A committee exclusively composed of military officers from the three services appointed by the king modernized the ordinances that Carlos III had approved in 1768 under the title, "Ordinances for discipline, subordination and service of my armies," and significantly included clauses that set limits to military obedience: "No member of the armed forces is obliged to obey orders which go against the law . . . in particular against the Constitution" (see Fernando de Salas López and Francisco Laguna Sanguirico, "Las Reales Ordenanzas en el Momento Actual de la Sociedad Española," *Revista Española de Investigaciones Sociológicas,* no. 36 [October–December 1986], 123–24).

53. Lieutenant General José Vega Rodríguez became chief of staff when Gutiérrez Mellado left the army for the vice presidency. A prestigious soldier, Lieutenant General Federico Gómez de Salazar was appointed Captain General of Madrid after serving in Valladolid and the Sahara. Lieutenant General Antonio Ibáñez Freire was assigned to command a military region then the Civil Guard and later became minister of the interior.

54. The first editorial article under the new direction announced that the journal would now support the army's modernization plans and that freedom of expression in the army had limits: "It is not the same to offer the High Command reasonable proposals for change as it is to propose the substitution of the High Command altogether" (*Ejército,* no. 456 [January 1978]: 3). Another editorial in December 1978 (no. 467) added: "A radical change is taking place in Spain, not yet concluded and which privately may please some more than others, but as military men we are compelled to respect and to serve"; "We cannot publicly criticize our Command, the minister, the government or the Constitution . . . and if our 'vocation' is to criticize [these institutions] then a good recommendation is to leave the army" (3–4).

55. Cassinello also played key roles in transition policies such as negotiations with Tarradellas for his return to the Generalitat (the government) in Catalonia and the uncovering of military plots such as the Galaxia affair (General Andrés Cassinello, *Recorded Interview,* Madrid, Fundación Ortega y Gasset, 2 October 1986). Gutiérrez Mellado, who had conflicts with military intelligence from his days in the HGS, weakened the powers of intelligence in the army staff and helped to strengthen the government service (Lieutenant General José Sáenz de Tejada, *Recorded Interview,* Fundación Ortega y Gasset, 24 September 1987; Lieutenant General Manuel Gutiérrez Mellado, *Recorded Interview,* Fundación Ortega y Gasset, 8 September 1987).

56. *Recorded Interview,* Fundación Ortega y Gasset, 9 May 1985.

57. Speech before the king during the celebration of the Pascua Militar of 1977 (Gutiérrez Mellado, *Al Servicio de la Corona,* 61).

58. "[The government's] fair play and decision are confirmed every day by us who are with him [the captain of the ship, the head of the government], with our own initiative. In the government we are four military ministers, whose professional history . . . may be analogous to the majority of officers who can be called typical of their class, but we do not admit anyone to exceed us in love for Spain, our King and the Army. Thus, nobody should think that we will weaken vigilance of our sacred mission of guaranteeing the honor, the sovereignty, the independence and integrity of our country" ("Conferencia Sobre las Fuerzas Armadas en la Capitanía General de Sevilla," in Gutiérrez Mellado, *Al Servicio de la Corona,* 86).

59. Gutiérrez Mellado, *Un Soldado de España,* 95–99.

60. Alfred Stepan, *Rethinking Military Politics;* Thomas E. Skidmore, *The Politics of Military Rule in Brazil: 1964–1985* (Oxford: Oxford University Press, 1988).

61. Guillermo O'Donnell, *Bureaucratic Authoritarianism: Argentina, 1966–1973, in Comparative Perspective* (Berkeley: University of California Press, 1988); David Pion-Berlin and Ernesto López, "A House Divided: Crisis Cleavage and Conflict in the Argentine Army," in *The New Argentine Democracy: The Search for a Successful Formula,* ed. Edward C. Epstein (New York: Praeger, 1992).

62. J. Samuel Fitch, "Military Role Beliefs in Latin American Democracies" (grant report no. 3, U.S. Institute of Peace, February 1993); Anita Isaacs, *Military Rule and Transition in Ecuador: 1972–1992* (Pittsburgh: University of Pittsburgh Press, 1993); Peter S. Cleaves and Henry Paese García, "State Autonomy and Military Policy Making," in *Armies and Politics in Latin America,* ed. Abraham F. Lowenthal and J. Samuel Fitch (New York: Holmes and Meier, 1986); Carina Perelli, "Los Militares y la Gestión Pública" (Montevideo: Peitho, 1990).

63. Arturo Valenzuela and Pamela Constable, "Democracy in Chile," *Current History* (February 1991); and Augusto Varas, "The Crisis of Legitimacy of Military Rule in the 1980s," in *The Struggle for Democracy in Chile, 1982–1990,* ed. Paul W. Drake and Iván Jaksi (Lincoln: University of Nebraska Press, 1991).

64. Stepan, *Rethinking Military Politics.* 72–79.

65. J. Samuel Fitch, "The Armed Forces and Democracy in Latin America: Toward a New Relationship" (discussion paper no. 46, Center for Public Policy Research, University of Colorado–Boulder, December 1988).

66. See, for instance, Alexandre de S. C. Barros, "Back to the Barracks: An Option for the Brazilian Military?" *Third World Quarterly* 7, no. 1 (January 1985).

67. The failure in attempts to create a defense ministry in Brazil and the difficulties encountered in such a creation in Peru attest to the restricted scope of changes considered by the military in these countries (Wendy Ann Hunter, "Back to the Barracks? The Military in Post-Authoritarian Brazil" (Ph.D. diss., University of California–Berkeley, 1992), 165–69 and 186–87; and Marcial Rubio, *Ministerio de Defensa: Antecedentes y Retos* (Lima: APEP-Friedrich Ebert, 1987).

68. Augusto Varas, *Los Militares en el Poder: Régimen y Gobierno Militar en Chile, 1973–1986* (Santiago: FLACSO-Pehuén Editores, 1987); Genaro Arriagada, "The Legal and Institutional Framework of the Armed Forces in Chile," in *Military Rule in Chile,*

ed. Arturo Valenzuela and J. Samuel Valenzuela (Baltimore: Johns Hopkins University Press, 1986); and Hunter, "Back to the Barracks."

69. Agüero, "Military and the Limits to Democratization"; David Pion-Berlin, "Between Confrontation and Accommodation: Military and Government Policy in Democratic Argentina," *Journal of Latin American Studies* 23 (October 1991).

70. In Spain the rise in terrorist attacks on the military by ETA could be seen as having a similar unifying effect, but, in fact, it helped galvanize hard-line positions more than it brought these positions together with those of the liberals.

71. Juan J. Linz and Alfred Stepan, *Problems of Democratic Transition and Consolidation: Southern Europe, South America and Eastern Europe* (Baltimore: Johns Hopkins University Press, forthcoming).

72. Thanos Veremis, "The Military," in *Political Change in Greece: Before and After the Colonels,* ed. Kevin Featherstone and Dimitrios K. Katsoudas (New York: St. Martin's Press, 1987).

73. See Lawrence S. Graham, *The Portuguese Military and the State: Rethinking Transitions in Europe and Latin America* (Boulder, Colo.: Westview Press, 1993).

Chapter 6: Obstacles to Regime Consolidation after the Transition

1. To use Giuseppe Di Palma's felicitous expression (*To Craft Democracies* [Berkeley: University of California Press, 1990], 144–45).

2. The view of democratization in terms of changing costs of toleration and suppression appears in Robert Dahl, *Polyarchy: Participation and Opposition* (New Haven, Conn.: Yale University Press, 1971), 14–16.

3. In September 1977 Josep Tarradellas, the Catalan leader before the Franquist regime, returned from exile to take over the provisionally reestablished government in Catalonia — the Generalitat — following an agreement with President Suárez. In December 1977 a General Council was provisionally established in Euskadi, while negotiations were started for future autonomy settlements pending constitutional definitions.

4. Peru faced a severe national integration challenge stemming from the marginalization of the vast Indian population of the highlands. In practice, however, this challenge did not have implications for the formal territorial organization of the state.

5. With these elections and the new constitution, the head of the government became accountable to Parliament and was elected by it, as any prime minister in parliamentary systems. The head of government retained, however, the traditional designation of *"presidente del gobierno."* Spanish prime ministers are referred to as presidents, and I follow that usage here.

6. AP-CD received 8 percent of the vote in the general elections of 1977 and only 6.1 percent in the 1979 general elections (José Ramón Montero, "Los Fracasos Políticos y Electorales de la Derecha Española: Alianza Popular, 1976–1986," *Revista Española de Investigaciones Sociológicas,* no. 39 [July–September 1987]: 10; on AP-CD, see also Rafael López-Pintor, "Francoist Reformers in Democratic Spain: The Popular Alliance and the Democratic Coalition," in *Spain at the Polls: 1977, 1979 and 1982,* ed.

Howard Penniman and Eusebio Mujal-León [Durham, N.C.: Duke University Press, 1985]).

7. This argument is advanced in Richard Gunther, "Democratization and Party Building: The Role of Party Elites in the Spanish Transition," in *Spain in the 1980s*, ed. Robert P. Clark and Michael H. Haltzel (Cambridge, Mass.: Ballinger, 1987), 38.

8. Juan Linz, "Europe's Southern Frontier: Evolving Trends toward What?" *Daedalus* 108, no. 1 (Winter 1979).

9. *Reconquista* (May 1979): iii, iv.

10. *Reconquista* (December 1979): 8.

11. *Ejército*, no. 474 (July 1979): 5–6.

12. Mérida, *Mis Conversaciones*, 142.

13. Ibid., 197–98. These evaluations were publicly challenged in an editorial in *El País* (25 September 1979). The government's disciplinary response to such serious indictments by the generals was merely to summon them to the capital (*El País*, 27 September 1979).

14. The council first offered the post to Lieutenant General Angel Campano, who was the most senior general, but he refused. Lieutenants General Jaime Miláns del Bosch, Antonio Elícegui, and Jesús González del Yerro were the other hard-liners considered (Lieutenant General José María Sáenz de Tejada, *Recorded Interview*, Fundación Ortega y Gasset, Madrid, 29 September 1987).

15. See General Gabeiras's speech commenting on the circumstances of his promotion and appointment in *Ejército* (January 1982, xiv); also see Lieutenant General José Gabeiras, *Recorded Interview*, Fundación Ortega y Gasset, Madrid, 15 December 1987. The appointment of Gabeiras was actually made by the new civilian defense minister, Agustín Rodríguez Sahagún, following the suggestion of Gutiérrez Mellado, who remained in the government as vice president for defense affairs.

16. José María Maravall and Julián Santamaría, "Crisis del Franquismo, Transición Política y Consolidación de la Democracia en España," *Sistema*, nos. 68–69 (November 1985): 105.

17. The putsch was planned for a day in November on which the king was traveling abroad and the president and the joint chiefs were out of Madrid (see "El Primer Golpe del Militar Tejero," Diario 16, *Historia de la Transición*, chap. 38). Tejero had already gained notoriety for the "Open Letter to the King of Spain," published in *El Imparcial* on 31 August 1978: "No. This constitution draft does not include some of the values for which we believe it is worth risking our lives. In it our dead are not found."

18. For this and other similar incidents, see Gutiérrez Mellado, *Un Soldado de España*, 107–8; and interviews with Lieutenant General José Sáenz de Tejada, Fundación Ortega y Gasset, Madrid, 24 and 29 September 1987.

19. In 1975, not long before his death, Franco defied massive domestic demonstrations and the pressure of heads of government from around the world by refusing to pardon ETA militants facing death sentences.

20. Juan Pablo Fusi, "Spain: The Fragile Democracy," *West European Politics* 5, no. 3 (July 1982). For the broader context of Basque nationalism, see Stanley G. Payne, *Basque Nationalism* (Reno: University of Nevada Press, 1975); Juan Linz, "The Basques in Spain: Nationalism and Political Conflict in a New Democracy," in *Resolving Nationality Conflicts: The Role of Public Opinion Research*, ed. W. Phillips Davison and Leon

Gordenker (New York: Praeger, 1980); Juan J. Linz, Manuel Gómez Reino, Francisco Andrés Orizo, and Dario Vila, *Conflicto en Euskadi: Estudio Sociológico Sobre el Cambio Político en el País Vasco, 1975–1980* (Madrid: Espasa Calpe, 1986); and Robert P. Clark, "Euzkadi: Basque Nationalism in Spain since the Civil War," in *Nations without a State: Ethnic Minorities in Western Europe,* ed. Charles R. Foster (New York: Praeger, 1980).

21. *El País,* 22 July 1978, 4 January, 26 and 27 May 1979, and 2 February 1980.

22. As Juan Pablo Fusi put it, "It was only because terrorism was linked to the regional question that it became a threat to the stability of Spanish democracy" ("Spain," 226).

23. Goldie Shabad, "After Autonomy: The Dynamics of Regionalism in Spain," in *The Politics of Democratic Spain,* ed. Stanley G. Payne (Chicago: Chicago Council on Foreign Relations, 1986), 139.

24. The Basque Nationalist Party withdrew all its representatives in Congress, in response to the government's attempt to initiate a "rationalization of the autonomy process," which Basque leaders thought would curtail their prerogatives. The government attempted rationalization in light of the pressures unleashed from all regions in Spain for the creation of their own autonomous communities, and that created a chaotic situation, which Spaniards referred to as "coffee for everybody" (see Diario 16, *Historia de la Transición,* chap. 41).

25. When Adolfo Suárez visited Euskadi in December 1980, the mayors of the PNV, the regional ruling party, with which the government had successfully conducted the negotiations for autonomy, declared him persona non grata, and many of the hosts were nowhere to be found to greet the president (see "Autonomía con Sangre en Euskadi," Diario 16, *Historia de la Transición,* chap. 41).

26. Gutiérrez Mellado, *Al Servicio de la Corona,* 144.

27. *Reconquista* (May 1979): iii–iv; (December 1979): 8.

28. General Juan Atarés Peña insulted Gutiérrez Mellado and the Constitution in a massive meeting with officers and NCOs in late 1978 but got away with a light internal disciplinary measure imposed by his superior, Lieutenant General Jaime Milans del Bosch.

29. See editorial comments in *El País,* 16 and 22 April 1990.

30. *El País,* 19 November 1978, 9 December 1979, 8 May 1980, 5 July 1980. Ironically, General Quintana Lacaci, General Atarés Peña, and Major Sáenz de Ynestrillas were all, much later and at different times, gunned down by ETA.

31. This double standard was exemplified also in the arrest of Major Santiago Perinat for denouncing the banning of the reading of *El País* and *Diario* 16 in military garrisons (*El País,* 15 December 1978) and the arrest of Captain José Luis Pitarch for statements made to the press (*El País,* 22 April 1980) (José Luis Pitarch, *Diario Abierto de un Militar Constitucionalista* [Valencia: Fernando Torres Editor, 1981]). On the action against the director of *Diario* 16, see *El País,* 2 February 1980; and the editorial on 29 January 1980. Also at the time film director Pilar Miró was prosecuted by a military court for a film that contained depictions of brutalities by the Civil Guard in the past (*El País,* 29 March 1980). In regard to attempts to reinstate the right of UMD members to return to the army, all parties in Congress, except Manuel Fraga's Coalición Democrática, submitted a bill to that effect in July 1980, resuming an initiative that,

on pressures from the military, Congress had been forced to drop in 1977. By different means the military again made it known that this would not be possible (see editorials in *El País,* 10 and 27 July and 28 September 1980).

32. *Ejército* (January 1980): ii.

33. *Revista de Marina* (February 1979): 214.

34. *Ejército* (January 1980): 3.

35. An emergency grand coalition including personalities of all major parties and,
in some versions, the military.

36. This statement appears in his article "Situación Límite" (An Extreme Situation), in *El Alcázar,* 8 February 1981.

37. Quoted in Pitarch, *Diario Abierto,* 99.

38. Royal Decree no. 1558/1977, which restructured organs of central administration of the state (*Diario Oficial del Ministerio del Ejército* [6 July 1977]: 82–85). Also important is the Royal Decree no. 2723/1977, which structured the defense ministry
organically and functionally (*Boletín Oficial del Ministerio de Defensa: Diario Oficial del Ejército* [8 November 1977]: 513-18).

39. See Ministerio de Marina, E.M.A. Reglamentos, *Ley Orgánicade la Armada* (y
Disposiciones Relacionadas con Esta) (Madrid: Servicio de Publicaciones del Ministerio de Marina, n.d.). For the army reform, see Royal Decree no. 3036/1976, which
ruled on the attributions, functions, and responsibilities of the chief of staff of the
army; Royal Decree-Law no. 8/1977, which restructured the Army Supreme Council; and Royal Decree no. 241/1977, which reorganized the army ministry. They
appear in *Diario Oficial del Ministerio del Ejército* (12 January 1977): 145-46; (10 February
1977): 561-62; and (28 February 1977): 801-3, respectively.

40. The orders of the minister of the army on the agencies to be made dependent
on the army chief of staff, which appeared in *Diario Oficial del Ministerio del Ejército* (25
April 1977): 353-58, reflect this kind of agency transfer.

41. The decree by which Rodríguez Sahagún was appointed minister indicated
that all his staff should come from the military (Miguel Angel Aguilar, "La Batalla
Perdida," *El País,* 3 January 1981).

42. One of those persuaded was the ministry's first and diligent undersecretary,
Admiral Angel Liberal Lucini, who later became the first chief of defense staff. Ear-
lier, upon his return in 1974 from the post of naval attaché in Washington, D.C.,
Admiral Liberal had prepared a memo for navy chiefs warning about the dangers of
enhancing the dominance of the army in the eventual creation of a defense ministry.
The navy had, in fact, not sought the creation of the ministry (interview with
Admiral Liberal, Fundación Ortega y Gasset, Madrid, 10 November 1987).

43. Royal Decree-Law no. 11/1977, which institutionalizes the Joint Chiefs and
rules on its attributions, functions, and responsibilities (*Diario Oficial del Ministerio del
Ejército* [11 February 1977]: 579-80). Significantly, the first chairman was an air force
general, signaling the desire to gradually diminish the dominance of the land army.

44. The board was composed of the president, the defense minister, the Joint
Chiefs, and seven other cabinet ministers and was chaired by the king. Also, the law
made the president responsible for the conduct of war (Law Which Regulates the
Functions of Supreme Organs of the State Concerning National Defense, *Boletín
Oficial de las Cortes,* no. 218 [26 December 1978]: 4612-15).

45. Mérida, *Mis Conversaciones,* 65.

46. A royal decree issued by the presidency in March 1978 specified for the first time that the dependency relations that previous laws established for the Joint Chiefs upon the president could also be delegated by the latter on the defense minister. The same decree, however, also instructed that "implementation of the missions assigned to the Defense Minister . . . *must be harmonized* with the responsibilities which have been assigned to the Joint Chiefs" (see Royal Decree-Law no. 836/1978 [27 March], which develops Royal Decree-Law no. 11/1977 [8 February], in *Boletín Oficial del Estado,* no. 102 [29 April 1978]; my emphasis).

47. Manuel Fraga, for instance, had argued in Congress against the clause of the 1978 national defense law, which assigned the conduct of war to the president.

48. *Reconquista* (August–September 1979): 7. In March 1980, in Congress, Rodríguez Sahagún still emphasized the need to "develop and consolidate the structures of the new defense ministry" and to "overcome the inertia generated by the existence, for so many years, of three different ministries" (*Diario de Sesiones del Congreso de los Diputados,* no. 77 [March 1980]: 5198). Socialist member of congress Luis Solana also argued that "the truth is that the Ministry of Defense is a ministry in which three old ministries have accumulated with three different models and ways of conceiving defense. Each one of the armies had a ministry and the three of them have accumulated in the new one" (ibid., no. 78 [9 April 1980]: 5240). Interviews with General Gabeiras (Madrid, Fundación Ortega y Gasset, 11 and 15 December 1987), who held different posts in the ministry since its creation until his appointment as army chief of staff in 1979, and Admiral Liberal (ibid., 20 November 1987), who was director general of economic affairs and then deputy minister of defense until his appointment as captain general in El Ferrol in 1983, confirm that little of substance was accomplished in this period.

49. Interview with Lieutenant General Federico Gómez de Salazar, Madrid, 3 July 1986.

50. For instance, in an article entitled "The Generals," Lieutenant Colonel (r) Angel Palomino wrote: "What we want is government and not that which is locked in La Moncloa ruining Spain. The generals are worthy of other treatment than the one received from the politicians . . . and it is therefore legitimate to think that [the generals] can and must present the situation, expose the problem and propose solutions to the captain general of the Armies: His Majesty the King" (in *El Alcázar,* 31 May 1979, 3).

51. *Revista de Marina* (February 1979): 214 (my emphasis).

52. The position of the Right was well expressed in the debate on the 1980 national defense law, which attempted to specify the prerogatives of the government. In this debate Manuel Fraga's group submitted a special amendment to include a role for the king in the decision-making powers of the government over the Joint Chiefs (see Amendment no. 139 by Coalición Popular, in Cortes Generales, *Ley Orgánica por la que se Regulan los Criterios Básicos de la Defensa Nacional y la Organización Militar: Trabajos Parlamentarios* [Madrid: Publicaciones del Congreso de los Diputados, 1984], 60). Manuel Fraga's and Miguel Herrero de Miñón's statements appear in Félix Arteaga Martin, "Reflexiones Sobre el Artículo Octavo de la Constitución Española de 1978" (paper presented to the First Iberoamerican Congress of Military Sociology, Madrid, September 1985).

53. Federico Trillo Figueroa, "Las Fuerzas Armadas en la Constitución Española: Esbozo de una Construcción Institucional," *Revista de Estudios Políticos,* no. 12 (November–December 1979): 111. The article also argued, however, against the overutilization of this view, maintaining that the link between the king and the armed forces could not be construed to suggest regal initiative in the mobilization of the military in defense of the Constitution (121–23). For another view in historical perspective, see Carlos Seco Serrano, "Relaciones entre la Corona y el Ejército," *Revista de Estudios Políticos,* no. 55 (January–March 1987).

54. See, for instance, Gutiérrez Mellado's guarantees to officers during a visit to the División Acorazada in 1978, in his book *Al Servicio de la Corona,* 172; and Rodríguez Sahagún's prudent promises regarding personnel policies, in his first speech in the Pascua Militar in January 1980 (*Ejército* [January 1980]: ix).

55. In his inaugural speech in the 1979 Congress, Suárez stated: "Consensus has ended. . . . We are now headed toward the realization of a government program conceived under the prism of a party program, coherent with the promises made before the electorate" (qtd. in Carlos Huneeus, *La Unión de Centro Democrático y la Transición a la Democracia en España* [Madrid: Centro de Investigaciones Sociológicas, 1985], 262).

56. The Socialists and the Communists also experienced losses in the regional elections to the benefit of the regional parties, although to a much lesser extent.

57. Study no. 1264, barometer no. 17, January 1981, Centro de Investigaciones Sociológicas, Madrid. On this, see also Huneeus, *La Unión de Centro Democrático,* 296, 313, 390–91.

58. See Bonifacio de la Cuadra and Soledad Gallego-Díaz, *Del Consenso al Desencanto* (Madrid: Editorial Saltés, 1981).

59. Fusi, "Spain," 227, 229.

60. For growth rates, inflation, unemployment, wages, and strike activity, see Juergen B. Donges, "La Insuficiencia de Productividad en la Economía Española: Causas y Remedios," in *España: Un Presente para el Futuro (I. La Sociedad),* ed. Juan J. Linz (Madrid: Instituto de Estudios Económicos, 1984), 100; and Richard Gunther, "The Spanish Socialist Party: From Clandestine Opposition to Party of Government," in Payne, *Politics of Democratic Spain,* 33. For wage increases, see Rafael López Pintor, "Mass and Elite Perspectives in the Process of Transition to Democracy," in *Comparing New Democracies: Transition and Consolidation in Mediterranean Europe and the Southern Cone,* ed. Enrique Baloyra (Boulder, Colo.: Westview Press, 1987), 87. On the perceived importance of unemployment, terrorism, and inflation, see Study no. 1240, barometer no. 13, September 1980 (N = 1180), Centro de Investigaciones Sociológicas, Madrid. For evaluations of the political and economic situation, see José Ramón Montero and Mariano Torcal, "Voters and Citizens in a New Democracy: Some Trend Data on Political Attitudes in Spain," *International Journal of Public Opinion Research* 2, no. 2 (1990).

61. The same polls that indicated high levels of concern with unemployment and terrorism and low evaluations of the political and economic situation also suggested, however, that economic discontent and political pessimism did not increase support for antidemocratic solutions. Although these low evaluations may have weakened the intensity of support for democracy—intensity that declined during 1980 and rose again sharply in 1981 after the coup attempt (Montero and Torcal, "Voters and Cit-

izens," 126–27)—it was concluded that the legitimacy of the system remained high (see also Juan J. Linz and Alfred Stepan, "Political Crafting of Democratic Consolidation or Destruction: European and South American Comparisons," in *Democracy in the Americas: Stopping the Pendulum*, ed. Robert A. Pastor [New York: Holmes and Meier, 1989], 46). I submit, however, that the military, when weighing alternative courses of action during critical junctures, does not wrestle with systems in general; it wrestles with concrete administrations and leaders and is, therefore, more sensitive to the popularity of leaders and governments than to inferences about "system" legitimacy.

62. Quoted in Sergio Vilar, *La Década Sorprendente: 1976–1986* (Barcelona: Editorial Planeta, 1986), 97. For UCD, see Carlos Huneeus, *La Unión de Centro Democrático;* and Leopoldo Calvo Sotelo, *Memoria Viva de la Transición* (Barcelona: Plaza y Janés / Cambio 16, 1990).

63. On 10 January 1978 Gutiérrez Mellado attended a meeting of the defense committee of the Cortes, chaired by Socialist Enrique Múgica. It was the first institutional meeting of a military chief with members of all parties, Nationalists and Communists included, to report on defense policy. After a long presentation of the minister's reform and modernization plans, committee members of all parties agreed to a statement that praised the meeting and the plans put forth by the minister (*Ejército* [supp.], no. 459 [April 1978]: 3–32).

64. David Gilmour, *The Transformation of Spain* (London: Quarter Books, 1985), 249–50; and Huneeus, *La Unión de Centro Democrático*, 282–97.

65. Emilio Attard, *Vida y Muerte de UCD* (Barcelona: Planeta, 1983), 183–84; Manuel Fraga, *En Busca del Tiempo Servido* (Barcelona: Planeta, 1987), 200–202; and Montero, "Los Fracasos Políticos y Electorales," 16. The formula of a "*gobierno de concentración*" vaguely suggested the creation of a strong government that included a broad coalition with individual members of the moderate Left, the Center (with the exclusion of Suárez and his closest entourage), the Right, and the military.

66. By this time only 10 percent of the army remained truly loyal to Suárez and Gutiérrez Mellado, according to estimates by Alberto Oliart, defense minister in the Calvo Sotelo government, which succeeded Suárez (*Recorded Interview*, Fundación Ortega y Gasset, Madrid, 20 May 1985). Suárez's resignation speech appears in Eduardo Chamorro, *Viaje al Centro de UCD* (Barcelona: Planeta, 1981), 32–36. On the meetings in Ceuta and Melilla, see José Oneto, *La Verdad Sobre el Caso Tejero* (Barcelona: Planeta, 1982), vii–viii.

67. Fraga, *En Busca del Tiempo Servido*, 231.

68. Oneto, *La Verdad Sobre el Caso Tejero*, i–xix.

69. Interview with Lieutenant General José Gabeiras, Madrid, 15 December 1987.

70. Fraga, *En Busca del Tiempo Servido*, 226; and Oneto, *La Verdad Sobre el Caso Tejero*.

71. See Oneto, *La Verdad Sobre el Caso Tejero*, ix; and Vilar, *La Década Sorprendente*, 76–78. An editorial in *El País* a year later expressly criticized "the maneuverings of a few individuals more or less representative of the PSOE in favor of a caretaker government presided by some prestigious military in order to displace Adolfo Suárez" (*El País*, 25 September 1982).

72. Interview with Lieutenant General José Sáenz de Tejada, Madrid, 29 September 1987.

73. Chamorro, *Viaje al Centro de UCD*, 40.

74. Fraga, *En Busca del Tiempo Servido*, 225.

75. In Juan Pablo Fusi's words, Suárez "secluded himself in his Moncloa Palace, haunted by the opposition, isolated from the public, frightened of parliament, fearful of his own party. Spain was ruled by the phantom of a silent and paralyzed government" ("Spain," 232).

Chapter 7: The Coup Attempt and the End of the Threat to Democracy

1. For an illuminating view of unintended change, see Albert O. Hirschman, *A Bias for Hope* (New Haven, Conn.: Yale University Press, 1971), 26–37; and Hirschman, *Rival Views of Market Society* (Cambridge, Mass.: Harvard University Press, 1992), 171–75.

2. Accounts of the coup attempt are found in José Oneto, *La Verdad Sobre el Caso Tejero* (Barcelona: Planeta, 1982); and Pilar Urbano, *Con La Venia Yo Indagué el 23-F* (Barcelona: Argos Vergara, 1982). See also Julio Busquets et al., *El Golpe* (Barcelona: Ariel, 1981); Ricardo Cid Cañaveral et al., *Todos al Suelo* (Madrid: Punto Crítico, 1981); and Oficina de Información, División de Relaciones Públicas, Estado Mayor del Ejército, "Golpe de Estado del 23-F," n.d.

3. One account revealed that the Joint Chiefs suggested that it should assume power since it was the top chiefs' duty to handle a "military situation." The king rejected the suggestion and decided, instead, to maintain the continuity of civilian rule by constituting a government of secretaries of state and subsecretaries, under the chairmanship of the secretary of state for security (*El País,* 18 February 1991, 13).

4. When, later, Colonel Tejero was ordered to give up and turn himself in, he replied that he only took orders from Milans; when Milans was ordered to withdraw his edict and to retrieve his forces, he replied that he only took orders from Armada.

5. This was the assessment made in handwritten notes by captain general of Madrid, Guillermo Quintana Lacaci, revealed in *El País* (18 February 1991, 14).

6. Diario 16, *Historia de la Transición*, chapter 44, page 661.

7. Sergio Vilar, *La Década Sorprendente: 1976–1986* (Barcelona: Editorial Planeta, 1986), 103.

8. General Manuel Gutiérrez Mellado, *Recorded Interview*, Fundación Ortega y Gasset, Madrid, 9 May 1985.

9. In fact, witnessing the movement of army jeeps in and out of Madrid and tuned in to radio broadcast of the coup, generals assembled at the air force headquarters sat and wondered whether that day would be observed as a national holiday the following year.

10. Alberto Oliart, *Recorded Interview*, Fundación Ortega y Gasset, Madrid, 20 June 1985.

11. *El País,* 8 and 24 May 1981; 3 October 1981; 5 November 1982. See also the editorial comments of *El País,* 31 May 1981.

12. See Richard Gunther, Giacomo Sani, and Goldie Shabad, eds., *Spain after Franco: The Making of a Competitive Party System* (Berkeley: University of California Press, 1986), 311; and Vilar, *La Década Sorprendente*, 118.

13. The church had distanced itself from the government following the divorce bill submitted by the justice minister, Fernández Ordóñez, who later left the party with the social democratic faction, and the CEOE, the employers' association, which earlier had rejected Suárez's interventionist orientations, now decided it could not entrust its representation to the UCD. Antonio Garrigues Walker, an influential leader of the liberal faction in UCD, still advocated in May 1981 a *gobierno de concentración*, formed by parties, generals, and representatives of the *poderes fácticos* (the powers that be: the church, business, and the military) (see Carlos Huneeus, *La Unión de Centro Democrático y la Transición a la Democracia en España* [Madrid: Centro de Investigaciones Sociológicas, 1985], 358 and 333–413; Diario 16, *Historia de la Transición,* chap. 47; and José Ignacio Wert, "La Campaña Electoral de Octubre de 1982: El Camino del Cambio," *Revista Española de Investigaciones Sociológicas,* no. 28 [October–December 1984]: 63–69).

14. *El País,* 28 July 1981, 8.

15. The defense minister revoked the award, ordered an investigation, and removed the general in charge of the case (*El País,* 4 November 1981).

16. *El País,* 6 December 1981. See also the editorial on 8 December 1981 (10).

17. *El País,* 11 December 1981.

18. At a meeting of the king with the supreme councils of the three armed services in March 1981 (*Reconquista,* no. 371 [April 1981]: 7).

19. Especially of those who had been surprised by his behavior during the coup. Prior to the coup many had been led to believe that the king had favored, from behind the scenes, a political solution with military participation.

20. *Reconquista,* no. 370 (April 1981): 7.

21. *Ejército* (January 1982): ii–vi.

22. *Reconquista,* no. 370 (April 1981): 7.

23. Ibid., 6–7.

24. According to Minister Alberto Oliart, there was a generalized attempt from military sectors to put pressure on the government in order not to take the conspirators to trial (interview with Alberto Oliart, Madrid, 25 November 1987). See also *Historia de la Transición,* book 16, chapter 46.

25. A large number of NCOs and lieutenants who participated in the assault on Congress were exempted from prosecution, partly as a result of Tejero's surrender agreement and partly as a result of decisions by the military prosecutor and the government. Government and military decisions on this were based on reports that army commanders wrote immediately following the coup on individual responsibilities and which exonerated a couple of captains general who had been hesitant in following orders from headquarters and a few commanders of army units—among them Villavicencio and Vicálvaro—who had in fact consented to abide by orders not to deploy forces or take control of public facilities only after these orders were insistently issued several times. Also, several officers in the Brunete Armoured Division were exempted from prosecution, despite their evident participation in preparing military units to follow orders from General Armada.

26. For instance, General Milans, sitting with the accused, stridently abandoned the room in protest against one witness's reference to the assault on Congress as an act of terrorism and to the deputies as hostages (see *El País,* 6 April 1982, 1 and 10).

27. *El País,* 18 June 1982.

28. *El País,* 29 September 1981, 1; and *Ya,* 14 August 1981.

29. *El País,* 5 June 1982, 10. For journalistic accounts on the trial, see Oneto, *La Verdad Sobre el Caso Tejero;* and Martín Prieto, *Técnica de un Golpe de Estado* (Barcelona: Grijalbo, 1982).

30. The Joint Chiefs issued a statement calling for a rejection of criticism of the sentences issued by the military tribunal (*El País,* 5 and 9 June 1982).

31. *Ejército* (January 1982): ii–vi.

32. An editorial in *El País,* on 25 September 1982, criticized "the silent acceptance by the government of the worrisome tendency shown in some military sectors to try to relate themselves with the King as supreme commander of the Armed Forces without going through the legal and constitutional Government customhouse." On 25 November 1982, after the elections, an editorial in *El País* insisted on this issue and hoped that with a new government the armed forces' subordination to political power would stand out, against "the insidious tendency to prefer for the Joint Chiefs an impossible *direct* dependence on the King, skipping the authority which corresponds to the government."

33. *Ejército* (January 1982): viii–ix. Alberto Oliart set a distinction between "command *over* the Armed Forces and command *in* the Armed Forces." The former, he argued, is assigned to the government and the latter to the chiefs of staff of the armed services.

34. Speech at the Pascua Militar of 1982 (*Ejército* [January 1982]).

35. *El País,* 8 August 1982.

36. Following a visit to Milans del Bosch in prison, a colonel was found carrying documents with plans for the putsch, which included the takeover of military command posts, broadcast stations, government facilities, and the Zarzuela Palace. The group of officers caught in the planning of the putsch already had presumably contacted fifteen or twenty other officers to help carry out the plan. Although skeptics thought the government had blown the incident out of proportion in an attempt to scare voters from voting for the PSOE, a special court in April 1984 found these officers — a group of colonels and lieutenant colonels — guilty of rebellion, sentencing them to twelve years in prison (*El País,* 4 and 12 October 1982; Vilar, *La Década Sorprendente,* 125; interview with Alberto Oliart, Madrid, 25 November 1987).

37. See Oneto, *La Verdad Sobre el Caso Tejero,* xviii. Most of the officers I interviewed confirmed the feeling of revulsion and helplessness which the behavior of the prosecuted chiefs produced in the army.

38. *El País,* 28 February 1981.

39. See Leopoldo Calvo Sotelo, *Memoria Viva de la Transición* (Barcelona: Plaza & Janés / Cambio 16, 1990), especially chapter 7.

40. An army general insisted, in 1982: "National Defense and 'nationalities' do not appear to be compatible. There is only one: that of the Spanish Nation. The term 'nationalities' leaves the possibility open to speak of their defenses, but by whom? in what way? and, most of all, against whom?" He added: "The Armed Forces view regionalism and the autonomies with concern if they lead to distort the concept of Nation and to the disintegration of the Fatherland. The autonomies are not in themselves a challenge to national sovereignty but they must be precluded from becoming

the basis for the creation and stimulus of separatist aspirations which sooner or later could cause serious conflict." However, he consented to LOAPA, which proposes that "the autonomies be only a manifestation and a module of power that consider their activities within the unity of the single power of the state. This is, in part, what is attempted with the LOAPA" (General Francisco Ríos García, "Repercusión del Desarrollo Autonómico en la Defensa Nacional y en las FAS," in *Las Autonomías en España,* Ciclo de Conferencias, Centro Superior de Estudios de la Defensa Nacional, Madrid, October 1982, 124–25). See also Luis Maldonado Escoriaza, "Euzkadi y la Historia," *Reconquista,* no. 382 (April 1982): 9.

41. According to President Calvo Sotelo, the government wanted to scare terrorists, to put pressure on France to move for greater cooperation with Spain on the matter, and to show the military the difficulties of the counterterrorist struggle. He wanted to prove to the military that army involvement in the combat of terrorism would have no impact on the outcome and that inflammatory statements by hardliners on the need for tougher measures against terrorism would be deflated (interview with Leopoldo Calvo Sotelo, Madrid, 10 May 1988). According to General José María Sáenz de Tejada, who at the time had been appointed commander of the Navarra Mountain Division, the measure was taken as a result of government concerns following the assassination of two lieutenant colonels, in Bilbao and Pamplona in March 1981. In his account the army did not request participation, and, furthermore, it did request later, in June 1982, that this participation be terminated because of poor results and the inappropriateness of police functions for the army (interview with José María Sáenz de Tejada, Madrid, 25 May 1988).

42. Calvo Sotelo, *Memoria Viva,* 48.

43. Eduardo Serra was appointed subsecretary, and Javier Palacios, a civilian as well, took charge of the Directorate for Economic Affairs.

44. "Ley de Dotaciones Presupuestarias de las Fuerzas Armadas," in *Información Comercial Española,* no. 593 (December 1982); Law 20/1981, *Boletín Oficial del Estado,* no. 165 (11 July 1981); and Law 48/1981 (11 January 1982).

45. Well before the proceedings ended, Calvo Sotelo had decided that he would appeal the sentencing (personal interview, Madrid, 10 May 1988).

46. These diverse postures were expressed in a meeting that the government held with the generals and admirals immediately prior to the decision to join the Alliance, a decision that nonetheless was adopted in full independence from the military (interview with Alberto Oliart, Madrid, 25 November 1987).

47. For instance, immediately following the assassination of General Lago, colonels at the Brunete Division started readying the troops and handing out ammunition. The captain general of Madrid, Lieutenant General Ricardo Arozarena, had to summon in his office all the generals under his command, ordering that nothing could be done without his own personal authorization. Shortly before the assassination, Arozarena, visiting the DAC headquarters, was warned by a colonel that officers in the DAC had met and sworn to take action the next time someone was hit (interview with Ricardo Arozarena, Madrid, 7 November 1987).

48. Voter turnout in this election was unusually high: 79.6 percent. The Socialists won in forty-one of the fifty-two Spanish provinces, and in municipal elections the following year (May 1983) they gained control of a majority of local governments

across the country. For an analysis of these elections, see the set of articles in *Revista Española de Investigaciones Sociológicas,* no. 28 (October–December 1984); and the epilogue in Gunther, Sani, and Shabad, *Spain after Franco.*

49. *Ejército,* no. 516 (January 1983): ii. The celebration of the Pascua Militar did not take place because the king was recovering from a minor accident, but the speech was widely distributed and published.

50. "El General Jefe del Estado Mayor del Aire a los Miembros de este Ejército" (memorandum circulated in the air force the day after the announcement of the Socialists' victory).

51. See Rafael López Pintor and Manuel Justel, "Iniciando el Análisis de las Elecciones Generales de Octubre de 1982 (Informe de un Sondeo Postelectoral)," *Revista Española de Investigaciones Sociológicas,* no. 20 (October–December 1982). See also Wert, "La Campaña Electoral"; and Mario Caciagli, "España 1982: Las Elecciones del Cambio," *Revista Española de Investigaciones Sociológicas,* no. 28 (October–December 1984). For a comparative discussion of electoral abstention in Spain, see José Ramón Montero, "Niveles, Fluctuaciones y Tendencias del Abstencionismo Electoral en España y Europa," ibid.

Chapter 8: Civilian Supremacy and Military Reform

1. See Donald Share, "Two Transitions: Democratisation and the Evolution of the Spanish Socialist Left," *West European Politics* 8, no. 1 (1985); Richard Gunther, "The Spanish Socialist Party: From Clandestine Opposition to Party of Government," in *The Politics of Democratic Spain,* ed. Stanley G. Payne (Chicago: Chicago Council on Foreign Relations, 1986); José Félix Tezanos, "Continuidad y Cambio en el Socialismo Español: El PSOE durante la Transición Democrática"; and Antonio García Santesmases, "Evolución Ideológica del Socialismo en la España Actual," both in *Sistema,* nos. 68–69 (November 1985). For a larger historical account of the PSOE's evolution see Richard Gillespie, *The Spanish Socialist Party* (Oxford: Clarendon, 1989).

2. Certainly, the military would have been less tolerant of a Socialist government following the first democratic elections than it was of Suárez's government of former Franquists. For changes in the PSOE, see Donald Share, *Dilemmas of Social Democracy: The Spanish Socialist Workers Party in the 1980s* (New York: Greenwood Press, 1989), 67–91; and Hans Jürgen Puhle, "El PSOE: Un Partido Dominante y Heterogéneo," in *Crisis y Cambio: Electores y Partidos en la España de los Años Ochenta,* ed. Juan J. Linz and José Ramón Montero (Madrid: Centro de Estudios Constitucionales, 1986).

3. Interview with Lieutenant General Emilio García Conde, Madrid, 24 May 1988. See *Reconquista,* no. 380 (February 1982), for a brief biographical sketch of the members of the Joint Chiefs.

4. See "Barcelona: Una Explosión de Españolismo," *Reconquista* (June 1981): 44–45. The Armed Forces Day, celebrated every year in a different city, was created during the tenure of Vice President Gutiérrez Mellado to replace the previous celebrations of Victory Day, which commemorated the victory of Franquist forces in the civil war.

5. Thus implicitly favoring the "occupational" model strongly rejected by the mil-

itary (PSOE, *Programa de Transición*, Twenty-seventh Congress, "La Defensa," 11–13).

6. Ibid.

7. See Enrique Múgica Herzog, "Las Fuerzas Armadas en la Democracia para Todos" (paper presented at Club Siglo XXI, Madrid, January 1979).

8. *Anexo del Acta del 29 Congreso (Política y Estrategia; Política Internacional)*, Partido Socialista Obrero Español, 21–24 October 1981, 18.

9. *Reconquista*, no. 395 (June 1983): 7.

10. Interview with Narcís Serra, Madrid, 22 December 1987. The Socialists had also acquired much experience in their active participation in debates in the Cortes on military and defense issues. See *Informes Sobre Funcionamiento y Trabajos del Grupo Parlamentario Socialista*, General Vice Secretariat, PSOE, 29th Congress, Permanent Committee of the Parliamentary Group, 46.

11. Wilfried Freiherr von Bedow, "Central Organizations of Defense in the Federal Republic of Germany," in *Central Organizations of Defense*, ed. Martin Edmonds (Boulder, Colo.: Westview Press, 1985), 72.

12. Federal Minister of Defense, *White Paper* 1979: The Security of the Federal Republic of Germany and the Development of the Federal Armed Forces (n.p., n.d.). See also Catherine McArdle Kelleher, "Defense Organization in Germany: A Twice Told Tale," in *Reorganizing America's Defense: Leadership in War and Peace*, ed. Robert J. Art, Vincent Davis, and Samuel P. Huntington (Washington, D.C.: Pergamon-Brassey's, 1985).

13. There had already been early skirmishes. As president-elect, Felipe González had requested the subsecretary of defense to postpone the letter of intention for the purchase of 90 F-18 fighter jets in the United States. The air force had originally requested 300, but the UCD governments reduced the number to 144 and pressed for a further reduction, which the air force finally accepted at 90. In 1983 the Socialist government issued a letter of intention for the purchase of only 72 airplanes, which led General García Conde, air force chief of staff, that same day publicly to declare it "a day of national mourning" (interview with former subsecretary of defense, Eduardo Serra, Madrid, 25 May 1988; and with Lieutenant General Emilio García Conde, Madrid, 24 May 1988).

14. The Royal Ordinances for the Armed Forces, approved in 1978, stipulate that no soldier is compelled to obey orders that imply acts contrary to the law or which constitute crimes, in particular "against the Constitution" (Article 34, Law 85/1978, 28 December, *Boletín Oficial del Estado*, no. 11 [12 January 1979]).

15. Royal Decree-Law 10/1977, of 8 February, established that members of the armed forces could not publicly express preference for any political option and banned affiliation or collaboration with any political organization, public expression of political views, and attendance at public meetings of a political nature (*Boletín Oficial del Estado*, no. 34 [9 February 1977]).

16. See Julio Canales Morales, "Política de Defensa, Política Militar," *Revista de Aeronáutica y Astronáutica*, no. 533 (May 1985).

17. Narcís Serra, "La Política Española de Defensa," *Revista Española de Investigaciones Sociológicas*, no. 36 (October–December 1986): 175.

18. With these reforms Spain swiftly caught up with the dominant features of defense organization in NATO member countries. The figure of chief of defense

staff, for instance, resembled the U.S. chairman of the Joint Chiefs, the German inspector general, or the British chief of defense staff—all positions created at different times in the postwar period and made responsible for the implementation of joint planning and joint structures.

19. Interviews with José María Sáenz de Tejada, Madrid, 17 November 1987; and with Miguel Silva Vidal, Madrid, 13 November 1987. See also the presentation by Lieutenant General Fernando Gautier Larraínzar to the conference "Spain in the 1980s," held at the Woodrow Wilson International Center for Scholars, Washington, D.C., 25–27 September 1985.

20. During the congressional debate of the bill the minister clearly pointed to the state of affairs in need of reform: "Until the past year each service-branch evaluated its own needs, whose total cost always appeared way above the real budgetary possibilities; past governments then decided to allocate the budget among the three service-branches so that they themselves would distribute it according to their own needs. This has been a clear example of the absence of joint action, a clear example of viewing defense as something based on the superimposition of efforts rather than on their coordination" (*Diario de Sesiones del Congreso de los Diputados,* 2d Congress, no. 79 [29 November 1983]: 3826).

21. Lieutenant General Sáenz de Tejada had joined the army as a volunteer— *alférez provisional*—at the outset of the civil war in 1936 and during World War II volunteered for the Russian Front with the División Azul. Later he held numerous positions in the general staff, specializing in foreign and domestic intelligence. Immediately prior to his appointment as army chief of staff, he was captain general of the First Military Region in Madrid. Admiral Liberal Lucini, whose father—an army officer—had been killed a few days after the outbreak of the civil war, had entered the naval school in the midst of the war in 1938. As a navy captain, he was assistant to navy minister Pedro Nieto Antúnez and later, besides holding different command posts, was naval attaché in Washington, D.C.; upon his return he collaborated with General Gutiérrez Mellado as subsecretary of defense in the newly created ministry.

22. *Boletín Oficial del Estado,* no. 2 (1 February 1984): 2618–22. For a summary presentation, see *Ministerio de Defensa: Memoria de la Legislatura (1982–1986)* (Madrid: Ministerio de Defensa, 1986), 60–69.

23. Interview with Eduardo Serra, Madrid, 25 May 1988. The top positions in the Spanish administrative structure are, in descending order, the minister, the secretary of state, the subsecretary, and the director general. In 1990 the subsecretary of defense was upgraded to the rank of secretary of state for military administration (Royal Decree 619/90 [8 May]) (*Ministerio de Defensa. Memoria de la IV Legislatura [1989–1993],* 76).

24. Ministerial Order 18/1985, *Boletín Oficial de Defensa,* no. 44 (1 April 1985).

25. Interview with Eduardo Serra, Madrid, 25 May 1988. For the post of subsecretary of defense the government appointed a young law professor, Gustavo Suárez Pertierra, who until then headed the government's office for relations with the Catholic church.

26. For instance, long-term matériel requirements were coordinated with national industry in order to enhance local industry and domestic research and development. Spending on research and development (R&D) was increased, and special efforts

were made to gain domestic compensations for purchase agreements abroad and to participate in joint ventures with other European countries for the production of combat fighter jets, frigates, and armored vehicles (see *Ministerio de Defensa: Memoria de la Legislatura [1982–1986]*, chap. 10; *Ministerio de Defensa: Memoria de la Legislatura [1986–1989]*, chap. 9; and *International Defense Review* 4 [1989]: 392). Also of interest in this regard are the annual presentations of the defense minister in Congress. For important previous efforts, see "Interview with Gabriel Peña Aranda," *Reconquista*, no. 377 (November 1981).

27. *Boletín Oficial del Estado*, no. 2 (2 January 1987): 75–80.

28. Interview with Gustavo Suárez Pertierra, Madrid, 10 December 1987.

29. *El País*, 1 November 1986, 16.

30. *Boletín Oficial de Defensa*, no. III (10 July 1985).

31. Ministerial Order 24/86, 13 March, in *Colección Legislativa del Ministerio de Defensa* (Madrid: Minister of Defense, 1986), 138–39. The chiefs of staff are appointed by the council of ministers following a proposition by the defense minister. The chiefs of staff command their respective armies under the authority of the minister, from whom they depend directly. The minister is charged with the conduct, coordination, and control of military personnel policy—functions delegated to the subsecretary—and is responsible for policies on the organization and deployment of the armies.

32. The three chiefs of staff strongly conveyed their opposition to the minister (interview with Lieutenant General José Sáenz de Tejada, Madrid, 17 November 1987), who nonetheless went ahead issuing a special ministerial order and making wide use of his new prerogatives. For instance, about 70 percent of the positions in the Zaragoza Military Academy (which forms army officers) had been assigned to new teachers by the end of 1987 (interview with Gustavo Suárez Pertierra, Subsecretary of Defense, Madrid, 10 December 1987).

33. Interview with Colonel Francisco Laguna Sanguirico, Madrid, 3 December 1987. See Ministerial Order 66/1985, November 22, in *Colección Legislativa* (1985): 258–59; Royal Decree 2078/1985, 6 November, in ibid., 240–41; Ministerial Order 37/86, 28 April, in ibid. (1986): 179–92. An explanation of the latter appears in *Ministerio de Defensa: Memoria de Legislatura* (1982–1986), 219–22.

34. The military especially resented the decision to allow conscripts to leave and return to the barracks in civilian clothes, because it would harm efforts to inculcate discipline and military spirit (interview with Lieutenant General Ricardo Arozarena, Madrid, 7 September 1987; see *Ministerio de Defensa: Memoria de la Legislatura (1986–1989)* (Madrid: Minister of Defense, 1989), 179 and 185).

35. Before announcing its decision, however, the government reassured the chiefs of staff that none of the beneficiaries would make use of his right to rejoin the army (interview with Lieutenant General José María Sáenz de Tejada, Madrid, 25 May 1988). This, together with the fact that the chiefs of staff were not compromised because the measure was adopted between the end of the mandates of the outgoing chiefs and the assumption of the positions by the entering officials, helped to placate any resistance to the this measure. Nonetheless, all these officers were later readmitted into the active reserve.

36. Lieutenant General Francisco Veguillas, a close collaborator of the minister, admitted during his assumption of command of the Seventh Military Region in Val-

ladolid in 1986: "We are suffering a reorganization which the military finds very hard to assume because it is us who will suffer from the personnel reduction already established in the army, the navy and the air force" (*Diario* 16 [11 April 1986]: 5).

37. A unified command brings together forces from the different services in a specific regional area or for the performance of ad hoc missions; a specified command is a centralized functional unit.

38. Interview with Admiral Angel Liberal Lucini, Madrid, 27 November 1987 and 4 December 1987. Regular participants in these meetings were the king, the president and vice president, the ministers of defense, foreign affairs, interior, and finance, and the four members of the Joint Chiefs.

39. Major General Ramón Fernández Sequeiros, "El Ciclo de Política de Defensa" (MS, Madrid, 5 June 1986), 6.

40. Upon taking over in 1981, Minister Alberto Oliart found that army directives still explicitly included the "internal enemy" as one of the major threats, jointly with Morocco and the Warsaw Pact. Despite the minister's attempts to the contrary, the army kept finding ways to retain the "internal enemy" as part of its threat definition (Alberto Oliart, *Recorded Interview*, Fundación Ortega y Gasset, 20 June 1985).

41. This reorganization removed the Directorate General for Defense Policy from oversight by the JEMAD and placed it directly under the minister.

42. Lieutenant General Gonzalo Puigcerver, "Hacia una Estructura Unificada del Mando Militar," *ABC*, 14 June 1987, 36.

43. *Ministerio de Defensa: Memoria de la Legislatura (1986–1989)*, 80–82. Part of the new measures included the decision to create a rapid deployment force with elite units from the three armed services under the direct command of the JEMAD. See Philip K. Scaramanga, "Spain's Rapid Deployment Force," *International Defense Review* 4 (1989): 435.

44. See Miguel Martínez Cuadrado, ed., *La Constitución de 1978* (Madrid: Editorial Mezquita, 1982), 282 and 312.

45. The Ley Orgánica de Fuerzas y Cuerpos de Seguridad (Organic Law on Security Corps and Forces) established that the director general of the Civil Guard would be appointed by the government following a joint proposal by the ministers of the interior and defense. This law also established that members of the armed forces commissioned in the National Police Corps had either to return to their original armed service or else retire (see Organic Law 2/1986, 13 March, on Security Corps and Forces, *Boletín Oficial del Estado*, no. 63 [14 March 1986]). As of 1 September 1987, the appointment of generals to the Civil Guard became the exclusive prerogative of the minister of the interior (*El País*, 1 September 1987, 13).

46. Some two hundred officers in this category, however, attempted to slow down the implementation of this rule (see *Diario* 16, 21 May 1986, 9). For a thorough description of the pre-reformed police, see Ian R. MacDonald, "The Police System of Spain," in *Police and Public Order in Europe*, ed. John Roach and Jürgen Thomaneck (London: Croom Helm, 1985); and, for a critical study of the reforms, see Diego López Garrido, *El Aparato Policial en España* (Barcelona: Ariel, 1987). Civilians also took over leading positions at the Santa Bárbara National Corporation, a firm producing a rocket launcher, cannons, ammunition, and machine guns for the army (*El País*, 15 December 1986).

47. Article 116 of the Constitution establishes that Congress cannot be dissolved, nor can its functioning be interrupted during the period of enforcement of any of the states of emergency. Also see Organic Law 4/1981, 1 June, on States of Siege and Exception, *Boletín Oficial del Estado*, no. 134 (5 June 1981); and Organic Law 1/1984, 5 January, which, as a reform of Organic Law 6/1980 (1 July), regulates the basic criteria of National Defense and Military Organization (ibid., 7 January 1981).

48. See the Organic Law on the Organization of Military Jurisdiction (Ley Orgánica 4/1987 de 15 de julio, de la Competencia y Organización de la Jurisdicción Militar), in *Boletín Oficial del Estado*, no. 171 (18 July 1987); the Organic Law on the Military Penal Code (Ley Orgánica 13/1985, de 9 de diciembre), in ibid., no. 296 (11 December 1985); and the Organic Law on Disciplinary Regime of the Armed Forces (Ley Orgánica 12/1985, de 27 de diciembre), in ibid., no. 286 (29 November 1985).

49. However, the text of the question submitted in the referendum imposed limits on the extent of integration in NATO (see Share, *Dilemmas*, 83). See also Esther Barbé, *España y la OTAN* (Barcelona: Editorial Laia, 1981); and Federico G. Gil and Joseph S. Tulchin, eds., *Spain's Entry into NATO* (Boulder, Colo.: Lynne Rienner, 1988).

50. Interview with Admiral Angel Liberal Lucini, Madrid, 4 December 1987; and Alberto Oliart, *Recorded Interview*, Fundación Ortega y Gasset, Madrid, 20 June 1985.

51. Narcís Serra, "Spain, NATO and Western Security," *Adelphi Papers*, no. 229 (Spring 1988); and Angel Viñas, "Spain and NATO: Internal Debate and External Challenges," in *NATO's Southern Allies*, ed. John Chipman (London: Routledge, 1988).

52. For a general discussion, see Antonio Marquina, "Spanish Foreign and Defense Policy Since Democratization," in *Spanish Foreign and Defense Policy*, ed. Kenneth Maxwell (Boulder, Colo.: Westview Press, 1991).

53. See "Plan General de Modernización del Ejército de Tierra," *Reconquista* (November 1982); Lieutenant Colonel Javier Pardo de Santayana, "Una Empresa Ilusionante: El Plan General de Modernización del Ejército de Tierra," *Ejército*, no. 517 (February 1983); Lieutenant General Ramón de Ascanio y Togores, "El Ejército Español: Modernización y Transformación," *Ejército*, no. 528 (January 1984); and Lieutenant Colonel Luis Gravalos González, "Ejército de Tierra," *Revista de Aeronáutica y Astronáutica*, no. 533 (May 1985): 471–82.

54. Lieutenant General José María Sáenz de Tejada, "La Reforma y Modernización en el Ejército de Tierra" (MS, April 1988). The laws on personnel reduction were Ley 40/1984 of 1 December, for the army; Ley 8/1986 of 4 February, for the navy; and Ley 9/1986 of 4 February, for the air force. These laws are summarized in *Ministerio de Defensa: Memoria de la Legislatura (1982–1986)*, 161–68; and *Ministerio de Defensa: Memoria de la IV Legislatura (1989–1993)*, 167.

55. The army's share of total military spending in personnel also declined from 60.3 percent in 1982 to 56.2 percent in 1989 and 39 percent in 1993, a decline largely accounted for by greater allocations to central organs in the ministry of defense (*Ministerio de Defensa: Memoria de la Legislatura (1982–1986)*, 302–4; *Ministerio de Defensa: Memoria de la Legislatura (1986–1989)*, 286 and 289; *Ministerio de Defensa: Memoria de la IV Legislatura (1989–1993)*, 303).

56. See "Ley Reguladora del Régimen del Personal Militar Profesional," *Boletín Oficial del Estado*, 20 July 1989.

57. For an austere and occasionally grim assessment of reforms, especially because

"personnel reduction was not balanced with an increase in military hardware," see Lieutenant General José Sáenz de Tejada, "La Reforma en el Ejército de Tierra" (MS, April 1988). Further reforms and reductions were envisioned as a result of a national defense directive (no. 1/1992) to accommodate the structure and deployment of the forces to a changing international situation.

58. *Información Comercial Española,* no. 592 (December 1982): 7-18.

59. With the purpose of diminishing the relative weight of personnel expenditure, Minister Oliart's budgetary law (no. 44/1982) established limits to the overall increment in defense expenditure: if total increment exceeded a certain limit, the allocations for investment would have to be reduced, thereby providing an incentive not to overstep these limits (*Información Comercial Española,* no. 592 [December 1982]: 7-18).

60. Amelia Díaz Álvarez, "Aproximaciones al Gasto en Defensa," *Papeles de Economía Española,* no. 37 (1988): 293.

61. See *Memoria de la Legislatura* (1982-86) and (1986-89). These methods of personnel reduction had previously been tried during the Republic under Manuel Azaña's military reform policies, and they stood well in line with deeply rooted Spanish tradition (see Michael Alpert, *La Reforma Militar de Azaña* [Madrid: Siglo XXI, 1982]).

62. Differences between both systems persisted in practice, however, and salaries for military personnel again began to lag behind. In addition, the system established in the law did not adequately take into consideration the hierarchical peculiarity of the armed forces when establishing criteria for setting different compensation items. The result was that salary differences between grades often were not as marked as desired (see General Rafael Hitos Amaro, "La Política de Retribuciones Para los Militares de Carrera en España Durante los Ultimos Cincuenta Años," *Ejército* [October – November 1979]; Colonel Emilio González Tapia, "Retribuciones Militares. Peculiaridades de la Carrera Militar: Sus Antecedentes y su Proyección de Futuro," *Ejército* (September 1982); "La Verdad Sobre las Retribuciones Militares," *Reconquista,* no. 406 (July–August 1984); and *ABC,* 29 May 1983, 26.

63. *Memoria de la Legislatura (1982-1986),* 172-76.

64. *El País,* 16 April 1989.

65. *Diario* 16, 16 July 1986, 11. The attack on the ministry injured nine persons, including an admiral who was holding a meeting with the ministry's director general of personnel (*Diario* 16, 22 July 1986, 13).

66. On negotiations with ETA, see *El País,* 11 August 1986, 12; 21 August 1986, 10; and 31 August 1987, 14; and Patxo Unzueta, "El Diálogo y la Negociación con ETA," *El País,* 31 August 1987, 9. For a journalistic account of military reactions, see "El Ejército Quiere Saber Qué Significa Dialogar con ETA," *Tiempo,* no. 279 (14-20 September 1987): 8-13.

67. For the implementation of the autonomies, see Joaquim Solé-Vilanova, "Spain: Developments in Regional and Local Government," in *Territory and Administration in Europe,* ed. Robert Bennett (London: Pinter Publishers, 1989). See also Juan J. Linz, Manuel Gómez Reino, Francisco Andrés Orizo, and Dario Vila, *Conflicto en Euskadi* (Madrid: Espasa-Calpe, 1986).

68. *El País,* 6 December 1987, 11.

69. *El País,* 18 February 1991, 13. For other episodes indicative of resistance in the military, see *El País,* 23 January 1986, 11; 24 January 1986, 14; 11 May 1986, 12; 12 May

1986, 13; 10 December 1987, 17; 27 April 1989, 16; and *Diario* 16, 6 February 1986; 9 April 1986; 10 May 1986, 5-7; 13 May 1986, 5-6.

70. *ABC,* 14 June 1987, 43.

71. The episode received broad coverage in the press, reflecting the novelty of the procedure and the uncertain expectations of the press on military reactions. See, for instance, *El País,* 22 March 1986, 18; 23 March 1986, 13; 24 March 1986, 14; and 27 March 1986, 12; and the editorial on 23 March 1986, 10, which criticized General Yrayzoz's conduct.

72. *El País,* 17 June 1987, 15; and 15 October 1987, 15.

73. *Tiempo,* no. 279 (14-20 September 1987): 10.

74. Generals sympathetic to the military policies of the government had supported restrictions to freedom of speech but only as temporary measures that should be revised later, "when civil society and the military world have consolidated a practice of respect for the law and their fellows' views" (General Ramón Salas Larrazábal, qtd. in *El País,* 7 May 1983). For a broad and thorough discussion of these issues, see Luis Prieto and Carlos Bruquetas, eds., *Libertades Públicas y Fuerzas Armadas* (Madrid: Ministerio de Educación y Ciencia e Instituto de Derechos Humanos de la Universidad Complutense, 1985).

75. Members of Parliament of Fraga's Partido Popular announced that they had received 1,461 letters from officers criticizing the bill and that their amendment proposals reflected this criticism, especially in regard to "the excessive and even abusive" prerogatives sought by the minister in the field of promotions and education (*El País,* 31 March 1989).

76. One-fourth of the air force pilots had requested transfer to the reserve in 1987, and 20 percent of the navy pilots had done the same, creating unsurmountable difficulties such as the danger of having more jet fighters than pilots. See, for instance, *El País,* 1 December 1987, 17; 3 December 1987, 21; and 1 August 1989.

77. *Anuario El País* 1990, 130-32. In this particular case protests were related to a clause that encouraged NCOs to remain as such by substantially raising their salaries. Demonstrating wives protested against the fact that their second-lieutenant husbands, former NCOs, would not benefit from those raises.

78. *Revista General de Marina* (February 1984): 167.

79. Ibid., February 1986, 179.

80. *Anuario El País* 1990, 131.

81. *El País,* 16 March 1989, 17.

82. See, for instance, James Schlesinger, "The Office of the Secretary of Defense," in Art, Davis, and Huntington, *Reorganizing America's Defense.*

83. For a critical assessment of accomplishments in the area of military education, see Félix Arteaga Marín, "La Enseñanza Militar: Estructuras de Cambio y Cambio de Estructuras"; and José María Riaza Ballesteros, "Líneas Generales de la Reforma de la Enseñanza Militar," both in *La Enseñanza Militar en España,* ed. Francisco Alvira et al. (Madrid: CIFAS-Consejo Superior de Investigaciones Científicas, 1986). On slow progress in the civilianization of defense intelligence (CESID, in the Ministry of Defense), see *El País,* 25 May 1986, 11; and 1 June 1986, 3-4.

Chapter 9: Outcomes Compared

1. See Harry J. Psomiades, "Greece: From the Colonels' Rule to Democracy," in *From Dictatorship to Democracy*, ed. John H. Herz (Westport, Conn.: Greenwood Press, 1982); Constantine Danopoulos, "From Military to Civilian Rule in Contemporary Greece," *Armed Forces and Society* 10, no. 2 (1984); and Nikiforos Diamandouros, "Regime Change and the Prospects for Democracy in Greece: 1974–1983," in *Transitions from Authoritarian Rule: Southern Europe*, ed. Guillermo O'Donnell, Philippe C. Schmitter, and Laurence Whitehead (Baltimore: Johns Hopkins University Press, 1986).

2. Thanos Veremis, "The Military," in *Political Change in Greece: Before and After the Colonels*, ed. Kevin Featherstone and Dimitrios K. Katsoudas (New York: St. Martin's Press, 1987).

3. See James Brown, *Delicately Poised Allies: Greece and Turkey* (London: Brassey's, 1991), chapter 2. Also see Constantine P. Danopoulos, *Warriors and Politicians in Modern Greece* (Chapel Hill, N.C.: Documentary Publications, 1984).

4. See Diogo Freitas do Amaral, "La Constitución y las Fuerzas Armadas," *Revista de Estudios Políticos* (Madrid) 60–61 (1988); Francisco Pinto Balsemão, "The Constitution and Politics: Options for the Future," in *Portugal in the 1980s: Dilemmas of Democratic Consolidation*, ed. Kenneth Maxwell (New York: Greenwood Press, 1986); and Thomas C. Bruneau and Alex Macleod, *Politics in Contemporary Portugal: Parties and the Consolidation of Democracy* (Boulder, Colo.: Lynne Rienner, 1986).

5. See Alvaro Vasconcelos, "Portuguese Defense Policy: Internal Politics and Defense Commitments," in *NATO's Southern Allies: Internal and External Challenges*, ed. John Chipman (London: Routledge, 1988); and Thomas C. Bruneau, "Defense Modernization and the Armed Forces in Portugal: Implications for U.S.-Portuguese Relations" (MS, July 1991).

6. See David Pion-Berlin, "Between Confrontation and Accommodation: Military and Government Policy in Democratic Argentina," *Journal of Latin American Studies* 23 (October 1991); Deborah L. Norden, "Democratic Consolidation and Military Professionalism: Argentina in the 1980s," *Journal of Interamerican Studies and World Affairs* 32 (Fall 1990); and J. Samuel Fitch and Andrés Fontana, "Military Policy and Democratic Consolidation in Latin America," *Documento CEDES* (Buenos Aires) 58 (1990).

7. See Paul W. Zagorski, "Civil-Military Relations and Argentine Democracy: The Armed Forces under the Menem Government," *Armed Forces and Society* 20, no. 3 (Spring 1994); Andrés Fontana, "Más Entendimiento entre Civiles y Militares," *El Cronista* (Buenos Aires), 18 June 1992, 17; and Rosendo Fraga, "El Debate sobre la Cuestión Militar," *La Nación* (Buenos Aires), 20 July 1992, 9; Rut Clara Diamint, "Cambios en la Política de Seguridad: Argentina en Busca de un Perfil no Conflictivo"; and Ernesto López, "Argentina: Desarme de hecho y Cooperación para la Paz," both in *Fuerzas Armadas y Sociedad* 7, no. 1 (January–March 1992).

8. Rosendo Fraga, "Permanente Inestabilidad: Frágiles Relaciones Cívico-Militares en Argentina" (MS, March 1991).

9. *Latin American Weekly Report: Southern Cone* 19 (April 1990): 7. For the negotiations on the transition, see Charles G. Gillespie, *Negotiating Democracy: Politicians and Generals in Uruguay* (Cambridge: Cambridge University Press, 1991).

10. Juan Rial, *Las Fuerzas Armadas en los años 90* (Montevideo: Peitho, 1990).

11. Proposals to shorten President Sarney's term were based on his accidental and unexpected accession. A compromise arranged by the moderate opposition to the military government had him run for the vice-presidency, but President-Elect Tancredo Neves died shortly before he was due to assume, and the presidential sash was bestowed on Sarney. Sarney was then supported by the military and a civilian coalition dominated by former supporters of the military regime (Frances Hagopian and Scott Mainwaring, "Democracy in Brazil: Problems and Prospects," *World Policy Journal* [Summer 1987]).

12. Eliézer Rizzo de Oliveira, "O Papel das Forças Armadas na nova Constituição e no Futuro da Democracia no Brasil," *Vozes* 82, no. 2 (July–December 1988).

13. Jorge Zaverucha, *Rumor de Sabres: Tutela Militar ou Controle Civil?* (São Paulo: Editora Atica, 1994); Wendy Hunter, "Back to the Barracks? The Military's Political Role in Post-Authoritarian Brazil" (Ph.D. diss., University of California–Berkeley, 1992); and *New York Times,* 19 November 1991, A3; *Brazil Report,* 15 August 1991; and *Latin American Monitor,* July–August 1991, 921.

14. On institutional conflicts over salaries, see "Itamar chama a guarda," *Istoe,* no. 1278 (30 March 1994): 34–39. On presidential lack of restraint, especially Sarney's relations with the military, see Scott Mainwaring, "Dilemmas of Multiparty Presidential Democracy: The Case of Brazil," *Kellogg Institute Working Paper,* no. 74. Domestic involvement was further complicated by the military's dilemmas in searching for a new mission, which included the battle against poverty. For an excellent presentation of these dilemmas, see Wendy Hunter, "The Brazilian Military after the Cold War: In Search of a Mission," *Studies in Comparative International Development* 28, no. 4 (Winter 1994).

15. Felipe Agüero, "Chile: South America's Success Story?" *Current History* 92, no. 572 (March 1993): 130–35; Brian Loveman, "¿Misión cumplida? Civil Military relations and the Chilean Political Transition," *Journal of Interamerican Studies and World Affairs* 33 (Fall 1991); and Rhoda Rabkin, "The Aylwin Government and Tutelary Democracy: A Concept in Search of a Case?" *Journal of Interamerican Studies and World Affairs* 34, no. 4 (Winter 1992–93).

16. The preceding military regime had been a case of "inclusionary corporatism," which did not rely in the kind of brutal repression that characterized authoritarian rule in Argentina, Brazil, Chile, and Uruguay. See Alfred Stepan, *State and Society: Peru in Comparative Perspective* (Princeton, N.J.: Princeton University Press, 1978); and Angela Cornell and Kenneth Roberts, "Democracy, Counterinsurgency and Human Rights: The Case of Peru," *Human Rights Quarterly* 12 (1990): 529–53.

17. See Marcial Rubio, *Ministerio de Defensa: Antecedentes y retos* (Lima: APEP-Friedrich Ebert, 1987); Sandra Woy-Hazelton and William A. Hazelton, "Sustaining Democracy in Peru: Dealing with Parliamentary and Revolutionary Changes," in *Liberalization and Redemocratization in Latin America,* ed. George A. Lopez and Michael Stohl (New York: Greenwood Press, 1987); and Cynthia McClintock, "El Gobierno aprista y la fuerza armada del Perú," in *El APRA: De la ideología a la praxis,* ed. Heraclio Bonilla and Paul W. Drake (Lima: Nuevo Mundo EIRL, 1989).

18. In a blatant display of autonomy the military reacted in 1993 to Congress's investigations on human rights abuses by mobilizing tanks in the streets of Lima.

See "In Peru, a 'Second Coup' Reveals the Upper Hand," *New York Times,* 2 May 1993, E-6. For references on Bolivia and Ecuador, see my article "The Military and the Limits to Democratization in South America," in *Issues in Democratic Consolidation: The New South American Democracies in Comparative Perspective,* ed. Scott Mainwaring, Guillermo O'Donnell, and J. Samuel Valenzuela (Notre Dame, Ind.: University of Notre Dame Press, 1992), 157–58 and 164–66 (and nn. 9, 10, 11, 35, 37, and 39); Anita Isaacs, *Military Rule and Transition in Ecuador* (Pittsburgh: University of Pittsburgh Press, 1983); and Catherine M. Conaghan and James Malloy, *Unsettling Statecraft: Democracy and Neoliberalism in the Central Andes* (Pittsburgh: University of Pittsburgh Press, 1994).

19. For an assessment of the same set of South American cases from the angle of military autonomy, see David Pion-Berlin, "Military Autonomy in Emerging Democracies in South America," *Comparative Politics* 25, no. 1 (October 1992).

20. Robert H. Dix, "Military Coups and Military Rule in Latin America," *Armed Forces and Society* 20, no. 3 (Spring 1994).

21. And these amnesties or impunity stood in stark contrast, for instance, with the prison sentence given Otelo Saraiva de Carvalho, a major leader and military figure in the Portuguese transition, for involvement with an illegal organization. In Uruguay episodes of contestation were much too recent: army refusal of presidential orders to confront striking police in 1992 and an obscure episode with the head of army intelligence. See "Tensa situación en Uruguay por actuación de militares," *La Nación* (Santiago), 12 June 1993, 8–9.

22. See Dimitri C. Constas, "Greek Foreign Policy Objectives: 1974–1986"; and Thanos Veremis, "Greece and NATO," both in *Greece on the Road to Democracy: From the Junta to PASOK, 1974–1986,* ed. Speros Vryonis, Jr. (New Rochelle, N.Y.: Aristide D. Caratzas, 1991); and George J. Tsoumis, "The Defense Policies of PASOK," in *Greece under Socialism: A NATO Ally Adrift,* ed. Nikolaos A. Stavrou (New Rochelle, N.Y.: Aristide D. Caratzas, 1988).

23. Kenneth Maxwell, "Portuguese Defense and Foreign Policy: An Overview," in *Portuguese Defense and Foreign Policy since Democratization,* ed. Kenneth Maxwell, Camões Center Special Reports no.3, Research Institute on International Change, Columbia University, 1991.

24. For these cases, see Jorge Zaverucha, "Civil-Military Relations during the First Brazilian Post-Transition Government: A Tutelary Democracy" (MS); and Louis W. Goodman, Johanna Mendelson, and Juan Rial, eds., *The Military and Democracy: The Future of Civil-Military Relations in Latin America* (Lexington, Mass.: Lexington / D. C. Heath, 1990).

25. This argument is developed more extensively in Felipe Agüero, "Democratic Consolidation and the Military in Southern Europe and South America," in *The Politics of Democratic Consolidation in Southern Europe,* ed. Richard Gunther, Nikiforos Diamandouros, and Hans-Jürgen Puhle (Baltimore: Johns Hopkins University Press, 1994).

26. J. Samuel Fitch, "Toward a Democratic Model of Civil-Military Relations for Latin America" (paper presented at the International Political Science Association meeting, Washington, D.C., 31 August 1988); and Alfred Stepan, *Rethinking Military Politics* (Princeton, N.J.: Princeton University Press, 1988).

27. Hunter, "Brazilian Military."

28. As J. Samuel Fitch put it, "The democratic professionalist alternative is difficult to sustain where military officers cannot practice their profession for lack of operating funds or where military salaries do not permit officers a minimum standard of living commensurate with other skilled professions" ("Military Role Beliefs in Latin American Democracies," U.S. Institute of Peace, Interim Performance Report no. 3, 13 February 1993, 15). An interesting comparative presentation of this argument is found in Wendy Hunter, "Contradictions of Civilian Control: Argentina, Brazil, and Chile in the 1990s" (MS, Department of Political Science, Vanderbilt University, n.d.). See also Lars Schoultz, William C. Smith, and Augusto Varas, eds., *Security, Democracy and Development in the Western Hemisphere* (New Brunswick, N.J.: Transaction Publishers, 1994).

29. In southern Europe, Portugal faced the combined tasks of enormous reductions in budget and personnel (from 282,000 in 1974 down to less than 40,000 in 1991) with the attempt to modernize equipment to tackle new defense postures, but enormous gaps remained between goals and deeds. See Lawrence S. Graham, *The Portuguese Military and the State: Rethinking Transition to Democracy* (Boulder, Colo.: Westview Press, 1993), 77; Kenneth Maxwell, "Portuguese Defense and Foreign Policy: An Overview," in Maxwell, *Portuguese Defense, 3*.

30. New democracies, however, are not evaluated solely on the basis of socioeconomic efficacy. Based on a study of Spain, Juan Linz and Alfred Stepan argued that democracy can be valued as the best political system even if its socioeconomic efficacy is negatively assessed: "The political perception of desired alternatives has a greater impact on the survival of democratic regimes than economic or social problems *per se*" ("Political Crafting of Democratic Consolidation or Destruction: European and South American Comparisons," in *Democracy in the Americas: Stopping the Pendulum,* ed. Robert A. Pastor [New York: Holmes and Meier, 1989], 46). Memories of atrocities and the lack of liberties under the previous authoritarian regime, they maintained, provide new democracies with additional capital of public confidence and support. (Although this would not apply to cases that were regarded as relatively less repressive and more successful in its economic program, as was argued for the case of Brazil in Guillermo O'Donnell, "Transitions, Continuities and Paradoxes," in Mainwaring, O'Donnell, and Valenzuela, *Issues in Democratic Consolidation*). However, the extent to which this "system-," or "regime-," tied capital is actually transferred without losses to specific administrations is unclear, especially in the face of extreme economic distress and the perception of government policy failure.

31. A vivid, and perhaps extreme, example of this problem was President Alfonsín's decision to resign to allow the assumption of President-Elect Carlos Menem four months earlier than it was legally due.

32. See Juan Linz and Arturo Valenzuela, eds., *The Failure of Presidentialism in Latin America* (Baltimore: Johns Hopkins University Press, 1994).

33. Carol Graham, "Peru's APRA Party in Power: Impossible Revolution, Relinquished Reform" (paper presented to the Latin American Studies Association International Congress, Miami, December 1989).

34. Gary W. Wynia, "Campaigning for President in Argentina," *Current History* (March 1989); and William C. Smith, "Políticas económicas de choque y transición democrática en Argentina y Brasil," *Revista Mexicana de Sociología* 2 (April–June 1988).

35. While support for Alfonsín's government declined dramatically in Argentina, attitudes toward democracy remained basically unchanged (see Edgardo Catterberg, "Attitudes towards Democracy in Argentina during the Transition Period," *International Journal of Public Opinion Research* 2 [1990]: 158 and 165-66). In Peru the combination of the disastrous economic situation inherited from the policies of Alan García and the escalation in the subversive war led to substantial public support for nondemocratic solutions, such as offered by President Fujimori's decision to break with the Constitution.

36. Kurt Weyland, "The Rise and Fall of President Collor and Its Impact on Brazilian Democracy," *Journal of Interamerican Studies and World Affairs* 35, no. 1 (1993).

37. Richard Clogg, *Parties and Elections in Greece* (London: C. Hurst, 1987), 192-216.

38. See Mario Bacalhau, "Transition of the Political System and Political Attitudes in Portugal," *International Journal of Public Opinion Research* 2, no. 2 (1990); Manuel Braga da Cruz and Miguel Lobo Antunes, "Revolutionary Transition and Problems of Parliamentary Institutionalization: The Case of the Portuguese National Assembly," in *Parliament and Democratic Consolidation in Southern Europe: Greece, Italy, Portugal, Spain and Turkey,* ed. Ulrike Liebert and Maurizio Cotta (London: Pinter Publishers, 1990).

39. In Chile the formation of a Center-Left coalition based on stable and disciplined parties since the resumption of democracy allowed its political system to overcome the institutional rigidities of presidentialism which it faced in the past. Still, the authoritarian legacy of Pinochet-appointed senators denied democratic governments sufficient majority for constitutional reform on military issues. For a broader discussion of problems of presidentialism and parliamentarism in different contexts, see Scott Mainwaring, "Presidentialism, Multipartism and Democracy: The Difficult Combination," *Comparative Political Studies* 26, no. 2 (July 1993).

40. A consensus confirmed in 1987 with Papandreou's praise of Karamanlis's performance "in upgrading the armed forces and safeguarding security" (Veremis, "Greece and NATO," 71).

41. Maxwell, "Portuguese Defense," 4.

42. Marcelo Cavarozzi, "Patterns of Elite Negotiation and Confrontation in Argentina and Chile," in *Elites and Democratic Consolidation in Latin America and Southern Europe,* ed. John Higley and Richard Gunther (Cambridge: Cambridge University Press, 1992).

43. See Scott Mainwaring, "Brazilian Party Underdevelopment in Comparative Perspective," *Political Science Quarterly* 107, no. 4 (1992-93); and Mainwaring, "Politicians, Parties and Electoral Systems: Brazil in Comparative Perspective," *Comparative Politics* 24, no. 1 (1991).

44. There were, however, signs toward the end of President Aylwin's administration, after the election of Eduardo Frei for the following term, that the parties of the Right might be willing to reconsider the veto exercised thus far on constitutional reforms. See "Derecha: Tiempos Nuevos, Vida Nueva," *Hoy,* no. 857 (20-26 December 1993): 19.

45. Laurence Whitehead, "Democracy by Convergence and Southern Europe: A Comparative Politics Perspective," in *Encouraging Democracy: The International Context of Regime Transition in Southern Europe,* ed. Geoffrey Pridham (New York: St. Martin's Press, 1991).

46. Although the presence of NATO was generally beneficial for the purposes of accommodating the military in democratization, it certainly was not a panacea. It will be recalled that NATO had unquestioningly accommodated authoritarian Greece and Portugal and that Secretary of State Alexander Haig, former NATO commander, had dismissed the 1981 coup attempt in Spain as merely "an internal affair" of that country.

47. For the international context of defense policy in Portugal, see Alvaro Vasconcelos, "Portuguese Defence Policy: Internal Politics and Defence Commitments," in Chipman, *NATO's Southern Allies;* and Walter C. Opello, Jr., "Portugal: A Case Study of International Determinants of Régime Transition," in Pridham, *Encouraging Democracy.*

48. Susannah Verney and Theodore Couloumbis, "State-International Systems Interaction and the Greek Transition to Democracy in the Mid-1970s," in Pridham, *Encouraging Democracy.*

49. Heraldo Muñoz, "The Rise and Decline of the Inter-American System: A Latin American View," in *Alternative to Intervention: A New U.S.-Latin American Security Relationship,* ed. Richard J. Bloomfield and Gregory F. Treverton (Boulder, Colo.: Lynne Rienner, 1990); and James R. Kurth, "The Rise and Decline of the Inter-American System: A U.S. View," in Bloomfield and Treverton, *Alternative to Intervention.*

Index

Coordinación Democrática, 71
Cortes, 19, 48–50, 53–54, 70–71, 74–76, 79, 81, 85, 88, 90–91, 94–96, 122–23, 135, 151, 165, 169, 201, 247n. 2, 268n. 16
Council of the Exchequer, 50
Council of Ministers, 45, 48, 53
Council of the Realm, 48, 50, 268n. 16
Council of State, 50
Counterterrorist struggle, 168, 228
Coup. *See* Military coup attempts
Court system, 137; military, 52, 73, 172, 177
Crown, 152, 165–66. *See also* Juan Carlos; King of Spain; Monarchy
Cyprus, 59, 66, 130, 240, 243

Dahl, Robert, 16
Death penalty, 88
Defense: budget, 20; policy, 186–87, 201–2, 204, 221–22, 233–34, 240, 244; spending, 206. *See also* National defense
De Gaulle, Charles, 167, 274n. 63
Democracy: concept of, 16, 17, 24; support for, 145, 175; threats to, 141, 144, 161, 167, 181, 229, 231; transition to, 3, 6, 7, 9, 10–11, 13, 16, 25, 55, 60, 62, 64, 66, 70, 97, 112, 118, 127, 135, 139, 153, 219, 223, 227, 229, 238, 241n. 1, 257n. 48. *See also* Transition
Democratic: consolidation, 10, 21–22, 38–39, 65, 67, 135–36, 139, 181–82; government, 18; inauguration, 39, 68, 79, 100, 112–13, 136, 138, 159, 162, 225, 230–32, 239; institutions, 70, 117, 146, 162, 181, 214; regimes, 6, 35, 68, 139, 181, 188, 197; rule, 25
Democratization, 3–5, 8–10, 13, 17–18, 21, 23–24, 26, 29, 36, 39, 43–45, 60, 68, 70–71, 73–75, 86, 97, 102, 107, 127–28, 131, 154, 161, 170, 174, 181, 184, 219–20, 228, 230, 233, 243–45
de Santiago, Lt. Gen. Fernando, 72, 74, 80, 108, 123, 147, 159, 270nn. 28, 31, 277n. 12
Developmentalism, 112
Di Palma, Giuseppe, 76
Díaz Losada, Gen. Angel, 212
Diez Alegría, Lt. Gen. Luis, 88, 270n. 29
Diez Alegría, Lt. Gen. Manuel, 113, 122, 123, 125, 281nn. 46, 47
Directorate General for Defense Policy (DIGENPOL), 191
Disappeared persons, 265n. 49. *See also* Human rights
División Azul (Blue Division), 107, 109, 184, 277n. 9

Eanes, Ramalho, 240, 242–43, 251n. 3
Economic: crisis, 127, 139–40, 154, 172, 237;

development, 111; integration, 243; transition, 34, 220
Ecuador: authoritarian regime, 29, 265n. 49; democratization, 248n. 4; electoral restrictions, 69; military, 127; transition, 60, 66, 69, 99, 239
Elections, 70, 74, 76, 85, 95, 162, 178–81, 183, 214, 225, 238–40; municipal, 154; regional, 137, 143, 169
Electoral college, 57
Elícegui, Lt. Gen. Antonio, 285n. 14
Elites: civilian, 10, 11, 22, 59, 61–64, 66, 68, 70, 95, 99, 102, 118, 137, 219–20, 231–34, 239, 241–42, 245, 264nn. 40, 45; military, 36, 64, 66, 182, 190, 211, 219, 233; in transition process, 3, 8, 9, 28, 30, 33, 43, 58, 63–66, 68, 70, 128, 139, 154, 230, 233, 247n. 2, 258n. 51
Empowerment, 26, 36, 44, 56, 147, 177, 197
England, 233
Escola Superior de Guerra (ESC, Brazil), 111, 120
ETA, 31, 70–71, 103, 140–43, 155, 168, 177, 210–11, 255n. 3, 274n. 68, 284n. 70
Eurocommunism, 104
Europe, 3, 77, 104, 187, 213; Central, 205; Eastern, 3–4, 205, 248nn. 6, 7; Western, 182, 215. *See also* Southern Europe
European Economic Community, 233
Europeanization, 182
Euskadi, 88, 137, 142–43, 153, 154, 269n. 25
External debt, 258n. 57

Factionalism, 13, 30, 36, 63, 93, 98, 136, 138, 153, 241
Factionalization, 103
Falange, 50, 53, 109
Falklands/Malvinas, 59, 66, 98, 130, 233, 242
Fascism, 50, 262n. 27
Federal Republic of Germany. *See* West Germany
Fernández Maldonado, Gen., 57
Fernández Miranda, Torcuato, 268n. 16
Fernández Ordóñez, Francisco, 292n. 13
Fernández Posse, Gen., 169
Fernández Teijeiro, Gen. David, 212
Fontenla, Gen., 144
Fraga, Manuel, 72–73, 85, 95, 97, 138, 152–53, 156–57, 175, 204, 268n. 18, 270n. 28, 273n. 58, 282n. 49, 288n. 52
France, 183, 252n. 23, 258n. 49, 274nn. 41, 63
Franco, Francisco, 7–8, 45–50, 53–55, 61–62, 68–69, 71, 74, 76–77, 85–87, 90, 93, 103–4, 108–9, 113, 119, 123, 125, 141, 158, 161, 183, 229, 259n. 3, 265n. 47, 269nn. 23, 27, 276n. 4

Franco Iribarnegaray, Lt. Gen., 271n. 40
Franquism, 5, 7–8, 10, 44–45, 51, 53–55, 57,
    61, 68–70, 72–73, 76, 78, 87, 90–91, 95,
    97, 103, 106–7, 113, 116–18, 122–23, 128,
    137–39, 141, 154–55, 167, 182, 185, 200,
    208, 210, 231, 241. *See also* Post-
    Franquism
Franquist: authoritarian regime, 3, 8, 10, 43,
    45, 58, 61–62, 103; bureaucracies, 122;
    elites, 63, 69, 72, 108, 156, 247n. 2; era,
    33, 52, 74; hard-liners, 71, 77, 91, 94–95;
    institutions, 5–6, 18, 44, 48, 71, 79, 104,
    124, 141, 147; legality, 75, 76, 91, 111;
    loyalty, 73, 126; reformers, 71, 91; state,
    44–45, 50, 53, 106
Frei, Eduardo, 307n. 44
Fueros, 137
Fujimori, Alberto, 228, 241, 307n. 35
Fundamental Laws and Principles, 68, 77,
    89, 260n. 10

Gabeiras, Lt. Gen. José, 123, 140, 144, 147,
    164–65, 280n. 28, 285n. 15
Galaxia. *See* Operation Galaxia
Galicia, 154, 169, 269n. 25
Gamboa, Adm. Marcial, 88, 270n. 29
García, Alan, 128, 228, 237, 239, 241, 307n.
    35
García Conde, Lt. Gen. Emilio, 178–79, 184,
    268n. 15, 296n. 13
Garrigues Walker, Antonio, 292n. 13
Ghizikis, Gen., 59
Gibraltar, 206
Gómez de Salazar, Lt. Gen. Federico, 83,
    113, 267nn. 11, 14, 268nn. 15, 21, 271n.
    43, 282n. 53
González, Felipe, 153, 156–57, 175, 183–86,
    204, 268n. 17, 296n. 13
González de Suso, Gen., 168
González del Yerro, Lt. Gen. Jesús, 116, 139,
    285n. 14
Gorbachev, Mikhail, 161
Greece: authoritarian regime, 29–30;
    democratization, 6, 59, 221, 248n. 4;
    external armed conflict, 33; GDP, 34;
    military, 6, 65, 130; transition, 39, 58–59,
    65–67, 99, 130, 219, 221, 229, 231–32,
    238–41, 243, 245, 266n. 57
Guarantees: for democracy, 24–25, 76; for
    the military, 63, 69
Gunther, Richard, 8
Gutiérrez Mellado, Lt. Gen. Manuel, 80,
    82–83, 85, 87, 88, 103, 105, 108, 123–26,
    128, 140, 144, 149–51, 156, 158, 176, 184,
    188, 268n. 21, 270n. 30, 271nn. 43, 48,
    272nn. 51, 52, 276nn. 4, 8, 279n. 28,
    281n. 37, 282nn. 53, 55, 285n. 15, 286n.
    28, 289n. 54, 290nn. 63, 66

Haig, Alexander, 308n. 46
Hard-line militaries, 94–95, 97, 100, 105–6,
    110, 113, 123, 126, 128, 136, 138–39, 159,
    168, 174, 181, 220, 232, 238. *See also*
    Franquist: hard-liners
Hard-liners, 71, 108–10, 113, 123, 126–27,
    135–36, 139, 140–41, 144–45, 153–54,
    161–62, 167, 177–78, 182, 220, 235, 241,
    245
Haya de la Torre, Victor Raúl, 229
Herrero Rodríguez de Miñón, Miguel, 152,
    169, 288n. 51
Human rights, 24, 59, 62, 67, 98, 130, 159,
    223–25, 227–31, 233, 235, 240, 242, 245,
    265n.49. *See also* Military trials
Hungary, 266n.3
Huntington, Samuel, 17, 20

Ibáñez Freire, Lt. Gen. Antonio, 83, 113,
    282n. 53
Individual rights, 135, 203
Iniesta Cano, Gen., 80, 278n. 15
Íñiguez del Moral, Lt. Gen. Miguel, 199
Initial conditions, 10–13, 39–40, 138, 219–21,
    231, 245
Immovilismo, 103
Intelligence agencies, 24
Interamerican Treaty of Reciprocal
    Assistance, 244
Italy, 257n. 48, 262n. 27

Japan, 3, 4
Jefe de Estado Mayor de la Defensa
    (JEMAD), 189–90, 197, 200
Joint Chiefs, 148, 150–52, 164–65, 170, 184,
    186, 188–90, 194, 199, 202
Joint Strategic Planning (Plan Estratégico
    Conjunto, or PEC), 189, 192, 198–99,
    202
Juan Carlos, 7, 48, 61–62, 69–70, 76, 109,
    146, 157–58, 164–65, 184, 264n. 46, 265n.
    47
Junta Democrática, 71
Juste, Gen., 163, 164

Karamanlis, Konstantin, 59, 97, 221, 231–32,
    238
King of Spain, 7, 22, 43, 61, 69, 71–72,
    75–77, 79–80, 84–85, 87–88, 90, 93–94,
    123, 125–26, 144–46, 151, 157–58, 163–66,
    168–75, 178–79, 189, 201, 211, 213, 260n.
    16, 293n. 32

Lacalle, Luis Alberto, 225
Lacalle Leloup, Lt. Gen. Álvaro, 184
Lago Román, Gen. Víctor, 168, 177, 294n. 47
Lanusse, Gen. Alejandro, 263n. 32
Larrazábal, Adm. Wolfgang, 266n. 57

Superior Council for Military Industries, 50
Supreme Council of Military Justice, 49,
   157, 203
Supreme Court, 50, 81, 173, 177, 203
Supreme Staff, 50–51, 53, 261nn. 18, 20

Tarancón, Bishop, 95
Tarradellas, Josep, 284n. 3
Tejero, Col. Antonio, 141, 163–68, 172, 174,
   285n. 17, 291n. 4, 292n. 25
Terrorism, 44, 52, 67, 99, 107, 136, 139,
   140–42, 144, 146, 154, 157, 159, 168, 172,
   210, 232, 286n. 30, 294n. 41. *See also*
   ETA; Shining Path
Torres Rojas, Gen. Luis, 145, 163–64
Totalitarianism, 71, 169
Transition: agenda, 44, 58, 61, 63–64, 68–70,
   72, 74, 77, 91, 267n. 4 (*see also* Reform
   agenda); civilian-controlled, 11, 30, 38,
   64, 101, 231, 244, 266n. 56; modalities,
   44, 58; outcomes, 38–39, 64, 219–20,
   230; process, 13, 29–30, 34, 36, 38–39,
   43–44, 58–61, 63, 65–70, 76–77, 86, 91,
   94, 101–2, 107, 123, 127, 137, 144, 152,
   170, 219, 228, 231, 233, 236, 240, 243,
   245, 247nn. 3, 4
Transition, military-led, 13, 39, 64, 66, 77,
   80, 87, 110, 136, 138, 143, 154, 219, 231,
   245, 257n. 43, 266n. 57
Trillo Figueroa, Federico, 152
Turia Operation, 163
Turkey, 59, 130, 167, 232–33, 240, 243

Uncertainty, 3–5, 11, 24–26, 70, 72–73, 76,
   87, 138, 236

Unión de Centro Democrático (UCD), 85,
   87, 95, 138, 153–54, 157, 162, 169, 174–75,
   177–78, 180–81, 184, 186, 204, 233, 238
Unión General de Trabajadores (UGT)
   (Socialist Labor Federation), 73, 79
Unión Militar Democrática (UMD), 86, 91,
   94, 101, 104–6, 124, 145, 152, 157, 186,
   197, 215, 272nn. 51, 52, 276n. 7
Unions, 80
United States, 4, 33, 35, 118–19, 187, 240,
   244, 296n. 13
Uruguay: authoritarian regime, 29, 53,
   56–57; democratization, 248n. 4, economic factor for transition, 35; electoral
   restrictions, 69; military, 110, 127, 129,
   130, 223; polarization, 32; transition, 39,
   60, 62, 66, 69, 99, 131, 225, 229, 230,
   234, 239, 241, 245

Valenzuela, Lt. Joaquín de, 168
Vega Rodríguez, Lt. Gen. José, 83, 113, 144,
   269n. 21, 271n. 43, 282n. 53
Veguillas, Lt. Gen. Francisco, 211, 298n. 36
Venezuela, 66, 254n. 25, 257n. 45, 264n. 41,
   266n. 56
Voluntary retirements, 209

Western European Union, 233
West Germany, 4, 35, 187, 253n. 23
Workers' Rights, 90, 105, 267n. 7
World War II, 4, 112

Yrayzoz, Maj. Gen. Fernando, 211